SECRET ENGLAND

SARAH BROWN

By the same author

Vegetarian Kitchen
Sarah Brown's Vegetarian Cookbook
Sarah Brown's Healthy Living Cookbook
Sarah Brown's Vegetarian Microwave Cookbook
Sarah Brown's New Vegetarian Kitchen
Quick and Easy Vegetarian Cookery
Vegetarian London
Sarah Brown's the Best of Vegetarian Britain

SECRET ENGLAND

SARAH BROWN

WEIDENFELD & NICOLSON
LONDON

First published in Great Britain in 1990 by
George Weidenfeld & Nicolson,
91 Clapham High Street,
London SW4 7TA

Copyright © Sarah Brown 1989

All rights reserves. No part of this publication may be reproduced, stored in a retrieval system, or transmitted in any form or by any means, electronic, mechanical, photocopying, recording or otherwise, without the prior permission of the copyright owner.

British Library Cataloguing-in-Publication data
Brown, Sarah
Secret England.
I. Title
914.204858
ISBN 0-297-81086-3

Printed and bound in Great Britain by
Butler & Tanner Ltd, Frome and London

Maps drawn by Julie Cleary based upon the Ordnance Survey map with the permission of the Controller of Her Majesty's Stationary Office
© Crown Copyright.

Contents

Acknowledgements vii
Introduction ix

Dorset 1
Wiltshire 26
The Forest of Dean 50
Shropshire 74
The Lancashire Coast 96
The Dales 123
Northumberland 148
Nottinghamshire 173
Warwickshire 198
Suffolk 223
The Chilterns 247
Sussex 273

Index 297

Acknowledgements

An unexpected consequence of writing this book was the chance it gave me to spend time with many friends up and down the country. Their local knowledge added greatly to my research, and their company on the walks made everything much more fun.

I would like to thank my sister Deborah for finding the Polissoir and much else about Wiltshire, as well as organizing a very good camping trip in Dorset; my mother who braved the waters of Chichester Harbour and chauffeured me around Sussex; my parents-in-law Sheila and Brian Street for weathering the blustering gales, barbed wire and bulls in Lancashire; Sally Street for helping with Warwickshire and Suffolk, contributing so much with her knowledge of bird life and her sense of humour; Dorothy Marsh who gave me a wealth of information on Shropshire and still had the energy to walk up the hills; Miriam and David Rosen for their navigation round the Dales and for introducing me to Silverdale; Elisabeth Brown for taking me to the lovely Hambleden Valley; and finally Pamela Knutson for being a tireless walker on many of my jaunts, six feet behind maybe but always there.

Thanks also to my agent Harriet Cruickshank for her support, and to David Roberts of Weidenfeld for his enthusiasm for the idea. I am grateful to my editor Amanda Harting for all her thorough work in bringing the book to production. My thanks to Moira Taylor for checking the text and to Julie Cleary for drawing the maps together with her many helpful suggestions. I am indebted to the Ramblers' Association, the National Trust and English Heritage for all the work they do to protect the countryside.

Above all, my thanks to Paul for taking this project to his heart and sharing so much with me.

Sarah Brown
January 1990

Introduction

This book is a celebration of the lesser-known places in England.

I've enjoyed travelling in England – for both work and pleasure. There are a wealth of scenes and sights right on our doorstep apart from those on the well-trodden tourist trail which takes in London, Stratford, York and the West Country. There's scarcely a corner of the country that doesn't have something to offer. This book is about exploring some of those corners, some near the main tourist trails, some a little further afield. I hope you will enjoy sharing these explorations with me, whether you are intending a quiet amble in the country or a more strenuous walk.

Another reason I enjoy exploring is that I'm an avid map reader. It has become more than a casual hobby because of the sport I follow. It is called 'orienteering' and is a combination of cross-country running and navigating with a very detailed map and compass. It has been compared to running for a train whilst doing the crossword! Orienteering events take place all over Britain, usually on Sunday mornings when most sensible folk are still in their beds, and you spend roughly an hour finding your way round the countryside.

The scenes and sights are from twelve areas in England, each area forming one chapter of the book. They are ideal for a short break, either a long weekend or a mid-week excursion, and I have written with that in mind. Although you may use a car, you probably don't want to spend all day in it when you're away, so the chapters don't cover too large an area. I hope, too, as they are areas selected from the whole country, that there should be several in easy range wherever you live. The walks vary in length but are generally four or five miles long, and usually come with an option for doing less, or even sometimes more. They are on footpaths, and also on canal towpaths, old railway lines, cliff tops, open fields and even over the water on the Sussex footpath ferry! There's no overall itinerary, I've just given some suggestions as to what else is nearby and in some cases local pubs or good tea rooms that might round off the visit.

I've started with the dramatic coastline of Dorset, worked my way round the country to the wild moors of Northumberland, and then back down to the hills of South Sussex. Along the way there's the meandering valley of the Wye, the quiet of the Lancashire coast, the beech woods of the Chiltern Hills, and the juxtaposition between country and industry in Nottinghamshire.

I've explained each walk in some detail, giving the length and the time you should allow, as well as some idea of conditions so you know whether to be well-booted or to wear ordinary shoes. I've pointed out the main features, given directions and tried to indicate where the path may be difficult to find! There are simple route maps given in the book, but I recommend you take the appropriate Ordnance Survey map which can be borrowed from your local library, if necessary.

Walking is an excellent way to enjoy the countryside and I find that a walk is the most satisfying way to absorb a place. It slows your pace so dramatically that you see and experience so much more. You have time to take in a view, notice the individual flowers of a hedgerow, look in shop windows, creep up on a rabbit or feel the elements on your face. Even walks that are popular never feel that crowded, especially when you compare them to a rush-hour trip in the London Underground. Now that I've done all the walks, I want to do them all again as there was so much to discover and enjoy.

Finally, here are some tips on keeping to the 'Country Code'.

Whilst I'm infuriated when I come across a footpath sign half buried in the undergrowth that points to a ploughed field or, worse still, a three-strand barbed-wire fence, I also feel sorry for farmers who have suffered at the hands, or rather the feet, of walkers. Once, I inadvertently let three sheep out of a field and it wasn't any fun playing sheepdog to get them back.

Please follow the well-known 'Country Code' on any of the walks in this book:

INTRODUCTION

LEAVE NO LITTER
LIGHT NO FIRES
SHUT ALL GATES FIRMLY
PICK NO WILD FLOWERS NOR PLANTS
KEEP DOGS UNDER CONTROL

Notes on the Key

Below is the key that explains the symbols that have been used for the maps which you'll find throughout the book.

The majority of maps have been drawn at a scale of 1:50,000 or 2 cm per 1 kilometer or $1\frac{1}{4}$ inches to 1 mile. Scale bars are included with all maps and where the scale differs from 1:50,000, the correct scale is given above the bar.

Happy walking!

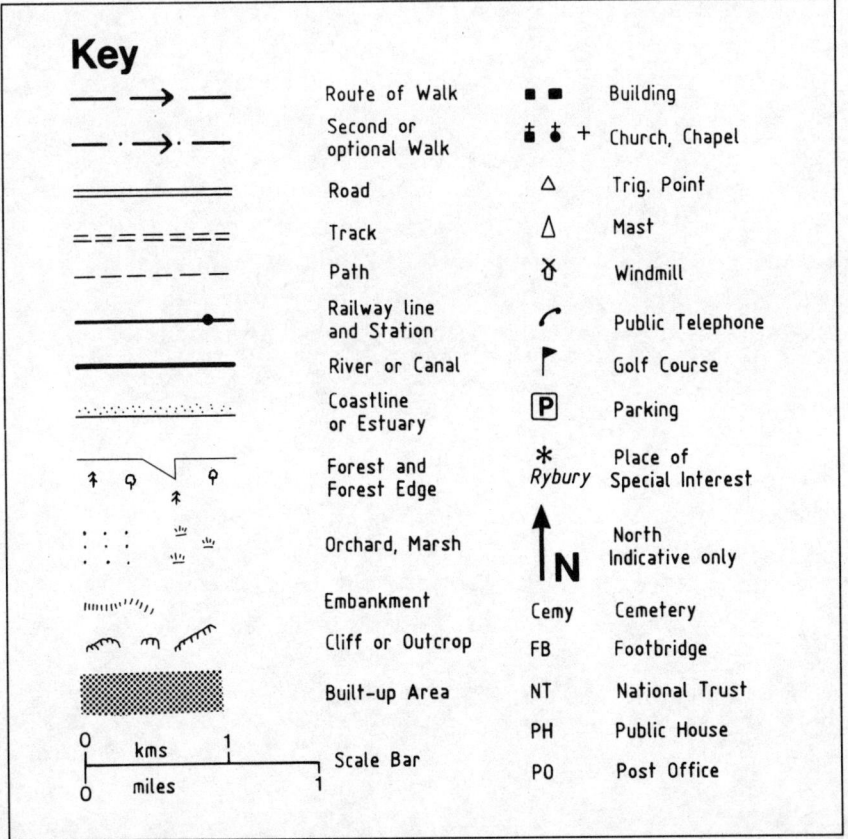

DORSET

The *Alice in Wonderland* expression 'curiouser and curiouser' seems to sum up Dorset perfectly, this county of curiosities, of which the most famous is Lulworth Cove, especially its magical fossilized forest.

There are many geological curiosities all along the coast. You don't have to be a rock buff to appreciate the precarious chalk stacks of Old Harry and his family; the dramatic black shale of Kimmeridge, and Chesil Beach, that inexplicable grading of rounded pebbles stretching for miles.

Inland too there are many unusual features, including the biggest swallow-holes in Europe and the richly textured Dorset heathland. The latter achieved fame through the novelist Thomas Hardy's Egdon Heath, but it is a tragically disappearing environment, fast going the way of Dorset's dinosaurs.

Man, too, has added a few oddities to the landscape – an obelisk that was once a street lamp, a lonely Norman chapel whose origins are a mystery and, further back to prehistory, a plethora of hill-fort earthworks, from the vast Maiden Castle to the sculptured Hod and Hambledon Hills.

Geologically there is great variety, true of virtually every English county, but all the more interesting here for being in such a small area. Many varieties of the stone are used for building: Purbeck marble, Purbeck-Portland (limestone that contains hardly any stone), Portland (which became popular under the patronage of Sir Christopher Wren), Purbeck Slate (no connection with real slate, as seen at Corfe Castle village), and Blue Lias (mined near Bridport). Other stones include Greensand, Flint in the chalk, and Dorset Cob which is in fact mud.

With no shortage of places to delight and intrigue, an extra bonus is the good walking. This is not just because the going underfoot tends to be good, but also because there is extensive way-marking to add to the opportunities.

I have set out two walks on the Isle of Purbeck, a most rewarding area to explore. It is a part that can be easily overlooked because its natural gateway, Corfe Castle, has a great capacity to detain. Further along the coast there is wonderful walking above, rather than on Chesil Beach.

Inland, there is a walk that takes in the heath and forestland around the home of T. E. Lawrence, where you can also see some of the most unusual and lovely church windows in the country, and there is also a visit to the chalk downlands in the heart of Dorset.

As well as the countryside, the towns of Dorset are very attractive. I've mentioned, especially, Dorchester, Wareham and Blandford Forum.

The Isle of Purbeck

The name belies the truth, as this is not really an isle at all unless you try to imagine the River Frome cutting off this little chunk of land. In spite of being a small area, there is a wealth of things to discover here. The walking is wonderful, with terrain which varies from heather and coastland to rounded hills and dense forests. The two most interesting towns are Wareham and Swanage. In addition, there are many small villages, plenty with a fascinating history, and much in the way of industrial history and geology too.

It is probably worth trying to stay in the area to save you retracing your steps along the main road through Corfe Castle. There are plenty of good bed and breakfast places, and I once camped in the height of summer and had no trouble finding a pleasant uncrowded farmsite.

I've described two of the many possibilities here. First is a heathland walk starting on the eastern coast, bringing you near Swanage. Second is one to the southern part of the Isle, which is handy if you want to explore Wareham later, where food is available from pubs on the pretty quayside.

Whichever way you go to the Isle of Purbeck, you'll probably end up passing Corfe Castle, as it is strategically placed on an isolated mound in a break in the Purbeck Hill Range. It is a very popular spot, ranked amongst the top ten in the National Trust's head count of visitors. Both the setting and the ruins are very attractive. They are made more interesting because many of the walls and towers that fell down when the building was seriously undermined in the Civil War still lie where they fell some three hundred years ago. Seeing these chunks of masonry in a state of upheaval – some would compete seriously with the leaning Tower of Pisa – gives you a sense of the strength of the place, and the power that was needed to demolish it.

If you decide to visit *en route*, it is best to wind your way around the narrow streets to the car-park provided for the castle. From there it is only a short walk back through the village. There is a car-park on the outskirts of the town, but parking here involves crossing the busy A351 and a roadside walk around the foundations of the castle.

From Corfe Castle it is only a short distance to the heathland and cliffs near Old Harry Rocks.

OLD HARRY ROCKS

OS Map 1: 50 000, Sheet 195
A circular walk of 5–6 miles (8–10 km). Allow three hours.

I feel as though I should start this walk with 'Roll up! Roll up! Hurry before you miss the spectacular heathland of Dorset!' Geographically, heath is a feature of sandy and gravelly soils of lowland Britain. Britain's heathland represents almost half of what is left in Western Europe, and the largest remaining areas are in Dorset. With the ravages of agriculture, mining and scrub succession, the area has dwindled to some 12 per cent of what it was two hundred years ago. The heath's decline has been further accelerated by afforestation since the Second World War. Man has intruded in other ways as well, with the exploration of natural gas and oil and the vast increase in housing in the county.

The disappearance of this environment is most worrying because of the range of wildlife that depends on the heath for existence, though you may have to be very patient to see some of these creatures. The Dartford Warbler, found solely on heathery heaths, as well as the nightjar and woodlark, are all now scarce in Britain, as are the native reptile species. There are only six types of these found in Britain, with the smooth snake and the sand lizard found virtually nowhere else but on this southern Dorset heathland. An encouraging move is Dorset County Council's recent launch of the Dorset Heathland Forum, which will endeavour to protect this valuable landscape.

The wild, unenclosed expanses that are left are a pleasure to walk in. In winter the landscape is coarsely textured with spiked thorn and deep brown heather, whilst through the warmer months the scene changes with bright patches of yellow gorse and soft purple-pink hues.

This walk takes you over part of the heath, and then onto contrasting grassy hills along to Handfast Point where the Purbeck Hills end abruptly at the sea.

The navigation is very easy as the paths are well way-marked. The beginning section and the final part are popular (sadly this evidence comes from the litter), but the main middle section is unlikely to be too crowded. I last walked here in the height of the August holidays, but by going in the early evening I encountered only a dozen people.

The going underfoot is very easy. Light sandy soil covers the heathland, and some of the boggier areas have been protected with gravel. On the downland section there is the typical short springy turf. It is a climb to get onto the ridge but then it is downhill to the cliffs. Around here there is no fencing or other barriers to prevent you, dogs, or children from falling off, and it is unwise to get near the edges as the turf can be slippery even in dry weather, so take great care. Dogs (and children) may be better on a lead on this part.

Car-parking and the start

Park at Middle Beach car-park, Studland. It is locked at 8 pm. If you are intending to walk later on a summer evening, you could use the southern car-park which is not locked until 11 pm.

Come out of the car-park, turn right past the little triangle of green and just beyond on the right is a footpath taking you to the main road.

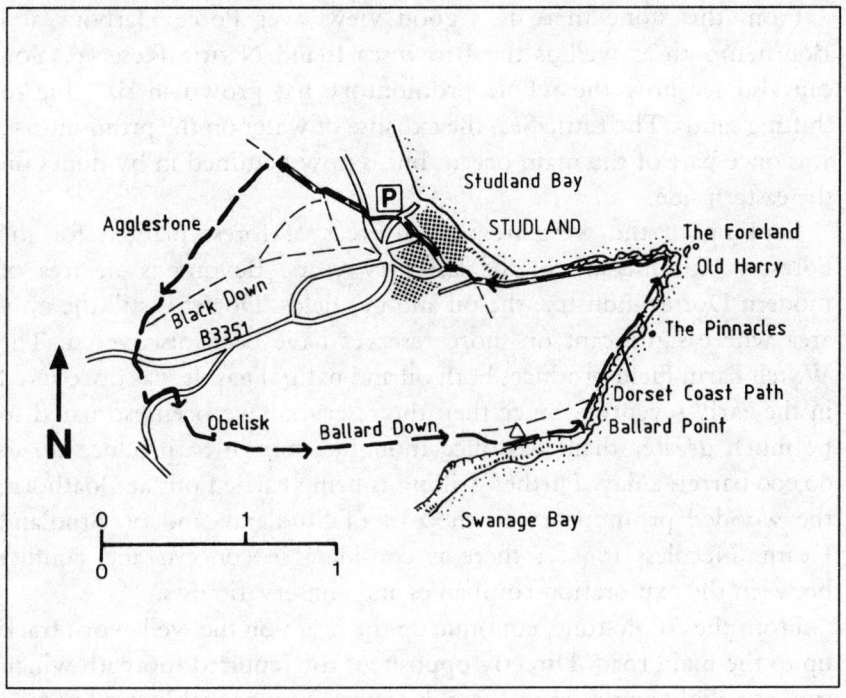

Cross this road and turn right, walking along the verge to the first main track on the left, a private road which is also marked as a bridleway and footpath. Fairly quickly you get onto the open heathland with its distinctive vegetation. Clear paths have been worn through the heather, which is no mean feat as it is a most resilient plant. You'll see the Agglestone looming to the left. Head towards that on any of the tracks.

The Agglestone is all that remains of the crust of sandstone that once covered the surrounding area. All the rest has been worn away by the elements, leaving this oddly shaped chunk, some 20 feet (6 m) high and estimated to be nearly five hundred tons in weight. It, too, is weathered, rather grey on the southern side, and reddish underneath, with the iron content of the rock; it's correct geological term is Ferruginous Sandstone. As usual with these natural curiosities, there are legends to explain their existence. Apparently, the Agglestone was thrown by the devil from the Isle of Wight to hit Corfe Castle, though he was somewhat wide of his mark.

From this stone there is a good view over Poole Harbour and Bournemouth as well as the Brownsea Island Nature Reserve. You can also see how the whole promontory has grown in size due to shifting sands. The Little Sea, the expanse of water on the promontory, was once part of the main ocean, but is now hemmed in by dunes on the eastern side.

Looking to the west are several areas of forest planted for the Forestry Commission in the last fifty years. Beyond is an area of modern Dorset Industry, the oil and gas fields. Dorset is still the only area where significant on-shore reserves have been discovered. The Wytch Farm Field produces both oil and natural gas. It was discovered in the early seventies. Since then the reserves have been estimated to be much greater than was once thought, enough to produce up to 60,000 barrels a day. Further drilling is being carried out at Goathorn, the wooded promontory to the east of Studland, and on Studland Heath. Needless to say, there is considerable concern and conflict between the exploration companies and conservationists.

From the Agglestone, continue up the heath on the well-worn track up to the main road. Directly opposite is the required footpath which runs at a slight angle across the golf course. You probably need to take more care here than going across the road. After the golf course, the path drops down through a slightly wooded area, and then out into the open where you'll see a gate down to your left. Immediately opposite this is the track leading up to the obelisk.

This obelisk was erected by George Burt, a Swanage stone merchant, to commemorate 'the introduction of pure water from the chalk formation to Swanage'. Surprisingly, in view of the amount of stone available locally, the obelisk was brought down from London where it had been used as a lamppost outside Mansion House. Burt's firm was London-based, and he transported all manner of things from the capital – wrought-iron work, balustrades and bollards, and the entire facade that forms the centre of Swanage Town Hall. In the Second World War the obelisk was dismantled in case it acted as a landmark for enemy planes. It was not re-erected until 1973.

From the obelisk there is a long ridge of downland that brings you beyond the trig point to the sea. These are the Purbeck Hills, which used to stretch as far as the Isle of Wight. Poole Harbour and the Solent were merely river valleys until the sea eroded the line. This part is called Ballard Down and it is owned by the National Trust. The ridge terminates in the dramatic cliffs at the northern end of Swanage Bay.

However much you are familiar with the sight from postcards of the cliffs, they are breathtaking. The contrast of their faces white against the blue-green sea, and the sheer drop suddenly ending the soft rounded contours of downland, is stunning.

Turn left along the cliff edge. Far below in the sea, you'll come first to a squarish stack and a shark's tooth of a pinnacle, and then to Handfast Point itself. This is described by Hardy as a 'windy, sousing, thwacking, basting Jack Ketch of a corner'.

At the far end are the Old Harry Rocks. There used to be Old Harry's Wife, but she got swept away in a storm in 1896. Local legend has it that the fishermen painted a black ring around the poor old widower. But the old chap isn't too lonely as the sea is already carving away future generations. You can see (without going too close to the edge) small arches that have already been eroded under the narrow promontories. These will be stacks in years to come, and will then, too, eventually succumb to the sea.

From here, in good visibility, you can see the Needles and the Isle of Wight, a distance of over twelve miles (19 km).

From Old Harry continue along the cliffs back towards Studland. Just beyond a small block of forest on the left is a short footpath bearing right that brings you to a tarmac road. When you get to the road, turn right. There is a short road walk back to the triangle of green that you passed at the start, and incidentally it passes the car-park that is open later in the day.

Isle of Purbeck Quarries Walk

The South-West Peninsula Walk is the longest long-distance footpath in the country running over five hundred miles (804 km) from Poole Harbour to Minehead in Somerset. But I'm not suggesting that for an afternoon's excursion! This somewhat shorter walk is based on the Purbeck Isle section of the footpath which takes you along and over a great many interesting sites, whether you are interested in geology, natural history, history or geography.

I have deliberately chosen a walk through the central part of the Isle of Purbeck as this will give you a taste of all the many possibilities. Probably once you've walked here, like me, you'll be planning when to come back.

Along the Cliff-Top

OS Map 1:50 000, Sheet 195
A circular walk of 5 miles (8 km). Allow 2½ hours and extra time if you want to visit Chapman's Pool.

As I mentioned, this is a fascinating area from many points of view. This walk takes you past exciting quarries along a glorious section of the coast from where you can see breathtaking cliffs, an enigmatic chapel perched on a rocky headland, and finally, a secluded bay, tucked away at the base of the cliffs. It makes a good picnic spot, even in the height of summer.

The going underfoot is excellent – on track and short turf. I can't, however, emphasize too much how careful you should be where the path gets very narrow along the edge of the cliff. There often isn't much more than a foot or two between you and the sheer drop to the sea below. Although at times hair-raising, it is exhilarating to walk here accompanied by the sounds of the ocean, the noise of the surf and the yelping sea gulls.

This walk is fairly energetic, for despite being given the title 'along the cliff-top', the coastline has a nasty trick of suddenly descending into a steep valley, offering no alternative but a climb up the other side.

The navigation is easy with a clear track down to the coast, and little route choice as you walk along it. The route back to Worth Village is also well signposted.

DORSET

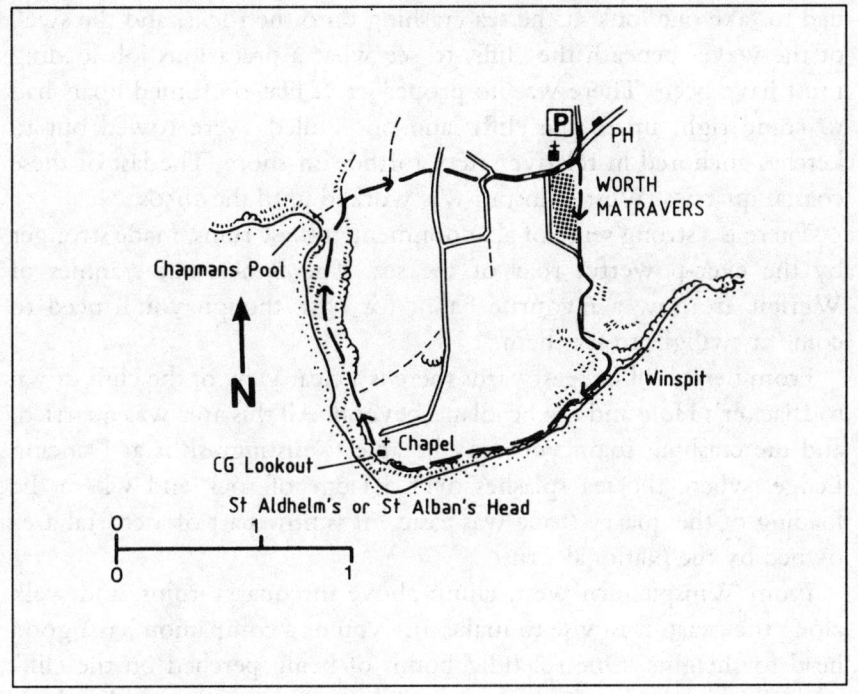

Car-parking and the start

There is a car-park, signposted from the village centre, just to the north of the village called Worth Matravers.

Start by walking into the village centre. Then, beyond the village pond to the left is a track, signposted Winspit. It starts alongside an attractive terrace of houses called London Row, and then soon comes out into open countryside, keeping along the valley bottom. On either side the sloping downland is covered with tiny ledges, a sure indication that ancient farming was once carried out here.

Apart from farming the other main activity in the area was quarrying. The stone was called Cliffstone, otherwise known as Purbeck Portland Limestone, and there were quarries all along this coast down as far as Swanage. At Winspit, where the track meets the sea, old quarry ruins and marks in the cliffs are evident where the blocks of stone were cut out. Once the blocks were cut, the hazardous business began of loading them onto ships for transport to Swanage Bay. I only had to take one look at the sea crashing onto the rocks, and the swell of the waves beneath the cliffs, to see what a precarious job loading must have been. There was no proper jetty. Flat-bottomed boats had to come right up to the cliffs, and once filled, were rowed out to ketches anchored in relative safety further off-shore. The last of these coastal quarries, West Winspit, was worked until the 1950s.

There is a strong sense of abandonment at these ruins, made stronger by the ever-powerful roar of the sea. The nooks and crannies of Winspit are now a favourite haunt for bats, though you'll need to come at twilight to see them.

From here, looking eastwards there is a clear view of the cliffs down to Blacker's Hole and the headland beyond. All this area was quarried, and the crashing foam you may be able to distinguish is at Dancing Ledge, where the sea splashes over a ledge of rock and where the loading of the quarry stone was easier. It is now part of a coastal area owned by the National Trust.

From Winspit turn west, climb above the quarry ruins, and walk along the coast. It is wise to make sure you or a companion has a good head for heights. One splendid bonus of being perched on the cliff-edge like this is the chance to see gliding birds so close at hand. (It helps to distract me from the trembling of my legs.) There are plenty of gulls wheeling round and you may also see terns and kittiwakes.

After a few ups and downs, the rocky headland of St Aldhelm comes into view below, and the small chapel dedicated to this saint is on the headland above.

The chapel is a charming place, unusual in being exactly square ($25\frac{1}{2}$ feet [8 m] apparently) and rather remotely placed; so remote that there are many question marks surrounding the origins of this building. It doesn't seem possible it could have been a parish church. One story is that the chapel was erected by a Norman lord who had come to this headland to watch his daughter sail away on her honeymoon. Suddenly a violent storm whipped up and the newly-wed's boat was dashed on the rocks below. The distraught father decided to build a sea-mark here so that other voyagers might not suffer the same fate. There was supposed to be a light forever burning on the top, but another mystery of the chapel is that no one can yet work out how a beacon could have been attached to the roof.

The interior of the chapel is quite simple with the most pleasing vaulting in each of the four sections. The very thick walls keep out the sounds of the wind and sea, adding to the calm atmosphere, so it is quite a shock to return to the elements.

From the chapel, continue round the cliffs. You get a good view west as far as Portland Bill. Much nearer you should be able to make out (without binoculars) Clavell Tower, built by the eponymous local landowner on the top of the Kimmeridge Cliffs. The cliffs themselves are very distinctive, comprised of black shale, known as blackstone, rather than the more familiar white chalk.

William Clavell had several unsuccessful attempts to extract useful deposits from this unusual rock. At various times the shale has been used for jewellery (by the Romans, for instance) and as an oil for Parisian street lamps, a scheme abandoned because of the terrible smell. Ironically, this is now the site of a profitable oil well.

I found it equally fascinating to think I was looking here at over a hundred million years of the earth's development. The top of the chalk that is part of the Purbeck cliffs is relatively young at sixty-five million years old, whilst the Kimmeridge Clay, with its distinctive grey appearance, comes from an earlier time of up to a hundred and eighty million years ago.

The oldest rocks were put down in the Jurassic Period, at a time when Dorset was a warm sea and ammonites lived in it in abundance. About a hundred and thirty-five million years ago, forces in the earth buckled the earth's crust, throwing up a land mass and leaving Dorset with a sub-tropical landscape covered by forest and both fresh and salt waters. When the land wasn't flooded it was covered with soil, known as dirt beds, which now contain the remains of plants and animals that lived at that time, including a great variety of Dorset Dinosaurs. The second main geological period is called the Cretaceous Period, which is when the relatively 'young' chalk deposits were laid down. Geologists are very partial to this section of the coast as the rocks are so well-displayed in the cliffs.

Looking at the cliffs is one thing, climbing them is another! This next part of the walk is very steep as the coastline drops away into a deep valley. There are some fairly primitive steps and a fence to help you on the way down, though not so on the side going up.

Once you get to the top, you'll soon catch sight of the bay known as Chapman's Pool. Its sweeping curve contains a clear sea, and its sheltered position lured me down, despite the thought of climbing up again. It is pleasant to swim here as long as you don't mind a shingly rather than a sandy beach.

To get down to the pool, carry on along the cliffs until you are almost past the bay. Here there is a choice of tracks taking you back to Worth Matravers via some fields and farmland, or down to the pool in a diagonal line. It is worth going down, especially if the weather is good enough for picnicking and swimming, but it will add a good half-hour to your walk.

If you are not going to the pool, just turn right at the way-marking sign and follow the route back to the village. The last part of this is on a road with no footpath, but there is scarcely any traffic. There is a pleasant café in Worth as well as a pub if you are, as I was, in need of refreshment.

Nearby Wareham is a fine riverside town, now made more pleasant with a new bypass. Up until the fourteenth century it was a port, but now only pleasure boats cruise their way up to the quay. It's a very picturesque spot with its square surrounded by old pubs, and a low curving bridge over the river. Just the place for a little refreshment. If you haven't had enough walking, there is a short jaunt around the huge earth banks built to defend the town in the days of King Arthur. On North Street there is the Saxon church of St Martin's where you'll find a T. E. Lawrence effigy in full Arab dress. Lawrence is somewhat of a local hero and there is an interesting walk around his former home.

In the triangle between Dorchester, Bridport and Weymouth there is some excellent walking both along the coast and inland. After a morning's ramble or longer in this countryside you are in easy reach of any of these three towns and all have something to offer.

As with the suggestions for the Isle of Purbeck, I have chosen to describe a walk around a central section as there is not only plenty of interest but it will also give you a chance to see what there is to come back for. It's the sort of area that looks intriguing, encouraging you to walk on further. There are also plenty of possibilities for day-long expeditions.

Abbotsbury

OS map 1:50 000, Sheet 194
A circular walk of 5½ miles (8–9 km). Allow 2½–3 hours.

This walk gives you the classic aerial view of Chesil Beach, an extraordinary geological phenomenon that quite frankly is best appreciated from above. The beach comprises some sixteen miles (25 km) of raised shingle. It is quite possible to walk on but exceedingly tiring. On the ordnance survey map the area is marked by a mass of black flecks, rather like a man who hasn't shaved for a day or two.

From the ridge above Abbotsbury, where you get the view, there is a large hill fort and a good view, too, over the north-western part of Dorset. The circuit goes on through Abbotsbury and then up another hill to the delightful chapel of St Catherine's.

The going underfoot is mostly good with springy foot-friendly turf below your feet, and a couple of tarmac road sections. There are two steep climbs, one on a narrow path that may be a little muddy in wet conditions, and one fast road to cross. The way-marking is excellent (although as you join part of a longer walk the signs point to places further on than you may wish to go). The village of Abbotsbury, the tower of St Catherine's, and the beach, are good landmarks to keep you on course.

Car-parking and the start

There is free parking at Chesil Beach, south-west of Abbotsbury. Follow the signs to the sub-tropical gardens from the village centre along the B3157 and then turn off onto a smaller lane. The first car-park is for the gardens. Further along is another one just by the beach.

Most walks have a natural direction, and having considered both ways round, I think the clockwise route is better, as you spend most of the way looking into views rather than turning back for them. The advantage of the other direction is that you get a better view of Abbotsbury, so if you were only going to do the there-and-back to the village via St Catherine's that would be best.

Start by walking westwards along the tarmac road for about one mile (1½ km). You'll soon be able to see the cliffs beyond Bridport rising some 600 feet (182 m) to the Golden Cap. Shortly beyond Lawrence's Cottage (no relation to T. E.) is a footpath off to the right going up Tulk's Hill. It is signposted Abbotsbury Hill Fort. Ahead, high on the hill, you'll see a very pretty thatched white cottage surrounded by dark trees, which is along the path of the walk. Aim for this, skirting around East Bexington Farm. There are yellow arrows to keep you on course.

Beyond the cottage, climb straight up the hill and then turn right towards the hill fort and Hardy's Monument. You are now on the section of the Dorset Coast Path where it takes a sweep inland to avoid Weymouth so the route is well signposted. Watch out for the busy road crossing. Just beyond you'll come to the ramparts of the hill fort.

This was an Iron Age construction comprising an impressive mass of ditches and ridges and making good use of a natural lump at the end of a long spur. It is one of about thirty in Dorset. Some of the forts were occupied by communities as well as being used for defence. Sites were chosen well, and from here you can see far inland across the lovely valley of the River Bride. The biggest of the villages is Litton Cheney, and to the right is Long Bredy. After the Roman conquest the forts were mainly deserted.

Carry on along this ridge. From here you can see Chesil Beach sweeping round to the Isle of Portland. The beach encloses a stretch of water known as The Fleet. At the far end is Fleet, the village made famous thanks to the novel, film and TV serial of the Moonfleet story, a tale of eighteenth-century smugglers. I vividly remember the film version with some terrifying scenes set in the moonlit graveyard.

Although Chesil Beach looks a formidable barrier it was breached by the sea in 1824, and most of Fleet village was destroyed. The landlocked lagoon that remains, called The Fleet, is a mixture of fresh and salt water. It is now an important nature reserve and the home of many birds and unusual flowers.

Inland, along the ridge, you should be able to see a small chimney-like tower. This is Hardy's Monument – for once nothing to do with the writer but with the captain of Nelson's 'Kiss me, Hardy' fame. Admiral Sir Thomas lived for the first part of his life at Portesham, the village that lies at the bottom of the hill, and the monument was erected after his death, to mark his heroics at Trafalgar.

Walk in the direction of the monument along the ridge for about a

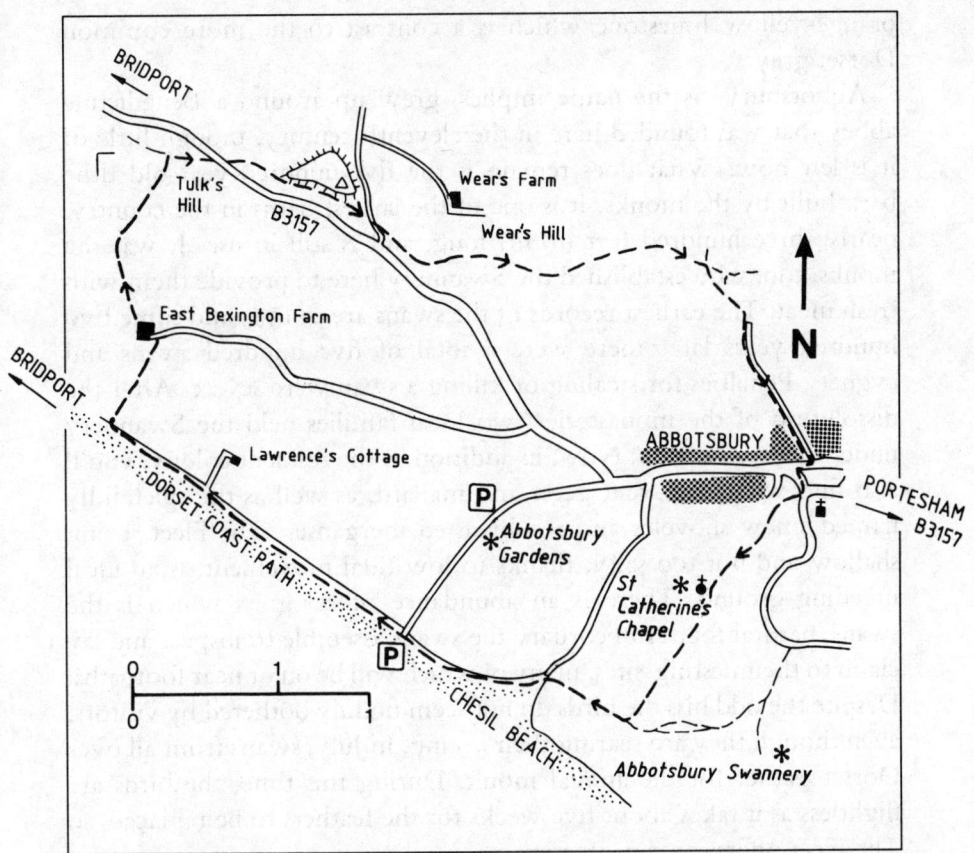

mile (1¼ km) and then there is a diagonal signpost pointing you down towards Abbotsbury. The path isn't particularly obvious here but it goes over some distinct lumps and bumps, evidence of more prehistoric earthworks, and down in the general direction of the village. From here you'll get a good view of St Catherine's, a tiny chapel standing on an isolated hill on the other side of the village, which the walk will eventually pass.

The track brings you out at the back of Abbotsbury Village. If you want a refreshment stop, there is a good place on the road to Portesham (open in summer only) and you may like to spend a little time wandering around Abbotsbury itself. It is rather a one-road village straggling out to the west for some way. What struck me first was the different stone used for many of the buildings here. It is a local, almost orange-yellow limestone which is a contrast to the more common Dorset grey.

Abbotsbury, as the name implies, grew up around a Benedictine abbey that was founded here in the eleventh century, though little of it is left now. What does remain is the five-hundred-year-old tithe barn built by the monks. It is one of the largest barns in the country, nearly three hundred feet (91 m) long, and is still in use. It was the monks, too, who established the Swannery here to provide them with fresh meat. The earliest records of the swans are in 1393 and some two hundred years later there were a total of five hundred swans and cygnets. Penalties for stealing or killing a swan were severe. After the dissolution of the monasteries two local families held the Swannery under their protection. Now, in addition to the resident colony, you'll also find widgeon, brent geese and mallard, as well as the splendidly named smew shoveler and red-breasted merganser. The Fleet, being shallow and not too salty, thanks to low tidal movement, is an ideal breeding-ground. There is an abundance of eel grass which is the swans' natural food. In February the swans assemble to inspect and lay claim to their nesting-sites, many of which will be on or near footpaths. Despite the odd hiss the birds do not seem unduly bothered by visitors, even though they are rearing their young. In July, swans from all over Dorset gather for the annual moult. During this time, the birds are flightless as it takes about five weeks for the feathers to be replaced, so The Fleet offers some protection.

Apart from the swans, there is a duck decoy dating from the seventeenth century. Some of the old ponds have been turned into reed beds to supply local thatching material, once again as fashionable as it was up until the nineteenth century. You can detour to visit the Swannery which is open between mid-May and September.

Once you have savoured the delights of Abbotsbury, finish the walk by climbing up the hill to St Catherine's. There is a footpath, signed rather quaintly with a picture of two monks hooded and habited, which goes out through a car-park at the back of the Ilchester Arms on the main street. Turn right along a small footpath and then left onto a very obvious track.

This chapel was part of the original abbey complex, but survived destruction in the time of the dissolution of the monasteries probably because it was a useful landmark for those at sea. Inside, the chapel is quite plain and simple, higher and narrower than I expected. On one wall is a little poem said by spinsters when they were searching for a husband, which is worth climbing up to the chapel to read.

Before you leave the hill, turn back to take in the splendid view of the village dominated by the huge barn.

To get back to the beach, head past the chapel towards the sea, dropping down over the pastureland to meet a footpath that goes to the Swannery. Here, turn right and walk back to the car-park.

Extending this walk is easy. There is a short loop marked on all the information boards called the hill fort loop, which takes you an extra half mile (1 km) further along the ridge above Abbotsbury to a summit called White Hill.

If you feel particularly energetic, you might like to go right along to the Hardy Monument, but that would be a much more substantial expedition.

Dorchester, a pleasant busy town, is an easy drive from Abbotsbury. It was a town as early as 100 AD, and you can walk over relaid Roman pavements in the Dorset County Museum, which is housed in a most curious Victorian building. There are many other interesting exhibits, but the archaeological display is particularly interesting. Much of the knowledge of our early ancestors comes ironically from evidence about death with the discovery of burial chambers and barrows. Be prepared for some pretty grim skeletons.

Clouds Hill and Culpepper's Dish

OS Map 1:50 000, Sheet 194
A circular walk of 5 miles (8 km). Allow $2\frac{1}{2}$–$3\frac{1}{2}$ hours, depending on whether you visit both Moreton Church and Clouds Hill.

It is easy to be deceived into thinking that all there is to Dorset is breezy ridges and dramatic expanses of coastline. The inland areas have quite a different feel, particularly some of the low-lying forested parts. This walk covers a good mixture of forest, open farm and heathland, as well as a glimpse of two hills in the distance. It also takes you to Clouds Hill, the home of T. E. Lawrence, now in the care of the

National Trust, and also to his burial-place near Moreton Church. The walk starts, though, with a geological curiosity – Culpepper's Dish.

The going underfoot is good on well-defined tracks, and the navigation is easy, once you have got a hundred metres from the car-park, the route being fairly flat. In winter, or after a good deal of terrible weather, the final section through the forest could be muddy, but there is a road option if this is the case.

Car-parking and the start

Park at the Culpepper's Dish Picnic Site which is on an unmarked road south of Briantspuddle.

The dish or swallow-hole is directly opposite the car-park, though it is not marked and only roughly fenced off from the road with a strand of barbed wire. Do not go plunging in to the undergrowth, however, as the hole is forty 40 feet (12 m) deep and over a hundred yards (91 m) across. It's quite a clamber down and even more of a scramble up so you may be content to gaze in wonder from the rim. Swallow-holes are caused by acidic water draining through the heath, eroding ground below the surface. The top-soil eventually falls into the space created, thus leaving a natural basin. There are many more such holes in this area, particularly around Affpuddle and Puddletown Heath. New ones have appeared in this century.

For the walk, cross back into the car-park and look for the little track on the far right of the car-parking space that leads you diagonally left behind the car-park into the valley. As I suggested, the first part is just a little tricky to navigate, but it a short-cut from the car-park to the forest track and it avoids going on the road.

At the bottom of this track, you'll come out at a crossroads of forest roads; take the one going south-west. It is the central one as you look away from the car-park.

You'll soon see a marshy area to your left known as Rimsmoor Pond, and then you'll come out into the open, under a vast power-line. Just carry straight on, even though the path narrows slightly, and eventually, having passed some houses hidden in woods to your left, you'll come to a road. The route continues directly opposite. It starts by taking you on a wide bridle-track which ends at a field. On the map the route carries straight on, but if you look down the bridle-

DORSET

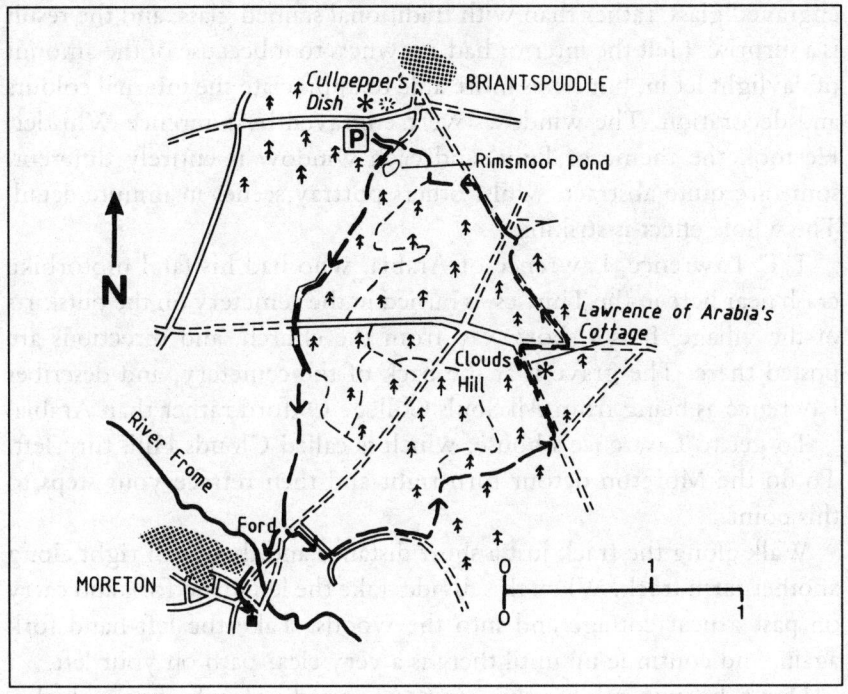

track to the left you'll see a yellow mark showing the route through the woods. I enjoyed this section, meandering through the quiet woods with a soft pine-needle carpet below my feet. The trees here have a gnarled and ancient feel, and there is a jungle-like quality to the undergrowth caused by the rhododendron bushes. This shrub is threatening much of the countryside by overtaking vast areas in woodlands and open spaces. Its dense structure starves nearby plants of light, and little wildlife is able to make use of it.

The trusty yellow splodges bring you over a small bridge and into fields. Across a couple of these and then around the edge of the third (a farmer has left a decent edge for walking on) and you join another forest road.

Here it is worth making a detour to Moreton, which adds almost an extra mile (1.5 km) in total. The church, although Gothic in appearance, was rebuilt during the eighteenth and early nineteenth centuries. It was then heavily bombed in 1940 and all the glass in the building was destroyed. The windows were subsequently replaced with clear engraved glass, rather than with traditional stained glass, and the result is a surprise. I felt the interior had a rawness to it because of the amount of daylight let in, but I was more able to appreciate the internal colours and decoration. The windows were engraved by Laurence Whistler. He took the theme of light, and each window is entirely different, some are quite abstract, whilst others portray scenes in minute detail. The whole effect is striking.

T. E. Lawrence, Lawrence of Arabia, who had his fatal motorbike crash near here in the Thirties, is buried in the cemetery on the outskirts of the village. It is a short way from the church, and directions are posted there. The grave is at the back of the cemetery, and describes Lawrence as being from All Souls College Oxford rather than Arabia!

To get to Lawrence's house, which is called Clouds Hill, turn left. To do the Moreton detour turn right and then retrace your steps to this point.

Walk along the track just a short distance and then turn right along another farm track. When this divides take the left-hand fork and carry on past a neat cottage and into the woods. Take the left-hand fork again, and continue up until there is a very clear path on your left.

Don't be put off by the ominous sounds of whirring vehicles, explosions, or the warning notices telling you not to pick up unidentified objects. Much of the surrounding area is used by the Army. Bovington Camp, home of the Royal Tank Regiment, is less than a mile away (there is a museum). What a mess it all is here with the ground sadly churned up by the tanks and heavy vehicles. It is a depressing contrast to the undisturbed forest earlier on.

Follow the path until very near the road. When it is in sight, turn left and follow the track that runs parallel. After a short distance it does seem to veer away from the road, but follow it on around a slight corner, climbing slightly. At the top, the main track curves away, but look out for a very small path to the right along the line of some old fencing. I did notice the odd yellow indicator mark along here. This path brings you back to the road and very close to Clouds Hill.

If you are walking when the house isn't open, take the footpath directly opposite which takes you around the back of the grounds on the way home. If you are visiting, walk along past the house, virtually hidden by dense bushes, to the car-park and entrance beyond.

T. E. Lawrence was stationed in the tank corps at nearby Bovington and he rented this little cottage from 1923. 'I don't sleep here but come out at 4.30 pm to 9 pm nearly every night, and dream, or write, or read by the fire, or play Beethoven or Mozart,' he wrote. The rooms are as Lawrence left them with his gramophone and 78's, and his leather settee. There were very few concessions made in the place to domestic activities such as cooking. Lawrence began living here permanently in 1935 when discharged from the Services. He wrote to Lady Astor that it was 'an earthly paradise' and nothing would drag him away. Sadly it was only days later that he was killed.

From Clouds Hill, go to the crossroads and turn right up the hill. Look out for where the footpath comes in on the right down some primitive steps. Here, cross the road and go through the gap in the bushes opposite. There's a very short steep descent and then veering right you'll come onto a sandy bridle-track. Follow this across the heathland, past the forbidding MOD notices. At the bottom of the slight valley join another track and continue on in the same direction. As this main track swings around the corner, look for signs of the bridle-track off to the left which then brings you out at a road junction.

Take the road opposite, signposted Briantspuddle, and follow this until you reach the power-lines. Here, if it looks dry underfoot, I suggest you make a short-cut through the forest, otherwise stay on the road. It is not terribly busy, but being so straight the cars tend to go rather fast.

For the woodland route, follow the course of the power-lines on the rough track. Just over the blind hill, you'll see a clear road-crossing. Turn right here and this route curves around to bring you back to the first junction that you encountered after leaving the car-park. Retrace your steps up the small path.

The Heartland of Dorset

OS Map 1:50 000, Sheet 194
A circular walk of 3 miles (5 km). Allow 1½ hours.

This walk introduces you to the centre of Dorset. It goes along almost a triangle of ridges that give extensive views to each point of the compass.

The hills of central Dorset are chalk-based like those of the Purbeck Range, and to the north there is a steep escarpment overlooking the Vale of Blackmoor. The walk starts close to Bulbarrow Hill, the second highest point (902 ft/274 m) in the county. In a roadside car-park there, you'll find a map table with direction lines picking out a few of the most prominent features in case you want to check up after, or even before, the walk.

The going is on grassy path and dirt track plus one section up a rather thistle-laden field, which wasn't too much of a problem. The route is quite obvious. There is one long but gentle climb.

Car-parking and the start

Use the car-park just south of Okeford Fitzpaine on the top of Okeford Hill. There are noticeboards in the car-park about the surrounding area, showing both footpaths and bridle-tracks as well as giving some details of local wildlife.

I like to do this walk in a clockwise direction, as it means you are always walking into a view. So start by crossing the road to the field opposite where you'll see a traditional beacon in the centre. There is a footpath on the map that goes across here, following the line of the ridge as far as the block of woods on the eastern edge of the field. Either it is so ill-used it has been forgotten, or it is deliberately ignored, because there was no satisfactory entrance to the field nor any way-marking. If you don't feel too confident navigating over an unmarked path, just enjoy the good view you get from the gate and then take the track to the right of the beacon field, which is virtually opposite the car-park.

From the gate or the beacon, you should be able to see Shaftesbury straddling a hillside some ten miles (16 km) away to the north. More eye-catching, perhaps, are the curiously moulded ridges of Hambledon Hill, nearer and just to the east. These ridges were once impressive hill forts, one of a pair in this part of Dorset. The other on Hod Hill is just obscured by the woods a mile or so south.

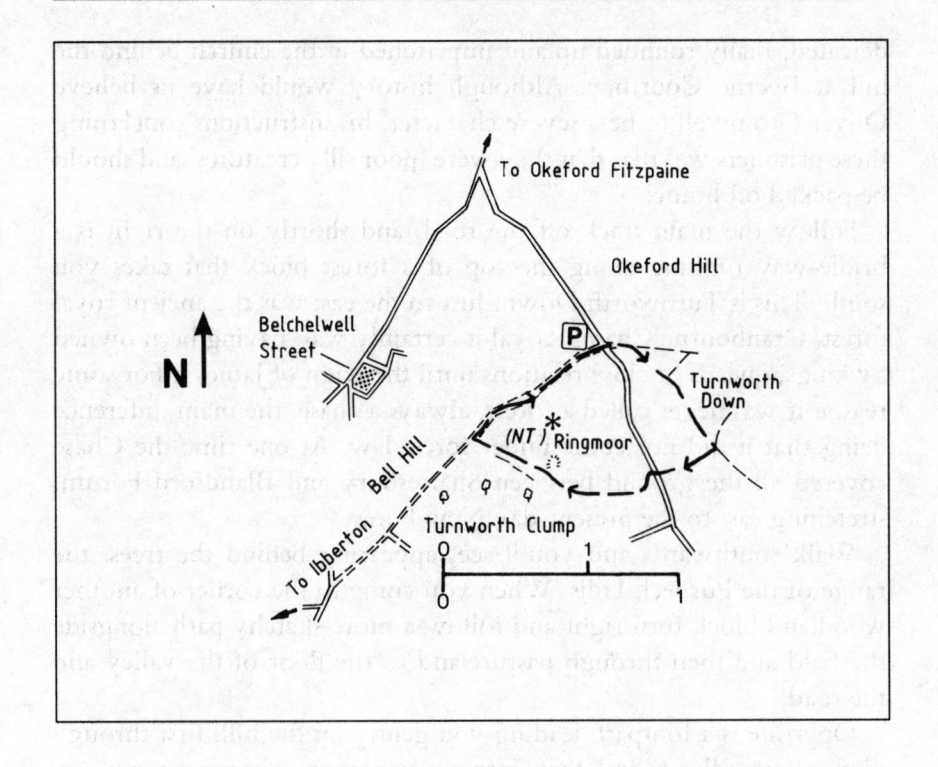

Although a visit to the hill forts is worthwhile, from this vantage-point it is easier to appreciate the effort that went into these workings, as the multiple ramparts are very clear. Evidence of settlements in the Iron Age as well as in Roman times has been found in the centre and some Neolithic enclosures found to the east.

This spot has also known activity comparatively recently during the English Civil War. A group of ordinary Dorset country folk – farmers, craftsmen, and labourers – were fed up with the indiscriminate looting and destruction of the soldiers on both warring sides. Armed only with clubs, hence their name Clubmen, they threatened a fight with anyone who plundered their land. A 'battle' was indeed fought, with some of Cromwell's troops from a Parliamentarian army. The Clubmen had the advantage of numbers but not of military discipline and were duly defeated, many rounded up and imprisoned in the church behind the hill at Iwerne Courtney. Although history would have us believe Oliver Cromwell to be a severe character, his instructions concerning these prisoners was that that they were 'poor silly creatures' and should be packed off home!

Follow the main track off the road, and shortly on the right is a bridle-way running along the top of a forest block that takes you south. This is Turnworth Down. Just to the east was the ancient royal forest, Cranbourne Chase. Royal it certainly was, having been owned by kings, queens or close relations until the reign of James I. For some reason it was never called a forest, always a chase, the main difference being that it did not come under forest law. At one time the Chase covered all the ground between Shaftesbury and Blandford Forum, stretching east to the present-day New Forest.

Walk southwards and you'll see, appearing behind the trees, the range of the Purbeck Hills. When you come to the corner of another woodland block turn right and follow a more sketchy path alongside the field and then through pastureland to the floor of the valley and the road.

Opposite is a footpath leading you gently up the hill, first through pleasant woodland, and then into open pasture where you can see, very faintly, the signs of raised banks indicating an ancient settlement. There are also slight marks left by prehistoric ploughing.

Keep climbing to the top of the ridge and you'll find a very obvious dirt road. Here you get a splendid view of West Dorset, the very flat Blackmoor Vale with the Quantock Hills, blue in the distance. Like the land to the east, this too was once all forested and known as the Forest of Blakemore. Significant areas were cleared from the fourteenth century, though permission had to be sought to 'reduce the land to cultivation'. Cleared areas tended to be irregular in size and surrounded by thick hedges. Some of these earlier systems can still be seen today, the lovely chequer-board pattern which has been created is a feast for the eye. The appearance of the downland has changed more recently. Modern farming techniques and agrochemicals make it possible to use the poor soils high up on the downs. Now the land is often ploughed where once only sheep roamed.

To the north, on the top of a thickly wooded hill, is a small triangular tower. This is Alfred's Tower at the famous romantic gardens of

Stourhead, some twenty miles (32 km) away, a National Trust property even more popular than Corfe Castle. Turn right from here and walk back along the track to the car-park. You will pass the signs on the left that direct you to the picnic site.

Whilst you are in this area you could easily visit Milton Abbas, a show village (for modern coach parties as much as anything else), or of much more interest and with a good bustling feel is Blandford Forum just six miles (10 km) east. I found it especially good to visit after this burst of countryside as I was encouraged to look at the buildings more closely.

There are two very significant dates in Blandford Forum's history: 1731, when the town was almost completely burnt down, and 1984, when the by-pass was opened. Although the name has strong Roman connotations, it may be derived from Bleagna, the Early English name for a freshwater fish. The town was founded at an important crossing-point, where the River Stour cuts through the chalky downlands. It was a lucky coincidence that after the eighteenth-century fire three established builders and architects were resident in the town – the brothers Thomas, John and William Bastard. Between them, they redesigned and rebuilt the town so all the buildings are virtually of the same period, something very unusual and curious.

There is an interesting town trail which not only introduces you to a fine selection of Georgian architecture but also to the town's ghosts: the black dog of Blandford Bridge and the headless sheep. There is also the town pump, a very fitting monument to the great fire, erected by the Bastard brothers and designed to provide water more for travellers than for emergencies.

WILTSHIRE

✦

Judging by the traffic shooting down, or more often jamming up the M4, there are plenty of people just using Wiltshire as somewhere to pass through *en route* to Bristol and the glories of the West Country. It wasn't until I had reason to visit Marlborough regularly that I realized within minutes of leaving the busy highway, there are some of the most splendid downland stretches in the south of England.

I was brought up near the Sussex Downs, which is why I feel an immediate kinship with this type of terrain. I'm always delighted by this countryside whether in howling gales, as often seems to be my luck, or on more typical days of clear skies and bright sunshine. What never changes is that wonderful feeling of space in downland such as this, making it the most marvellous 'all weather' countryside. The breadth of these Wiltshire downs is impressive with tremendous opportunities for walking. Once in the heart of the downs, you get the feeling of being in a great rolling sea. All around you is the wave-like sweep of the hills. The rhythm and curve of the land gives a soft rather than a dramatic quality, quite different from the hills of the North. Patches of forest and field remind you there is civilisation, modern that is, whilst evidence of the many settlements, henges, tumuli and barrows that abound in this county are signs of a civilization long ago.

Nowadays, these downs are mainly deserted apart from grazing sheep and profusions of wild flowers, but it wasn't always so. Wiltshire is brimful of sites of early habitation, from curious stone circles and spooky burial chambers to amazing earthworks that make me wonder when a Stone Age bull-dozer will be discovered. A great deal has been unearthed literally about the doings, peaceable and otherwise, of these early tribes. I particularly like some of the names given to them by historians, such as the 'Early Beaker' people. But there is still a sense of mystery about many of the sites, their meaning and origin, that I find most compelling. Even when I see marvellous constructed models of how massive stones were hauled out of the valleys sometimes nearly forty miles, I still find it hard to imagine it actually happening with the organization and manpower that must have been involved. How did primitive man have the time to build ceremonial sites for festivities? My primary school teaching taught me that he was supposed to be struggling just to stay alive!

The combination of the wonderful open land, mostly very accessible, and so much history to see makes for exhilarating walking. I've described three longish expeditions in this area. Although all across downland, they are surprisingly different in character. One takes in the site of a dramatic battlefield (slightly younger in age than prehistoric), another is a wander down one of the most impressive ancient earthworks in England, and the third, a treasure hunt for one of the most exciting finds I've come across.

Something else I discovered about Wiltshire while researching these walks was that there is much more to this county than the downs. When you arrive back in various wind-blown states from the hilltops, there are many sheltered places well worth exploring. There are of course a fair share of National Trust and English Heritage properties, but I found the market towns also very attractive with plenty to see. It was this discovery that really prompted the 'Downs and Towns' theme for this area, which I hope is an ideal mixture.

I've concentrated on three towns which I like the more I visit them – Marlborough, Devizes and Bradford-on-Avon. Like the downland walks I've described, they are quite different from each other except that each has a friendly feel and is as yet unspoiled by blatant commercialism. I enjoyed a stroll around each of these towns for different reasons and found they all have good features nearby such as forest or stretches of canal that are ideal for shorter, less-energetic expeditions than those over the downs.

When I began exploring North Wiltshire, I started off at Marlborough, as that is always the place I come to first from London. Then I travelled west to Devizes and Bradford-on-Avon. If you base yourself in or near any of these three towns, then all the walks and tours I have suggested are within easy reach.

In Search of The Polissoir

OS Map 1:50 000, Sheet 173
A circular downland walk of 6 miles (10 km) with possible additions of 3 miles (5 km). Allow 3 hours.

If you only have limited time, don't miss this downland walk which starts just outside Marlborough and takes the best part of a morning or afternoon. For an all-day expedition, you can extend it to visit the extensive prehistoric sites at Avebury as well. Otherwise, return to base and then drive to Avebury instead.

It is a marvellous walk, quite suitable for all weathers as indeed I found out when first completing it in high winds and driving rain. Do try to pick a day when at least the visibility is good, as the views over the sweeping downland are wonderful. The going underfoot is mostly soft short grass with little mud so it is excellent for both runners and walkers. You can take dogs but there are quite a few stiles to cross where they may need helping over, and be aware of grazing and other livestock.

This walk gives you the essence of the downs, taking you into the middle of softly curving lands that at once enfold you, and give you the feeling of being on top of the world. The fun of this jaunt is finding The Polissoir. It is a Sarsen stone, which was used as a sharpening bench for axe-heads and arrow-heads about 500 BC. There are two known examples in Britain, of which this Wiltshire one is the finer.

Car-parking and the start

Take the A4 out of Marlborough towards Devizes. About 1 mile out of the town is the village of Manton on your left. Go a little further on to a turning on your right signposted Manton House and Hollow.

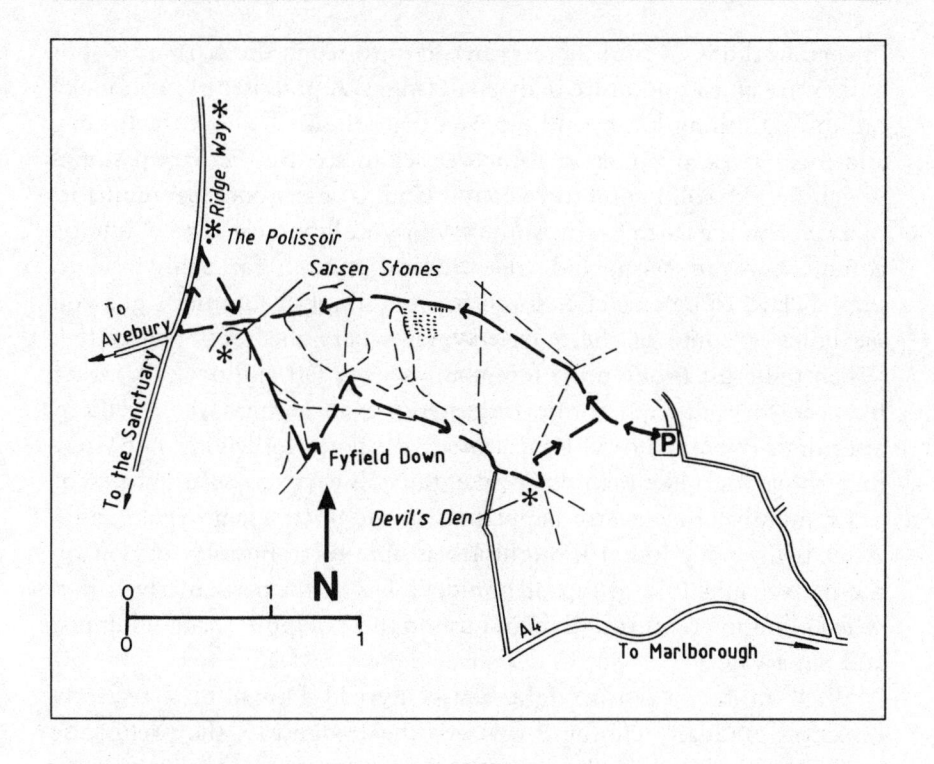

Drive (or walk) up here about three-quarters of a mile (1 km) and find a small hard-standing car-park.

The walk starts along the dirt track towards Manton House and then turns left onto the downs. Immediately you turn off the road, you see the open sweeping countryside ahead and can feel the soft grass beneath your feet. This part of the walk crosses a training area for race horses known as The Gallops. You'll have to be up pretty early to catch sight of the horses as they've usually done their training before 8 am. The route here is discreetly marked with way-posts and takes you on a diagonal line across the hill. Over to the south you should see a range of hills which includes Tan Hill, the highest point in Wiltshire and ahead, further west, Oldbury Castle topped by an obelisk.

After about half a mile going west, there's a fence marking the boundary of Fyfield Down. It is an area of land owned by the Nature Conservancy Council and encloses some ancient field systems known as lynchetts or cultivation terraces. These can date either from Celtic or medieval days. I find them rather hard to see in this particular spot as they are almost no more than small ridges. A practised eye can make out distinguishing lumps and furrows that tell much about the history and former use of the land. Much easier to see are the Sarsen stones which lie like solid confetti over the land. These stones are remnants of a layer of the earth's crust some seventy million years ago. Climatic conditions were warm and wet, tropical enough for palm trees to grow. Hard to believe after some anaemic English summers, but you see holes in some of the Sarsen stones where the roots penetrated. When the crust broke up, a few chunks were left and do look rather like a lot of sheep quietly grazing, hence their name, Grey Wethers, after their resemblance to a local breed of sheep. In driving rain, they look more rock-like than sheep-like, but it is easy to confuse the two.

I remember the reverse happening to me once when orienteering. After being very lost, I thought I was able to re-position myself on the map thanks to a group of boulders. I was not particularly happy when plunging on through them I found these helpful 'rocks' all upped and ran away.

Walk more or less straight across Fyfield Down in a westerly direction gradually climbing towards the Ridgeway, the prehistoric track, leaving Fyfield and going onto Overton Down. On the southern tip of Overton spur, a couple of miles away, is the site of The Sanctuary, a rather odd prehistoric site where concrete posts now mark the post-holes of a Neolithic timber building.

Once on the Ridgeway, you may meet with a number of walkers as it is a fairly popular section of this long-distance walk. You can decide at this point to go down to Avebury and explore the prehistoric sites. Another good reason for going is to sample the irresistible food served at Stones Restaurant which is conveniently in the centre of Avebury Village. This is a straightforward walk (four miles/6 km) downhill there and uphill back.

Whatever your decision, first go to seek out The Polissoir. It is not only an achievement to find, but a good excuse for turning back towards Marlborough and tea at The Polly on the High Street.

On reaching these crossroads (or tracks), where the route ahead goes to Avebury, turn right up the Ridgeway towards Barbury Castle. Walk about 400 yards and you'll see a wooden stile on your right (this is your route back). For the moment walk on just beyond, you'll see a brown Nature Conservancy noticeboard at the end of the reserve, and fifteen feet or so beyond it, also on the right of the track is a metal gate. Climb over this and look across the field, downhill, slightly to the right. You should see a large triangular stone about 150 yards distance. Walk to this stone, and then carry on, keeping on the same line for another twenty-five feet (8 m) or so. Slightly to the right is The Polissoir. It is a horizontal Sarsen stone like many of the others, except you can tell you've found the right stone as on the top there is a shallow smoothed-out bowl where the axe-heads were sharpened. It is curiously silk-like to the touch. Beside the bowl are clear grooves made by sharpening arrow-heads. It is strange to think of the activity that must have taken place in this part of the world so long ago in what is now just a barren field, virtually deserted, except for sheep and stones.

For the route home, go back to the wooden stile I mentioned on the Ridgeway, climb over and follow the path slightly left down another ridge for about a mile (1.5 km) and then turn eastwards dropping down into a valley. You'll soon see why this part is known as the Valley of the Rocks. It is an incredible sight, as though there had once been an almighty river washing these stones along which suddenly dried up, leaving them grounded. There are masses of rocks here, and it was from this site, apparently, that stones were taken to both Avebury and Stonehenge. They were lifted by means of sledge, roller and a good deal of prehistoric grunting and expletives I should imagine. Getting them as far as the Salisbury Plain can have been no mean feat.

Follow the Valley of the Rocks down, crossing into Fyfield Down again. Depending on the conditions, it can be pleasantly sheltered after the enforced airiness of the open downs. Ahead you'll see a rock construction, which seems small at a distance, known as the Devil's Den. It is actually in private land, but it is possible to get quite close without trespassing. This group of stones was once a neolithic burial chamber that was covered by a long barrow some two hundred feet (61 m) long and 130 feet (40 m) wide. The cap stone is about ten feet (3 m) square and very thick. It is an unusual position for a barrow to be as they were more often set on the skyline rather than the valley floor.

Now for the homeward stretch. Climb up the hill following the line of the fence, go past the end of The Gallops and on to the dirt track again. From here it is a short walk back to the car-park.

Avebury

If you decide not to extend the Polissoir walk to include Avebury, it is only a short drive from here and worth it. There is a large free car-park which is well-signposted.

Known as the Avebury Complex, there are several different aspects to explore. The main feature is the Great Circle, pricked out with standing stones, which is nearly a mile round. In some parts the ditch surrounding the area is so deep it is staggering to think of the amount of labour that went into constructing it, especially if you go to the bottom and clamber up the sides.

Within the grand circle are two smaller circles and some standing stones remaining. There are some splendid stories concerning some of these stones on the inner and outer rings. One apparently swivels round at midnight, another is named The Devil's Chair.

Apart from the stone circle there is also West Kennet Avenue, formed by parallel lines of stones extending well over a mile in the direction of The Sanctuary. Almost due south is Silbury Hill, an enormous man-made mound whose purpose has yet to be discovered. Beyond this is West Kennet Long Barrow.

Whilst the pattern of stones remaining at Avebury is less complete than Stonehenge, the whole site is more impressive being larger and older. But what I find most appealing is the accessibility. You can wander where you like as there are virtually no restrictions except polite requests not to deface the stones.

One of the aims of this book is to find places to explore that perhaps haven't had all the glory they deserve, and at the moment, Avebury is still in the shadow of its more famous sister, Stonehenge. However, a theme park is being developed, and a new car-park to accommodate the growing number of visitors. I do hope it won't lose its magic if it becomes a tourist bus stop. I expect, though, that early risers and those who venture out in all weathers will probably still have much of the place to themselves.

Around and about Marlborough

If you have an extra day in this area, it is worth visiting Marlborough. A wander through the town is ideal, too, when the weather is really foul, or you feel like a more lazy time. Nearby is the ancient forest of Savernake where there is good woodland walking which is likely to be sheltered.

I was pleasantly surprised on my first visit to Marlborough to find much more to the place than the eponymous school. The town has a delightful warm atmosphere thanks to the soft colours of many of the buildings, many of which date from the mid seventeenth and eighteenth centuries. A large part of the town was destroyed by fire in 1653. This was a major calamity and the town never really regained its importance, but that halt in its development probably means it is more pleasant to visit today.

One sign that is an obvious indication of the town's former prosperity is the main street, broad enough to be a dual carriageway and still leave room for the market stalls in the middle. The town boasts that it has the widest high street in England. The building of the M4 also helped Marlborough tremendously by taking away the burden of heavy traffic along the main street.

It is very pleasant to stroll along the High Street and discover some of the little alleyways leading off where there are some older buildings which survived the fire. Look out particularly for The Green. This is a grassy area, as you might expect, surrounded by pretty houses, some in lovely pastel colours, and is the site of the early Saxon settlement that was the beginning of Marlborough.

The ends of the main street are marked by two attractive churches. St Peter's at the west end, if you are keen on architecture, is worth a look as it is an elegant perpendicular design.

It is easy to while away a couple of hours here, having a wander by the river, a browse in the shops and something calorific at the Polly Tearooms to be found in the High Street. The town is busiest on the market days of Wednesday and Saturday. If you have time it is only a short drive to Savernake Forest.

Savernake Forest

This is one of the ancient Royal Forests, now owned by the Marquis of Ailesbury. Present day Savernake is some sixteen miles (25 km) wide and comprises 4,000 acres (1618 ha). It used to stretch as far north as Ramsbury and south to Pewsey. However, what is left is quite grand enough for me. Although I find it hard to imagine how you go about designing a forest, much of what is left was created by Capability Brown. He was responsible for constructing The Grand Avenue which is a four-mile drive (for carriages, not cars) from north-west to south-east. Halfway along it is his original circus where eight walks cross, known appropriately as Eight Walks. I suppose it has become more impressive over the years as the trees lining the paths, gigantic oaks and beeches, are now awesome. The walks are still very obvious but the once-formal paths have an appealing ragged quality thanks to natural undergrowth, giving the place the friendly feel of a well-worn carpet. Savernake is a good area for walking and, though popular, large enough not to get crowded. There are parking spaces off the A4 and also at Cadley to the west of Savernake. From both spots it is easy to get to Eight Walks and the Grand Avenue, both features of the forest not to be missed. It is also worth making a circular tour to the Ailesbury Column, standing in a rather isolated position just inside the southern edge of the forest. It seems a bit of an oddity, more so perhaps as it was in fact built to mark the recovery of George III's sanity. From here you can look right down to Tottenham House (now a prep school) and appreciate Capability Brown's wonderful approach to the house.

If you have driven to Savernake rather than walked from Marlborough, it is worth taking a slight detour back through Ramsbury and Mildenhall (pronounced Mynall). These are both attractive villages lying in the River Kennet valley. The valley itself is very pretty. Along the road are plenty of footpaths to the river. I have swum in the Kennet but it is only to be advised if you were brought up, as I was, by someone who took a delight in bathing in water the temperature of Scottish lochs. It was very cold.

Devizes and the Battle of Roundway Hill

Devizes is a good starting-point for a day of explorations and, as with Marlborough, you may find you need more than a day to fit everything in.

I usually find a place to park beside the canal at New Park Street. This car-park is signposted Kennet and Avon Canal Wharf Centre, quite a new development, in part due to the restoration of this canal. There is a good information office here, several craft shops and a small café. It is also the start of the walk to Roundway Down and as the parking is only five pence per hour, it's not too costly to do it.

The Battle of Roundway Hill

OS Map, 1:50 000, Sheet 173
A circular walk of 6 miles (10 km). Allow 3–4 hours.

There is an opportunity to make a short-cut on this walk. Most of the route is very clear and on good track, road, or typical downland grassy paths. At the end, though, there is a section that is likely to be a bit muddy. It is mostly flat or gentle gradients apart from the steep climb and descent to and from Oliver's Castle. This walk is suitable for dogs.

It is unusual to get such a good country walk leading straight out of a town. I like it too because of the terrific views over the Avon Valley and far beyond but one of the highlights is the dramatic site of the Battle of Roundway Hill.

Britain is filled with battlefields from Celtic skirmishes to full-scale military operations. Many of the sites I've visited have been rather disappointing, considering their importance in our history, and are now just scruffy pieces of land where you need help from the elements to give the place atmosphere. Not so at Roundway Down; here the formation of the land played a very important part in the outcome of the battle. Little changed today, it makes the whole event come alive.

Car-parking and the start

Park your car by the canal off New Park Street, as mentioned.

To start the walk, look for the bridge just by the canal information office, which leads over to a cemetery. This is the bridge you come over to finish. Don't cross here but walk eastwards along to the next bridge and cross the canal there. Ahead is a pair of splendid iron gates with a little opening on one side. This track is known as Quaker's Walk. After the rather grand start at the gates, the track ends rather abruptly at a road. The avenue of trees is still there, even though some smaller saplings make it a little unkempt, but I've known walks that start in a much less-promising fashion.

Where Quakers' Walk joins a lane, directly ahead is a track leading across a field for two hundred yards towards the few houses that make up the village of Roundway. Already you can see ahead the direction of the walk, going up the hill. At the village there is a little footpath to the left which then brings you onto a small road. (Here you can make a short-cut by turning left along the road and merely following it as far as Iron Pear Tree Farm, which is on the way back. You get some views of the battlefield escarpment, though it is not as good as going to the top.)

To continue, turn left down the road and almost immediately, on the other side of the road, is a stile and an obvious path under a large pylon that leads you up over Roundway Hill. Just climb this to the top. If you want a breather, pause to take in the view. Southwards, Devizes is spread out below you. Behind, a little to the east, is Etchilhampton Hill and beyond that, on a clear day, you'll see Salisbury Plain rising sharply from the Vale of Pewsey.

At the top, follow a metalled road, which changes to a dirt track, until you reach the edge of the woods. To the left is Oliver's Castle; Beacon Hill lies ahead, King's Play Hill a little to the right of that and Morgan Hill, with distinctive twin masts, to the far right. These hills surround Roundway Down.

The desperate battle which took place here was between Royalist forces and Parliamentarians, in 1643. The Parliamentarians, under General Warren, should have had the upper hand as they were vastly superior in number and had already forced the Royalist infantry to take cover in Devizes. All they needed was to see off the Royalist

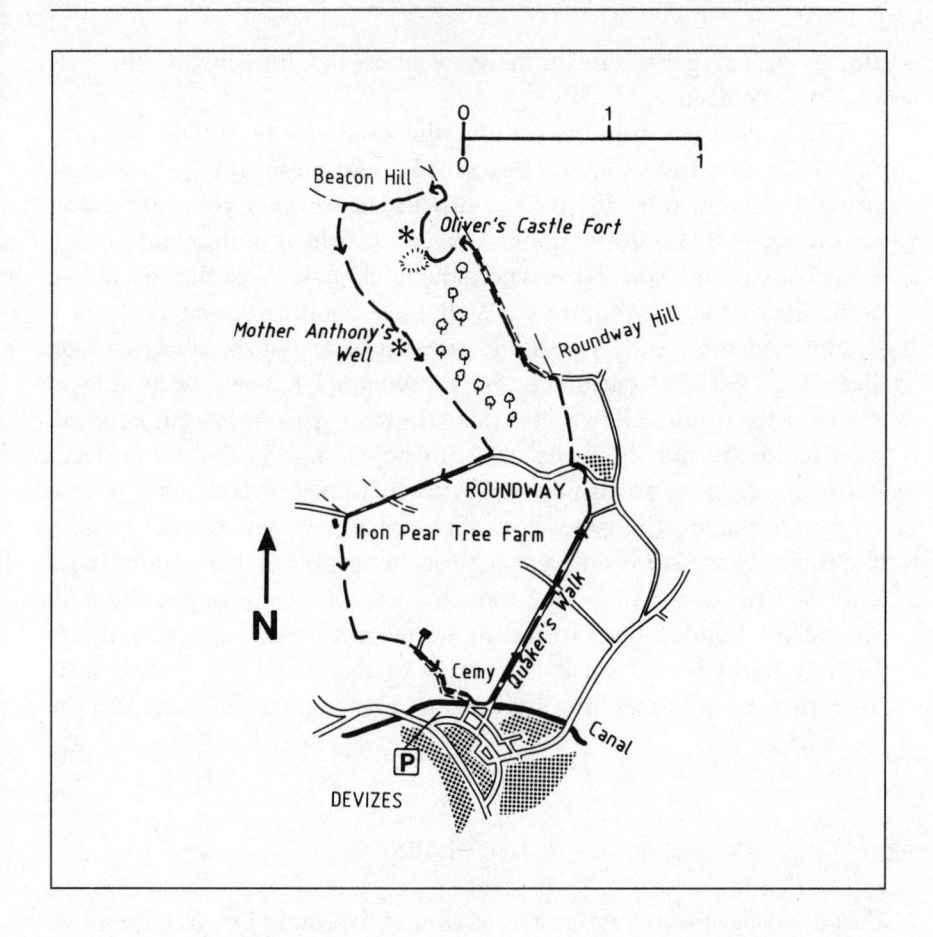

cavalry who had come from Oxford to give support. However, after the start of the battle between the two cavalries, General Warren's forces broke ranks and charged away from the flat plain towards Oliver's Castle with the Royalists coming in hot pursuit. Then, to the horror of the front riders, they found themselves at the top of the 300-foot sheer escarpment with no choice but to plunge over the edge. Some of the Royalists were unable to stop themselves going over too. It is understandable that the area at the bottom here is known as The Bloody Ditch. It is worth going over to Oliver's Castle, just on the edge, and having a look at the fatal slope. Oliver's Castle, by the way, is a misnomer and has nothing to do with Cromwell. It is actually the site of a prehistoric fort. Apart from looking down the slope, don't forget to take in the view across to Chippenham, the Vale of North Wiltshire.

The walk then continues along the ramparts of Oliver's Castle, skirting round the valley to Beacon Hill and down the gentler slope towards Netherstreet Farm. A footpath then brings you back along the bottom of the slope, under Oliver's Castle and after just over a mile, back to the road. Near where the track passes The Bloody Ditch, is the site of Mother Anthony's Well, once a source of water.

Now on the road, you should turn right and walk along to Iron Pear Tree Farm, a curious name for which I haven't been able to discover the origin. Here there is a little grassy space that leads between two buildings and the footpath from here, somewhat muddy, leads across the fields towards Devizes. After a couple of stiles you do need to turn left along the valley bottom towards a newish house. I found the route a little confusing and part of the trouble was the four-strand electric fencing for the sheep blocking off where I thought the path should be. I ended up skirting the house and garden and scrambling under a barbed-wire fence. The drive of this house goes into a little lane, then it's a short climb back to the bridge over the canal and the car-park.

Devizes

Try to save some energy for a look around the town. Devizes is unusual in still retaining virtually all the original medieval street pattern that was laid down when the castle was built over eight hundred years ago. The town trail (available from the Museum and the Tourist Information Centre) shows the plan very clearly and has good suggestions for a walk taking in all the buildings of importance. It is certainly worth going to the market place which is unusually spacious. Nearby are some interesting old streets; the oddly named Brittox, St John's Street and St John's Alley which brings you to Long Street and the Museum. Though small, the museum is certainly worth a visit if you want to find out about the Early Beakers. There is a huge amount of information on prehistoric sites and their inhabitants. (It also happens to be the headquarters of the Wiltshire Archaeological and Natural History Society.) What I enjoyed most were the many reconstructions and models showing the development of places such as Avebury, which you can take in on a fleeting visit. Allow plenty of time if you want to read all the small print. The Museum is particularly good value on a Monday (free), otherwise 75 pence.

For a shorter walking option at Devizes, and again somewhere more sheltered in awful weather, it is worth going to the Kennet and Avon Canal. A part that is particularly interesting is the Caen Hill flight of locks which is just west, out of the town on the road towards Trowbridge. My experience of lock staircases was just seeing a steady procession of them going up a long incline. At Caen Hill, though, there are individual rectangles of water beside each lock. I thought they were cleverly designed little parking-bays to give more energetic bargees a chance to overtake the Sunday drivers. In fact, these side bays, or pounds, were built to extend each lock sideways, compensating for lack of length as the canal at this point climbs a very steep hill unusually quickly. This flight of locks is one of the wonders of canal engineering, and is most interesting to see. You can park at the top of the flight and walk down to the bottom where you get the best view.

A Walk along the Wansdyke

OS Map 1:50 000, Sheet 173
A circular walk of approximately 6 miles (10 km). Allow 3 hours.

This is another wonderful downland walk within easy reach of either Marlborough or Devizes. It is quite different in character from the one over Fyfield Down. Here you walk mainly along the edge of the escarpment, sweeping around the curves and folds in the land, all the time conscious of the contrasting flatness of the plain below. Although you may not find another Polissoir, you may well see an abundance of wild flowers, have a close encounter with one of the nine Wiltshire horses, and finish with a wander along the Wansdyke.

The going underfoot is good all the way on short grassy tracks, except for the very last part. Here the route crosses a field used frequently for livestock, so it tends to become churned up as soon as there has been any hint of rain.

You can take dogs, they probably won't bother the White Horse but there are sheep and other livestock grazing, so take a leash.

This walk will take longer than one on the flat as there is a fair amount of climbing ending up at the highest point in Wiltshire. The views on a clear day are naturally worth it.

Car-parking and the start

If you are coming from the Devizes direction, the best drive, not in terms of time but interesting places, is via Urchfont (picture-postcard village), Marden (henge monument) and Honeystreet as this is an excellent place to see the chalky horse directly opposite, almost as though the road leads you straight there. Follow the road through the little village of Alton Barnes and there are various car-parking spots along this section. At the bend there is a quarry with possibilities for three or four cars, and further up a small lay-by with room for three. When the ground is completely dry, there is a wide track entrance too on the right-hand side by the lay-by, but it is impossibly muddy in wet weather. These car-parking directions rather remind me of an old family guidebook for rock climbing which recommended one place with the advice 'car-park space for one!' So it pays to come here early.

From the quarry at the bottom, the route goes up a gently rising grassy path to Walker's Hill. From the other parking spots, the route is still up the hill to the west of the road. Walker's Hill is an appropriate name as I certainly didn't feel any inclination to run up the steep sides. Another excuse for not running is the opportunity to scan the ground for wild flowers. Depending on the season, you may find cowslips, wild thyme and varieties of orchids.

The ground at the top of the hill is curiously pock-marked with mounds and ridges, evidence of much activity in former days. The ridge is a most dominating feature, and clearly a useful power-base. It was the site of a battle between the Saxons of Wessex and the Ceawlin of the Thames Valley. It was something more than a scuffle between rival teams of supporters as the Anglo Saxon Chronicle states dryly 'there was great slaughter here'.

Skirt around this hill, continuing west, and suddenly the White Horse appears in front. Green is sometimes a more accurate adjective, depending on how many weeds are poking through the chalky surface. Last time I visited, though, he had just been spring-cleaned and gleamed in the sunshine. This horse is the largest of the nine Wiltshire Horses, and despite having something of a primitive touch, most are much younger than prehistoric. This was was marked out in 1812 when there was quite a fashion for commissioning chalky cutouts. On a well-chosen site, such as this, they make excellent landmarks, so much so that during the war they had to be re-turfed, and were not uncovered until 1945.

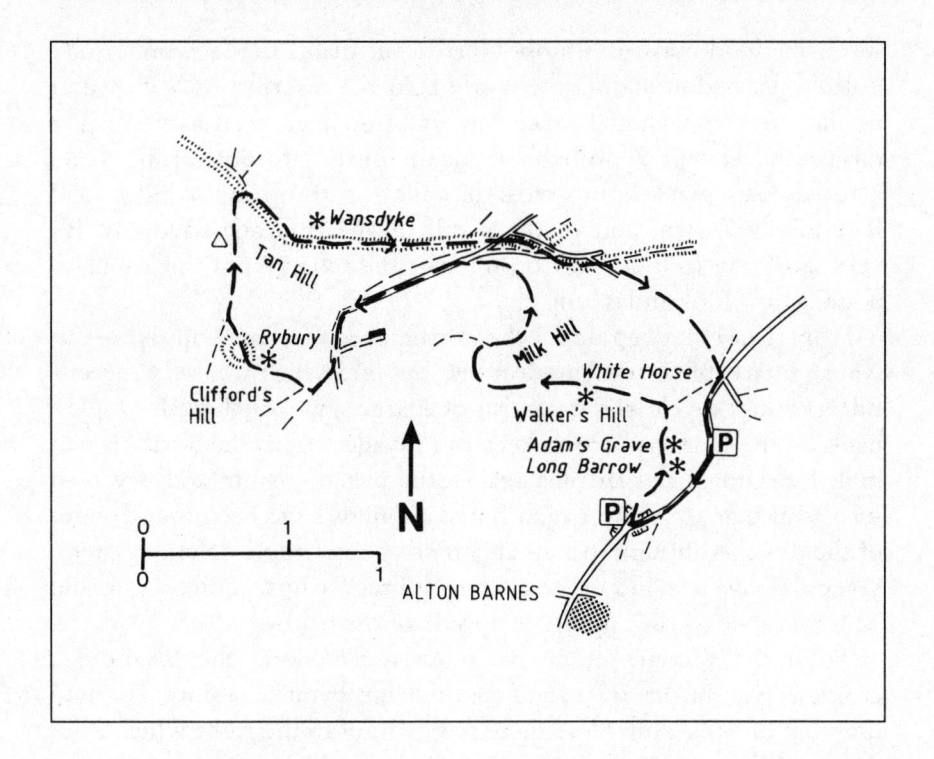

From the White Horse the route goes on west around Milk Hill, and then sweeps along the side of a huge and pleasing valley with views across to Tan Hill. Don't lose any height, but contour around the valley until you join a dirt track leading along the far edge. Follow this track downwards to the valley floor. This can be a sheltered respite from the wind, much appreciated by the little colonies of free-range pigs that live here. The route then goes up the hill to Rybury Camp, named after an iron-age fort of which there were many in this area.

Now for the final climb to Tan Hill, the highest point in Wiltshire. There is a trig point here, though the hill itself, as with many high spots on the downs, is almost more a flat plain. It is a wonderfully isolated place, dominating the world below, yet surprisingly it used to be the site of an annual sheep fair. It must have been a spectacular meeting-place, which probably made up for the effort of getting there. The views are marvellous; across the valley are the group of hills round Roundway Down, and to the north the Marlborough Downs. It's very satisfying to look back on some of the routes from this vantage-point – they look miles long.

From Tan Hill drop down the northern side to the Wansdyke, this was a remarkable Dark Ages frontier, but one which was very successful. As you'll see clearly, it consists of a large single ditch with a higher bank on the southern side to keep out invaders from the north. It was built by Romanized Britons against the pagan onrush, and it was so successful that as yet no pagan burial grounds have been found south of the dyke. Although it is an apparently very simple defence system, you only have to stand in the ditch to appreciate how difficult it would be for anyone to rush up the steep side of the bank.

To find the route home, walk eastwards along the Wansdyke, crossing over the dirt track, and continue until you have skirted around the back of Milk Hill. Here there is a path off to the right which leads down a valley and back to the road. If you parked at the quarry at the bottom of the hill, then it's about a mile down to your right. There isn't a café to greet you at the end, but it's only a short way to Devizes, Marlborough or Avebury for tea and cakes.

Bradford-on-Avon

After the well-organized streets, tidy terraces and spacious centres of Marlborough and Devizes, Bradford-on-Avon comes as a lively contrast. Here the marvellous higgledy-piggledy houses eagerly jostle together, all apparently trying to jump into the river Avon at once!

You get somewhat the same feeling if you are driving through. There almost seems to be a conspiracy urging you to the river as routes through the town, from the North and East, hurtle you towards the ancient bridge. Just over this, though, is a small car-park which is an excellent stopping-place. (Be warned, it is used as a market place on a

Thursday.) From the bridge there are some splendid townscapes looking across the river. Bradford rises above you with clusters of roof-tops, precarious terraces and twisting streets. It is well worth walking round this part of the town. Either get one of the good town guides from the Tourist Information just by the bridge or simply meander up the hill and over to the left. Don't be put off by the horrendous traffic, especially the gigantic lorries on the two narrow main streets. At least they can't follow you down the small side streets. Needless to say, the lady in the Tourist Information said there had been a bypass planned for years which had never arrived. It will be a blessing when it does.

The side roads are joined zig-zag fashion by smaller streets to lead you up the steep hill. At the top, the lanes are squashed into narrow alleyways and steep flights of steps, giving you the impression that every inch of space is used. Grander houses, belonging to former merchants and mill-owners – there used to be many here – tend to be on the lower part. Higher up are perched small terraces, once weavers' cottages, built into the side of the hill. They have pocket-sized precarious gardens avalanching down the cliff. At the very top, known as Tory, there is a delightful little church and a post-box. I should think the postman here is fit as I noticed there were four collections scheduled a day and I couldn't see any opportunity to bring up a van. Perhaps he has a mountain bike!

From the churchyard at the end, there are terrific views down onto the river and over to the massive tithe barn at Barton Farm. It's almost like seeing an aerial photograph.

Looking down the hill onto the jumble of houses below, I could well believe the famous Bradford story about the discovery of a Saxon church in the middle of the town at the end of the last century. It had been completely hidden by surrounding terraces of houses, and was made more difficult to spot because it had at some time, been altered to resemble a tiny house. Now, it's easy to see as space has been cleared around it, leaving a tiny well-kept garden. There are many signposts to 'The Saxon Church' around the town bringing you to Church Street, appropriately, in the lower part of the town near the river. It is the smallest church, at least in this country, that I've ever seen. The inside, which is minute, is quite plain, cool and quiet. A very old font is the only furnishing. I noted one comment that the church rather resembled a double dog kennel. Lucky dog!

If you've enjoyed wandering around the town, it is easy to finish off the day with a pleasant stroll of about four miles (6.5 km) to Avoncliff, a small hamlet to the west. The walk goes from Bradford on the south side of the river to Barton Farm and the Tithe Barn, then along the river a short way to the Kennet and Avon Canal. The towpath takes you to Avoncliff (about ¾ mile), past the weir which provided power for Bradford's many mills. The canal crosses the river here via a Georgian viaduct built by John Rennie. Once across the aqueduct, simply turn right and come back to the centre of Bradford on a not-too-busy road.

Spending a morning pottering around Bradford, without the walk to Avoncliff, still leaves you time to go to Lacock, the charming village owned by the National Trust, later in the day. Another claim to its fame is as the birthplace of Henry Fox Talbot, who is credited with the invention of modern photography. There is a photographic museum here, and Lacock Abbey, where the Fox Talbot family lived, is open to the public. Lacock itself is interesting as very little has changed here since the eighteenth century. There are many features to look out for and some delightful houses and excellent pubs; though perhaps, strictly speaking, I should call them 'inns'. As usual, when wandering around a place, I got in the mood for a 'proper' walk. At Lacock I found a little-used path going along the side of the abandoned canal.

The Old Canal and the Coach Road

OS Map, Sheet 173
Approximately 5 miles. Allow 2½ hours.

This walk takes you quickly into some typical Southern England countryside, a mixture of buttercup-filled fields and hawthorn hedgerows set in a lush valley between the river and the old canal. In the second half, there are lovely views over the Avon Valley. The route isn't signposted and I had the feeling along part of the way that I was making the first tracks.

Some of the going underfoot is on good tracks or metalled road but the route along the canal embankment can be very wet. Adding to the problem is the fact that it is a grazing area for cattle and inevitably the land gets churned up. But there is space to pick a relatively dry route after bad weather. I think it's worth making an effort to get into this pretty countryside as you are likely to have the place to yourself.

There is a good car-park provided for all visitors to Lackock just by the entrance to the Abbey and the Fox Talbot Museum. Here is a good view over a low wall to the Abbey grounds and the splendid front of the house. Start or finish this walk with a stroll around the village. The plan of Lacock is easy to understand with East Street, West Street, High Street and Church Street forming four sides of a square. Although it is now described as a village, Lacock was in fact a thriving market town in the eighteenth century, with plenty of local trades such as spinning, weaving, chair- and hurdle-making. The busyness of the place then was probably the reason for the surprisingly wide streets. While the towns nearby developed with the Industrial Revolution, Lacock's growth was curtailed, partly because the Talbot family, owners of the Abbey, insisted that the new railway was kept well away. So the town diminished to village status, remaining much as it was in its heyday. Matilda Talbot gave the whole village to the National Trust in 1944. Wandering around Lacock is a little like going around a large open-air museum. Every building is interesting in some way and no two houses are alike. The local guidebook encourages the sharp-eyed to note all the different door-knockers, boot-scrapers, etc. Although the place is preserved, I don't find it precious and thankfully it is free from all those notices starting 'Do Not . . .' which often appear in picturesque places put up by irate residents. There is a feeling of everyday life going on, certainly in the pubs!

For the walk, go down East Street, turn right at Church Street and then left up the little lane over the pack-horse bridge at the Bide Brook. This is a quintessential brook full of gurgling water, spotlessly clean, with signs of the ford used in former days. Carry on up the lane, almost head-high with cow parsley and its strong aroma of summer, then take a footpath diagonally across an open field. You can glimpse Bowden House from here, on the right, as well as Naish Hill, where the walk eventually goes. I almost persuaded two American ladies from Tennesssee to come along on the jaunt, but they were content to get as far as the river and be photographed by the charming pair of thatched cottages there, complete with bright red post-box set into the low wall. 'Yous'al have a good time' was the parting drawl.

The bridge at Reybridge takes you over the Avon, and just beyond are some raised pavements built in case of flooding. It used to happen two or three times a year, though the water runs so low in the summer it is hard to believe it's possible.

Immediately over the bridge, there is a stile into a field (dogs on lead; no access to river) and a track across the field leading to a stile descriptively known as 'squeeze belly'. It was certainly too much of a squash for the dogs as they had to be lifted over. Immediately opposite, there is a narrow path which ends up in a large field. Aim to the left, through a large gap in the hedge, and you'll then see the embankment of the old canal.

This was the Wiltshire and Berks Canal, built as a branchline of the now well-restored Kennet and Avon Canal and linking up with a canal at Swindon. It was in use for nearly a hundred years before being abandoned in 1914, which I suppose is almost as good a record as some of the smaller railway branches. Nature had made a pretty good job of reclaiming this place. The tow-path is quite overgrown, and the canal bed full of reeds and rushes. It hardly seems possible that such an isolated spot was once so busy.

Walk along the embankment, following the path through a narrow wooded part until it opens out onto fields. This stretch is so pretty with its lush green meadows, the quiet river, and gently sloping valley. (It was here I found the most teacherously muddy parts, but there is room to pick your way round.) Adding to the romance is an old hump-backed brick bridge in the distance going over the canal, now out-of-use. This makes a good turning-round place if you want a shorter stroll.

Just beyond the bridge is a little gate and a path leading over the bed of the canal (water-free), and another gate into a field. This last gate was impossible to open as the chain had been stapled too close to the catch. I climbed over, but noticed a path that would have done going to the left. This would be a good route in winter or early summer but I think later on in the year it could be very overgrown.

Turn left anyway, either along the bottom of this field, or along the path below, and then across the next field. Here there is a rusty gate, topped with an orange sack that looks as though it is suposed to be a marker. Beware! Beyond, is a very wet marsh! I thought it was better to go up to the right, and cross through the little copse. You may see a bale of straw and a feeding-bin for pheasants here. Once through the copse, climb up the little slope to the edge of the field. Basically you need to aim diagonally to the far corner. If the path is overgrown with crops, you can walk around the edge of the field to the left. Carry on until you meet a large gate, and then a track; go through another gate and you will eventually come to a metalled road. Turn right, and I'm afraid there is no choice but a long steady climb up to the top of Naish Hill. It is very easy going, though, passing through spacious fields, a small wood and then up over more fields. At the top, it swings around to the right and joins an unclassified road. Stop for breath and admire the panorama, with Chippenham in the distance and the hills near Bath to the west.

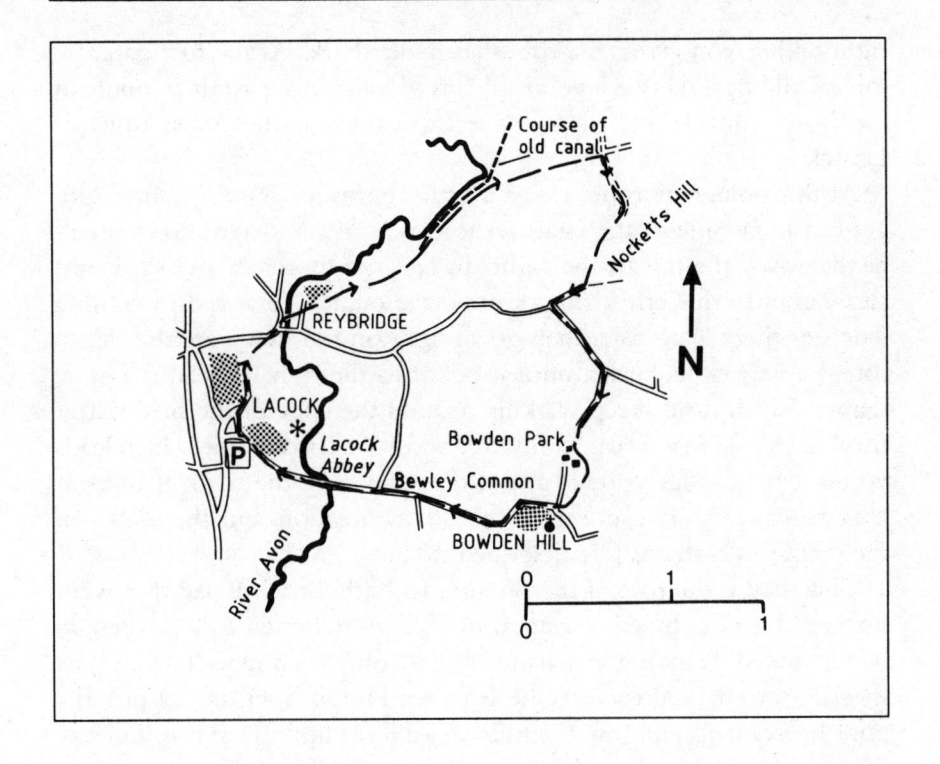

Turn left at this road, past the Naish Hill Quarry, which is still quarried for sand, and along past a group of cottages and farm buildings. Where the road curves slightly, there is a metalled road on the right taking you across the top of Bowden Park. At the first gate, by some buildings, there is a good stile provided. Once past the woodland there are some lovely views over the valley of the Avon towards Lacock.

At this point, the route is just a little confusing. You are aiming to get to the far side of the estate. Ahead is a private drive and the road bends down the hill to the right. In fact the footpath, (which is not clear) goes to the left skirting around the estate. You need to climb a fence, as there is no stile, then go straight on following another fence round a vegetable garden until it bends to the right. Ahead is a gate, ignore this! Instead, keep walking around the edge of the field. After fifty metres there is a large holly tree and a well-made stile which leads you out by a lodge cottage and little pond onto the road. (I think it may be easier to find going in the other direction, but the walk, on the whole, is better as I've described it.)

This road is the part of the London to Bath Coach Road that went through Lacock. It was a very well-used route, one of the earliest to be turnpiked, bringing in a handsome income no doubt. There was a special levy charged to keep the Bowden Hill part repaired. I pity the poor horses struggling up the hill as you'll see how steep it is. Luckily the road is lined with wide grass verges, great for walkers, and I can imagine the coaches swinging around the corners as they hurtled down the hill. Turn right down the hill following the road. It opens out onto Bewley Common, and then the Abbey and its lovely grounds comes in sight. This part goes over the line of the old canal and was once known as The Wharf, though there is now little to see. You now cross the Avon on a long and narrow bridge back to Lacock by the car-park. Today it is quite safe, but parish records show that the bridge was often in a ruinous state, I expect with overuse from the heavy coaches.

For sustenance after this expedition, there are good pubs supplying food and drink all around the village, more remnants of the old coaching days, as well as The Stable Tea Rooms just near the Abbey.

During the season, the Fox Talbot Gallery of Photography, named after William Henry Fox Talbot, is open. Some of his original calotypes and first cameras are on show as well as modern exhibitions of photography. I like particularly some of the sepia prints and postcards of skeletal leaves and trees, and the evocative picture of a child's rocking horse.

The grounds and cloisters of the Abbey are also open. Lacock Abbey is so-called because the present house used the site of an Abbey dissolved in 1539. Much of the medieval building remains. I found the exterior and grounds much more interesting than the endless portraits on show inside.

Lacock does attract a fair share of visitors, though I was quite surprised to read in the *National Trust News* that we (visitors) average out to less than a thousand per week. Invariably it will be more crowded at weekends. There is plenty of elbow room and as I found with the Tennessee ladies, not many people venture beyond the boundary.

The Forest of Dean

The area described in this chapter lies in two counties, Gloucestershire and the now-merged Herefordshire and Worcestershire counties.

The Forest forms a triangular area bordered by one of England's major rivers, the Severn, on the east and by the Wye on the West. Both rivers meet south at Chepstow. The third river of the region is the Monnow, which runs further west to join the Wye at Monmouth. Both Chepstow and Monmouth have military connections, as with so many places near borders. The largest town on the northern edge of the area, is the market town of Hereford, where the Wye turns upstream towards Wales.

The land is largely agricultural, with small settlements and narrow lanes criss-crossing it. Much of this has been here for years, with people living by much the same values as their predecessors over the centuries. It is beginning to undergo more change than ever before, as new houses infill old villages, and commuters and retired people arrive in quantity. Luckily a large amount of countryside remains to explore.

The phrase 'a richer dust', from Rupert Brooke's poem 'The Soldier', makes a good theme for this chapter. The poet, with several others, had strong connections with the area and found inspiration in this lanscape. His poetry brings to mind an England that is romantic and rich in terms of the land. These elements come to mind when exploring the Forest of Dean.

The central part of the region is lush, reflected in the warm red soil turned by the plough, and the building stone which shades from terracotta red to soft pink in the villages and churches. Stone, too, has been used here to great effect by inspirational medieval sculptors and luckily their work has endured well through the centuries.

The area of the Forest of Dean has not only yielded timber but also a wealth of coal and iron, hewn out by the Free Miners. Old workings add another dimension to the landscape, as do the stories of the bitter conflicts between the various groups over rights to the Forest.

There is so much to discover here and so much to see. The vistas on any walk are incredibly varied because of the complex landscape. There is very little that is straight or flat. Every lane seemed to have a dip or a bend, any view starts by looking over ridges, between a jumble of hills and hollows and beyond, in most directions, to distant mountains.

Two walks are included in the central part. Further west there is a ramble across the pleasant common of Ewyas Harold, which is between Monmouth, Hay-on-Wye and Hereford. I've also suggested a couple of interesting ideas for the Forest of Dean. Finally, to the south-east, there's a chance to step back into the seventeenth century, minutes from a main road, at the tranquil water gardens at Westbury. That short walk makes an ideal introduction or finale to a few days around this region.

Sculptured Landscape and Churches

OS Map 1:50 000, Sheet 149
A circular walk of $5\frac{1}{2}$–6 miles (up to 10 km). Allow 3–4 hours.

This walk goes along part of the Wye Valley near Brockhampton and into the hills behind the village of Fownhope. With its constantly undulating route, it captures the essence of the Herefordshire countryside. What makes it different from other hilly areas such as the Chilterns or Dales is the complexity of the undulations. The land is rather like kneaded bread, moulded in all directions, making it quite hard to work out the predominant hill or main valley, except of course with a major feature such as the valley of the River Wye. The difficulty in working out the hills is reinforced by characteristically thick, high hedgerows alongside many of the roads.

This expedition also focuses on a different side of Herefordshire, its architecture. You can see two very different styles of church architecture on this walk. One church is relatively modern, designed by a follower of the nineteenth-century Arts and Crafts Movement, and the other has a striking example of the work of the Herefordshire School of Norman Sculpture. Whilst you are in the area it's easy to visit another comparatively modern church at Hoarwithy, which seems transplanted from Northern Italy. The style of this one comes as quite a surprise in the heart of the English countryside. Further on at Kilpeck is a beautiful Norman church, one of the finest examples of the work of medieval sculptors.

The Herefordshire School of Norman Sculpture, or travelling workshop, as it actually was, came into existence around the middle of the twelfth century. There was probably a principal master and several apprentices travelling to work on commissions, mostly in Herefordshire but also in neighbouring counties. First evidence of their work is in the north of the county at Shobdon. Inspiration for their sculpture came from a wide variety of sources: Anglo-Saxon, Viking, French and North Italian. It is characterized by intense and dramatic carving with vivid gestures, curving drapery, expressive fertility symbols and a touch of the comic with characterful facial expressions and upside-down angels. The most dazzling example of the work of this school is at Kilpeck, which is about ten miles (16 km) away, and a half-hour drive round the back roads of some lovely countryside. The walking around Kilpeck itself wasn't as rewarding as this area, but you can get a taste of the style, though of a more conventional subject, in Fownhope church at the start of this walk. Here there is a tympanum, now moved inside the church, showing the Virgin and Child with hands raised in a gesture of blessing.

This walk is on a mixture of surfaces; path, field, track and road. It is best to be prepared for some muddy areas, and also for some steep climbs. The route away from the Wye Valley includes quite a hill, as does the path up to Capler Camp later. For a very short expedition, you could start at the church of Brockhampton and then just walk up to the top of Capler Hill for the views.

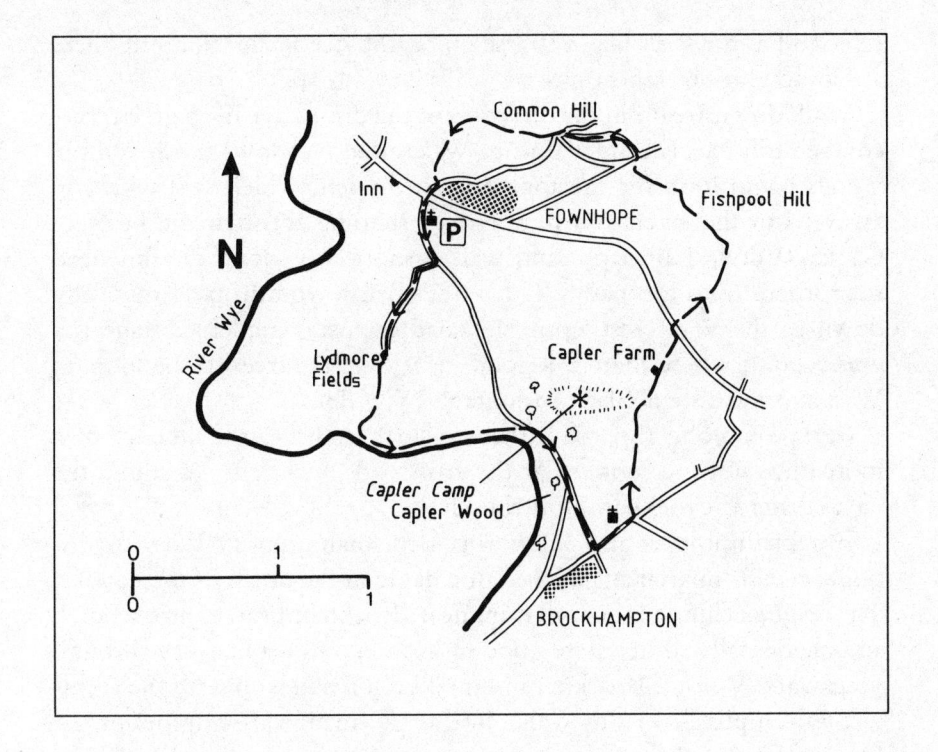

Car-parking and the start

There is plenty of parking in the village of Fownhope. It is a very attractive village with a mixture of old, new, and new that would like to look old. Finishing your walk here gives you an opportunity to visit The Green Man, a local inn with a long history. It was once a courthouse and a judges' room. The landlord here in the early 1800s was Tom Spring, otherwise known as the Bare-Knuckle Champion of All England.

From the church, walk up the minor road in the direction of Brockhampton. After a very short distance, on your right is a rough lane by a house called Lydmore Fields. Turn up here, climbing the slight hill beyond the houses, and after some way there is a farm on the left. Just round the corner is a gate and a faint path that leads round the edge of the first field, but then head towards a small house in the trees. Here it is possible to climb over a wooden stile, turn left and join the path along the river.

This is one of the many meanders of the wiggly Wye. It is a broad river and as the trees begin to rise up on the steep bank opposite there are some glorious reflections.

Walk downstream in the direction of the distinctive deep green tree-covered hill that is Capler Camp. Where the meadows finish and the woods begin look for the footpath on the left, which will take you away from the river to a minor road running through the heart of Capler Wood. Turn right and walk a short way along the unfenced road (there is no footpath). The woods below you drop dramatically down to the Wye. Just along the road opposite Capler Cottage is a grassy point where there is a good view over the trees to the looping Wye and the distant Black Mountains of Wales.

Carry on along this road; there is little traffic so the absence of a footpath is not too serious. At the crossroads, turn left and round the next corner is Brockhampton church.

Brockhampton is also known as Brockhampton-by-Ross to distinguish it from a village of the same name in the north of the county. The original church is now in ruins near Brockhampton Court, a hotel, and incidentally somewhere good to get a cup of tea halfway through your walk. Visiting Brockhampton Church fits in well with the architectural emphasis on this walk. Just as the medieval sculptors of the Herefordshire School developed their own unconventional style, the designer of this new church took an equally individual approach, but nearly eight hundred years later.

This 'new' church, despite having an appearance of medieval solidity, was built at the beginning of this century. It was designed by W. R. Lethaby, a member of the Arts and Crafts Movement and a follower of William Morris. The Arts and Craft Movement, founded in 1888, had a considerable effect on architecture with its stress on craftsmanship, its conscious effort to use local building materials, and its theme for ornament taken from nature.

A striking feature of the design is the steeply-pointed arch that is used in the porch, transepts and chancel, and which is echoed with lozenges in some of the larger windows. The whole design gives a tremendous feeling of uplift. Inside, the sharp arch is used again, adding a strong upward ambience to the interior.

Continuing the Arts and Craft theme there are two romantic, brilliantly coloured tapestries on either side of the altar. These were made from a Burne-Jones design by the William Morris company.

Don't miss, as I nearly did because of the fading light, the wooden choir stalls carved with an assortment of wild flowers. The designs have all been transferred into embroidery and the motifs used on the hymnbook covers.

From the church carry on up the road and just before it forks there is a small lane to the left with a farm at the end and a broken down fence, but no sign of a stile. The footpath, according to the farmer I spoke to, goes around the field to the right and then up the hill. There isn't a well-defined track but the hill, of some 600 feet (200 m), is certainly obvious.

Head for the right-hand side of the Capler Camp entrenchments. There is a farm building here and at the back is a flat, grassy stretch that marks the boundary of the camp. It's worth walking around to appreciate the strength of the site. It was probably an Iron Age settlement, built by fugitives from Western France who came up the Wye Valley. The Valley was a traditional trading route as well as a useful migrant path for those fleeing and those invading. Along the route various hill forts were built, usually on scarps overlooking the Valley, which in those early times was thickly forested. The western part of Capler Camp goes right to the edge of the scarp. No need to build more than one ditch for defence here. To the south and east the man-made defences were required to be more substantial and you can see the lines of the extra ramparts.

Go back to the farm buildings and look for the footpath sign, a yellow arrow which goes off the main track to the left. This section of the walk joins the Wye Valley trail. The Wye Valley walk goes from Chepstow to Hereford covering fifty-two miles (83 km). There is a complete pack with maps and directions available at local Tourist Information Centres. The standard of the way-marking is good.

The descent from Capler Camp is very steep but there are steps which make it easier. Follow the path and yellow arrows to the farm lane. Here turn right to the main road, and then left a short way down the road to a farm lane on the right. Walk down the farm lane and look out for the signs which divert you along field edges around the farm. Just nearby there used to be a chapel dedicated to St Dubricus, the only dedication to this saint east of the Wye and a reminder of the time when all of the land to the west as far as the Monnow was known as Archenfield, an area more Welsh than English, which remained Celtic until the twelfth century.

Follow the path up the ridge to Fishpool Hill. Looking all around you will see a complicated topography of ridges and valleys. Ahead is a distinctive geological area called the Woolhope Dome, an outcrop of Silurian Limestone. The fossil-rich limestone prompted a group of naturalists to found the Woolhope Society of Naturalists and Archaeologists in 1851, a club which still meets today.

From the ridge the path goes into a wooded nature reserve. The path is very obvious and there are occasional information boards about plants and animals to look out for.

Once through the woods, you'll come out in an open space where you need to bear right (the left fork goes to Fownhope along the road and provides a short-cut home.) Cross the minor road and follow the track immediately opposite, and then shortly after take the little path signed off to the right. This carries on through the woods, climbing above some common land. You can catch glimpes of the village of Fownhope dominated by the church spire. The path then goes down through a knee-high wild meadow, absolutely packed with flowers. Just beyond is a meeting of six roads, known locally as Six Ways. It was here I met Trixie and her owner also out for a twilight walk. They were worried I would 'go astray' and so accompanied me on the last part back to the village. As we walked I absorbed some of the local colour. The route was known as Jacob's Ladder. Why was that? 'Well, it be steep,' came the reply. To find this path, keep on following the Wye Valley signs from Six Ways. This is virtually straight on towards Cherry Hill. As the path flattens out a little, there's a very obvious fork off to the left. Take this and drop steeply down to a hedge-lined plateau, then turn right towards the small isolated cottage. Jacob's Ladder is the path that runs below the cottage and then curves round the edge of the fields and into the back of a new housing estate. Make for the vast red barn, and just around the corner is the church.

There is so much of interest to see in this small area including more woodland to explore at Haugh Wood to the north – an area owned by the National Trust – and little churches at How Caple and King's Caple.

I've already mentioned the extraordinary touch of Tuscany in the church at Hoarwithy. The best approach to that village is along the

King's Caple road. Just at the point where you drop down to the Wye, St Catherine's Church comes into sight, built high on the side of the next valley. I saw it first with brilliant afternoon sunshine adding a glow to the red sandstone of the church. That, coupled with the parched red earth around, was a very un-English scene. Even if you saw it in the pouring rain, the outline of flattened tower and rounded cupola would still make you think twice about whether you were still in England.

The present church was built around an existing chapel on the orders of William Poole, the vicar of Hentland, who also paid for the work out of a legacy he inherited. It was begun in 1885 and continued for nearly twenty years. Several craftsmen came from Italy, and some from St Paul's in London.

You approach the church along a warm brick-lined passage up shallow steps. Towards the top, arch upon arch takes you into the short cloister walk running along the southern side. It is a perfect place to see down to the village and over to the hills beyond. The floor is a faded mosaic. Inside, there is even a Byzantine feel. Four marble columns, with richly ornate capitals, support the inner cupola, and behind is a golden ceiling mosaic. There's a plentiful use of marble elsewhere, including the beautiful altar which is inlaid with huge squares of lapis lazuli and agate. It is a remarkable piece of architecture, and I hope realized the vicar's dream.

A Corner of Poets

Dymock is a small village some five miles (8 km) south of Ledbury, just inside the borders of Gloucestershire. This part of England, with its romantic rural feeling, and numerous isolated spots hidden by wooded hills, must have seemed a perfect haven as a retreat to a group of poets before the First World War.

Lascelles Abercrombie and his wife Catherine were the first of the group to come here. They rented a cottage just outside the village in 1911. A year or so later they were joined by Rupert Brooke and John Drinkwater, then by Wilfrid Gibson, and a year later by Edward Thomas and Robert Frost.

They all stayed in the area within a few miles of each other, spending time together reading and discussing their latest poems. Catherine Abercrombie organized the distribution of a quarterly periodical 'New Numbers' which included some of their new work.

The coming of the war split the group up, Frost returned to America and Abercrombie worked as a munitions inspector in Liverpool. Thomas enlisted and was later killed in Flanders in 1917. Rupert Brooke, who is today perhaps the best known, died in 1915 of blood poisoning. His war poems are some of the most famous, and he died a national hero.

The poets found great inspiration in the landscape around Dymock. 'All set in the blue of the sky, green of the fields and leaves, and that red, that red of the soil.' Thus it was described by another poet visiting in 1916.

This walk goes through the countryside associated with the poets, to the house that was rented by the Abercrombies, and beyond to Ryton Firs, an impressive tree-covered ridge that also features in some of the poems.

Apart from being a poet's corner, this area is known also as Daffodil Crescent, since in the spring there are masses of wild daffodils growing in the nearby fields. If you are there at the right time of the year, it is worth going on the local 'Daffodil Trail' to see the best of these spring flowers.

OS Map 1:50 000, Sheets 149 and 150
A circular walk of 6 miles (10 km). Allow $2\frac{1}{2}$–3 hours.

The going underfoot is mixed with some paths across fields, road and bridle-track, and woodland rides. The worst parts are over the farm lands at gates where cattle tend to churn up the land especially in wet weather.

Inevitably for this landscape there is little walking on the flat, except down by the river, but the undulations are quite gentle. There is plenty of livestock around, sheep, cattle and some horses, plus game birds in the woods, so dogs will need to be kept on leads.

Although the route is quite complicated, the paths are, in general, well marked with yellow or blue directional arrows, as there have been several projects to encourage more walking in this area. Even so, some parts are likely to be overgrown.

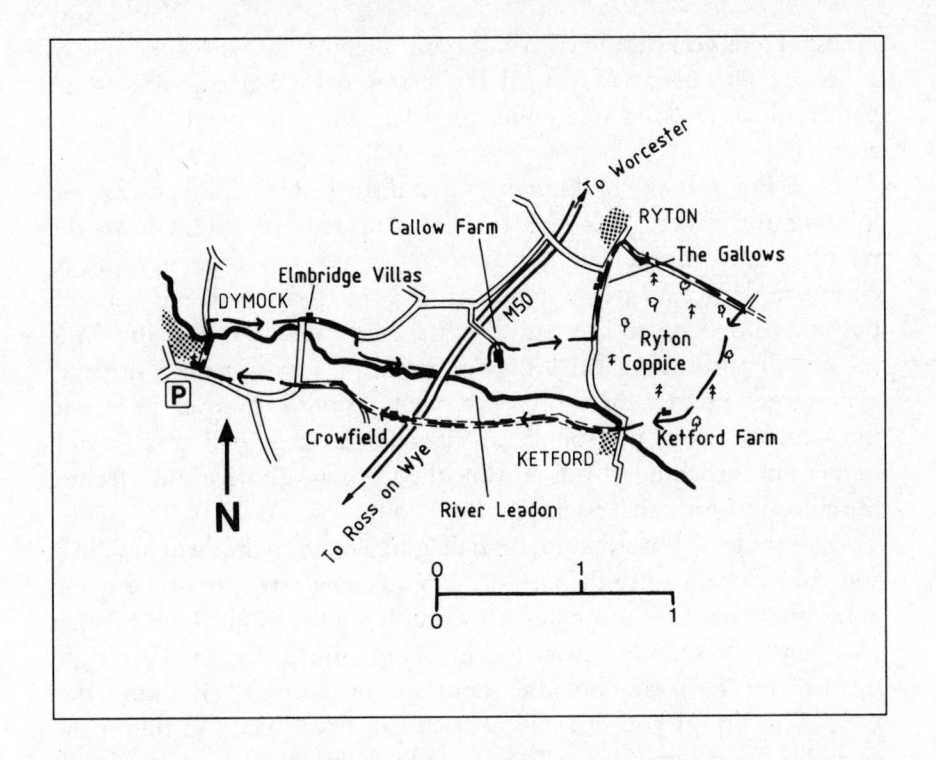

There is a longer version of this walk developed by the Windcross Public Paths group. They have also documented a walk through the wild daffodil fields called the Daffodil Way, and are at present way-marking a Poet's Path-2 which will go to the north of this area.

Car-parking and the start

There is parking space for several cars at the Parish Hall just by the church on the B4126.

Start at the church, going to look first at the display about the Dymock Poets that is at the back of the nave.

Go north of the church to the kissing gate, and then cross the meadow diagonally right where there is a stile onto the road. Turn left and cross over the tiny River Leadon, not really much more than a little brook. Follow the path along the edges of the fields and the route of the river until you come out at a minor road bend. Follow the road to the left and after a quarter of a mile (500 m) look for Mill

House. Here you should turn right and then go down by the side of a house. The peace may well be shattered by barking dogs. The path leads down to a stile taking you left, virtually parallel with the river.

It was not only the barking dogs that disturbed the rural peace I was looking for. There was also the constant roar of traffic from the relatively new motorway, the clattering of a distant train, and just to complete the scene, a low flying jet! I wondered whether it was still possible to find much inspiration in the landscape, but what drew me on was the promising ridge of woods ahead. I was in for a surprise. Having gone under the motorway, walking with my back to it, and the wind blowing the sounds away, I felt as though I was leaving modern noise behind. It was possible then to get a glimpse and a feeling of the countryside that so inspired these poets.

Once under the motorway, head diagonally left to the farm buildings and cross the stile onto the farm lane. You can go straight on here, but as the alternative led more quickly away from the traffic, I headed that way, and it was the one place I didn't find a footpath sign. Turn right towards the farmyard but then continue on a dirt track almost due west. This brings you out into a vast field. I was lucky to find it full of stubble and bone dry too, so I could march boldly across. In the middle of the growing period I suspect I'd have been less fortunate, and would have had to walk around the edge.

This is a very pleasant valley, with the first of the gently rounded hills immediately in front and a steep ridge of powerful green beyond that.

Aim for the huge glasshouse on the other side, where there is an exit from the field, and then turn left along this narrow hedge-lined lane. You pass The Gallows, which was the house used by the Abercrombies, and the scene of many a literary lunch or supper. Catherine wrote about these evenings listening to poetry: 'I lay on a stoop of hay and listened and watched the stars wander through the elms and thought I had really found the why and the wherefore of life.'

Carry on along the road about 150 yards to a bridle-path on the right. This climbs up gradually running along the side of a wood. Looking over to your left, you get glimpses of the pretty Malvern Hills with their distinctive outline, rising up to the Herefordshire

Beacon in the far distance. Looking straight ahead the church on the horizon with the outline of a stumpy tower belongs to the curiously named Redmarley D'Abitot, which sounds more like a stain remover than a village.

This bridle-track ends at a junction with a lane where there is a gate into a large expanse of pasture land. Go diagonally right up to the woods at the top of the field to a little path leading through the woods. This was alive with baby game birds skuttling around in a haphazard fashion, and probably not too happy at the sound of distant gun fire.

The path splits into two bridle-ways. Take the lower one and follow this down the bottom edge of the woods. All this is part of Ryton Firs, of which Abercrombie wrote: 'All the meadowland Daffodils seem/Running in golden tides to Ryton Firs.'

At certain times of year, this path may end in shoulder-high bracken. But don't despair; if you push on a little you'll find a gate into the field and a reassuring yellow marker. This path runs along the top of the next two fields and then circles round the left of Ketford Farm.

Join the farm lane and walk down to the road, then turn left and cross over the River Leadon. It is a little confusing here as you expect from the map to be in the hamlet of Ketford, but the sign was for Pauntley which is apparently the parish name.

Almost immediately beyond the bridge is a track to the right, and then a gate on the right marked with a blue arrow. This path goes along the top of the fields and then into a wooded area, where you can climb to a good viewing point. From there you can see the obelisk at Eastnor Park on the Malvern Hills. The immediate view is of a patchwork of fields of very contrasting yellow and dark green.

A very obvious bridle-path goes back in the direction of Dymock. Where it joins a lane, the footpath is opposite. It goes around the edge of the cricket pitch and then out onto the main road just before returning to the starting-point at Dymock Church.

Abbey Dore

The Golden Valley, a beautiful name for a beautiful place, stretches down from near Hay-on-Wye to the rather unromantic A465 trunk road at Pontrilas. This peaceful valley, about twenty miles (32 km) long, and just a few miles wide, is extraordinarily lovely on the right day. It provides a spacious home for the gentle course of the River Dore until it joins the Monnow. There is quite a bit of confusion about how the Valley came to get its name. Possibly it was a misunderstanding by the Normans when the Welsh for water, 'dwr', was thought to be the French 'd'or' – of gold.

The most southerly village of the Valley appears at first to be a much-expanded, sprawling modern development. It has the curious name of Ewyas Harold, which I can't help but think of as Eyewash Harold, with an image from the Bayeux Tapestry. It doesn't seem very promising, but the heart of this village around the old church is charming.

The village was here at the time of the Doomsday Book, and was one of only five boroughs in the county. It was here too that one of the first defensive earthworks to be called a castle was built, in 1051. Now the castle has gone and even the tourists tend to bypass the place, heading further up the valley. There is though, just behind the village, a rambling common, one of the very few true commons left in the south. Communal grazing rights are enjoyed by those living nearby (but dogs are the predominant quadruped that I've seen there). It's a marvellous place for wandering, plenty of soft grass avenues through bushes and bracken, and with a definite hill shape, providing views in nearly all directions. It's quite different from anywhere else in the vicinity. Over the hill from Ewyas Harold is the church of Abbey Dore, and a lovely Court Garden. This walk includes all these places.

OS Map 1:50 000, Sheet 149
A circular walk of a minimum 4 miles (6 km). Allow 2 hours and extra time to enjoy the Abbey and the Gardens.

The walk can be easily lengthened by spending more time on the common. This can be deliberate, or even accidental if the navigation causes trouble!

The going underfoot can be a little soggy over the fields leading up to the common and on the narrow footpath that is used for the descent, but the walking on the common itself is excellent.

The navigation is a little confusing on the common itself as paths

THE FOREST OF DEAN

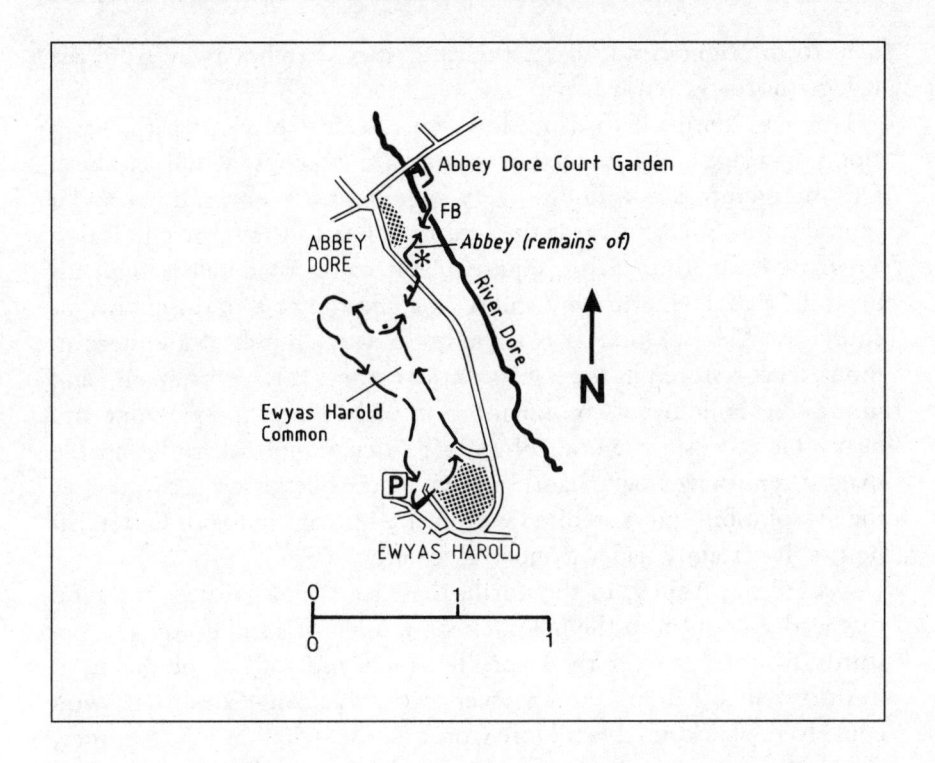

lead in all directions. It's small enough to enjoy being a little lost, but you may end up doing a bit more than you expect.

Car-parking and the start

Park in the centre of Ewyas Harold village, close by the church.

Starting at the church, walk past the village store to the left and then turn up the little lane on the left heading up the slight hill. At the T-junction at the top there is a footpath straight ahead up across some fields. This continues in the same direction, coming out shortly at some houses and a rough road. Here, turn left and walk along the road until it peters out into the common. This tract of land is exactly what you'd expect a common to be – wild, but not quite. It is covered with bands of rough heather and gorse cut through by broad grassy avenues. Although the land is high it undulates quite definitely and beyond there are views of wooded hills and ridges. Carry on upwards, tending over to the right-hand side of the ridge that stretches away from the village (north-westwards).

Don't be tempted to drop down on the first obvious path. Keep along the ridge and as you come around a small copse you'll see ahead a classic picture-book house – very square with four windows and a central door. Walk towards this and then just to the right you'll find a narrow footpath that drops quite steeply to the road below and ends up at the pub. Here, turn left and walk along the road to the enormous church of Abbey Dore. This is the presbytery church of a Cistercian monastery, restored in the seventeenth century. It is a very strong and impressive building, a combination of Early English stonework and heavy Herefordshire wood. Note in particular the oak roof and the magnificent carved oak chancel screen. The Abbey itself decayed after the Dissolution, but is credited with being one of the major Cistercian houses. It certainly had a wonderful location.

Behind the Abbey, to the north, there's a couple of decrepit gates that lead you out into the field. Go straight across, and go on across a sturdy footbridge over the river. Turn left and follow the daunting security fence (I didn't realize sheep were that dangerous!) until you come to the back of Abbey Dore Court Gardens. To find the entrance, turn right and then left along a track which brings you onto the road at their car-park.

This garden must surely be an inspiration for all potential Percy Throwers, or anyone looking at a jungle outside their back door! Exactly twenty years ago this garden was a mass of undergrowth and rubbish, with no organization, not much in the way of tree or plant varieties, and all paths obscured. Wandering now around the very distinctive areas, it is hard to think a wilderness could ever have been here. Where there were once head-high nettles, there is now a herb garden, and impassible brambles have gone to make way for a winding riverside path.

Over the river is the area known as St Stephen's Meadow which used to belong to the Abbey. Here there is now a large pond and rock garden.

The garden makes an excellent turning-round point for this walk, not least because they now have a small tea-room on site. It was started because it was taking visitors so long to get around. For serious plant lovers, the boast of the garden is that it is home to the National Sedum

Collection. On entering (there is a charge) you get a detailed map showing the layout and notable plants to look out for as you saunter around. Don't miss the two stone figures by the house, they look as though they have just stepped out of *Alice in Wonderland*.

After visiting the garden, Abbey, or both, retrace your steps to the little house on the common. You could head straight back to Eywas Harold from here, but to get views on the other side, keep going on up past the house, climbing virtually to the highest point of the common. You won't go too far because a fence delimits the boundary of the common. At this point start to make your way left, heading slightly downhill and in the direction of Ewyas Harold. You should end up at a small private house just below the ridge where there is a narrow path taking you down to a lower road. From here there is another footpath leading across fields to a small road in a new housing estate at the back of the church. You may not find this exact path but on exploring I discovered that there are a variety of ways down off the common back to the village.

While you are in this area, it is worth going downstream (the River Monnow, which the Dore runs into nearby) to Grosmont, an old ruined castle where you can enjoy a good view from a semi-ruined tower. You just creep into Wales going along this route. It is somewhat ironic that this is now Wales, as Grosmont and the neighbouring Skenfrith Castle and White Castle were built as a triangle to keep out the troublesome Welsh! Owen Glendower was defeated here by the man who was to become Henry V. Now the sounds of battle have well and truly vanished and this is a peaceful part of the countryside. Grosmont itself is a very pretty little place, really tucked away in the many undulations of this countryside. I stayed at a secluded riverside campsite nearby, and had a good meal in the local pub.

The Forest of Dean is a huge area, some 120,000 acres (48,562 ha), covering the wedge-shaped part of the country where the Wye meets the Severn and stretching northwards to Ross-on-Wye. Only about a quarter of this is tree-covered now, with much of the rest being farmed. The forest has played many roles over the years, from being a royal hunting ground, to being a great mining area, a source of timber particularly for ship building, and also grazing land for commoners.

All these claims on the forest have produced a very turbulent history with rioting almost into the present century.

The Ancient Britons discovered iron-ore deposits and started mining in the forest, work that was continued by the Romans and subsequent settlers. The outcrop mining created a different landscape with its pits and rifts and piles of excavated rock. Timber was used for charcoal burning to smelt and forge the ore in the forest. As well as making the usual nails, horseshoes, etc., there was a vast industry for making crossbow bolts. The castle of St Briavels, in the heart of the Forest, was one of the great arsenals in the country, producing over half a million of these quarrels, as they were known, during the thirteenth century. It is not known exactly how the miners in the Forest of Dean came to enjoy the title 'Free Miner' along with certain rights and privileges, particularly the use of free timber. It might have been to do with their service to the king in the Middle Ages, not just in the making of ammunition, but also in their tunnelling skills during sieges. Forest of Dean miners worked at sieges as far away as Berwick and Dover.

Apart from the miners, the Commoners held rights to grazing and pannage (rights to fatten pigs). There was a slight curb on the Commoners and the Free Miners when the Forest was deemed a Royal Hunting Forest in the days of Edward the Confessor. It kept that title over the centuries, but by Tudor times the crown wanted to protect the forest more for its timber than for hunting. The reason was ships. It was not only a great age for trade and exploration, but also the time when England was emerging as a naval power. A timber shortage was feared and Acts of Parliament were passed to check the rights of both the Free Miners and the Commoners within the forest.

A later act allowed enclosure of the forest, and in 1657 the first deliberate planting of trees. Rioting came from both the miners, fearing the loss of their traditional right to free timber, and then from the Commoners whose grazing rights were threatened by enclosure. There are records of fences being torn down, enclosure hedges being uprooted and fires being started. This battle continued on and off for some 250 years, with the miners losing their right to free timber in 1808, and the last riot by the Commoners occurring in 1898, when 11,000 acres were enclosed for replanting.

Small wonder that this tremendous opposition has produced the legends that the inhabitants of Dean are an aggressive bunch and a law unto themselves.

Since the Great War, the forest has been managed by the Forestry Commission, and the arrangements between interested parties seem to have become more amicable. Although up to 5,000 animals graze here, the commission has the power to enclose new areas of planting so the young shoots have a chance to grow into trees. Mining does still go on, but not on the scale of former centuries. The last commercial iron ore was produced in 1944 and the last coal mine closed in 1965, but there are still nearly a dozen small mines in the forest.

Walking in most areas, you'll still see many sheep wandering on the roads and quietly nibbling in the car-parks and the shelter of the woods. Deer too, once completely exterminated in the forest, in a rather drastic attempt to prevent poaching, have also been re-introduced. All over the forest you'll come across evidence of mining activity, with old quarries, railway lines, pits and tunnels and flattened charcoal hearths serving as a reminder of this area's colourful activity.

There is useful information at the Dean Heritage Centre and at the numerous Forestry Commission car-parks.

As there is so much to choose from, I've described here a couple of oddities which might easily be overlooked – Puzzle Wood, a small privately owned area, and the Sculpture Trail, a way to see the forest through modern eyes.

Puzzle Wood

OS Map 1:50 000, Sheet 162
Puzzle Wood is about ½ mile (500 m) from Coleford on the road towards St Briavels.

I have not given a distance or time allowance for this walk as it might be the shortest or the longest walk in the book depending on how quickly you solve the puzzle.

The paths, which are the puzzle, are laid out in such a way that you can end going around in several circles, and one fern and rock-filled hollow begins to look surprisingly like another. But feeling lost adds to the atmosphere of the place as it is in fact a tiny (less than a half-mile wide) area.

Puzzle Wood was part of the Lambsquay Mines which were some of the first mines in the area, dating back nearly three thousand years. The mines were opencast and the ore was iron. The rocks were first cracked by the simple means of being heated by fire and then suddenly cooled with cold water, causing fractures. The ore was then hewn out. The workings have changed the face of the land with scowles (a corruption of an old word for caves), pits and passages.

Whilst it has been possible to find out about the early history of the mines, there is a long period when this wood just lay undiscovered. It was in the latter part of the 1800s that the property was bought by the Turner family. By this time, all the old workings were well and truly overgrown. There is nothing raw about the mining remains left here. The piles of rock and chiselled cliffs and caves have been invaded with ferns, mosses, and creepers. Yew, an iron-loving tree, grows well, and on the outskirts of the wood are carpets of bluebells in the spring, and the unmistakable smell of wild garlic and its tiny white flowers. Turner, far from cleaning up the wood, left it as it was, but added paths and bridges plus the odd strategically-placed seat to make exploring the wood easier and a real adventure. It was for the family's own pleasure but also as a playground for the children. The wood was sold to the Watkins family at the beginning of this century and is owned today by a descendant of that family.

You can lose yourself completely here both in space and time.

The Forest Sculpture Trail

OS Map 1:50 000, Sheet 162
A circular trail of 4 miles (6.5 km) marked by blue-ringed posts. Allow 2 hours.

I first came across the idea of a forest sculpture trail whilst on an orienteering training exercise in Grizedale Forest, near Lake Coniston, Cumbria. Coming head on with a huge but static deer gave me a terrific fright until I realized that the animal was made of brushwood.

I then enjoyed discovering the many other sculptures and seeing the use the artists had made of the environment.

The trail in the Forest of Dean is equally imaginative and makes a most enjoyable walk, almost a treasure hunt as you search out each different work of art. The treasure hunt means it will appeal to those with children particularly. You can get the small leaflet giving you details of the trail either from the Forestry Commission offices and campsites in the Forest of Dean, or the Dean Heritage Centre near Cinderford.

If you are without a leaflet, go to the Beechenhurst Picnic Site and car-park on the B4266 just east of the junction of the B4234 and the B4226 (the same road as Speech House). The trail begins there and you can find it by following blue-ringed wooden posts each of which is marked with an arrow to show you the direction in which to continue.

The sculptures themselves are not pointed out in any way. Some of them, like 'Place', a massive throne, are very obvious indeed, whilst some of the more subtle, like 'Falling Crowns', are more difficult to spot.

Fifteen artists were involved with this venture which was developed over a period of four years. Each artist was asked to respond to and interpret the character of the Forest of Dean, bearing in mind aspects of its history such as the mining or timber production. They were also asked to look for specific sites in the forest that would enhance the work.

The result is a fascinating variety of sculptures; some are naturalistic, some abstract, some made from natural materials that may eventually be reclaimed by the forest or the elements, others made from distinctly man-made materials which, because of their setting, are not eyesores but rather serve to highlight a feature of the surroundings.

Everyone who sees them has their personal favourites. I think mine must be 'Crossing Place' where a herd of deer is crossing over a small pond. Some of the herd are already across, others are swimming in the water whilst the remaining ones are poised on the bank. The animals themselves are most effective but what is most striking is the way the artist has captured the timid approach the deer make towards the water, and the overall sense of silence.

★　　★　　★

Westbury-on-Severn seems little more than an attractive cluster of houses that one rushes past whilst on the main road from Gloucester to Cinderford, just before you get to the Forest of Dean. In fact, it's worth pulling off the road and pausing here awhile. You'll discover a pleasant meadowland walk to the broad River Severn, the garden cliffs that lie on one of the banks, and, hidden from sight only yards from the main road, a fascinating, fully restored seventeenth- and early eighteenth-century water garden laid out in the Dutch style. It is one of the rarest types of garden to have survived in this country. I found a couple of hours disappeared here effortlessly, and on continuing my journey I felt surprisingly refreshed. It may not surprise you to find that I also discovered here a good village tea-room that also serves light snacks.

A Walk Around the Water Garden

OS Map 1:50 000, Sheet 162
A circular walk of 1 mile (1.5 km). Allow $\frac{1}{2}$ hour for the walk and then time to explore the gardens.

This is one of the shortest walks in the book, and is very easy. It is ideal if you are on the way to explore the Forest of Dean and the Wye Valley or if you are travelling, since it makes a good break in the journey.

Although only a short ramble, there are likely to be some wet and muddy patches as the route goes over several fields. Some of these are grazed meadowland where the grass will be short (but may be wet), but on the way back the route crosses a cultivated field, making wellingtons the preferred footwear at some times of the year.

The navigation is easy as the River Severn and the church spire at Westbury are landmarks which are not easily missed.

Car-parking and the start

Driving in from the Gloucester side of Westbury, look out for the National Trust sign to the garden pointing you to the left. I think it is best to go on a short way beyond here to the next turning, just by a pub. This lane leads to the church and there are several end-on parking spaces.

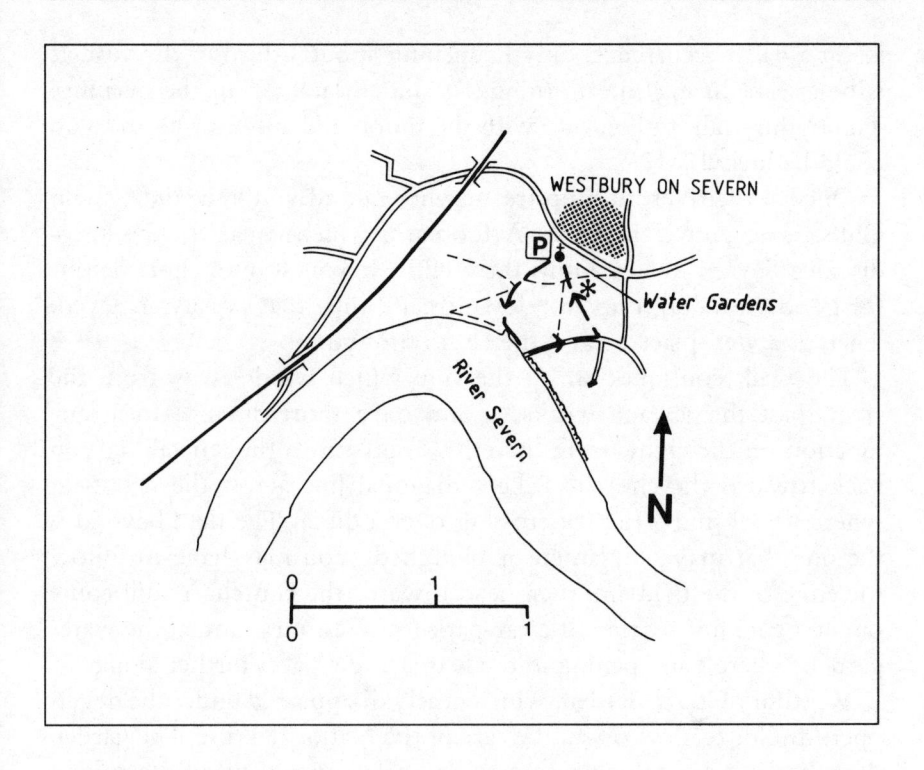

Walk down the lane by the church and at the end you'll come to a gate into some flat meadows. The path goes over the side of these along a little stream. After crossing two fields, you'll come to the side of the River Severn. Its broadness is impressive, particularly here as this is a point where it swings round in a huge final loop before straightening out into the estuary and the Bristol Channel.

It is the meeting of the river and the tidal estuary that creates the phenomenon known as the Severn Bore. At the turn of the tide, best at a full moon near the spring or autumn equinox, when the currents are at full strength, the waters of the sea rush up the estuary slap bang into the oncoming river. The result is a huge wave which then heads upstream. This quantity of water comes to a narrow gap just around the corner from Westbury, which it forces into. The first wave is followed by a second and third wave and then by the full force of the tide, a foaming and bubbling mass. Unfortunately this phenomenon is not a daily occurrence, only happening about a third of the year. It is best seen during the mornings, or much later on in the evening. Time your walk to coincide with the moon and a good tide and you could be lucky!

Once at the river, turn upstream where ahead you'll see the Garden Cliffs rising above the river. A footpath, which is part of the long-distance Severn Way, climbs these cliffs. If you want a short detour for good views both up and downstream, then that's easily achieved. There is a well-placed seat if the climb tires you.

The walk continues on up the lane which winds away from the river, past the sewage works (!) and on a short distance to a lane junction on the right. Here there is a footpath to the left taking you back towards the church. Take a diagonal line across the first field where you'll find a rickety crossing over a ditch. The field beyond is the one that may be planted or ploughed. You may have to follow the edge of the field and then head towards the church. You'll come out at a gate just by the little car-park for Westbury Court, the water garden. There's an opening in the hedge a few paces further along.

Westbury Court Garden, which nearly disappeared under the developers' bulldozers, is now in the care of the National Trust. The garden dates back to a time when society had a different view of the role of gardens, nature and man's place in the scheme of things. The layout is rigid and formal; long lines of water, grass and bushes echo a parade ground. I find it fascinating to imagine visitors to the garden in the early days, and what they thought of them. I wonder what visitors will make of them in another two hundred and fifty years?

Once through the entrance of Westbury Court Garden, it is as though you have stepped back to the early days two centuries ago, with the only reminder of the modern world being, sadly, the noise of traffic on the main road. The formal layout and calm waters of the canals have a tranquil air. The garden is small, but I found being able to take in the entire area at a glance one of the attractions. Viewing the scheme as a whole was one of the intentions of the original designers and to do this they built an elegant brick summerhouse with a first-floor viewing room. This is known as the Tall Pavilion. It's a typical Dutch device, giving access to a vantage point so the spectator can appreciate the composition. Originally you would have been able to see further afield to the Severn.

A Colchester family first owned the estate and began the work on the garden in 1696. The site was lovingly maintained and extended over the next hundred years. Still surviving are some quaint records referring to early work amongst which are:

"1702 21 May, paid Mr Wells 2,000 sparagus plants, mat £1:6:0"
"1703 18 Jan, paid tyling the somerhouse £1:10:0"

The next two hundred years tell a very different story. The original house was demolished, and eventually the property was sold to a speculator who had planning permission for ten houses on the site. The garden pavilions were ruined and the canal became stagnant and overgrown. Luckily, Gloucestershire County Council refused permission for various inappropriate developments, bought the land, and offered the garden to the National Trust. There are pictures in the Pavilion that show its state then. Looking at the scene now it is hard to believe. Much early work was done by volunteers and, as is often the case, a huge anonymous donation enabled a serious programme of restoration. Even the Tall Pavilion was so beyond repair that it was completely demolished and reconstructed in old materials.

Luckily, the form of the garden survived in an engraving by Kip, so it has been possible to recreate the layout to give the feel of what it would have been like at the end of the seventeenth and early eighteenth centuries.

In the corner, diagonally opposite the Tall Pavilion, is a tiny walled garden, which is a mass of roses, lily of the valley, pinks and hollyhocks. There are seats where you can enjoy this charming spot, made more fascinating by the knowledge that every flower planted was known about in Britain before 1700. The gardeners have been able to use the original planting records as a guide.

Apart from what has been planted quite recently, there are some ancient trees that survive at the southern end near the Pavilion on the Ilex Oak Lawn. The Holm Oak growing here, thought to be one of the oldest in the country, is some 400 years old. It is interesting to find that this tree does not feature in the engraving, possibly because it added an unwelcome touch of asymmetry. Nevertheless it survived.

SHROPSHIRE

'The blue remembered hills' was A. E. Housman's description of the hills of Shropshire, a most apt choice of words for hills are in profusion in this county.

It seems a much-neglected region, keeping its delights well-hidden, under a bushel of barley, probably, since it is this commodity that has brought much of the farming wealth to the county. Maybe it's just that the locals are canny and don't want the place filled with trippers. They wish them instead a speedy journey west to Wales, north to the Lakes or south to the West Country.

Shropshire is a marvellous place to explore. My first holiday was near Ludlow when I was about ten; more recently I have been going to biannual orienteering events called Springtime in Shropshire, which has been a splendid way to get to know the less-populated part of the county, namely, the hills.

Hills are in profusion in Shropshire. If they had all been only a little higher it would be considered a mountainous region, especially the southern half. As it is, the hills are smaller than most mountains and are that much more accessible and rather more personal. I was struck by the fact that many are known individually rather than as ranges. The well-known Wrekin juts suddenly out of the plain near the ever-growing new town of Telford, looking for all the world like a pyramid from one side and a recumbent whale from the other. The Long Mynd represents 5,000 acres (2,023 ha) of heather and bracken-covered moorland plateau. Less well known is the much excavated Brown Clee, Shropshire's highest hill which rises to 1,772 feet (540 m).

The walks specified in this chapter are not necessarily better designed for fell runners; there is some climbing, but it is often gentle, and a common way you'll encounter the hills is as a good view rather than a summit conquered.

The countryside is not the only thing to explore as this county has its fair share of delightful market towns such as Much Wenlock and Ludlow. Shrewsbury, the county town, lying snug in a meander of the broad River Severn, is almost the centre of the county and makes a good starting-point for most expeditions.

The roads emanating from the town are all horrendously busy, but if you head off down the minor roads and back lanes, you'll soon find rural Shropshire.

The ideas I've set out in Shropshire will take you to the hills in the south-west and south-east of the county, the Stiperstones and the Clees, respectively. North of Shrewsbury is less markedly hilly than south, but I managed to find an interesting hill there to explore.

As Mary Webb, a Shropshire-born author, writes, 'Shropshire is a county where the dignity and beauty of ancient things lingers long.' I hope you'll experience some of that in your travels here.

The Stiperstones

The Stiperstones is the name given to a range of hills on the south-western side of Shropshire, almost into Wales. Although not far from the busy A488, this area could be light years away from the modern world. The rugged profile of the land has a powerful atmosphere, unchanged by time and steeped in legend. Are you going to brave the Devil's Chair on 22 December when all the ghosts of Shropshire gather on the hill?

More ghosts lurk on the south-western flank of the Stiperstones, where a busy mining settlement called The Bog once thrived. It is now a lonely site with ruined buildings and signs of old workings. But less than a hundred years ago men and boys worked in the local mines whilst the womenfolk looked after smallholdings. Little remains of the community since decline of the industry towards the end of the nineteenth century with only the mining of barytes, a heavy white mineral, continuing until the 1920s. The last building, a corrugated iron community hall, which was the Miners' Institute, was knocked down some fifty years ago. The Miners' Arms, once a pub, is now a private house.

This walk starts on the site of the former mining community and goes round, via another deserted village, to the dramatic ridge of the Stiperstones with its legendary Devil's Chair.

OS Map 1:50 000, Sheets 137 and 126 (though the bulk of the walk is on Sheet 137)
A circular walk of 5 miles (8 km). Allow $2\frac{1}{2}$–$3\frac{1}{2}$ hours.

The going underfoot on the first part is the most pleasant, on track and grassy path. Returning along the ridge of The Stiperstones it is very rocky and you'll need to take good care. It is quite slow going. There are some hefty descents and a huge haul up to the top, which again will be quite slow.

Car-parking and the start

The car-park is at The Bog, not what you may think but a gravelled area within easy reach of The Stiperstones. Here you'll also find a series of information panels telling you about life in the mining heyday of the nineteenth century.

I prefer to save the Stiperstones Ridge for the last part of the walk as I find going in this direction means you get a better view of the Devil's Chair and you walk towards extensive views at the start.

Walk up the road from the car-park to the corner of the hairpin bend. Here there's a stile and path, with three more stiles to cross leading up to an obvious track along the lower slopes of the Stiperstones Ridge. You will see some of the rocky tors (or peaks) towering on the horizon, but more of them later.

Follow the track as it continues between the fences, ignoring any paths that seem to lead up or down the hill. After $1\frac{1}{2}$ miles (2 km), there's a fence corner and the path then goes down the hill through a patch of gorse and bracken. You come out at a stile into a field. You can see far across the Shropshire Plain with the hills of Wales rising to the left.

Here, go down to the far side of the field and then turn right, following the field boundary as it goes downhill and then meets the road. Turn right and walk into the village of Stiperstones.

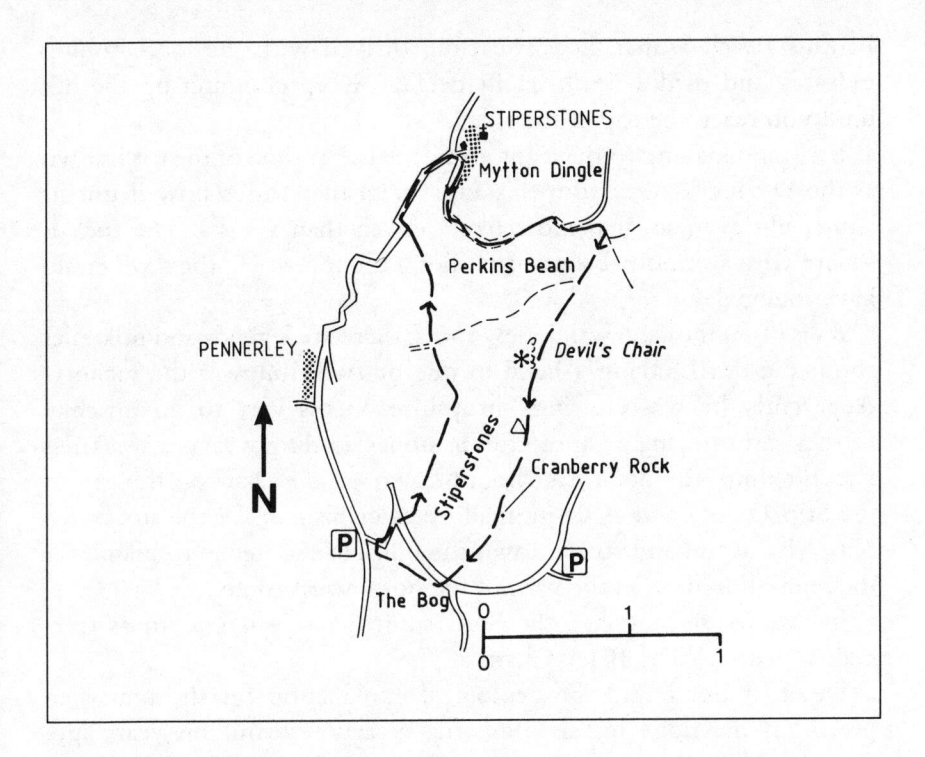

Opposite The Stiperstones Inn is a lane which winds round past several cottages, some almost hidden below you, and then gradually ascends the steep slope of the ridge. This is a broad valley dramatically enclosed by the towering hills on either side. The name for these valleys in local dialect is 'dingle'. Strictly speaking it means a valley that is slightly wooded. Here, on both sides of the path, are scatterings of small trees shedding a dappled light on the ground.

Some of the trees would be more at home in an orchard than a forest, the distinctive damson, for instance. It is so common in Shropshire it is nicknamed the Shropshire plum. In autumn, its delicate leaves turn a brilliant yellow, adding a vibrant colour to many a hedgerow and garden. There may well have been an orchard or two on this lane as there are remains of many houses on either side of the path. Some buildings are still quite recognizable, whilst all that remains of others is tumbledown walls and foundations. This was the old village of

Perkins Beach which, like The Bog, thrived with the local mining industry and died a death on its decline. Keep climbing up the hill until you reach the top of the ridge.

If you look along to the right you'll see the outline of the tor known as the Devil's Chair. From this angle it's easier to see how it got its name, but even so, it is more like a couch than a chair. The rock is square with a smoothed-out curve along the top where the devil could have lounged.

As is often the case with lonely spots, there are legends and folk tales about the devil having a hand in one or two things in the vicinity. Apparently he was crossing Shropshire on his way to do mischief further east carrying an apron full of stones. Feeling weary, a weakness I didn't think the devil had, he sat down on the chair on the top of the Stiperstones and as he jumped up after his nap, all the stones fell out of his apron and rolled down the hill. He's someone to blame for the many boulders on the path of the homeward route.

In the Welsh language the Stiperstones Range is known as Carneddan Tuon – The Black Chairs.

Devil or no, I find the geological explanation for the pinnacled profile of the ridge just as dramatic. Nearly 500 million years ago, there was no ridge here, just a vast beach of pure quartz sand and pebbles. Volcanic eruptions, which created Snowdon in Wales, caused waves in the land here that folded the accumulated sediments and created the ridge. The remaining sculpturing is the result of erosion. The softer rock layers were gradually worn away, and during the Ice Age intense frost shattered the quartzite leaving the jagged angular tors.

The first tor you come to on the ridge is known as Shepherd's Rock. Here, turn right and walk along the wide rocky track through the Scattered Rocks (the devil's work) and up to the Devil's Chair. Beyond is the trig point at Manstone Rock and finally Cranberry Rock, probably named in honour of the bilberry, whinberry and cowberry, known locally as cranberry plants. These occur mixed with heather all over the slopes around the path.

From this ridge there are splendid views. To the north-east are the distinctive Wrekin and Caer Caradoc and the long upland tract to the south-east is The Long Mynd, stretching over ten miles (16 km). Incidentally, the road between The Mynd and The Stiperstones, which goes alongside the River East Onny and then to Habberley, is absolutely beautiful. The near hill to the south-west is Corndon Hill, which is in Wales.

From Cranberry Rock the path drops down to the road. Cross over and immediately opposite is a stile and a clear path leading right over the fields and then through the gorse and brambles to come out just above The Bog car-park.

Much of the atmosphere of this region, with its brooding air has been captured in the novels and poetry of Mary Webb. She was born near Much Wenlock, but lived for many years near Pontesbury just to the north of The Stiperstones. Her own story of her struggle against illness, financial hardship and lack of literary recognition, is fascinating. The little money she did have would often be spent on the poor, children especially. It was only after her death and posthumous praise by the then Prime Minister, Stanley Baldwin, that she achieved fame. Recently her novel *Gone to Earth* was made into a film for television and much was shot at Stiperstones Village. She not only captures vividly the quality and colour of the countryside of Shropshire but describes many of the ways and customs of the farming folk. For example, the hiring day at market where people came with a symbol of their trade, to get employment for the next year, such as a cook with a wooden spoon, or a blacksmith with a horseshoe in his hat, and the 'love-spinning' where neighbours got together to spin for a girl about to be married.

From Stiperstones it is worth driving just a little further west to the north of Corndon Hill to explore another intriguing area. On top of the Rowls is Mitchell's Fold, the most complete of three prehistoric stone circles in the area. From here, go down to the village of Priest Weston, and turn north towards Middleton Hall Farm where you'll come to Middleton Church with its unique and characterful carvings. Not to be missed.

Only a handful of folk live hereabouts, but in the nineteenth century Middleton was a thriving area thanks to the profitable mining industry. In 1872, Waldegrave Brewster came as rector to the parish. He was an energetic young man who kept careful note of events at the church, even down to details of the temperature and rainfall. He wanted to enrich his church, and found he had a flair for carving, particularly in wood. He set about all the pew-ends and the desks and bench-ends for the choir boys, carving not only abstract patterns but a marvellous series of heads. The carvings took him twelve years. Each one is different, some bearded, some jolly, and some stately. My favourite is a marvellous beaky woman in a mob cap, the archetypal Judy. I wonder if any of the parishioners recognized themselves.

To the north of Shrewsbury the land flattens out into an undulating plain which continues into Cheshire. Far from becoming monotonous, the countryside continues to be varied and interesting, with a patchwork of fields to all horizons. Of course, some of the patches are larger than they used to be as many hedges have been grubbed up to make way for the plough. Occasionally you'll see two or three well-spaced oak trees in a large field. These would once have been part of hedges, before field rationalization, but now they stand in isolation. The oak flourishes in this part of the county and farmers will tell you it's a sign of the rich quality of the land. Shropshire oak has been much sought-after by shipbuilders, and was used extensively in housebuilding and interior panelling. One of the best examples is the lining of the chamber of the House of Commons.

There are still patches of woodland and numerous small lakes known locally as 'meres'. The Shropshire Union Canal threads its way through the county passing by the main towns of Market Drayton, Whitchurch and Ellesmere. The latter is the place to find Shropshire's lake district with nine meres to the south and west of the town. These are a haven for wildlife and many kinds of waterfowl. To the south of Whitchurch is Brown Moss, an area of woods, heath, marsh and tiny lakes, created partly through peat cutting and drainage. It's rich in birdlife and unusual wet-land plants such as water plantain and water violet.

The plain is not quite all marshes and meres for there is one outstanding hill in the area – Grinshill. A short walk starts from Corbet Wood and with a bit of a climb you can get to Grinshill Summit for a glorious panorama of South Shropshire and the Welsh borders, complete with helpful viewing-table.

Corbet Wood and Grinshill

OS Map 1:50 000, Sheet 126
A circular walk of minimum 2 miles (3 km). Allow 1 hour and upwards.

The going underfoot is either on sandy wooded paths or on rough track. It's quite a climb up the hill, but is only a short sharp shock.

There are numerous paths going through the wood, though the main ones are quite obvious. It is a small enough area not to get too lost. In my experience, though, you can accidentally go in too small a circle and not enjoy the whole area, so I have suggested the route through the woods to the villages of Grinshill and Clive, leaving the climb to the summit until the end.

Car-parking and the start

To find the car-park, turn off the A49 at Preston Brockhurst in the direction of the village of Clive. About $\frac{3}{4}$ mile (1 km) up the road is a turning to the left marked Corbet Wood Picnic Site. Drive some way up this rough lane and just after the massive quarry workings on the right is the picnic site at the end of the lane. This is Corbet Woods which were owned by the Corbet Family until given by Sir John Corbet to the council in 1972. The Corbets were a well-known Shropshire family with estates at Adderley, near Market Drayton, and a seat of power at Moreton Corbet, where you can still see the ruins of the castle damaged by Cromwell in 1644.

You'll notice that the quarry is still being worked. The area around Grinshill and Corbet Wood has been quarried since Roman times. The stone was used to build Viroconium, the large Roman capital near the present-day village of Wroxeter. For hundreds of years, Grinshill remained one of the most important quarries in the county. Two types of stone were available here, both essentially sandstone. At the bottom of the hill a red stone was quarried that ranges in colour from a warm pink to a rich earthy hue. From quarries on the top came a white or rather greyish stone. This was used to build many of the elegant buildings in Shropshire such as Attingham Park, but it was also sought-after all over the country.

Take the footpath that curves round the edge of the car-park starting at the noticeboard. It is not immediately obvious when you drive up, as once off the car-parking plateau, the path descends very quickly into the woods. It's like walking down a warm earthy tunnel, I imagine rather like a rabbit must feel, as steep banks rise up on either side.

After a short distance, at a T-junction, there's another small plateau, though here there is not always such a good view because it's surrounded by dense trees whose summer foliage restricts things considerably. Here, turn left and continue down the hill. At the bottom at another T-junction, turn right. This track brings you around the base of the woods with open fields to your left.

At a third T-junction, you can climb straight up the very steep slope ahead if you want to get to Grinshill Summit. Alternatively, save that for later, and turn left. Where the track starts to bend right, you can make a quick detour into Grinshill Village, which is most attractive, full of a variety of interesting buildings with all sorts of styles represented. The common theme is grand! There's a pub called the Elephant and Castle, a reminder of the Corbet family who used both symbols as part of their emblem.

Loop back to the woodland track by the church, and here turn left going under the daunting crags of Grinshill Hill. I think it is probably a good idea to be aware of their height so that when you finally reach the top, you pay proper respect and don't go bounding over the edge.

This track brings you out at Clive, another pretty village (no link with the famous Shropshire-born Robert Clive, from Moreton Say). Turn right up the road, then right again down another rough lane beyond the church. (Incidentally this lane leads straight back to the car-park.)

Carry on up this lane until you have passed the school, and then take one of the paths to the right which takes you to Grinshill Summit. It is worth waiting for. The views are tremendous and the viewing-table helps point out many distant features.

To get back to the car-park, follow the path off to the north-east. If you haven't got a compass don't worry, it's a case of either going back where you just came from, going over the cliff, or taking the alternative route to the north-east. This eventually joins the rough lane that runs from Clive to the car-park, so turn right. If you veer right earlier you'll end up on one of the woodland paths through Corbet Wood, which gets you back to the car-park, too.

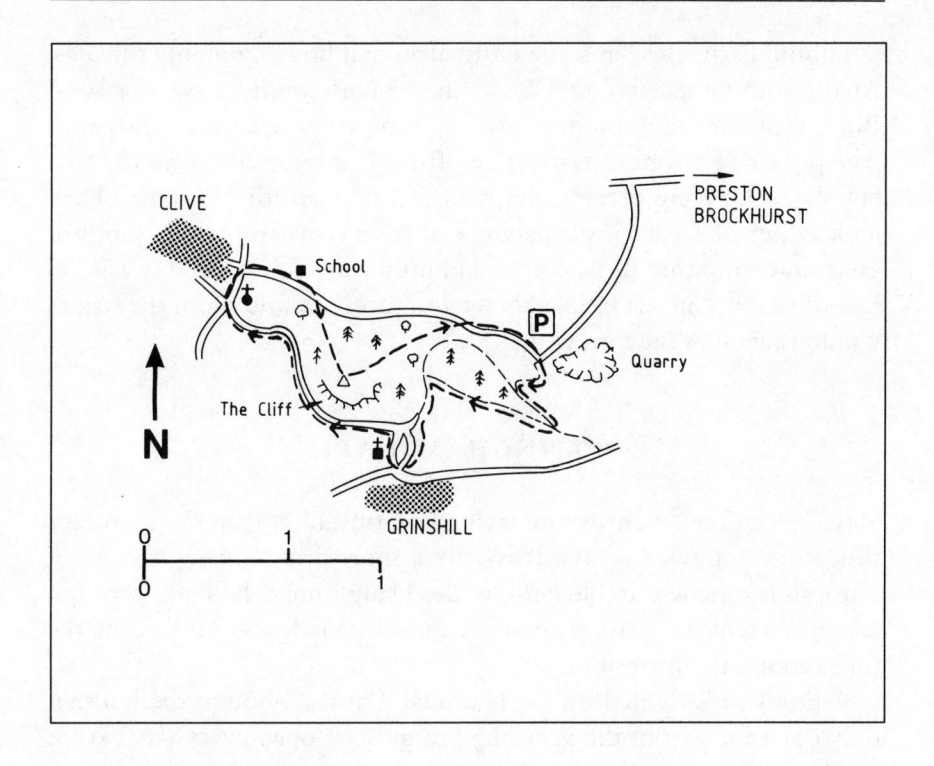

North Shropshire has a solid traditional feel about it, but in farming terms there's an interesting break in tradition just near here at Pimhill Farm. It has been pioneering the organic farming of cereals for three generations. The farm is off the main A528 Shrewsbury to Wem road.

The wheat grown at Pimhill Farm was originally milled just for use within the family, but in 1949 the Mayalls switched to organic methods, rejecting the use of chemicals. Needless to say, suspicion was rife amongst neighbouring farmers, old heads were shaken and there was a belief that no good would come of it. Forty years on, this flour, with a healthy reputation amongst wholefooders like myself, is very popular indeed. The Mayall family use traditional grinding methods too, only producing half a tonne an hour, which they feel gets the best out of the grain. I've made many a loaf with their flour and always found it superb. At Pimhill you'll find a well-stocked farm shop, cereal products, organic fruit and vegetables, and some immense Shrewsbury biscuits.

Pimhill Farm also has some unusual animal breeds, notably the pigs. Apart from Gloucester Old Spot, they have recently crossed a Wild Boar with a more domesticated sow to produce what are called Iron Age piglets! The ones I saw ranged from being just a few weeks to a few days old, lying pretty helpless under the warmth of a lamp. They look rather like a stack of marrows as their coats are striped (no, not green but a mixture of slate grey and mustard yellow). As this was the first litter born on the farm, they were waiting to find out if the stripes would remain as they grew up.

Attingham Park

Having seen the extensive quarrying at Grinshill, it seems a good idea to see the stone put to use. It is only a short drive, through some of Shropshire's richest arable land, under Haughmond Hill and through Upton Magna to Attingham Park, an elegant house on one of the finest estates in Shropshire.

Attingham is owned by the National Trust. Although the house is only open for part of the year, the grounds are open every day except 25 December, so you can call in just to see the exterior of the house in its parkland setting. I like the contrast of the formality of the house and grounds with the rural surroundings.

The main house was built by a little-known Scottish architect, George Steuart, and is built with grey Grinshill ashlar. It also made use of a product of one of Shropshire's other industries, cast iron. This was one of the first houses to use cast iron for window frames, here used for the gallery. The frames were made by the local Coalbrookdale company.

There are some attractive Regency interiors to enjoy especially 'The Boudoir', as well as a collection of silver and French and Italian paintings and furniture.

The surrounding estate is what really tempted me and it is ideal if you are in the mood for a gentle stroll. The now mature park is considered one of Humphrey Repton's most successful designs. The Mile Walk takes you down to the placid River Tern which meanders through the estate. From here you can go across a bridge into the Deer Park and then come back to the front of the house. These walks are laid out in a little map available at the house and all the routes are easy to follow.

Between Wenlock Edge and The Long Mynd is a delightful backwater and a walk here gives you marvellous views of the well-known hills such as The Wrekin, The Lawley, the harsh-sounding Caer Caradoc as well as the North Shropshire Plain. There are also some enchanting gardens to see and one of the best brick-built houses in Shropshire.

If you are planning to be in Shropshire in the late summer, do try to pick a day when the fascinating Preen Manor Gardens are open. Preen Manor is part of the National Gardens' Scheme. It is a charitable trust made up of over two thousand private gardens which would not normally be open to the public. All gardens in the scheme open on limited days and the entry fee goes to a number of different charities. There is a book published by the scheme, listing opening times.

The house at Preen Manor has an interesting history. It was built as part of a cell for the twelfth-century Cluniac monastery which was centred at Much Wenlock. It was surrendered to the crown in 1534, but appears to have remained unaltered as a manor house until the eighteenth century, when a south wing was added in the same style as the church. Most of this building was pulled down in the nineteenth century, and in 1870 new owners commissioned the architect, Norman Shaw, to build a substantial mansion. Pictures show that the house towered over the church, but it was short-lived and was demolished, apart from its Gothic porch, less than fifty years after its erection. A smaller house was built in the 1930s.

The present owners have spent the last decade restoring the gardens here. Many of their ideas are new, such as the pebble garden and ornamental kitchen garden. They have also discovered several features of the Victorian age, for example, a bowling green and formal parterre with commanding views of distant Wenlock Edge. Clever use of arches, steps and avenues have been made to lead you round from one area to another. My main impression, apart from the beautiful plants and flowers, was the inspiration and creativity of the place, and the sheer hard work that makes it possible.

OS Map 1:50 000, Sheet 137
A circular walk of 5–6 miles (8–10 km) with an opportunity to make a substantial short-cut. Allow about 3 hours, and longer if you are viewing the gardens and having tea.

The going underfoot is mixed. There are lanes and farm tracks, as well as several paths across fields, but nothing seemed too muddy. There are several gentle climbs, but this walk tends to be one where hills are viewed at a distance rather than walked over.

The route is clear apart from a short section between Broome and Plaish, and on the way back from Plaish, above Holt Farm, I had to make a guess at where the track was supposed to be.

Car-parking and the start

The best place to park is by the church at Church Preen, which is just off the lane that runs through the village.

It is certainly worth visiting the churchyard to see what is reckoned to be the oldest tree in Europe, a yew some fifteen hundred years old. It is quite remarkable that it is still alive as most of the base of the tree is hollow and higher up there is a metal band holding the spreading trunk together. Despite its appearance, the tree regularly shoots new wood, and there are a profusion of berries.

Look, too, for the headstone which is on the outside of the church wall. The story goes that a local man was so fond of his horse that he wanted to be buried with him in the churchyard. 'Not on,' said the vicar. So the best they could do was bury the man in the churchyard, and his horse just over the wall, hence the unusual placing of this headstone.

If Preen Manor Gardens are not open then go back up to the lane that leads north out of the village and turn right in the direction of Maypole Bank. There's a lengthy lane walk, about $\frac{3}{4}$ mile (1 km) where you can look over to Wenlock Edge and The Wrekin beyond. From this side, the thickly wooded scarp of the Wenlock Edge is awesome. It runs in an unbroken escarpment from Benthall Edge, near the famous Iron Bridge, down to Craven Arms. Shropshire is not the place you would expect to find the Barrier Reef, but you can imagine Wenlock Edge to be England's equivalent. The limestone rock was deposited when Shropshire was covered with a tropical sea, forming a barrier to one side. Over time the sea has gone, but the rock remains. It is an area rich with limestone-loving trees such as ash, yew, spurge laurel and spindle, and plants such as orchids and quaking grass with its distinctive fragile spikelets covered with heart-shaped purplish tufts.

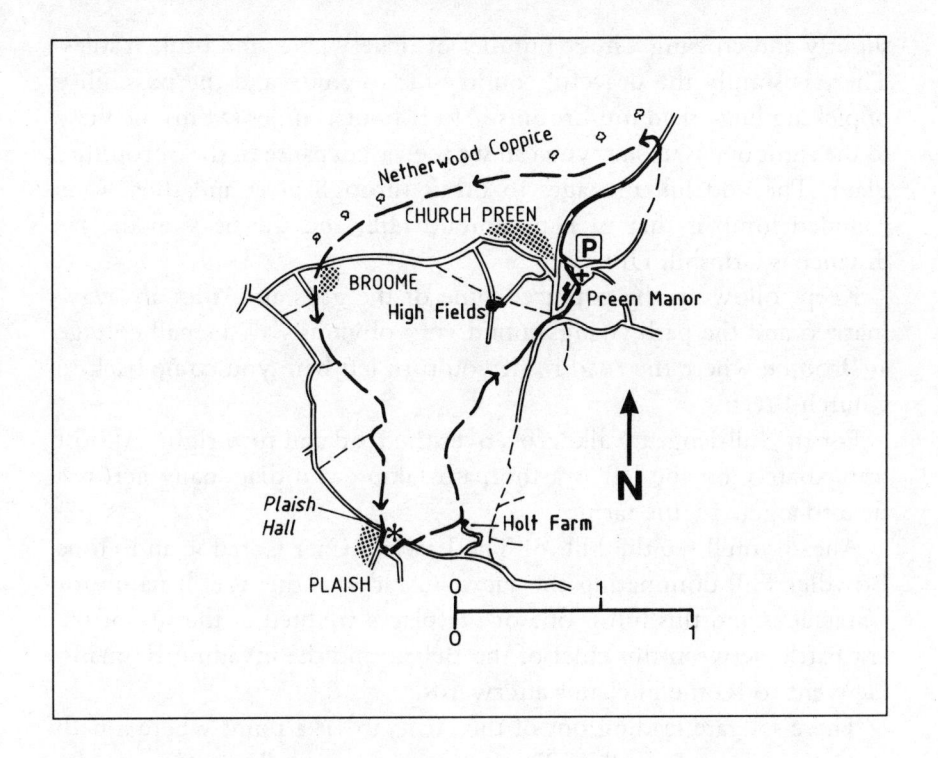

Some of Wenlock Edge isn't as green as it might have been due to the quarrying activities which cover the area with a fine white dust. Limestone from here was used for the building of the nearby Buildwas Abbey, and Wenlock Priory and Church.

Follow the lane until you see the private drive of Preen Manor estate to the right, just by a small lodge. If the gardens are open, it is possible to go through the estate to this lodge.

Just beyond is a farm on the left and a track leading around the buildings to fields behind. Head up to the gate on the left; once through that, cross over the hedge boundary and make for the edge of the Netherwood Coppice, which you'll see running in front of you. The walk goes to the left, following the line of the coppice, climbing slightly and crossing a huge number of rickety gates and broken stiles. There is simply the peaceful countryside to enjoy and the possibility of picking huge field mushrooms. After about 1½ miles (2 km) the view to the right opens up and you can see the vast expanse of the Shropshire Plain. The odd hill manages to break through now and then. One rounded lump is that of Haughmond Hill, and the peak in the far distance is Grinshill Hill.

Keep following the coppice; some of the gaps and stiles are way-marked and the path swings round very obviously to a small cottage at Broome where the road is. (If you turn left here you come back to Church Preen.)

For the full-length walk, cross over the road and turn right. Almost immediately on the left is a footpath taking you diagonally across a field to a gate by the farm.

Ahead you'll see the hills of The Lawley, Caer Caradoc and Hope Bowdler Hill dominating the view. Caradoc is the Welsh name for Caractacus and this hill is one of the places credited as the site of the last battle between this chief of the Belgae and the invading Romans. He went to Rome in chains afterwards.

There's a gate leading out of the farmyard at a point where a path goes down into the valley. The first part down to the stream is quite clear, then it gets rather faint. By this time, though, you should be able to see a small farm by some woods ahead, two fields away, which is where you need to end up.

At this farm, the route on the map varies from what is actually possible, as the footpath through the woods beyond is overgrown. I got put on the right track by two farmers, alike as two peas in a pod. I said they were so similar they had to be brothers, and the jovial response was, 'Father's inside in the house and he ain't much different!'

You need to turn right down the farm lane which goes towards the road, and once over the bridge, there's a gate on the left. Go through this and then straight across the next two fields. At the third field, there is a low barbed-wire fence with no obvious crossing-point. It is rather broken down in the middle where frustrated walkers have had to climb over.

On the top corner of the field, you'll see a gravelled track which brings you out on the lane directly opposite Plaish Hall, a very fine example of a brick-built house, 'H'-shaped and dating from around

1540. Look closely at the chimneys for they have a rather sad tale to tell.

The house was commissioned by William Leighton, who was the Chief Justice of Wales. He was keen to have the finest ornamental chimneys in Shropshire. On asking who was the best craftsman to do the work, he found out that he had just sentenced the man to death. Pulling a few legal strings, the craftsman was given a stay of execution and built the striking chimney stacks that remain on the house today. After the work was done, the judge had him hanged (some say from his own work) giving the story of a somewhat gruesome ending. Local gossip is that the house has never been a very happy place to live despite the beautiful setting.

Walk to the far side of the hall, turning left, then left again along the lanes. Just on the corner where the lane bends to the right, there is a rickety wooden section in the left-hand fence which marks a footpath leading diagonally across the field towards Holt Farm. At the bottom of the valley is a stream crossed by a very sturdy bridge. The overhanging branches of a tree, which almost act as a barricade, make the crossing tricky. Once over the bridge, walk to the farm, where you'll see a track going to the left taking you up a slight incline in the direction of Church Preen. Just up the hill, the track runs between two small areas of wood. It is after this that the way is confusing. I scrambled over a vicious fence onto a path along the top of a field where you can make your way downhill to a farm track that goes directly to Church Preen. If you end up at High Fields Farm, (there is also a very clear track leading there) you can also walk to Church Preen very easily.

From this part of Shropshire you can easily reach Much Wenlock, an ancient market town. It's worth going there via the school (now a private house designed by Norman Shaw which survived better than his manor house). This is marked on the map by a crossroads between Church Preen and Hughley. You may have noticed signposts to it at some of the road junctions.

A Saxon abbey was founded at Much Wenlock in the seventh century AD, and then a Benedictine priory was built on the same site in 1080. A small town grew up around the priory, gaining importance in the fifteenth century, when it was given a Royal Charter. When the priory was dissolved, the town continued thriving, but was never to be part of the industrial expansion of nearby Coalbrookdale.

There is plenty to explore through the centuries here – extensive priory ruins, the beautiful sixteenth-century, half-timbered Guildhall, seventeenth-century inns and the Victorian Corn Hall and Agricultural Library. I found some very good homemade elderberry and apple jam, rather with the consistency of Summer Pudding, in a small café on the High Street, one of the highlights of my visit to this lovely old town.

Brown Clee

South-east Shropshire is dominated by the Clee Hills, a range that includes Brown Clee, Titterstone Clee and Cleehill.

Brown Clee has the distinction of being Shropshire's highest hill, yet it is not so well-known, nor so well-visited as some of its lowlier neighbours. Don't let the thought of the climb put you off as it is only a gentle ascent and a most rewarding view. The boast is that you can see seventeen counties from the top, at least that was in the days before reorganization and the loss of counties such as Flintshire and Carmarthen. Nevertheless, from the top you can look down over Southern Shropshire. Arable farmers from the north of the county may dismiss the region as mere 'cow country', but the rich grazing meadows, the smallholdings and the rural settlements are most agreeable.

It has not always been a case of living off the fat of the land. The area was settled in the Iron Age, when it is believed that most of the area would have been forest. The settling tribes built forts on all three Clee summits with a fourth, Nordy Bank, as probably an outpost or lookout station, on a western spur of Brown Clee. Later Saxon farmers deserted the windswept tops, looking for shelter in the valleys below and formed a number of settlements. But many of these communities have not survived, in part due to the Black Death but also because the living eked out was small and the medieval peasant migrated to areas where there was more work. Several deserted villages are marked by isolated churches and grassy mounds where once houses might have stood.

Centuries later the population here grew again, not for farming but for mining, as the top of each of the Clees was found to be formed of a highly resistant volcanic rock, and below were some rich coal seams, the highest in the British Isles. There are abandoned workings on Brown Clee and some quarrying still goes on at Titterstone.

This walk takes you past the Iron Age fortifications along the ancient 'straker' ways, used first by the farmers to drive their cattle and later by the womenfolk to carry coal down the mountainside. It also visits the remains of a deserted medieval village. There is much to absorb and enjoy in this constantly varying area.

I have been up Brown Clee in very constrasting conditions. Once there was such a fierce gale that I was almost on my knees at the top. Recently, when coming from Nordy Bank I picked a strange day. Though the mist was lying thickly in the valleys there was a feeling that the sun was going to win the day. At least this was the case amongst the locals in the pub at Ditton Priors where I called in for coffee before setting off. There was a hint of blue in the sky and after climbing only a short way, I suddenly found myself above the cloud with the whole Brown Clee ridge in brilliant sunshine, looking just like a huge rock rising out of a grey sea.

You can approach Brown Clee from the Cleobury Mortimer side but I've chosen to describe the route from the north-west as this brings you to a lesser-known area of Shropshire. It is well away from any busy roads and in fact the most difficult navigation is finding the start.

OS Map: 1:50 000, Sheet 137
A circular walk of 5 miles (8 km). Allow $2\frac{1}{2}$–$3\frac{1}{2}$ hours depending on whether you detour to get to the summit.

The going underfoot is on grassy paths, dirt track, road and field. It is mostly dry except for the area near Five Springs where you'll have to pick your way around the marshy patches. Lower down there are some muddy parts over the fields, especially near the brooks.

The navigation is quite simple over the hills, as the summit of Brown Clee is marked clearly with a pylon. The route down is on part of the Shropshire Way, which is way-marked with the buzzard symbol, and the walk down to Abdon Village is obvious, though it is not so clear on the way back.

Car-parking and the start

You'll need to find the minor road that runs along the side of Brown Clee from Hillside to Cockshutford. I approached from Ditton Priors (leaving Cleobury north on the B4364). You could also wend your way from the B4368, leaving at Diddlebury.

Aim for Nordy Bank which is shown on the OS Map (GR 575847). It is just above a bend in the road and there you'll find roadside parking.

Take the wide track from the road bend which skirts round the north of Nordy Bank, the vast fort covering a spur between the hills. The path winds up the hill. Ahead there's a pylon marking a quarry on a hill-top, over to the left the deep valley of Five Springs, rich in autumn with burnished bracken. Beyond rises the slopes of Brown Clee.

Keep following the track up the hill until you get very close to the top of the ridge. Then you can take a less obvious path to contour round to the top of Five Springs. There are certainly five shown on the map, but you may feel the amount of marsh around means there should be more.

The woods at the top are part of the Burwarton Estate, owned by Lord Boyne, which covers the slopes to the south-east.

Walk along the slight plateau in the direction of Brown Clee to the boundary walls. Just beyond, in the bracken (and easier to spot in winter) is a small memorial tablet to German and Allied airmen who were killed on this hill during the Second World War.

Follow the path on up to the summit. The fort on top was known as Abdon Burf, but much of the earth work has been sliced away with later mining activities. The top stone was called 'dhu stone', taking its name from the Welsh for black, as this is a black basalt. It was used for sett, the traditional square cobblestone, and also for kerb-stones.

Leave the summit, dropping down the south-west side until you meet a very clear dirt track, which goes down the hill to the right. This was known as a Straker Way, created by drovers taking their cattle to market and later used by the miners. It is marked with the soaring buzzard symbol which also marks the long-distance footpath called The Shropshire Way. Follow the track down to the road.

On the road, turn right and then left at the next junction. A short way down here on the left is a footpath across the fields.

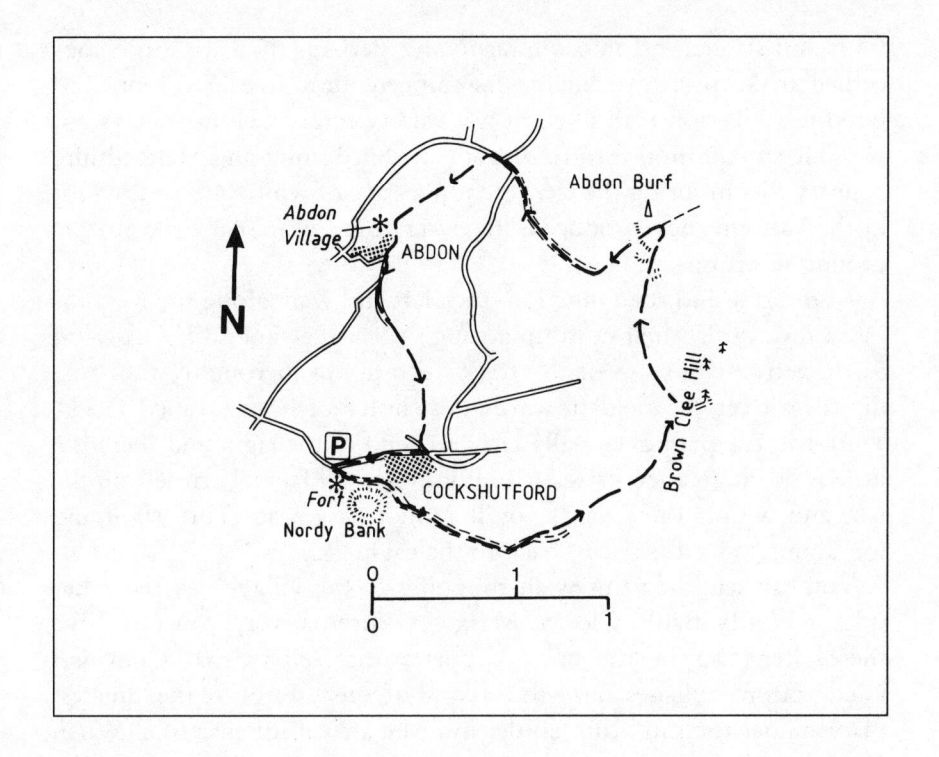

Follow the arrows down the hill, aiming for the village of Abdon. For part of the way, there is a section which seems to be hollowed out, as though it was the course of a sunken track or green lane. It could well have been more obvious when the medieval community of Abdon was here. On the lower fields to the right is the isolated church which once stood in the midst of other village buildings. Now all that is left are grassy mounds and the faint tracings of what might have been a street. The modern hamlet, just a cluster of houses, is some distance away. You'll need to head off to the right to explore the church and village. Then come back to the path and cross over a tiny brook to a lane past a couple of houses which brings you out on the road through the village.

If you look to the right you may see guardians of the village – three sheepdogs lying full stretch in the middle of the road. Even when a car came round the corner they were in no hurry to move. Instead they gave the occupants a good look over and then casually got on all fours and strolled off into the farmyard. Perhaps they are more concerned to keep an eye on the magnificent pear tree in the orchard opposite, a Tetton Hall Dick. It is a variety rarely seen nowadays but was once a common feature of both the Shropshire and Staffordshire countryside. In spring the trees are just a cone of white blossom, whilst in the autumn they produce a mealy textured pear that drops to the ground in profusion.

At the lane and road junction, turn left and walk along the road for just a few yards, then head up a rough track that goes diagonally off to the left. At the top of the track keep going in roughly the same direction over the fields towards the cluster of houses called Cockshutford. The path eventually curves round to the right and there is a little footbridge over a stream and onto a small lane. Turn left up the lane and within a few yards you'll come to the road. Turn right and it is about 500 yards ($\frac{1}{2}$ km) back to the car-park.

You can lengthen this walk by going to the village just the other side of Nordy Bank, Clee St Margaret. Alternatively you can drive there later. Despite the lines of poetry that tell us that Clun and Clungunford (villages in the south-west of Shropshire) are the 'quietest places under the sun', this hamlet must be a rival for that title. When I stood in the churchyard even the birds were quiet. Remarks in the visitors' book all note the peacefulness.

The church has an early Norman chancel with one original tiny window set into the thick walls. The exterior is very striking with its herringbone masonry. It isn't in a regular pattern, more a mass of stones going in all directions, some set on the diagonal, some laid flat. It's as though a group of workers were responsible, all contributing their own little design. In amongst the jumbled pattern there is supposed to be the outline of a fish, an ancient Christian symbol, possibly red herring! The chap repairing the wall of the house next door, who knew all about it, tried to outline the shape for me but by the time we'd both had a good look at the wall, we reckoned to have found a shoal of fish instead.

From this area you're within easy reach of what I think of as Shropshire's prettiest town, Ludlow. This was Mortimer territory, belonging to one of the powerful English families. They built the castle here which is among the most impressive of those constructed along the Welsh Marches.

Ludlow was a planned town but it hardly resembles new towns as we know them in the twentieth century. The walls were begun in 1233, and the main streets run south and are connected by smaller lanes, with the hub of the town being the Butter Cross. Leave a good half day to explore the town with its range of buildings showing the wealth of different ages. Among the fine black-and-white timbered houses, the best-known is the Feathers Hotel which dates from the beginning of the seventeenth century. You'll also find many Georgian brick buildings, particularly in Broad Street.

Ludlow is a good place to get decent food, of the pub variety as well as wholefood snacks.

The Lancashire Coast

It is very worthwhile taking the road to Wigan Pier. There is an excellent exhibition here of Lancashire life staged in extensive waterside buildings. With the help of actors, many of the scenes are vividly recreated and I would dare anyone to defy the schoolmistress. My visit here inspired me to take a closer look at Lancashire, especially the developments along the seashore.

Seeing the life of the workers caught up in the industrial changes made me understand why the local coast was described rather uninvitingly as 'The Lancashire Lung'. It must have been a wonderful escape from the terrible factory life and the 'satanic mills'; a life-saving breath of fresh air.

The benefits of the sea – bathing in it, breathing in its air – were a discovery of the nineteenth century. It was the start of seaside hotels, bathing machines, fun fairs and promenades. Improved transport, especially the coming of the railways, meant a day release for thousands going over to enjoy the pleasures of the coast. There was something for everyone. Imagine the mill workers and their families setting off in their Sunday best for their annual day out at Blackpool, or the genteel folk strolling in Southport's Botanic Gardens.

Although the various resorts continue to change they have maintained their individual characters. The Blackpool area attracts the masses, Southport includes the refinement of fashionable shopping and many golf courses. But there is so much more to this coast than an endless succession of resorts. In fact they are all rather spread out. Separating these bigger developments are large tracts of coast that should remain undeveloped thanks to the efforts of the National Trust's Enterprise Neptune, and so on. These reserves are fascinating even if you only have a limited knowledge of bird life, flora and fauna as the countryside itself is so interesting. The duneland walking is quite an experience, even more so if you are trying to do any running! The nature reserves in the north are a complete contrast and I think Silverdale is one of the prettiest places I have ever seen.

I have chosen four very different areas to give you an insight into the potential of this coast. You may want to take four days over it, or more, depending on if you want to make an extra visit to Silverdale, or spend time in the interesting towns of Lancaster or Southport. Equally, you might just make use of one of these days as a break from swishing up the M6 to the Lake District and beyond.

I have set out the expeditions along the coast from North to South, cheating slightly by coming inland to Ribchester to catch a glimpse of the Romans.

Silverdale

If you do nothing else along this coastline, do take time out to go to Silverdale and Arnside. It is a tiny area, nestling on this coast just between the Lake District and Morecambe. I fell for the place completely. It seems to have absolutely everything, except all in miniature: cliffs, crags, shore and sands, marsh, meadow and mountains in the distance. An added joy is that the area has escaped commercialism, and that will probably go on being the case now that so much is a conservation area. The natural beauty is left to speak for itself. There are a plethora of nature reserves and National Trust-owned open spaces – Warton Crag, Arnside Knot, Eaves Wood, Gait Barrows and the very well-known bird haven at Leighton Moss. All this within a circle of probably less than a five-mile radius.

The main walk I have described will take the best part of a day if you do the whole circle, and takes you through some very beautiful unspoiled parts on well-defined paths. There are ample opportunities for shorter circles and other areas can be saved for a second visit.

Kilns and Crags

OS Map 1:50 000, Sheet 97
A circular walk of 7–8 miles (10–12 km). Allow 4 hours.

This walk has several short-cuts and a very good coffee shop about halfway round at the Wolf House Gallery. Take into account when you are planning the walk that the Gallery is closed between 1 pm and 2 pm.

The going is mostly easy on very good footpaths. Some parts may be muddy and watch out for slippery limestone poking through the surface after rain. There are two quite testing hills and gentle undulation round the rest of the way. The countryside varies constantly and is never dull. In fact you might get a touch of adventure with wild life ranging from bulls to eagles and a footpath described as 'over the Cliff!' – but I survived to tell the tale.

Car-parking and the start

Drive through Warton and take the Old Coach Road up a fairly steep hill just out of the village. Just where the road flattens out, look out for a signpost on the left, 'Crag Foot' bridle-path (marked in red dashes on the OS Map). On the road here there is a wide grass verge with room for a few cars, and a small, walled, gravelled area that could be used as a car-park too.

The route begins up the bridle-path signed to Crag Foot, which climbs quite steeply through the woods.

A few minutes up the hill take the path signed 'Concessionary Path Warton Crag' which takes you across the boundary wall to the left on a path that climbs up to the summit.

The name Warton Crag applies to the whole hill which is the southern tip of a ridge of limestone running north to Yealand Redmayne. There are chunks of limestone poking through much of the undergrowth, though the craggiest part faces south and is a popular climbing area. At the top there is a large clearing including a trig point and beacon, erected as part of the celebrations for the Armada anniversary, though this beacon site had few connections with the Channel. It was used to give warning to the rest of the county of

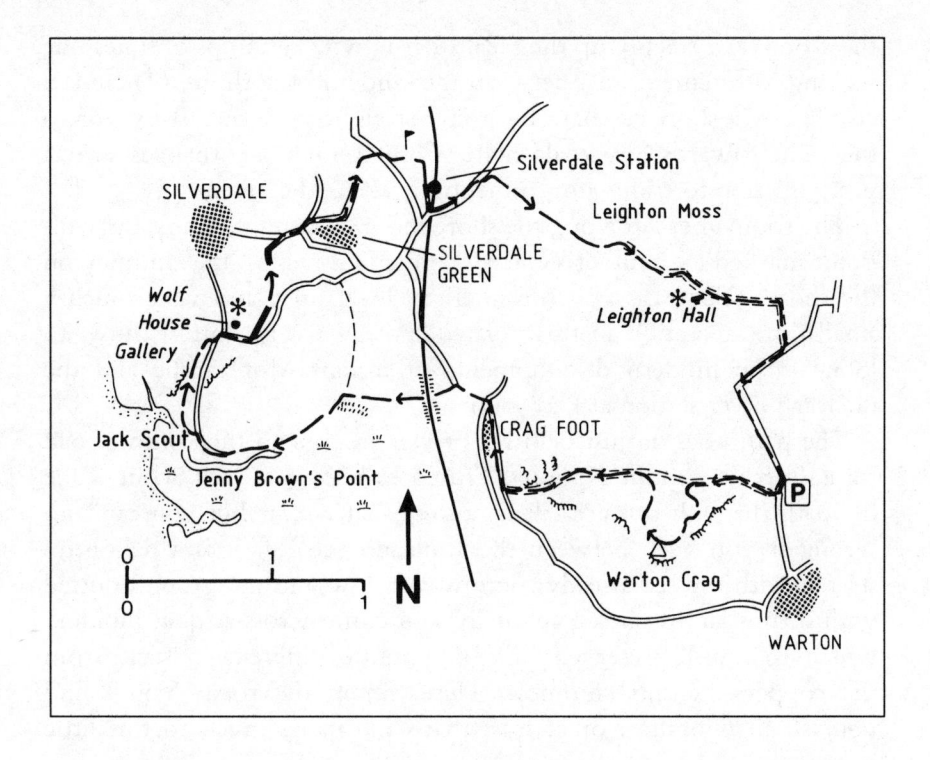

Scots approaching from the north. The signal would come from over Morecambe Bay, which the Romans called The Great Bay. It is an excellent vantage-point with the Lake District Mountains visible in the distance.

To continue the walk, turn back inland and take the path signed Crag Foot which brings you back to (but further along) the bridle-path. Here, turn left and follow it down to the road. Turn left down this quiet lane to the road junction where there is a slender chimney. It was built for smelting copper, which was mined nearby.

The road curves round, crossing the bottom of Leighton Moss. At a slight bend, just before a bridge, there's a footpath off to the left taking you to the headland tip known as Jenny Brown's Point. I encountered my bull going along this embankment section. He managed a half-hearted snort in my direction before being diverted by the cows.

Even without the presence of the bull, I thought this was a most interesting section of mixed marsh, sand and close-cropped turf. Ahead, the woods rise steeply up the Heald Brow with outcrops of limestone making a pavement area between the land and the shore. (There is a chance for a short-cut here by going straight up Heald Brow, or to the right towards Silverdale Station, but remember, there is such a pretty section to come, not to mention cake and coffee!)

The route goes left along the shoreline and round to Jenny Brown's Point marked by another slender chimney known as 'the chimney on the shore'. This was also for smelting local ores, and very much a small-time operation in this isolated spot. What a contrast, now, to look at the modern developments of distant Morecambe and the nuclear power station at Heysham.

The path goes on just below a private house and then onto a road for a short way to the National Trust area known as Jack Scout. Take the path through this area. It is not especially clear but you can't go wrong if you keep between the wall and the sea. It is a delightful stretch with the sea already some way below and the ground dotted with shrubs and bushes. Eventually you come across a squat building which is a well-preserved lime kiln, quite different in style from the copper-smelting chimneys. Here, rejoin the road. You'll find yourself in Gibraltar, or at least that's the name given to this little area.

Just a short way down the road, peeping out from the trees, is the Tower House, often visited by the Victorian novelist Elizabeth Gaskell, who said she could never tire of Silverdale. At the T-junction, turn right and you are at The Wolf House Gallery. It is an ideal stopping place, really the sort I'd like to have on every walk. The main gallery is housed in a Georgian farm building. There's a framing studio in the coach house and a textile workshop in the dairy. You may need a cheque-book too. It's not that the food is expensive but the range of pottery and paintings on sale is as tempting as the coffee and cakes.

I thought the leaflet was wrongly printed when it said they were closed for lunch. But that is how it is. The coffee bar apparently started by accident when they decided to serve people a drink whilst they were browsing over the pictures. That side of the business has grown and there are four or five tables huddled together at the end of one of the shops. There is plenty to look at whilst munching an oat datie or a very fresh scone washed down with a goblet (pottery) of fruit juice.

The hardest thing about this visit is getting going again! But luckily I decided not to stagger off with a terracotta pot but come back for a second look (and cake).

To continue the walk, carry on up the road and look out for the signpost on the left to Wood Well. Follow the path through the woods to find the well. It is not the picture-book variety but a large, walled pool. Before the advent of extensive mains water supply, storing water in a porous limestone area such as this was necessary to ensure settlement.

The well is in a pleasant picnic area. Just behind is one of the best footpath descriptions I have seen: 'The Green – Over the Cliff'. And it is true. The path does just go straight up and over the cliff. There's no need for crampons and carabinas, the cliffs are only about 20 feet (6 m) high and the rocks are formed in such a way as to make a natural staircase for someone with pretty long strides. Despite my fear of heights, I managed the ascent.

At the top, follow the cliff edge to the left and then bear right into the woods to join a path which brings you out onto an open piece of grassland, then to the road at Silverdale Green. Here, turn right up to a junction and then left up Bottoms Lane. Soon, you'll see the footpath to the right to Burtons Well, which is hidden way down in the woods and not in such good condition as Wood Well. The water, very shallow, was jet black. The path leads out into a beautiful wild meadow full of slender grasses and delicate flowers. There is a wooden bridge and some duck-boards in the centre to take you over the little stream, and then on up some more steps, man-made to a regulation height this time, to a lane. Although it doesn't look very promising, the route goes straight ahead over the wall through some brambly undergrowth and out onto the golf course. the route shown on the OS Map goes directly across down the shallow valley but the path swings right and the exit from the golf course is diagonally across to the right. There are plenty of golfers to set you on course. A rather unfriendly notice near the exit tells you not to loiter, so I suppose it's fortunate that the path hasn't been 'accidentally' obliterated.

More or less opposite the golf-course exit is the little station of Silverdale and a T-junction where you turn left towards Leighton Moss. On the corner is the RSPB (Royal Society for the Protection of Birds) bird reserve centre and further up the road on the first major track on the right, is the causeway across the marshes. A little way down is the signpost, Public Hide.

Seeing these wild marshes made me appreciate how quickly nature works. Only eighty years ago, this whole area was reclaimed by drainage and used as farmland but, since 1917, it has reverted to the wild and is now a mixture of freshwater and seawater marshes. The extensive reedbeds and jungle of marsh grasses are a haven for birds and otters where they can hide well away. Or so they think. Halfway across is a well-constructed hide (five-star category as hides go I'm sure) with wooden benches and places to rest your elbows. There are small windows looking over the central lake. It is the visual equivalent of eavesdropping because you are so close to the birds. Do leave some time to absorb the scene and watch the flurrying, fluttering and feeding. If you arrive nearer dusk you may catch a glimpse of an otter or two.

Leighton Moss has something to offer all year round. In spring and autumn it is home to many birds of passage. In the winter months there are flocks of finches, and it's a bad weather refuge too. In summer it is the butterflies and dragonflies that may catch your eye. Behind the lake you can see Farleton Knot rising in the distance.

Once you can bear to drag yourself away, the walk goes on along the causeway and through the farm buildings on the other side, then up towards Leighton Hall. This is the home of the Gillow family, celebrated cabinet-makers, who started their business from the imported hardwoods brought by ship to Lancaster. It is an impressive building surrounded by parkland and you only have to glance behind you to see why anyone would choose to build here; the view across the valley and to the mountain skyline ahead is breathtaking.

In the near distance you can see a reddish gash across Arnside Knot, one of the nearest hills. This is a scree slope of small loose stones, created through glacial action along the side of the crag. The scree material is known locally as 'shilla'. It is not only the feature that is striking, but the thought that after the glacial period when plants slowly covered the area, one of these may have survived that period.

Leighton Hall is open to the public in the afternoons and, weather permitting, there are displays of eagle flying mid-afternoon.

The drive leading out of the Leighton Hall park is private, but there is a footpath up the hill following the line of wooden pylons. At the top, turn right along the wall until you come to a stile that brings you

THE LANCASHIRE COAST

out on to the main road. Here, turn right and it is a short distance back down to the start.

If you have time, do explore the northern part of Silverdale around Arnside, because it is equally as interesting. The village isn't particularly pretty but the small winding roads have a pleasant leafy feel. The token promenade lining the Kent Estuary is rather quaint, giving a touch of the resort to this genteel spot. The eye-catching feature is the huge railway viaduct that takes the main railway line over the river to the opposite coastline known as Furness.

This part of the bay is over-shadowed by Arnside Knot, some 500 feet (152 m) high, which is an area owned by the National Trust. You can drive quite high up to a wooded car-park, which is a good place for picnics. Do climb the short way to the Toposcope, a map of the mountain sky-line of the Lake District, which helps you identify nearly the whole range of peaks. I saw as far away as Skiddaw, which is north of the Penrith to Keswick line, and in really good conditions you can see to the Isle of Man.

There is a very good short walk from the car-park, if you've come here for a second day. Just go downhill on the obvious path from the car-park, it will eventually bring you out onto a small patch of meadow. Here, turn right and descend quite steeply through the woods on and on until you reach a well-hidden caravan site. On turning into the site, there is a sign to White Creek, or Far Arnside. Take the path to Far Arnside. It starts off in the woods but then comes out into the open on top of the low crags just above the sands. It's a wonderful little track with splendid views over the sands. You may not be alone. Morecambe Bay is favoured by the bird world and, in winter, there may be up to a quarter of a million waders present. The rich mud flats are excellent feeding grounds, and the low crags ideal for roosting.

Follow this little track as it dodges in and out of the woods along the bay until you reach another caravan site. Carry on through this to Hollins Farm, where the route to Arnside Knot is signposted. It is a slow ascent through woods and quite hard to find the trig point at the top as it rather hidden amongst trees with no distinctive path. If you are just wanting a view, the Toposcope and Mountain Indicator are easier to find.

From here it is a short distance back to the car-park.

The National Trust produce a leaflet with three different walks around Arnside Knot lasting from forty-five minutes to two hours. One of these walks takes you to the south-facing scree slopes I mentioned earlier. (You are asked not to walk on these.) There are also some interesting notes on the geology and natural history of the area. The map on this leaflet is not drawn to scale and a little confusing to say the least! I suggest you still take the OS map as well.

Lancaster

I expect that for many people Lancashire is a county with lots of people and plentiful industry, an image created by the successful television programme 'Coronation Street', or perhaps the stick figures and chimneys captured by L. S. Lowry paintings, or some of George Orwell's writing.

It was not always so. At the time of the Civil War in the 1640s there were few towns and people and it was not ranked amongst the powerful counties. It was the Industrial Revolution that made Lancashire more important and created the popular image. There was an explosive growth of urban areas throughout the nineteenth century. My husband's great-great-grandfather moved to Liverpool from the town of Wirksworth in Derbyshire, earning a living as a cowkeeper and beerseller (milk and beer deliveries, I wonder?) The 1841 census records that all his neighbours were so-called immigrants, from counties such as Cumberland and Westmoreland, moving towards the hub of industry and better employment opportunities.

Lancaster is the administrative town of Lancashire, and is at the opposite side of the county from the big urban centres. Although now best-known for its university and civic buildings, it too has an industrial side that preceded and foreshadowed the huge growth in the south of the county, and, on the whole, was of a rather more human scale.

Modern Lancaster has the feel of an inland city. There is just a tree-lined quay and some drunken warehouses to remind you of a busy maritime past. But it was the link with the sea that established the site, giving seventeenth- and eighteenth-century Lancaster its prosperity. It was this link which was the spur for much local, and later county-wide, industry, leaving the legacy of many fine buildings. Exploring the coastal area between Lancaster and the nearby port of Glasson gives fascinating insights into the industrial developments here.

Earlier, there was a Roman settlement on the present-day site of Lancaster. The Romans realized the strategic importance of a site which had a commanding view of the surrounding hills, close to a river that could be forded at low tide and yet was navigable by ships at high water.

It was nearly a thousand years later that the first bridge was constructed over the River Lune and not until the end of the thirteenth century does the first-known written reference of Lancaster as a port occur.

Large-scale importing of goods began in the seventeenth century with profitable trade routes established to the West Indies and America. There were imports of rum and cotton, sugar and timber. Businesses were built up on these commodities. The first sugar refinery was established in 1680 by John Hodgson, a local merchant. This was considered the first factory, as opposed to cottage industry, a move that was to change the face of Lancashire. Another local man, Robert Gillow, used the imported mahogany to found a high class cabinet-making business, the name of which still survives today.

Within less than sixty years, the silting up of the River Lune and subsequent threat to the port of Lancaster, meant a search by the city's merchants for an alternative downstream harbour. The choice on the Lune Estuary was either Sunderland Point on the northern banks, which was found to be unsuitable, or Glasson, a spot on the southern bank. In 1779 The Lancaster Port Commission decided to build at Glasson.

Glasson Docks was some distance from Lancaster and needed both a railway and a branch of the Lancaster Canal to strengthen trade. Sadly it was just too late. A general trade depression at the end of the Napoleonic Wars meant the end of the trans-Atlantic routes. Though there was still coastal trade, Lancaster was never again to be amongst the leading north-west ports and was unable to compete with booming Liverpool.

Today, the defunct railway line and quiet canal are a boon for walkers and an ideal way to experience this part of the coast.

Glasson Docks and the old Port of Lancaster

OS Map 1:50 000, Sheet 102

As the whole circuit from Lancaster to Glasson, via the coast and then back along the canal, is 16 miles (26 km), it is more of an expedition for the really energetic, or for those who might stay somewhere on the way. I have therefore divided the walk into two linear walks, one down the railway and one down the canal, as you may find the length of these an easier alternative.

The navigation on both these walks is straightforward. The railway track is well-signed, and the canal route is obvious.

Car-parking and the start

There are plenty of public car-parks in Lancaster. To be near St George's Quay, follow signs to the Maritime Museum and Castle. There is a park on Richmond Hill which is also handy for the bus station. Free three-hour parking is available on the Quay if you are only doing part of the walk.

If you want to be near the canal, aim to park near the Town Hall on Nelson Street or on Thurnham Street, both of which are close to the Tourist Information Centre.

Get a bus to Glasson Docks (Ribble Motor Services) and then choose either the old railway route or the canal route back to the city.

I found the sight of Glasson Docks a notable contrast to the rest of the coastline. The small marina is filled with bobbing boats, their tall masts and colourful sails a pleasant relief in both shape and colour to the flat grey-green marsh grasses and intricate creeks that surround the area.

It is unusual to find in Britain a place with a relatively short history. Glasson is exactly that. Before the creation of the docks here, there were really no more than a few farming families. With the building of the main wet dock in 1787, big enough to hold twenty-five merchantmen of at least 200 tonnage, there was sudden expansion. Within a few years the population had grown enormously and it is easy to imagine the old harbour at work. There were sandstone quays and warehouses, a dry dock and a shipyard, plus the Customs House and Harbour-Master's Cottage. Cargoes came from across the Atlantic, and from nearer at hand, to provide essential materials and food for a surprisingly large hinterland. The port is still operational, but now it deals in mainly animal feed from the Netherlands rather than the more romantic cargoes of rum and molasses.

Before leaving Glasson, walk up to the top of Tithebarn Hill for a splendid view of the Lune Estuary. On the far bank is Sunderland Point, and, on a clear day, you'll see the Lake District mountains beyond.

The Old Railway Line

OS Map, 1:50 000, Sheet 102
A walk of 5–6 miles (8–10 km). Allow 2½–3 hours.

This route is very well-marked and easy to follow as it traces the course of the old railway line. There is virtually nothing left of the railway to be seen except for the old Station-Master's House at Glasson and the Crossing-Keeper's Cottage at Conder Green (near where the path crosses the River Conder on the railway bridge). Large stretches of very straight path are a clue to its origins, though in summer the undergrowth creeps up around either side, making it seem so narrow that I could scarcely believe there was room for a train.

The Glasson–Lancaster Line was built by the London and North Western Railway Company. In its heyday there were four passenger trains a day. These shut down in 1930, though a goods train ran for several more years, and the whole line shut down in the Sixties, a decade in which British Rail's mileage shrank by a third.

There are no directions to give, really, except stay on the track! After about three miles (5 km) you reach the crossing-point at Aldcliffe; there is a choice of continuing straight on along the old track or taking a path to the left which brings you around the marshes of the Lune Estuary. This whole area is a Sight of Special Scientific Interest (SSSI). Look out for the population of wintering wading birds such as the redshank, and wildfowl such as mallard in the autumn. These marshes were once grazed by sheep and so the predominant vegetation is grass.

At Marsh Point the path meets the edges of modern industrial Lancaster and from here it is a short walk up to St George's Quay.

This is a delightful part of the city overlooking the River Lune. Now quiet, this quay was once a hive of activity, graced with tall ships and probably resounding with taller tales. The Quay was built to cope with the booming trade with America and the West Indies and at one time it dealt with more tonnage than Liverpool. Cargoes were stored in the vast quayside warehouses. In the midst of these is the fine Customs House, designed by a member of the Gillow family, Richard, an architect rather than a furniture-maker.

This building now houses the Maritime Museum where I spent a happy hour or so. There are two sections, one in the Customs House and the other, a new exhibition, is set out in the warehouse next door.

There is plenty on the history of the port, the present-day fishing industry, and the various developments along the coast. I liked some of the striking contrasts between old and new. One room is very high-tech, full of pipes and bright primary colours, all relating to the Morecambe Gas Field, whilst the neighbouring room is a reconstruction of an old warehouse scene with the soberly dressed labourers manhandling giant rum barrels.

I enjoyed the two short videos about the port and the history of Morecambe Bay. I hadn't realized Lancaster's involvement with the slave trade. I wonder if there are similar fictional folk tales here to match those of Liverpool where lots of people thought slaves were kept in cellars under the cobblestones by the Pier Head. The slave trade brought a prosperity to some that was hard to give up. So much so that the Lancaster merchants sent in a special petition to Parliament opposing Wilberforce's Abolition Bill.

Only on the way out will you find out just how high above the ground you are as the staircase descent seems endless. It must have required some effort to haul up all those barrels.

As a final inducement to visit the museum I should tell you that the management have even found room for a tiny café.

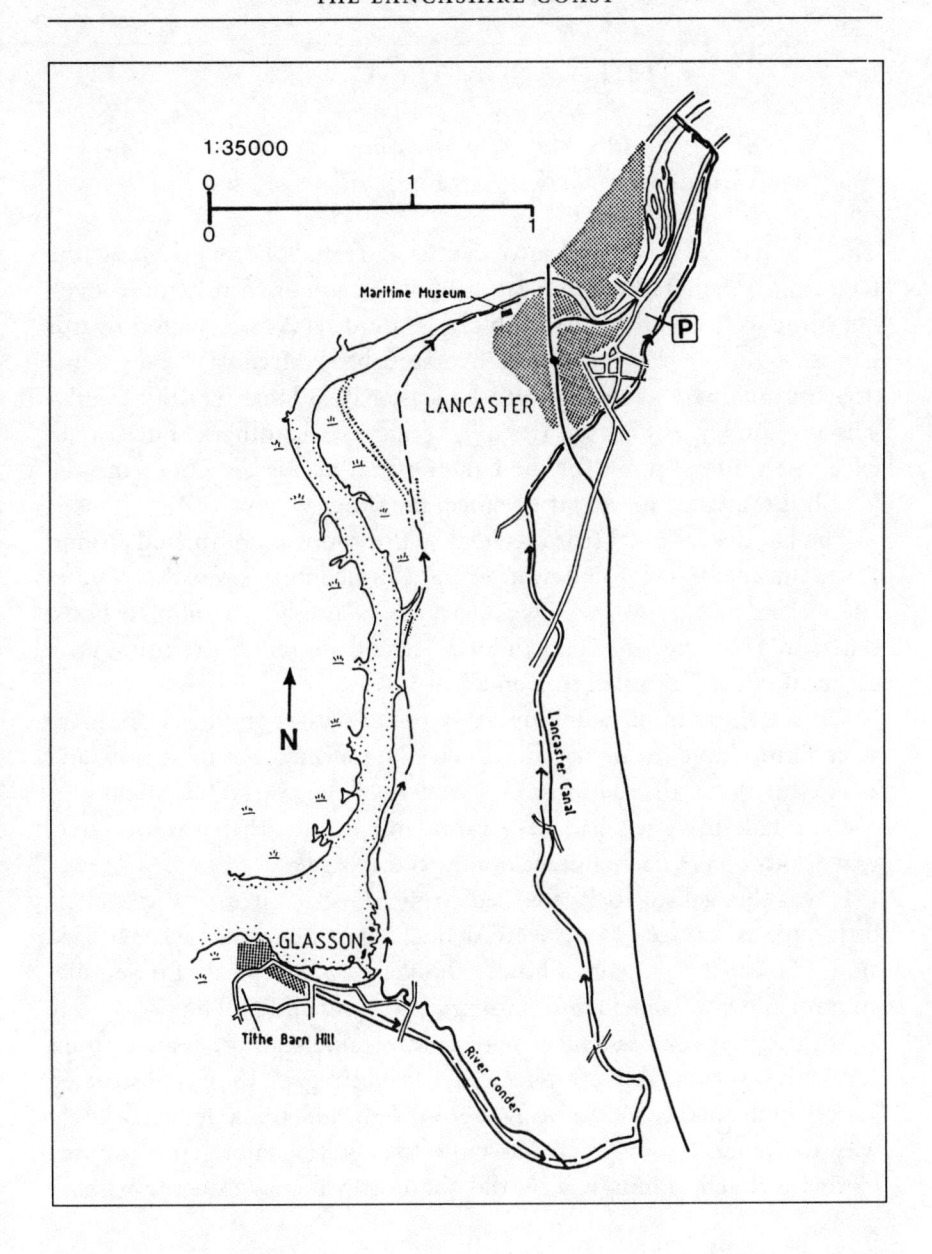

THE LANCASHIRE COAST

The Lancaster Canal

OS Map 1:50 000, Sheet 102
A walk of 6–8 miles (10–12 km). Allow 3–4 hours.

The alternative way back into Lancaster from Glasson is along the Lancaster Canal. The route is easy to follow, and obviously quite level, but some sections of the towpath can be muddy. As you walk towards Lancaster the scene is dominated by the Ashton Memorial. The memorial and the park were given to Lancaster by a local wealthy family. The monument is high on the hill, acting as a landmark, but also an excellent vantage-point for the Lake District in one direction, and the Welsh mountains, in the far distance, the other way.

The Lancaster Canal from Kendal to Preston was completed around 1800. But the branch to Glasson wasn't finished until some thirty years later, even though Glasson was desperately needing a fillip to boost trade. In 1826 the first load of stone set off down to Preston, and a cargo of salt sailed north to Kendal.

On the short branch-line up the Conder Valley there are six locks which must have meant a slow start to the journey, but these now add a pleasant visual diversion to this section of the walk. The main part of the canal, however, had a forty-one mile stretch that was lock-free, which must have been a great bonus to the bargees.

It was the lack of locks that led to the development of the packet-boat express service. These were slender, light boats that were hauled along the canal by a pair of horses. To keep up the speed of nine miles an hour the horses needed changing every four miles! The boats were well fitted out for passengers with comfortable seating, heated cabins and refreshments. After looking at, and sitting in the reconstructed packet-boat in the Maritime Museum, I should think it was a great way to travel, far more comfortable than jolting along the country roads by coach. Though how did the horses manage on the narrow path?

One of the first boats in service was called the *Water Witch*, a rather daring name given the links that Lancashire has with witches, even though that was some two hundred years earlier. The name is still preserved by a canal-side pub which is handily sited where you come into Lancaster.

Walk along through the town with its wharves and warehouses to the Lune Aqueduct. It is a magnificent work, over 600 feet (182 m) long, carrying the whole canal high over the River Lune. Built by John Rennie, it was completed nearly two hundred years ago. From here you can see the modern motorway bridge spanning the Lune further upstream. Progress!

There is a footpath here that joins up with the old railway line if you are going to do the complete circuit.

I've concentrated on the maritime history as it was what I became interested in as part of the walk, but there is much more to Lancaster. Some very good leaflets are available from the Tourist Centre. Just two or three minutes from there, along Brock Street, is a cosy little wholefood café called Libra. Great for soup if you are washed out and windswept as I was. On milder days they have a small garden eating area. There is a good choice of full meals, snacks, or just coffee and cakes.

RIBCHESTER

This village is the nearest place on the coast that gives you the flavour of inland Lancaster. The familiar grey stone houses, despite their steely colour, still have a friendly appeal. The village is attractive, and although I came in search of Romans, I looked at the other things on offer such as the Museum of Childhood. This will appeal to devotees of dolls and dollshouses of which there are endless variations packed into several tiny rooms. My lasting memory of the place is the Pathe News video on the flea circus (commentary and Carry On-style puns by Sidney James are certainly up to scratch). I hesitate to give away all the gory details or come up with any more irritating jokes, but after seeing the owner feeding the fleas with the comment, 'They feed off him and then he feeds off them', I was grateful for the steep staircase which jettisoned me into the street for a good breath of fresh air, ready to tackle the Romans!

Roman Fort on the Ribble

OS Map 1:50 000, Sheet 103
A circular walk of 4 miles (6 km). Allow 2 hours.

This walk explores the delightful valley of the River Ribble. It starts with the Romans, and then leaps some thousand years to a tiny twelfth-century chapel in the fields. Climbing north from the river, there's a view to the southern side of the valley and an impressive range of hills, linked with seventeenth-century tales of witchcraft. Road and track bring you back to the riverbanks and you finish with a pleasant stroll along the Ribble, where I discovered the secret of good cheese and tomato sandwiches.

The route is fairly obvious as a clear track takes you most of the way up the first (and only) hill. Then it's back to the river via road and farm track. There are, however, two short stretches of road with no footpath so you do need to be alert. The river path is well marked and just a little narrow in places. The going over the fields may be boggy in places, and so are occasional stretches of the riverside path.

Car-parking and the start

There is a good-sized free car-park in Ribchester where it is just a short walk down to the Roman fort and the Museum.

Ribchester, or rather Bremetennacum as the Romans called it, is in a remote area, and it seems odd now to think it was picked as the site for one of the largest forts in Britain at the time of the occupation. It was then a highly strategic spot. The Ribble Valley provided significant access to the other side of the Pennines and this was also the point where the main road west of the Pennines, from Manchester to Carlisle, crossed the river. It was possible from here to defend both the north/south as well as the east/west routes. Ribchester was set up by Agricola, the Roman governor who established a system of roads and garrisoned forts to enable him to extend the frontiers of the Empire north to the Forth and the Clyde.

The Romans staffed this huge fort with some of their fiercest men. The first occupants were units from Spain, then later heavy cavalry from Samatia, an area that is now the Balkans. I have often wondered, especially when visiting some of these far-flung outposts in typical British weather, what it must have been like for these soldiers imported from more clement climes. Apparently records have been discovered that mention veterans settling in the area, evidently liking it enough to stay. Having served their time as soldiers they became horse breeders and farmers.

Sadly, little now remains of the fort, as much was built over by the construction of St Wilfrid's Church and most of the rest was swallowed up by the changing course of the river. In 1988 English Heritage had a project to excavate an area on the north of the site, near where there are clear remains of the old granaries. The day I last visited had been preceded by torrential rain, and the excavators were involved in the depressing task of hoovering up the water from the dig before any further progress could be made.

Some interesting finds have been made in the past. The finest is a ceremonial cavalry helmet which was found on the river bank when the river changed course. The genuine article is now in the British Museum, but an impressive replica is in the little museum on the site of the fort.

Other finds include a pretty set of coins and the romantic engagement ring engraved with the words *Ave Mea Vita*: Greetings (to thee whom I love as dear as) my life.

Whilst visiting the fort and little museum, take the chance to see the church. I have never seen so many table-top tombs grouped together, it gives the impression that the churchyard is just being set up for the parish summer banquet.

From the church follow the signs along the banks of the Ribble around to the site of the Roman Bath House. You can work out from the ruins, and the information at the side, the progress of the bather through the different rooms. I don't think the fleas stood much of a chance, especially with the rather vicious-sounding metal scraper used to get rid of the dirt. I should think after treatment with that the sauna at the end would have felt like a blissful release.

From here walk out of the village on the B6245 towards Blackburn and at the stone bridge, just as you leave the village, take the little lane on the left to the Stydd Almshouses and St Saviour's Chapel.

The almshouses are extraordinary. They are set on two floors with a staircase up to a grand arched balcony. In the courtyard is an old well, though it is long disused. The surrounding area looked very neglected, though work was going on at the adjacent Catholic church, and the lane is marked with new signs. I learned from the Canon of St Wilfrid's that the almshouses are being modernized as part of a housing project. Once finished they should be splendid to look at and live in.

Carry on up the lane by the side of the almshouses, towards the farm buildings. As you get nearer, what looks like a stone barn turns out to be the little church of St Saviour's. The church was built by the Knights Hospitallers and was abandoned in the time of Henry VIII. It still seems a little neglected, but services are held here on the last Sunday of summer months and at special times such as Harvest Festival and 'Carols by Candlelight' on Christmas Eve. The lonely setting must add to the atmosphere of the service. On Christmas Eve 1775 a Catholic bishop was buried in this Anglican church, an interesting example of local religious toleration.

If you want to see inside St Saviour's, ask for a key from the rectory or the churchwarden's house as one is usually available.

From St Saviour's, continue on the track through the farm and out onto the fields. In a little valley just to your left is the course of the old Roman road, where just a short section is still used as a road. The track is quite clear until about halfway up the hill when it disappears into a marsh. You should make your way to the top of the hill. There are some small outcrops of rock visible and a stretch rather like moorland around the little summit. Here, I disturbed a hare who bolted with enviable speed over the brow of the hill.

At the top you get a good view of the Ribble Valley and the ridge of hills on the far side. As you look along the ridge, far over to the left, there is a huge sloping hump which is Pendle Hill. It features prominently in the days of the so-called Pendle Witches, a gaggle of women who lived in Pendle Forest, begging for a living and cursing those that didn't pay up. When someone who'd been cursed died immediately afterwards, there began a long witch-hunt lasting over twenty years, with many ending up on the gallows at Lancaster.

From the hill, carry on over to the farm and down the drive to the minor road. Here, turn right and follow the road past a junction on the right (there is no footpath on part of this section). Just beyond is a large farm lane going downhill to the Ribble. This is a pretty track;

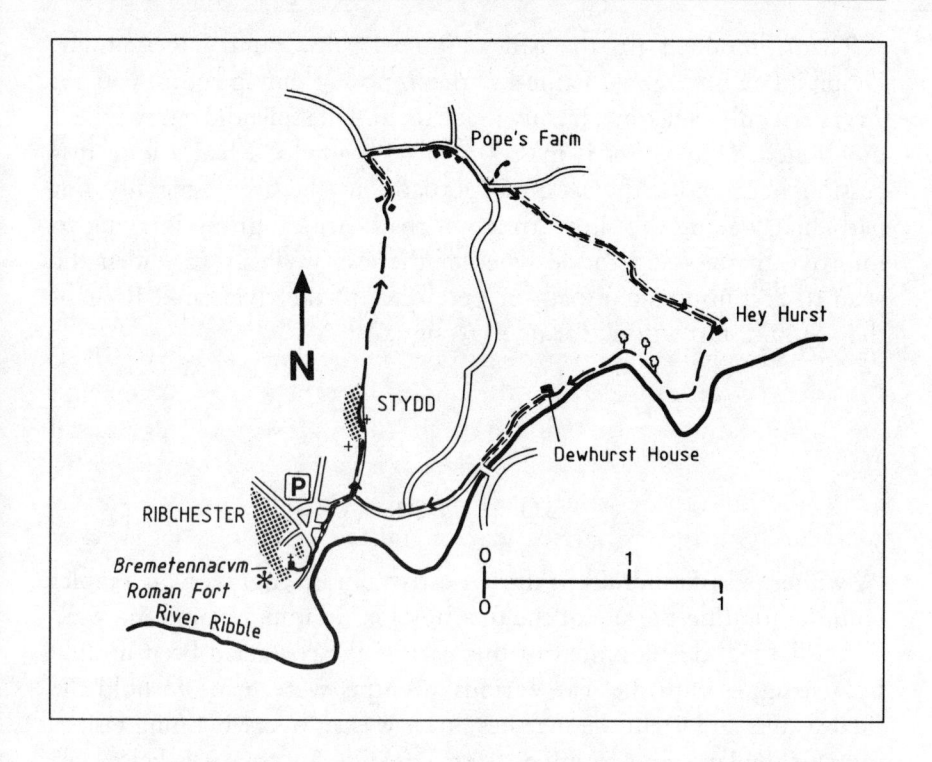

on either side there's an untidy hedgerow of flowers and foliage in abundance. Follow this right down to Hey Hurst Farm where it meets up with the long-distance Ribble Way and then drops down to the river.

This part of the Ribble is a delight. The river meanders lazily around in a loop, but whilst giving the impression of sluggishness, the water is in fact moving at a terrific rate. As you turn back along this track to Ribchester, the route is signposted with a wiggly R and W signifying the Ribble Way. This is a long-distance footpath going from the Ribble Estuary, near Preston, over seventy miles (112 km) to its source high in the Pennines of North Yorkshire. Our small section keeps close to the river, or climbs just slightly to meadows above. Soon you will see an elegant road bridge where the Burnley road is carried over the river.

Be warned! I'm afraid the last section of the walk back to Ribchester has to be endured rather than enjoyed as there is no choice but to walk along the busy road which in places lacks any sort of footpath.

Thank goodness for the Miles House Farm Country Restaurant. Despite the rather grand name and the imposing dining room, you get a very friendly welcome, freshly made tea and the splendid sandwiches I mentioned. (The secret is masses of black pepper.) I had a long discussion here about the lack of footpaths in the area generally but particularly along this short stretch of road. A local group is trying to improve matters and to see whether there is any way to widen the road to accommodate a path or get access to the riverbank. Perhaps they should start a book for us all to sign.

Southport

'A wilderness of sandhills' is the evocative phrase engraved on a tablet commemorating the site of the first hotel in Southport, built in 1792.

Until 1772, development of this part of the coast had been limited by a struggle with the sea. Various attempts were made to hold the tidal waters and drain the marshes but it was an overwhelming task as most of the land for five miles (8 km) around Southport is below sea level. Eventually a combination of huge embankments and sluices enabled land to be reclaimed. Even today there is a pumping station working continuously to keep the water levels down.

The coast became fashionable once bathing came into vogue at the end of the eighteenth century. South Hawes was a popular location, and an enterprising chap decided to open a summer lodging house. It was first known as the South Port Hotel and was to give the town its name, marking the beginning of substantial development along the coast.

I did find some sandhills – enough for a 'wilderness' – south of the town, where over the years the sea has receded two miles. The stretches of dunes left behind have a tenuous grip on the world, held together in most areas by marram grass. This was planted, often with the labour of school children, to prevent erosion. The difficulties of developing the whole area is a blessing as it leaves a coastline rich in nature reserves and interesting places to walk.

Walk from Formby Point to Southport Pier

OS Map 1:50 000, Sheet 108
A linear walk of 7–8 miles (10–12 km) using public transport to get to the start. Allow 3–4 hours.

This is a splendid walk if you are in the mood for the lonely sea and the sky. I love the barren feeling on the extensive sands, but found, too, a surprising variety of landscapes – lunar-like dunes, scented pine forest and different types of vegetation, many beginning with the prefix 'sea', but like the distinctive sea holly quite unlike their land cousins. You need a special vocabulary to describe features here such as 'mobile dunes' (shifting sands?), 'fixed dunes', and 'slacks'.

This walk works best as a linear walk and there is good public transport. Get the train from Southport to Freshfields. This provides a good preview of the walk, and should ensure you start with pleasant anticipation. The walk is basically north along the coast to Southport, and the pier makes an excellent landmark to aim at as a finish. Trains leave Southport about every quarter of an hour and take roughly ten minutes to get to Freshfields Station.

For a much shorter, and circular alternative, park (there is a charge) at the nature reserve at Freshfields and then do a short circuit cutting up the beach along Gypsy Wood Path.

From Freshfields Station head west towards the beach down a very pleasant leafy road about ¾ mile (1 km), which leads you directly to the nature reserve. These so-called Formby Hills are four hundred acres (162 ha) of duneland and forest owned by the National Trust. Despite a desert-like appearance, paradoxically they mark the start of an oasis of wildlife. The pine woods just before the dunes are now home to large numbers of red squirrel. (The pet shop on the corner by the station is the place to get stocked up with peanuts.) The red squirrel is a native of England, unlike the more common grey one, which is an American import. Remember that, like the rest of us, the squirrels are sensitive to the weather. On the evening I last visited I went armed with goodies. It was a rain-drenched night so I didn't expect many people to be about. I was right, but nor were there any squirrels. In better weather, there are plenty to see. They are really very tame and easily tempted by nuts. My consolation in the pouring rain was seeing a Natterjack toad plopping around the track in a very endearing fashion before diverting into the woods. He seemed rather far from home base but perhaps had been encouraged by the general wetness to journey further afield.

The main squirrel reserve is to the left of the road. If you wander around here, the path eventually joins up with the Woodland Path, which leads down to the sands more or less at Formby Point. It is a deserted, windswept part of the world, and it's strange to think it's less than 10 miles (16 km) down the coast from here to the massive dockland container port at Seaforth. The proximity to the port has had its benefits, though, as it may account for the number of rare plants found around Formby Point. The theory is that seeds from distant lands get carried over in cargoes unloaded in Liverpool. They are then carried north on the tides to end their journey here.

From the nature reserve turn north and walk along the beach. I enjoy this sort of area most in terrible weather. It is so exhilarating being out in a high wind under a rain-leaden sky on these sands. When the light is grey the sea and sand blend together as if they are one vast ocean beneath a heavy sky. The water takes on a different, more threatening tone and the green marram grass of the dunes looks almost like a metallic pink hair-do standing up in the wind. The walk seems to go on for miles, and so it does for at least two! The challenge is rounding the headland. Rather like climbing mountains where there is only ever one more ridge, you think there is only one more corner until Southport Pier comes in sight.

Carry on along the beach to Ainsdale Nature Reserve. It starts shortly after the National Trust boundary ends. The two reserves are separated by one of the half dozen or so golf courses along this stretch of the coast. I can see where these places get the idea for bunkers but managing a flat piece of fairway must have been a challenge.

This reserve is bounded by four major paths. Fisherman's path goes along the southern edge (and also, incidentally, back to Freshfield Station) and the path along the sea edge is known as Dune Path North which brings you through the 'Slacks'. This is the term for the wet hollows along the dunes which encourage a different type of vegetation, much of which seems to have a sea-side bias with sea holly, sea spurge and sea buckthorn. Sea holly is one of the easiest to recognize and is a most striking plant. It is shaped like holly, but has paler leaves

THE LANCASHIRE COAST

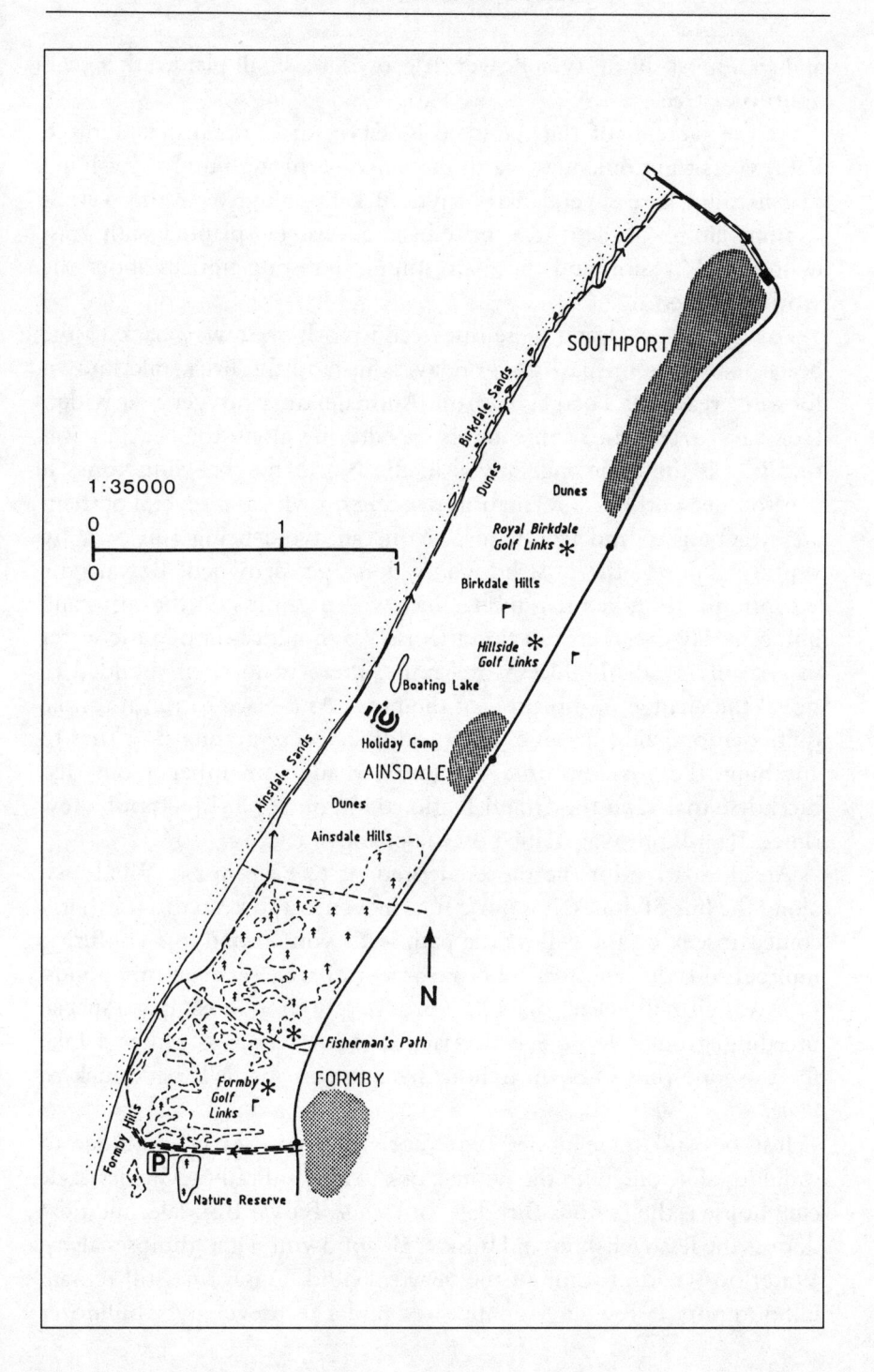

and an almost thistle-type flower. It grows as a small plant rather than a shrub or tree.

At the far end of the Ainsdale Reserve, the path (called Pinfold Path) veers right, inland towards the railway, through more low-lying marshland where several parts have duck-boarding over the wettest sections. Some of these areas have been intensively planted with grass to stop soil erosion and there are some interesting notices about the work going on.

For Southport, leave these dunes and work your way back to the beach, continue on past the holiday camp and the brick pile known for some reason as Toad Hall. From Ainsdale, the sands get ever wider. Don't be surprised to come across cars driving along the beach. I was told it was the done thing, well in the North maybe! Sometimes it gets to look a little like formation-dancing on wheels if several of them are sweeping to and fro at once. You can avoid being run over by venturing out to the tidal line, only don't get drowned! Beware the incoming tide. A red flag flying may well mean it's on the turn, and innocent day dreamers can find themselves shoulder-high in the water in no time at all. Unlike Morecambe, there is no siren sounded to signal the change of direction of the flow. As a place to run it can be quite demoralizing because it can feel like you're getting no closer to anything. To pass the time you can try and remember about that racehorse that won the Grand National at Aintree in Liverpool a few times; Red Rum was trained on these sands.

An alternative for the more energetic is to keep just off the beach along the line of dunes. It is quite an achievement to keep to a northerly route. In seeking the valleys the path leads you around in a confusing number of twists and turns. I came across a pretty series of tiny ponds. One was virtually heart-shaped, appropriately enough as this is a special breeding ground for the Natterjack Toad. I fear it is rather a hike for the lone one I saw near Formby but perhaps he'll have luck *en route*.

Just beyond these dunes two more golf courses lie shoulder to shoulder. The one with the white clock tower and rather Thirties-style club house is the famous Birkdale, or rather, Royal Birkdale, and next door is the less well-known Hillside. Beyond you'll get glimpses along Waterloo Road of some of the very splendid houses that still remain in Southport. A few have disappeared under the developers' bulldozer and where one house once stood, ten or so are squashed into the space. Southport attracted a good deal of money in the past with the gentry flocking here from Manchester. The done thing was to live 'the right side of the railway tracks', that is, the sea side.

Now the pier should be well and truly in sight, and on a reasonable day Blackpool Tower and seafront are clear across the water of the Ribble Estuary. The last stretch up to the pier goes past the attractive municipal gardens and the gaudy fairground. If your legs are tired you can take the little miniature railway down the length of the pier, which is roughly opposite the station you set out from, if you need to get your bearings.

Rumour has it that this lengthy pier was built in an attempt to catch up with the disappearing tide. Southport nearly had the distinction of being a seaside resort with no sea, as the beach got bigger and bigger and the sea further and further away. You'll see an extensive seawater lake at the end of the walk, which is the consequence of some imaginative thinking at the end of the nineteenth century. This artificial lake, called the Marine Lake, was created next to the promenade. It has since been extended, and is now home to championship dinghy racing. The area around the old part is one of water, gardens and bridges, and is very genteel, in keeping with the character of the town. This personality was not accidental. The town's leading citizens in the latter half of the nineteenth century decreed that building leases were only granted for developments that were not of an industrial or offensive nature. This policy was continued to the end of the century in a deliberate attempt to keep the town for the 'well to do'.

Much of Southport has weathered this century very well. A highlight is Lord Street, the main shopping street with many balustrades, colonnades and intricate iron work. It is said to be second only to Edinburgh's Princes Street amongst the high streets of Britain. A new 'Victorian' bandstand is to be built (to replace the one they pulled down!) and Wayfarer's Arcade is particularly attractive. Go in through an ornate portico and the narrow approach opens out into a spacious galleried area, enclosed by an arched glass and iron roof.

There is a good town trail focusing on Lord Street which describes the most notable buildings. You'll get this from the tourist information centre in front of the library and arts centre.

My favourite place for a touch of Victoriana is just outside the town centre in the Botanic Gardens. These gardens are quite small with formal areas primly laid out with small geometric beds of flowers. To the right of the museum and café is a most unpromising looking building with corrugated-iron roof, no windows and a small scratched brown door at one end. But open this and you are into another world. Behind here is a jungle of ferns officially called The Fernery. You don't even need the squawk of the odd parrot and a touch of humidity to believe you are in the tropics with the effects of giant fronds and dripping water. Cheese plants and rubber plants are enormous. At the far end are little stone steps giving you a verdant view over the top of this forgotten jungle.

The Botanic Gardens are to the north of the town centre, near the village of Churchtown which, although swallowed up by Southport, retains a different character and is a good place to find a pub.

Just out of Southport, Rufford Old Hall is another spot to escape from crowds, except at weekends. This is an old house owned by the National Trust. It is best to be a member as you will have to pay for some sort of entry fee, even if you are only calling for a drink at the excellent café.

Ruffold Old Hall was built early in the fifteenth century by Sir Thomas Hesketh. The cumbersome title is due to the fact that the Hesketh family moved into Rufford New Hall some three hundred years later.

The Hall was originally the central part of a house with two wings. Both of these disappeared when the east wing was rebuilt in brick. The Great Hall is preserved in its original state. It is probably the last place you would expect to come across Shakespeare, but there is evidence to show that he came here with a troupe of strolling players. The impressive room would certainly have been a wonderful setting for theatricals. The grounds are also very attractive and there are some tables provided for picnickers.

A visit to the original Hesketh family home makes an appropriate end to a tour of this region, as it was due to the efforts of that family that the first successful embankments were built to the north of Southport, and much of the low-lying land reclaimed from the sea.

THE DALES

'The Dales' is the name traditionally associated with the middle region of the Pennines that is the north-west part of Yorkshire. It is an area of high fells, with twenty mountains over 2,000 feet (609 m) high, and a variety of valleys providing routes and supporting settlements. The valleys are called dales, a word that has come from Norse, hence the name of the area.

In fact there are about fifty dales in the area covered by the Yorkshire Dales National Park, although only a handful are well known; Wensleydale and Swaledale have given their names to cheese and sheep, respectively. Lesser-known dales can, however, boast even more memorable names, such as Arkengarthdale or Crummackdale, and their scenery is as fine as that of the better-known ones.

Much of the Dales is marked by both natural and man-made activity. On one level this explains the theme of a 'riddled landscape' which I have taken for this chapter. There is, however, a second meaning to do with discovering the distinctive character of the land – solving its riddle, if you like – and its preservation, which is one of the prime objectives of the National Park. Here, not everything is immediately explicable. The landscape itself is intriguing with some curious plantlife and strange geological phenomena. Many localized words are used to describe the scene – gill, sett, rigg and scar – which give clues to the origins of the early settlers. There are many visual riddles to answer that reveal much about former invaders and the variety of ways in which the land has been used. This is of course also true of many areas of Britain, but I think it particularly applies here because the apparent emptiness of the Dales makes it easier to focus on features.

The landscape itself is certainly riddled. On the surface there are pot-holes, shake-holes, caves and mines. Above the ground, there's a rash of small stone barns dotted into every field. A huge network of stone walls divides the valleys into piecemeal areas whilst underground there are vast networks of passages. In the southern part of the area, many of these have been created naturally by the action of water on the porous limestone rock underlying the surface. There are tunnels and caverns, underground streams and channels. You may think you are looking at a solid mountain, but in limestone country it may well be on the way to being hollow.

In the northern part of the region, it was the search for rich mineral ores that lead to the excavation of the landscape. The mining heyday was towards the end of the nineteenth century. Thousands were employed here, something that is hard to believe when you stand on a windswept lonely fell. All that remains to serve as a reminder of the activity below ground are some deserted tips, old kilns and shafts.

Thanks to the creation of the National Park, much is being done to preserve the Dales and encourage visitors to enjoy its many qualities. There are, especially in the summer months, plenty of tourists. Well-known attractions such as Aysgarth Falls and Bolton Abbey are generally crowded, as are well-publicized tracks such as The Three Peaks Long Distance walk over Pen-y-ghent, Whernside and Ingleborough. It has started to get the nick-name 'the Three Peaks Motorway' not only because of the crowds, but also because the trampling of many feet have caused serious erosion.

I have chosen walks which, I hope, will bring you to less-frequented places. In the limestone region of the south, there is Crummackdale with its spectacular scenery. From Wensleydale, you can easily get to the Dales lesser-known lake – Semer Water. Just further north, though completely different in mood, is Swaledale. Here there is an industrial legacy to see as well as some pretty waterfalls. Finally, Teesdale, often overlooked beyond the boundary of the park in Durham, differs entirely in character from its Yorkshire counterparts and is well worth a visit.

Karst Country

OS Map 1:25 000, Outdoor Leisure Sheet 2: Yorkshire Dales, Western Area
A circular walk approximately 8 miles (11 km). Allow $3\frac{1}{2}$–$4\frac{1}{2}$ hours and an extra hour if you want to look around the caves.

This walk takes you into the heart of a different world, the Karst country of the Southern Dales. The landscape is dominated by limestone, which makes it quite different from neighbouring terrain. The name originates in Yugoslavia, taken from the region Karst, which is famous, too, for its limestone features. I find the word is curiously onomatopoeic, suggesting the naked white rock and craggy quality of the landscape.

The limestone crags and outcrops revealed are all exposures of the Great Scar Limestone, a slab of rock laid down some three hundred million years ago underneath a shallow tropical sea, which solidified under layers of shale and sediment. Huge earth movements lifted and folded the rock, creating a number of faults in the region. Further shaping of the landscape occurred during the Ice Age. Glaciers carved out broad valleys with steep sides scraped clean to leave daunting cliffs. On the plateaux, the top-soils were removed by the action of the glacier. The vast flat areas that remain are known as limestone pavement. Torrents of melting water flowing fast across the frozen ground created gorges; the more aggressive the stream, the deeper the ravine.

These events gave a broad structure to the land, leaving the familiar profile of the hills with their flat summits and the dales between them. The action of rainwater on the rock has created many smaller features which are part of Karst country. The water is absorbed by the rock, with a gradual dissolving taking place. This leaves evidence of masses of surface and subterranean features such as clints and grikes, sinks and swallow-holes, caves and pot-holes, all of which can be seen and explained on this walk.

The walk is energetic, not just because it is longer than most in the book, but also because there is a fair bit of up and down with some parts quite steep. You'll also be lucky to find a day without wind; wind in your face on the top of the Dales is something that I find particularly tiring. Do wrap up well, even if it is warm and sunny when you set off from Clapham Village, for it is snug in the valley and conditions will change once you are out in the open.

The route is fairly easy to find as most of the tracks are well walked and there are a reasonable number of signposts, but don't attempt this walk unless you are fairly confident about reading a map, and I would advise a compass for safety's sake. These words of warning are not meant to put you off, but it is best to be well prepared on any upland region.

One other note of caution. Be very careful on limestone after wet weather as it is treacherously slippery. Apart from rocky areas, the going is good, being on track and short turf.

If you haven't time for the whole route, you can go as far as the Norber Erratics, worthwhile for the good view of the Moughton Scar and dramatic Crummackdale.

Car-parking and the start

Park in Clapham Village in the official car-park which adjoins the National Park Centre in the middle of the village. There is a small charge.

From the car-park turn right and follow the lane to the church, forking right there along the lane signed Austwick, and then turn sharply right. This is Thwaite Lane, an ancient pre-turnpike highway. It now passes via a tunnel under the grounds of Ingleborough Hall. There is another tunnel, now blocked, which was the former impressive tradesmens' entrance to the Hall itself.

Follow this track for about one mile ($1\frac{1}{2}$ km), ignoring the main track off to the left signposted Selside. Look out for a signpost on the left by the side of a sturdy stile. This points you up over the fields to the outcrops of rock above the road known as Robin Procter's Scar. Climb up to the base of the cliffs and walk in an easterly direction. Some way along here you'll start to see large boulders, dark grey in colour, which contrast quite strongly with the white of the limestone. In geological language, these are called 'erratics' – a splendid term which is applied to rocks that shouldn't really be where they are! These lumps of rock were once half a mile away and were carried here by massive glaciers in the Ice Age, then dumped by the melting ice. Some of the boulders rest on pedestals of limestone, which indicates how the

THE DALES

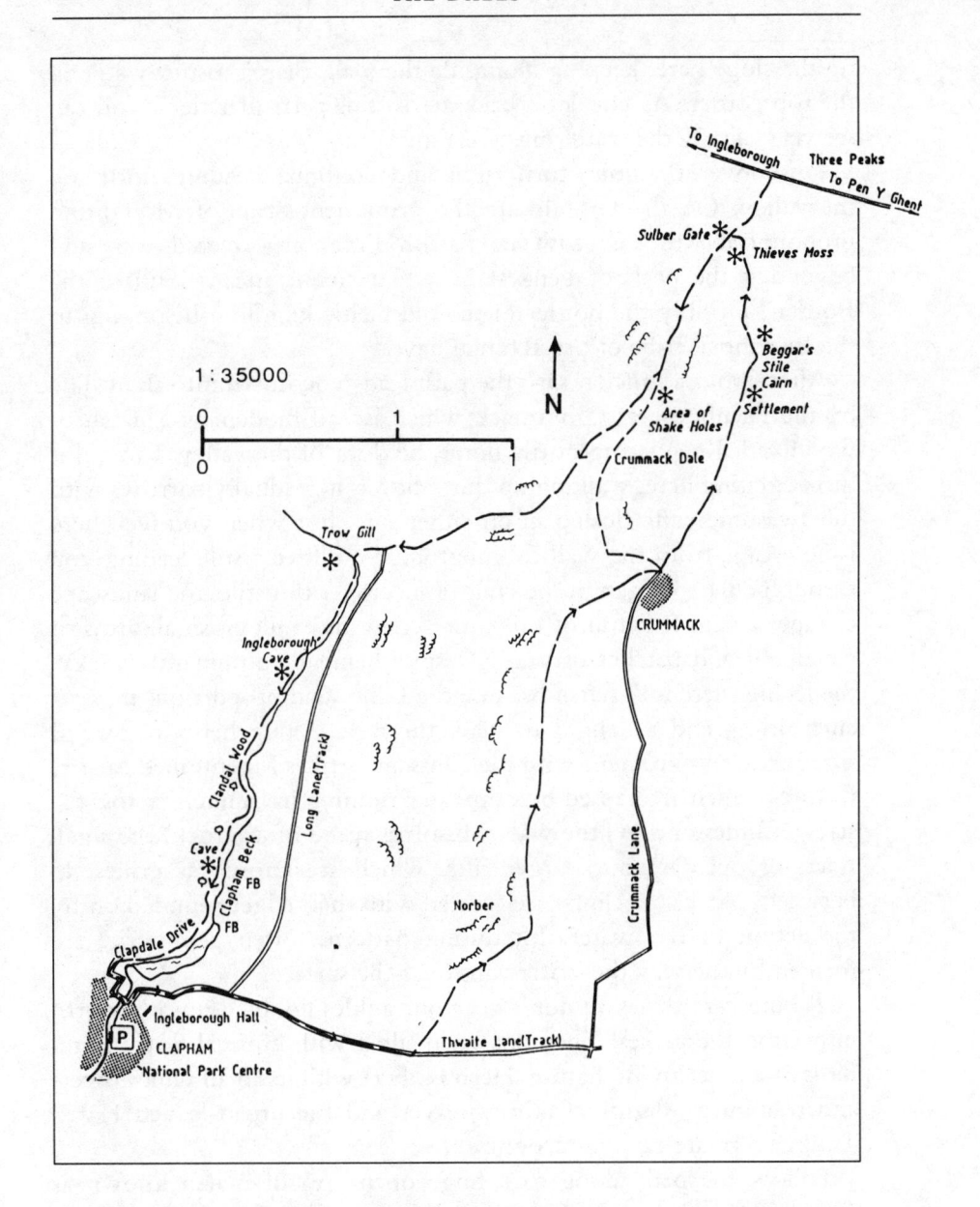

surface has been eroded since the erratics were originally deposited.

Walk along the bottom of the scar, almost parallel with Thwaite Lane below, and then swing north, heading towards Crummack. Eventually you'll come to an uncrossable stone wall, but if you climb up the slope here, keeping alongside the wall, there's a sturdy stile in the top corner. As you look back across this particular field, you can see very clearly the scattering of erratics.

Once over the stile, turn right and continue heading north up the valley. On the far side are the prominent Scars of Moughton, pronounced Moot'n, with its flattish limestone-covered top, and beyond is the peak of Pen-y-Ghent. The name means 'Hill of the Border', possibly the border of the old Celtic kingdom belonging to the Brigantian tribe of pre-Roman days.

After about a mile ($1\frac{1}{2}$ km) the path leads you down into the valley by the farmhouse at Crummack which is half hidden by a patch of woodland. Keep going north along the floor of the valley. I found it most exciting here, walking up the valley as it gradually narrows with the awesome cliffs closing in on either side. Just when you feel there is no escape from the wall of limestone, you'll see a stile leading you through a narrow gap in the crags. Once over this stile, the landscape changes again. It is full of miniature crags and valleys, small areas of pavement and patches of grass. Despite being predominantly rocky, the feeling here isn't harsh because the Lilliputian proportions make it enchanting, and a delight to walk through. Along here are several small areas of pavement with the clints and grikes I mentioned earlier, features which are caused by rainwater running in 'runnels' across the slabs of limestone. As the water dissolves more of the rock, the small fractures open up into larger rifts, which are known as grikes. In between, blocks (or clints) are created with their edges rounded off by the action of the water. Interesting patterns, often geometric, are formed by the way the water runs over the surface.

Taking care that you don't get your ankles gobbled up, it's worth inspecting the grikes. They are often filled with unusual flowers and ferns of a lime-loving nature. Herb Robert with its small pink flowers and triangular, slightly feathery leaves and the broad-leaved Hart's Tongue fern are easy to recognize.

Follow the path along to a huge open area of marsh known as Thieves Moss. I thought I had stumbled upon the Thieves' Graveyard itself! Just by this open area is a patch of limestone pavement dotted with thin slabs of limestone, all standing upright like tombstones (or sharks' teeth). It is quite extraordinary the way the erosion has created these shapes.

Look for the gate to the left of Thieves Moss. The route home is through the gate to the left, but you can make an interesting little detour to the right to Sulber Nick, only some 200 yards (200 m). Here, you'll see there is a signpost to Ingleborough, the final peak to be crossed on the famous Three Peaks route. This is a twenty-three mile (37 km) slog, starting and finishing in Horton, beginning with Pen-y-Ghent and continuing with Whernside. Some parts are rather well trodden, and even helicopters have been used in protection work. Once a year the route is the scene of a fell race – winning time a bit under three hours if you'd like to compare.

The route back to Clapham from Thieves Moss follows a southerly grassy path. Keep bearing to the right as there are several places where unmarked paths fork off left. The green of the grass is a pleasant contrast to the bare limestone, but you'll find plenty of evidence that this is limestone country. It is here you'll come across shake-holes which are rather like giant geological egg-timers. Once again, these are features caused by water erosion which creates hollows below the surface. The boulder clay above eventually trickles into the space, hence the egg-timer, leaving a conical depression on the surface. Shake-holes may only be a yard across, but as the path leads down into the valley of Clapham Beck, you'll see two unusually large ones on the other side of the valley, both several yards wide.

Streams disappear and reappear quite unexpectedly throughout this landscape, leaving sink-holes (where the water sinks into the ground, sometimes through minute fissures) and pot-holes, large vertical shafts. Just above the shake-holes on the far side of the valley is the pot-hole, Gaping Gill. Here Fell Beck, a sizeable stream, drops 360 feet (109 m) below ground in an unbroken fall of water, the deepest in Britain.

You can go back down to Clapham Village along Long Lane which meets up with Thwaite Lane, but I think it is more interesting to cross to the other side of the Clapham Valley and come back via Ingleborough Cave.

Go down the path at the entrance of Trow Gill, an attractive wooded ravine. This is now a dry valley, but it was created by glacial meltwaters which gorged into the limestone during the Ice Age. The stream that once ran here now probably uses the underground system through Gaping Gill and Ingleborough Cave. You can scramble up Trow Gill, but pick a dry day as the exposed stone is slippery. There are some beautiful trees, lime-loving ash and mountain ash or rowan, as well as many different ferns and lichens, flourishing in the sanctuary of this sheltered spot.

Carry on down the track, and you are likely to meet people in the entrance to Ingleborough Cave. You may like to time your walk to take in a tour of the cave as well. I find the thought of all this underground water carving out a secret landscape quite fascinating. The tour of the caves tells you something of the miles of linking passages between Ingleborough and Gaping Gill. The visit lasts nearly one hour, and it is a good idea to have warm clothing. There is a charge.

To get back to Clapham from the cave, carry on down the trail which is called Clapdale Drive. You'll see on the gate that there is a small charge (15p) for going through the Ingleborough estate. You pay at the cottage on the outskirts of Clapham Village. This part of the walk is on the Reginald Farrer Nature Trail and leaflets are available at the cottage.

Reginald Farrer was born in 1880 at Ingleborough Hall. He became an explorer and plant collector, being particularly interested in the Far East, especially the remoter regions of Asia such as Burma and Tibet. He brought back hundreds of species, some of which survive today. Curiously some of these are rhododendron, a lime-hating species which survives here by growing in patches of slaty rock, exposed by the displacement of strata in the North Craven fault and used very cleverly by Farrer. Sadly he died of diptheria when only forty.

Farrer's father, James, and his uncle, Oliver, were also influential in shaping the local landscape. They started in 1837 by unblocking the barrier of stalagmite that was holding back an underground lake in Ingleborough cave, thus draining the cave. Then, later, they created the lake at Clapham by damming the beck. You'll pass by this lake near the bottom of the trail. Simply follow the track into the village passing by the church and back to the car-park.

There are two good places to get snacks, one in the village centre, and the other just a little way further on. The latter has slightly later opening times which I found useful.

Semer Water

OS 1:25 000, Outdoor Leisure Sheet 30
A circular walk of 5 miles (8 km). Allow 2½–3 hours.

This is a fascinating walk through the centuries, around Yorkshire's largest natural lake and a chance to see the influence of man on the landscape over the last two thousand years. The canvas on which this influence is seen is distinctive, and quite unlike the other areas in this chapter. It is limestone scenery, but different from the other limestone country of the Karst further to the south. There the rock was a single structure, the Great Scar. Here, the formation of the land is due to many strata, called the Yoredale Facies. This is the name given to the layers of limestones, shales and sandstones that were built up in cycles of time over the Great Scar limestone. Different weathering of the different layers give the sides of the valleys a terraced appearance, with delicate ribbons of limestone running almost horizontal along the flanks of the dale.

The going underfoot is mostly good but be prepared to get wet feet. There are some marshy or muddy patches near Crook's Beck and around Semer Water itself. Much of the route goes across fields where the grass can be wet, and the hill climb is on virtually unwalked territory, so unless the sheep have been especially diligent, the grass will be long there too.

The navigating is easy as Semer Water is mostly in sight to help you keep your bearings. There are good footpath signs except for the short part that climbs up to the ridge above the Roman road.

There is livestock around the lakeside and sheep on the hilltops so dogs will need to be kept under control.

Car-parking and the start

The best route to Semer Water is from Bainbridge on roads signposted to Countersett. I suggest this mainly because it means the views around the lake will be more of a surprise than if you approach on the high road from Burtersett.

Anyone wanting a day's expedition could walk instead from

Bainbridge, adding an extra four miles (6 km) in total. Semer Water is a lovely spot for a picnic.

The lakeside car-park is at the north-east edge of Semer Water. There is a small fee to be paid at the farm near the beginning of the walk. After paying, I explained that as I was already *en route* I didn't want to go back to put the ticket on display, which seemed to be all right. I don't think they have wheel-clamping arrangements here yet!

From the car-park, turn right and walk towards Low Blean Farm (the place to pay for the parking), then the footpath you need turns off to the right, taking you through the meadows alongside the lake.

Semer Water is one of only two natural lakes in the Dales, the other being the more famous, and more crowded, Malham Tarn. Semer Water is larger, but to my mind no less lovely. It was formed in the Ice Age by glaciers which chiselled out a deep bed, and then dumped debris at the far end to form a natural dam. Local folklore has a much more colourful story about the lake's origins. The tale tells of a wandering hungry angel who was refused food by the inhabitants of a city in this valley, on the site of the present lake. Only a poor crofter further up the hill shared his food with the angel. The city was cursed by the angel with a rhyme that caused the lake to rise and drown the selfish inhabitants sparing only the small croft. Over the years the water level has been known to rise and fall quite dramatically, and on one occasion signs of a Bronze Age settlement were seen, so who knows?

Nowadays, the water and surrounding marshland are a designated site of Special Scientific Interest (SSSI). Access to the shore is not permitted. Interesting wildlife collects here, including many species of mayfly which are quite difficult to spot. It is more likely that you will see bulrushes and water lilies, wintering birds and possibly whooper swans. These are birds known for their loud trumpeting call. They can also be distinguished by a yellow patch just above the bill, like the Bewick swan, but the whooper is bigger.

Follow the path across the fields, negotiating some very narrow stiles to the ruined chapel.

This is the old church built in the seventeenth century for the inhabitants of Stalling Busk, the hamlet just up the hill. There is enough of the building left to see the unusual design with the pews arranged around a central pulpit. The church fell into disrepair as it was felt to be too far from the village; a new church was subsequently built in the village centre.

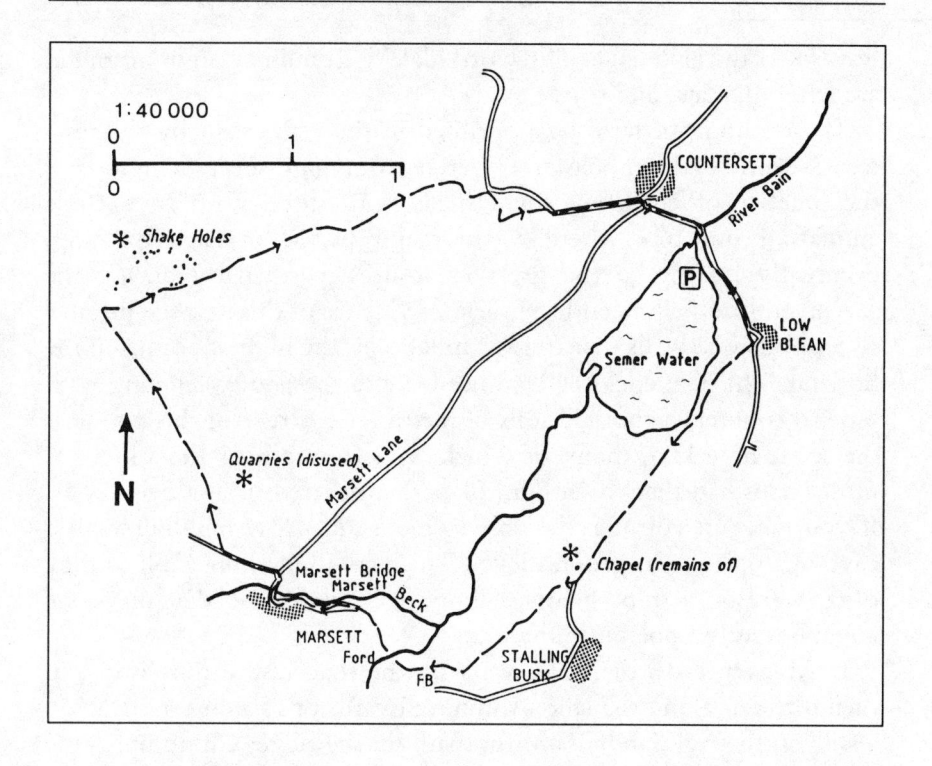

Carry on along the footpath beyond the church across more fields until you reach Busk Lane and a footbridge across Cragdale Water. Turn right down the track, crossing over Raydale Beck, and then follow the track into Marsett.

There are many 'setts' such as Marsett, Countersett and Burtersett in this area. The word 'sett' is from a Norse word for a house, 'saetr'. Over the years this has evolved to become 'seat', 'sett' or 'side'. It was more typical for Norse settlers, who came to The Dales between the seventh and eleventh centuries, to live either in isolated houses or with just two or three together rather than in village communities. They would graze their stock in the valleys in the winter and come to these higher reaches in the summer months. Even today many of these 'setts' are relatively small hamlets joined by ancient lanes. The Norse settlers not only contribute to today's pattern of the landscape with these far-flung hill farms, but also by the evocative names they gave to many features of the landscape. The word 'dale' is Scandinavian in origin, as are fell, gill, beck, and scar.

The tradition of farming flourished in the Dales, and by the thirteenth century, the monasteries were encouraging sheep-farming and the practice of enclosing small fields with stone walls to exclude animals. From 1600, there was a major period of farm building, eventually leading to the great enclosures, particularly during the seventeenth and eighteenth centuries. Evidence of this is in the massive sweeps of stone walls that run for miles over the highest points on the horizon. The new enclosed land needed clearing and sweetening with lime to counteract the acid soils of the moors. A relic of this period is the squat lime kiln, many of which were dotted over the valleys as most farms had their own kiln, or perhaps shared with a neighbour. If you look up you may be able to see a squat low building with a cave-like opening at ground level. This was a lime kiln, built as they often were on a slope below a limestone outcrop, so that the stone could be easily tipped into the top.

In Marsett, cross the beck, walk up the road just a short way and then turn left along the lane. A hundred yards or so along this track is a stile on the right and a faint footpath up the ridge. Climb up to the ridge-top where you should turn around for a splendid view of Semer Water. Behind is Addleborough with its flat profile. Here is a good place to stop and look over the valley to see the impact of a thousand years of settlements on the landscape. First imagine much of the land was covered with woods. Look for small irregular fields, cleared by early settlers, which contrast greatly with the enclosures of the 1600s and 1700s which took in huge areas of upland moor. The 1800s marked a time of quarrying and mining, and there are remains of workings to the right and an old track up the hillside. Far over to the right, towards Raydale, is a twentieth-century imposition, a dark blanket of conifers which has relentlessly crept over many British hillsides. Compare it with some of the small remaining areas of ancient woodland that remain, such as the little patch of variegated trees just below on this side of the valley.

From this ridge, to the north, you get a good view over Wensleydale and beyond to Great Shunner Fell, which is on the route of the Pennine Way.

To take further steps back in history, you can go over the ridge and drop down to a magnificent Roman road. This was built by the Roman general Julius Agricola in the first century AD during the campaigns against the Brigantes, one of the native peoples of Britannia. The road linked the small fort at Bainbridge with the important centre at Ribchester (see page 112).

To get back to Semer Water, stay on top of the ridge and follow the faint track until it goes sharply down the side of the hill, above a patch of woodland, and then joins a small road. You can walk down the road, but there is a footpath that takes you over another couple of fields, lower down, where you can join the road through Countersett. Then go over the sturdy bridge across the River Bain, which has the merit of being the shortest river in Britain. From here it is a short walk back to the car-park and the lakeside. Just here is a huge boulder, known as the Carlow Stone, which was transported here by a glacier, and dumped when the ice started to melt, though rumour has it that it was thrown by a giant off the top of Addleborough.

Turner featured this stone in his watercolour impression of Semer Water. The view now is perhaps a little busier than it was in his day. Gone are the motley collection of cattle, but there is still the wonderful expanse of water reflecting the sky, and the far hills diminishing into the blue distance.

From Semer Water, you can easily reach Hawes, a busy popular town higher up Wensleydale where there is a good information centre and the expanding Upper Dales Folk Museum.

Further up, towards Sedbergh, is the Sedgwick Geological Trail, named after the celebrated local geologist Adam Sedgwick and opened in 1985, two hundred years after his birth. It explains a good deal more about the Great Limestone Scar, and the influence of the rocks on the surroundings.

The Beadbonny Ash

OS Map 1:25 000, Outdoor Leisure Sheet 30, Yorkshire Dales: Northern and Central Areas
A circular walk of 6 miles (10 km). Allow 3–4 hours.

The 'Beadbonny ash' of the title, from Gerard Manley Hopkins' poem 'Inversnaid', came straight to mind when I saw the rowan tree in full berry leaning over the magical pool and waterfall at the top of this walk near Keld in Swaledale. It is the most wonderful setting, and on a good day you will certainly want to have a picnic here to make the most of it. Try to go late in the year even though the weather will be more chancy, because the rowan berries out in their full glory are a marvellous sight.

For me, Swaledale has a split personality, making it all the more fascinating to explore. On the one hand is its striking natural beauty with a 'wouldn't-it-be-nice-to-live-here' feel. On the other is the story of a tough life eked out of the land. In times gone by, as well as shepherds there were thousands who came to find prosperity through the mining of a variety of ores, particularly lead. Broken chimneys, collapsed tunnels and spoil tips remain on the landscape as forlorn evidence of this former industry.

Swaledale is hardly the standard picture of 'the industrial north' but, at the height of the lead-mining days of the eighteenth and nineteenth centuries, it was a major industrial centre. A census taken in 1851, when the industry was at its height, shows the population in Swaledale and the neighbouring Arkengarthdale to be nearly 7000. Mining wasn't just a preserve of the late 1800s, the Roman invaders were attracted by the prospect of lead, and ingots have been found which date from this period. In medieval times, the monasteries owned large tracts of the north. They used the land for farming, but were also able to make good use of their rights to mine. Lead was needed to cover the huge roof areas of churches, and documents record the export of lead to be used at York Minster.

This walk starts from the village of Muker, a thriving community in mining times, and loops round to Keld, then back along the River Swale. It is possible to look at remains of lead-mining activity while getting a chance to see stretches of heather on Kisdon Plateau and the glorious wooded ravine at Swaledale Head – all terrain that contrasts well with the Karst country further south.

The going underfoot is on good track, apart from a small section just as you drop down to Keld where it feels as though you are walking along the course of a stream for a few yards. There is a slow steady climb to the top of Kisdon, and then an easy descent. The return from Keld is flat apart from a short climb at the beginning. You may, however, want to do a little more scrambling to get down to see the waterfall in the heart of the gorge, but more of that later.

Navigation is relatively straightforward, with a road route option if you get off course, and the River Swale to follow on the way back.

Car-parking and the start

There is a small car-park on the southern bank of Straw Beck just as you drive into the village of Muker (pronounced Mewker) from Gunnerside and Ivelet.

Walk over the beck and into the village. Immediately, there is evidence of the importance of this former mining community. Amongst the sober grey-stone houses is the chapel, and the grandly named Literary Institute, both of which were built in the prosperous mining era.

Leave the main road and head into the centre of the village. Behind the Post office is a track that passes two more isolated houses and starts to wind up the hill. (You can follow the low path alongside the river but there is more variety if you climb the hill.)

Take the left-hand fork and follow the winding track up the hill. As you reach the plateau on the ridge, the path passes through almost a corridor of stone walls. At the top of this you meet the Pennine Way long-distance footpath, which skirts the north of the hill. Don't follow that route, but go on this track a little further, then fork right and follow the track, climbing again towards the top of Kisdon Hill. Here you are following the grimly named Corpse Way. This is an old route used by the locals to carry their dead from the upper part of the dale down to the church at Grinton which had a licence for burials. I imagine that on many days it was a grim task across this windswept plateau. The heathery moorland is a more cheering sight, sweeping across the hill and contrasting with the neat green enclosures of the valley below.

At the top are some old workings with a disused shaft, a tip, and a curious digging into the track itself, which seemed to lead nowhere.

The path now descends very gently, giving views over the valley and the steep-sided hills beyond. I was struck by the number of tiny barns dotted in practically every field. Although these were mainly built in the sixteenth and seventeenth centuries, they reflect the influence of the Norse invaders hundreds of years previously. Dale farmers used to practise methods of husbandry which were common in parts of Norway and the Alps. The technique was to have summer and winter pasturing, moving stock higher up in the warmer months and leaving new grass to grow in the valleys. The stone barns were used to shelter small numbers of stock or young animals, and the hay was kept in the loft above. In the square kilometre around Muker there are apparently over sixty barns. Many are now redundant due to the amalgamation of farms and a change in farming practice. They are consequently falling into disrepair. The loss of these little stone edifices would completely alter the character of the fields so there have been conscious efforts on behalf of the Dales National Park Committee to restore and revive barns, but as shelter for people not animals.

Follow the path around the side of the hill, and down the steep descent. You will see the road from Thwaite to Keld far below in the valley. When you get fairly close to the road, near the stream known as Skeb Skeugh, (a name that must surely have Nordic roots), on a part where the path turns a sharp corner left, look out for a triangle of rough open land to the right. At the top of this is a stile taking you on around the back of the hill to meet up again with the Pennine Way.

I found the first part of this path quite wet and rocky, but it soon came out into some drier terrain. Don't be tempted to drop down too early to join the main Pennine route, as you'll find yourself at the top of some impassable crags. Keep following the path around the corner of the hill; the path you need comes into sight below, and there is then just a short descent. Turn left.

A short way along here is a sign down to the Kisdon Force Waterfall, which is worth the detour. A feature of the Dales is the numerous and attractive waterfalls. An added pleasure is the way all the waterfalls seem to have a different character. They are given a variety of names – falls, spouts and forces, all seemingly well-matched to their meaning. Falls are where the water cascades over several shallow ledges of stone. Spouts are jets of water, as a stream rushes down a steep hillside. One of the most impressive of these is Cautly Spout on the Howgill Fells, which is about half an hour's walk to its foot from the road. If it rains during your time in the Dales then it will be even more impressive. Forces are where water is squeezed from a broad river into a narrow gorge and then tumbles eagerly over huge slabs of rock.

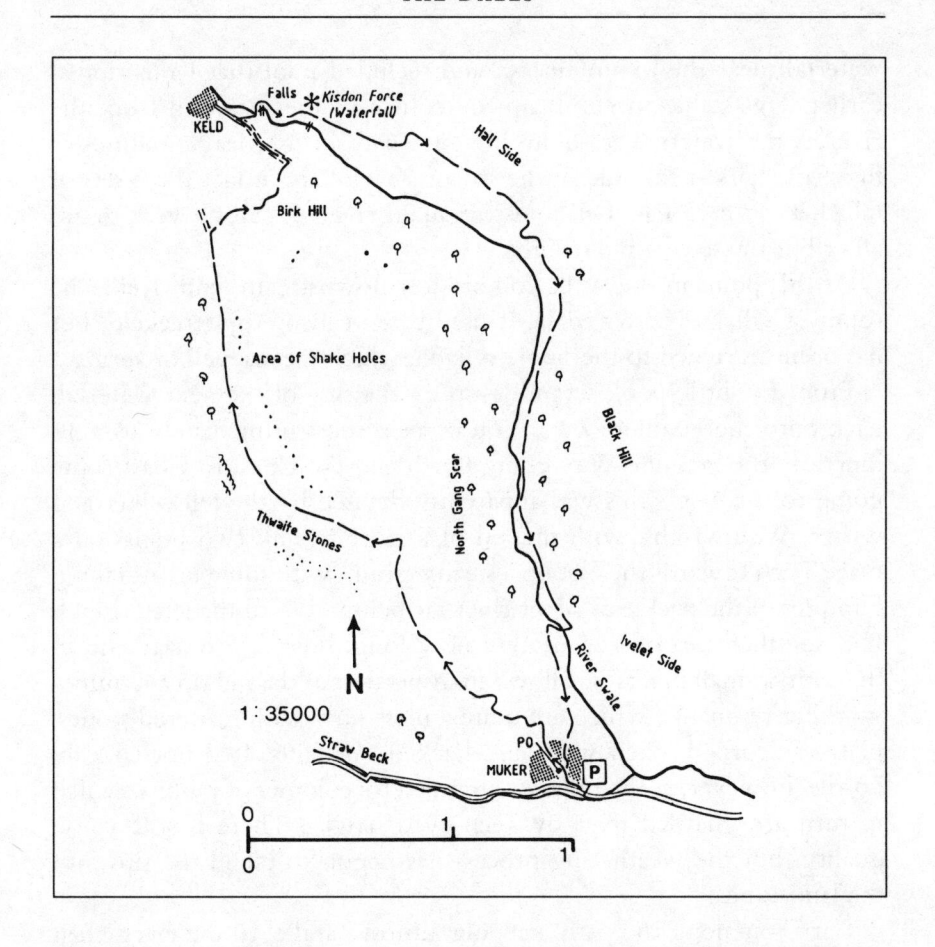

If you are not detouring to the river, simply follow the path above the woods until you reach a right-hand turn that descends to the footbridge over the Swale.

It was just down from this footbridge that I found the pretty waterfall near the mountain ash and secluded pool that I mentioned earlier. I was able to climb up the course of the waterfall from the river as the waters were quite low and had shrunk, leaving almost a flight of stairs at the side of the stream. There are in fact three sets of falls here, where East Gill joins the main river. It's not a very grand affair but the setting is a delight.

At this point in the walk you are just downstream from Keld, the topmost village in Swaledale. It used to be called Appletreekeld, but has been shortened to the single syllable which means well or spring.

From the little pool, scramble up by the side of the next waterfall back onto the Pennine Way. You come almost immediately to a T-junction, the Pennine Way going north and the Coast to Coast route going to the east – this was apparently devised by the fellwalker and writer, Wainwright, with the aid of a ruler to link two points on a map. Turn towards the east up a steady climb, with some breathtaking glimpses of the trickle of silver river far below. Up to the left is Beildi Hill, another area of lead-mining now long disused. From a bend in the path, a small diversion allows an inspection of the old tip and mine-working remnants, which are quite a mess now with scattered stones, piles of debris, broken walls and hacked out cliffs. It is not entirely hostile, however, as the hollows are filled by colonies of rabbits, which in turn are guarded over by keen-eyed hawks. There is still a raw quality, but the weathering process has begun to blend the tips into the landscape.

Carry on along the path, keeping almost parallel to the river, then bearing right below a ruined farm called Crackpot Hall, to cross the foot of Swinner Gill. There's another old ruin here that is also related to the Beildi Hill lead-mining. It's an old ore-processing place. Often there is a sign of mining activity near water, as water power was much used in the mining process. Wheels were built to grind the rock and drive the sieves used to separate the ore. Nearby smelting mills were also driven by water power.

After this, follow the path all the way along the river to the footbridge which takes you back over the flower-filled meadows to Muker.

Further down Swaledale are many other lead-mining communities such as Gunnerside and Reeth. Above Gunnerside, there is a walk to the Old Gang Smelt Hill which is now being restored. It's interesting how these industrial remains are now seen as valuable parts of our heritage, rather than eyesores.

Lower down the dale, the museum at Reeth has some interesting displays on the life of the lead miners and the rise and fall of the industry.

If you head up Swaledale into Garsdale you come to the attractive town of Sedbergh (sounding more like Sebber with local pronunciation). The centre has recently been given a facelift, with the central part cobbled with granite sett stones (square cobbles) and sandstone flags along the pavements. This main street is lined with old buildings interspersed with alleyways and yards. There is a solid old-fashioned air about the place which makes it well worth a wander.

Barnard Castle and Tees Dale

Barnard Castle, 'Barny' to the locals, is a friendly market town with one main street. This is Galgate, attractively wide and lined with trees. It sweeps around to the market place and the seventeenth-century market cross building, octagonal in shape, used over the years as a butter market, town hall and a lock-up.

The town is built on a scarp above the River Tees, which flows on, by a circuitous route, to disgorge into the North Sea near Middlesbrough. By then the river has more of an industrial character, reflecting its surroundings there. But here in the upper reaches of the dale, it is most attractive. One might hardly think that Teesside and Teesdale involve the same river.

As this dale lies outside of the main area of the national park, it tends to get a little overlooked. I have, however, enjoyed many rewarding walks around here. Some of these are well way-marked by the council, forming a series of short loops around Barnard Castle. There is a further series based around Cotherstone (pronounced Cutherstun) which is a village just to the north-west, another area well worth exploring.

Leaflets about these excursions are available free from the Tourist Information Centre.

You may find yourself following in the footsteps of one of England's best-known romantic painters, Turner, renowned for his expressionistic studies of light, colour and movement. He came to Teesdale painting many views and buildings, of which the best known are one to the south of the town, Egglestone Abbey and Mill, and another that you'll see on this walk, Barnard Castle from the Tees.

OS Map 1:50 000, Sheet 92
A circular walk of 3 miles (5 km). Allow 1½ hours or if 9 miles (15 km), allow 4–5 hours.

Whilst the longer walk merits a day's expedition, and you'll probably enjoy the picnic spot at Cotherstone, or the village pub, you can get a pleasant sense of the countryside from the shorter loop. The shorter walk is way-marked with the number 2 on yellow arrows as it is one of three routes that go in a circle from Barnard Castle.

The longer loop, the length really governed by the first crossing available over the River Tees, takes you to some gorgeous riverside settings, into the attractive village of Cotherstone, and then back along the Tees.

The going underfoot is fine, with just one field ploughed, but otherwise foot path, track, or old railway line. There are two short climbs, and quite steep descents. The route back along the Tees goes through quite a lot of grazing land so there are a number of gates to open (and close).

The navigation is not difficult as you can follow the numbered arrows to start with. When you leave this route, there is one spot where you need to look quite carefully for the path, then you'll be guided most of the rest of the way by the river.

Car-parking and the start

Apart from market day on Wednesday when some of the parking is taken over by stalls, you can usually find space somewhere on the main street, or in the large car-park by the Tourist Information Centre on Galgate.

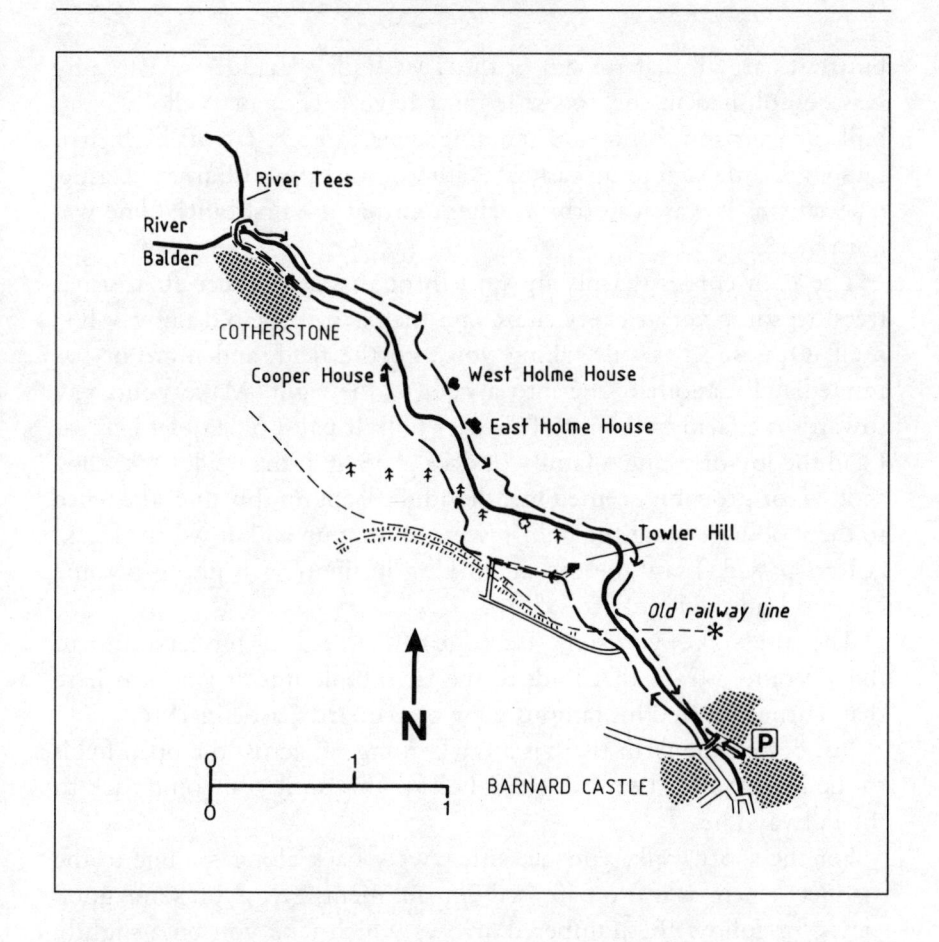

Walk down Galgate to the Post Office, which is just near the top of a green by the castle. Take the wide tarmac road by the childrens' swings down to the river. There is a substantial footbridge, the Tees Aqueduct Bridge, from which there is a good view of the castle.

Over the footbridge, turn right on the road, and almost immediately there is a kissing-gate and a track going across open pastureland. Follow the track for half a mile (1 km) and then fork right over a cattle grid and small stream past a cottage. Continue on the track just a short way and then take the narrow grassy path to the right, which climbs up towards the impressive remains of the former railway line. The buttresses are all that remain of the Tees Valley Viaduct which sadly was demolished in the 1960s. It must have been a marvellous sight, built of iron and stone, and standing over 130 feet (39 m) high. It is rather a shame to find no railway, either to or beyond Barnard Castle, especially as it was at nearby Darlington that the first official line was born in 1825.

The path curves sharply upward through some spruce (Christmas trees) to some very rickety steps, and then across the old railway line itself. Opposite is a stile taking you into the field, and more or less immediately, another stile into a field to the right. Make your way towards the farm buildings of Towler Hill. It pays to be quiet here, as I had the joy of seeing a family of deer playing in the field. Once they spotted, or probably scented me, the adults leapt nimbly over the fence to the woods, leaving the poor fawns running up and down the track. After I passed, I saw the parents lurking in the trees waiting to come out and lead the family to safety.

The route takes you along the edge of the field, then over a stile to the left onto a track that leads to the farm buildings. It was near here that Turner painted his famous view of Barnard Castle in 1816.

Just before the farm there is a track going off across the open fields to the left towards two oak trees. Follow this until you come back to the railway line.

For the short walk, you can either walk back along the line to the viaduct which, as it is on a raised embankment, gives you some good views, or follow the numbered arrows which take you on a slightly different route back to the cottage where you branched off to the viaduct.

For the longer walk, turn right up the track just before the railway line. In fact this was the Cotherstone branch of the railway that eventually went to Middleton-in-Teesdale. After a few hundred yards look out for a gap in the hedge on the right. This is easy to miss when the rosebay willow herb is in full flower.

Go straight across the field, keeping to the left of the spur of wood on the other side, then follow the hedge round until you see a path through the wood on your right. This descends quite steeply through a short strip of dark dense wood. It makes a splendid sight when you come suddenly to an open plateau with the river below. When I came here once in the fading light of evening, I emerged from the wood to find the space filled with rabbits, rather surprised at being so rudely interrupted and in a flash, they were gone.

Climb up towards the log cabin and then along the fields to Cooper House Farm. Just beyond the farm you join way-marked Walk 2 of the Cotherstone series.

In most of this section you are in sight of the wide river, and there are many places where you can get quite close to the banks.

The route drops down a slope to a stream, and then bears slightly left heading towards Tees View Farm. Beyond the farm you continue on the track until it turns left and then there is a grassy track which runs parallel to the river, past the old mill. Just beyond here is one of those isolated graves that are sometimes encountered. This one belongs to Abraham Hilton, a local benefactor, who died in 1902.

Carry on along the path and down the slope of Hallgarth Hill. This was the site of a twelfth-century castle owned by the Fitzhughs, who were the medieval lords of Cotherstone village. The last of the Fitzhughs fell to his death, with his horse, over one of the deep gorges cut by the River Tees. The place is known as Percy Myre Rock and is about one mile ($1\frac{1}{2}$ km) upstream.

The village of Cotherstone is extremely attractive, and blessed with a good pub if you feel in need of a pit stop. The village began as a small agricultural community in Anglo-Saxon times, and it was not until the nineteenth century and the coming of the railway that many cottages were refurbished and new houses built. I sampled the locally made Cotherstone Cheese, which is now available as far afield as London, but it is obviously best in its home location. It is a smooth white cheese with a surprising tang.

For the homeward route, take the first bridge, over the River Balder (named after the Viking God) — a boundary river between two ancient parishes.

Turn right and then cross the River Tees on the next bridge. Take the right-hand fork following the river around a wide grassy area which is a good place to picnic.

Beyond, downstream, is a path climbing up through the woods onto farmland. For the next mile or so, just keep parallel with the River Tees but some way above it. The route is well-marked with yellow arrows and appropriate stiles.

Once past West Holme House and East Holme House, look for the track that turns sharply off to the right which takes you down to the river. It is quite a steep descent and ends in a field. On the left-hand side of the field is a gate and the track leads close by the river.

I was struck here by the noticeable change in sounds from the water. One minute there was plenty of gurgling and splashing as the water cascades over mid-stream boulders, then suddenly there is silence where the river trawls over a smooth bed. The gorge is dramatic and rocky outcrops are exposed up the sides. This part is known locally as Rock Walk, and ends with two boulders where you can make a wish as you pass through. Beyond is a stone staircase framed by dark yew trees. The woods here are called Flats Woods and are all part of the Raby Estate.

The Raby Estate occupies a large tract of land to the north of the River Tees, with a castle at the attractive village of Staindrop. There are hundreds of farm buildings and cottages on the Estate, all of which are duly whitewashed by the tenants as part of their agreement. The origin of this, according to local stories, goes back to a lord of the manor, recently married and anxious to show his estate off to his new bride. When he began to point to the dwellings in the distance, she wasn't satisfied that they stood out sufficiently, and so from that day they have all been painted white.

If you go further up the dale towards Egglestone, there's a view from the road that is a mixture of rich green, dotted very noticeably with white buildings.

As you go through this stretch of woodland, you'll see many other paths through the woods which are not public rights of way, but permission has been given by the Raby Estate for the public to wander here.

The path ends by crossing Percy Beck, a small tributary of the Tees. Go round to the right and you will come back to the Tees Aqueduct Bridge.

While you are in this area, it is certainly worth going, on foot or otherwise, to the ruins of Egglestone Abbey. They are set close by the River Tees, and from there to the meeting of the waters at the striking Greta Bridge it is only a short way.

On all my walks here, I enjoyed the rich quality of the countryside with plenty to divert the eye – little buildings, softly sloping fields and heavily wooded gorges. It's tempting to feel it's rather cosy, but don't be entirely deceived. Go only a few miles out of Barnard Castle and you come across stretches of moors with little more than the rustle of grouse and the scurrying of sheep. Then it is easy to imagine the bitter winds of winter.

NORTHUMBERLAND

Northumberland is the least-populated English county. But whilst it may lack folk it is rich in unspoilt countryside and interest, much from the ever-turbulent times on the border.

A large piece of the county is reserved as one of Britain's ten National Parks. It well deserves this status, for the countryside is lovely, strong and appealing, open but with plenty of detail, somewhat wild, and often with a wonderful clarity to the views. Not surprisingly in view of its location, it's the least visited of the National Parks. I regard this as an attraction not a detraction. There has been heavy afforestation in the area of the Park, with some 20 per cent now covered with a monotonous green coat of conifer. The percentage would be even higher if the middle of Kielder Forest had not become a reservoir. Another 22 per cent is given over to the Army for some of the largest training areas in Northern Europe. Red flags often decorate the landscape warning the public off, and the booming of artillery is as much part of the rural sounds up here as the fluttering of the game birds and the bleating of sheep.

The Park is under threat from these two interests. But threats are nothing new for Northumberland. As a border county, invasions, wars and raids were a principal influence until comparatively recently. Not surprisingly, it's a terrific place to study fortifications, from the small dwellings known as 'peles' and 'bastles', through the fortified houses of the slightly more landed gentry, to the magnificent castles that are amongst the best-known in the country.

To recall the names of the historic families that lived here starts to sound like passage from Shakespeare with the Nevilles, Greys and, perhaps the most famous, the Percys, for Hotspur was one of them. Their lands and castles, their rivalry with the Scots and with other families, create much of the background into which a visit is woven. Think of a time when the country was ruled not by ministers such as the Secretary of State for the Environment, but by dukes such as the Warden of the Northern Marches.

There is plenty of excellent walking as this is a most spacious county. The Pennine Way finishes here with the last forty miles being a wet slog across the central Northumbrian Hills of the Cheviots. The Cheviot Hills can be quite bleak and forbidding or wild and romantic, depending on your point of view. I competed in a mountain marathon on these hills, crossing such atmospheric spots as Bloody Bush Edge and Windy Gyle, tramping along the old drovers roads of Clennel Street and The Street, then camping in the heart of the hills. On the second day, the cloud descended and I vividly remember climbing through the drifting cloud to a lonely ridge with peat hags (soft parts of the moor), an unforgettable feature of the Cheviot landscape, looming out of the mist. The stillness and the gloom were awesome. Walks such as this are memorable as long as you are well-prepared for inclement conditions and prepared to rely on a compass bearing or a companion who can navigate.

Not every venture has to be a mammoth expedition for the hardy hill walker. There are plenty of other good walks in this area, through most attractive valleys, and on kinder fells than Cheviot. The coast, too, is fascinating to explore with its golden sands and rocky headlands.

The ideas in this chapter cover a classic hill walk, inspections of relics of fortification, a look at the older landscape of the moorland and fell, and at some of its oldest inhabitants, the Wild White Cattle at Chillingham, as well as some estates of historic families. Each walk is near something of interest, so I expect you'll find that the days up here get full very easily. All are extensive enough to give a hearty day in preparation for matching refreshment.

Chillingham

This suggested day is the furthest north we get in this book. You may feel you're in a far-flung wild outpost. Bear in mind that all things are relative; the warden at the cattle park told me that the Greys, the ancestral family of this area, moved here from Wark-on-Tweed because it was right on the border, and life here was much easier.

Chillingham and its area are full of interest, and there is at least a day of very worthwhile exploring to be had. Sights include the Wild White Cattle, Chillingham Castle and the Church, both set in extensive grounds, and there's good walking from nearby Hepburn Forest to what I think is one of the best, and incidentally most easily accessible, viewpoints in Northumberland. The cattle and castle are not open in the winter, but I should think Northumberland is not a choice for many people at that time of year, anyway.

Chillingham Castle has been owned by the Greys since the thirteenth century. It was a major fortress of the borders, enjoyed many royal visits, and endured several sieges. The castle fell into decay in the 1930s but has been recently restored and is now open to the public.

St Peter's Church in Chillingham is known for the mid-fifteenth century tomb of Sir Ralph Grey and his wife Elizabeth. This is a much-decorated tomb-chest, with alabaster figures of the two principals on the top. Its purpose was image-building, to assist the establishment of the Greys here at Chillingham. It certainly leaves a powerful impression.

The Wild White Cattle of Chillingham

A certain amount of mystery surrounds this herd of pure white cattle. It's thought that their ancestors were not imports from the Romans but oxen who lived in Britain in prehistoric times, roaming wild over the great forests that covered the northern part of the country. The existing herd has been corralled here for the last seven hundred years, since the castle of Chillingham was given permission to enclose its lands by means of an estate wall. Wild and fierce beasties such as these, with their wicked horns, were unlikely to be stolen by a party of cattle thieves from the north, but they made a good source of food. There are scant records on the herd, going as far back as the seventeenth century, when a total of twenty-eight 'beastes' were in the herd, and the numbers haven't increased by that many since. Now the herd stands at around fifty, as more grass has been available due to the recent mild winters, and the three hundred acres (121 ha), which is now the province of the herd, will support just about that many. There is no culling here by man, only by nature in terms of the fittest surviving and the resources of the land limiting the numbers. 'Wild' as a description of the cattle is no joke. They are not treated by vets, nor will they eat grain or concentrates or accept a calf who has been handled or fed by man. The bulls are hefty fearsome animals but the cows can be equally aggressive, especially if they have young.

To visit the cattle you need to go to beyond the entrance to the Chillingham Estate to where there is a small amount of roadside parking. After obtaining a ticket from the warden's house, walk through the estates to a sort of wooden bus-shelter amongst the trees. Here you need to wait for some minutes for the warden, who is generally patrolling the park with the previous party of visitors. As he says, the cattle know how to take care of themselves, it is the visitors who need looking after.

The warden accompanies you to find the cattle and is more than willing to answer questions. A marvellous sense of anticipation is built up as you're never quite certain what you'll come across. I saw two young calves playing around a watchful mother; not twins, though, as there has never yet been a multiple birth, nor for that matter a calf that isn't anything but pure white.

As to the cattle themselves, they have quite a different look from the present domestic type. For one thing the cows don't look like travelling milk-floats staggering around with distended udders. They have a lean look, and as the warden pointed out, are still built with strong forelegs to carry them away from trouble, rather than cattle today, which have been bred to have a good hindquarters, or 'rump', to satisfy the butcher.

Another surprise was seeing the flock of sheep contentedly grazing in the park, co-exisiting very happily with the cattle. As we turned to return to the bus-shelter, there was movement in the wooded area ahead of us some thirty yards away. That animal there, said the warden calmly, is the king bull. One look through the binoculars made me see why. He was a massive beast with impressive horns and a classic bull neck which was coated with short rough hair. Only the fittest and strongest bull is king. Whilst king, he is the one to sire the progeny, thus ensuring a strong line runs through the herd. He remains leader until another bull is successfully able to challenge him in a contest. Curiously the fighting doesn't often result in a death, only the loser slinking away from the herd for a while to lick his wounds before being accepted back.

Seeing these animals brings you close to a fascinating piece of living heritage.

Ros Castle

OS Map 1:50 000, Sheet 75
A walk of 3 miles (5 km) but longer is possible. Allow $1\frac{1}{2}$ or up to $3\frac{1}{2}$ hours if you want an extended walk.

Although the name might imply otherwise, this is not a fortress but a hill, given to the National Trust in memory of Sir Edward Grey of 'the lights are going out all over Europe' fame. He frequently used to climb to this spot to enjoy the view. Although not a fortress itself, it does provide a view of several: Lindisfarne, Bamburgh, Dunstanburgh, Chillingham certainly, and some literature claims more.

You can drive very close to Ros Castle, but if you want a short walk, park at the Hepburn Wood picnic site.

There are several way-marked walks which start at the picnic site. Each walk follows a different coloured arrow. The green is the shortest (allow about an hour) and it takes you mostly on forest roads, the first part of which used to be a carriage drive created by the former owners.

The orange markers (allow $1\frac{1}{2}$ hours) take you partly along the green route but then higher up the hills beyond the forest boundary to Hepburn Crag camp. This is a small hill fort dating from 2000 BC. You get good views of Chillingham Park from here.

Most exciting of all, though, is a longer walk to Ros Castle.

Follow the orange markers through the wood up to Hepburn Crag Fort and then across the road. Ahead is the steep conical hill of Ros Castle rising out of the bracken-covered moors. There are vague traces of earthwork ramparts as this too was once the site of an Iron Age hill fort. Despite the commanding views from the top, no one ever capitalized on this site for a castle.

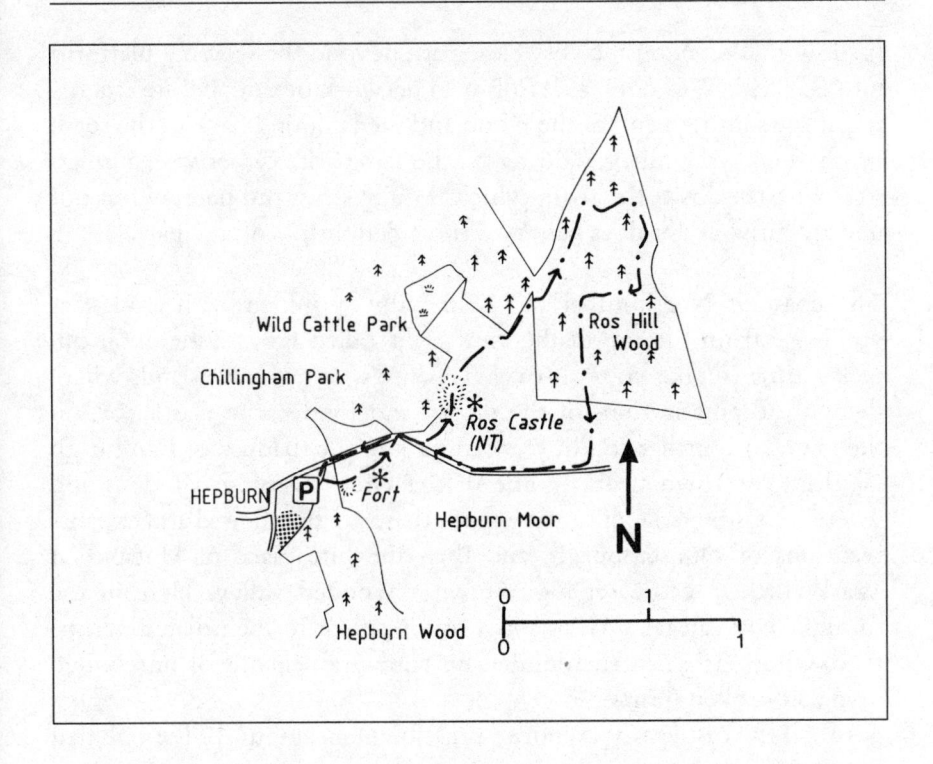

There are several paths leading up the very steep slope to the summit's trig point. Above this is a stone-built platform with direction and distance indicators on three sides. I was lucky on my second visit here to pick a perfect day for viewing. I strongly recommend that you take binoculars.

You can see right across the estates of Chillingham Castle to the imposing range of the Cheviots. The profiles of Cheviot and Hedgehope Hill are easily picked out. Scotland is to the north and the Simonside Hills to the south. Looking the other way, towards the coast, even with the naked eye you can pick out the castle on Holy Island as well as the massive fortress at Bamburgh and the skeletal one at Dunstanburgh. Further round to the right, amongst hills, are the town of Alnwick, and the more distant Newcastle.

Having had your fill of all the sights, follow the way-marked walk (yellow markers), on the very clear path beyond the viewing platform into Ros Hill Wood. Here it follows a network of rides before emerging at the southern end of the wood and then coming back to the road. From there you can get down to the car-park. Otherwise, just go straight back down the road, which is quite steep and narrow but not unduly busy, and it does pass by a most delightful cottage garden.

The coast of Northumberland is liberally sprinkled with castles, as you'll see from the top of the viewpoint called Ros Castle. You can pick a time to take yourself over the causeway to Holy Island, where there are dramatic ruins of the priory and Lindisfarne Castle, or, on the mainland further south, you can park in the shadow of Bamburgh Castle. (The town is also home of the Grace Darling Museum and several restaurants.) Continuing south there are the rugged and expansive ruins of Dunstanburgh, and then the birthplace of Hotspur at Warkworth, a castle set high above a wooded valley. Here in the summer you can take passage in a rowing-boat to the isolated hermitage, whose origin is surrounded by romantic legends of unrequited love and broken hearts.

Of all the castles my favourite must be Dunstanburgh, the one that demands the most exercise to reach – even the warden gets there on foot! I think the absence of the car helps to give a better sense of what the castle might have been like in its prime, even though it is much ruined compared to the others.

Dunstanburgh Castle

OS Map 1:50 000, Sheet 75
A four-mile (6 km) there-and-back walk, with potential to extend along the coast. Allow 2 hours to include a visit to the castle.

'In wonderfull great decaye' was how Dunstanburgh was described in 1550. This wasn't written for tourists, of course, but it's exactly the phrase to describe the castle of Dunstanburgh for visitors nowadays. The combination of remaining stonework and the setting make it a very special site, and it's even better because no cars can get to it. If possible, pick a day when there is plenty of weather about in order to fully appreciate the castle.

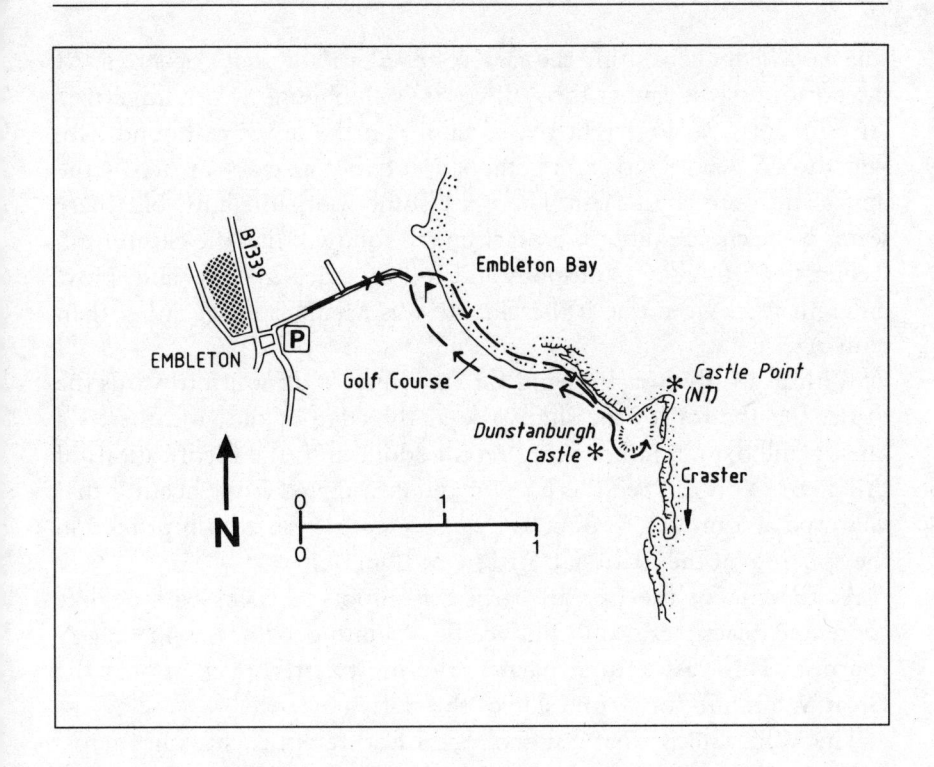

You can approach it from Craster, the little town to the south, or from Embleton, a village to the north. I prefer the northern approach as from Embleton Bay you get the splendour of the severe cliff of the Great Whin Sill on which the castle is built. The northern approach also offers the option of extending the walk at the end to include a coastal nature reserve.

The going underfoot is fine, as you have the choice of walking by a path alongside the golf course, or on the sandy beach. The area around the castle is all grassed. This walk is mainly level going, with a short climb at the end up to the castle.

Car-parking and the start

Park at Embleton village car-park, or by the roadside which leads down to the links. Then walk down the lane to the golf course. The lane has a hedge separating the cars from pedestrians, so it's no strain. At the bottom of the lane is the golf course's clubhouse, which advertises refreshments. Passing right by, certainly on the outward-bound trip, you should head south along the side of the fairway, or across the dunes and onto the beach. There are some footpath signs, but there seems to be choice about the exact line to follow. I like the clean, fresh feeling here; the bay is unspoilt and full of a rich golden sand. How different it all would be if the climate was Mediterranean rather than semi-Arctic.

With probably just the wind for company, walk south towards the castle. On the top of the slight rise at the edge of the sand there's a line of pillboxes, a rather more recent addition to the fortifications of this coast. You can see the lines of the corrugated iron sheeting that was used as a mould – rather as the wooden pattern was imprinted in the concrete of the National Theatre in London.

At the end of the bay are large sea-smoothed rocks basking like contented black seals, and above, the daunting cliff rises in craggy contrast. This vast natural barrier, the most easterly outcrop of the Great Whin Sill, forms one side of the castle's defence.

The Whin Sill is a natural geological feature which stretches across northern England. It was formed by a lava flow solidifying underground between other rock. Over millions of years, erosion and faulting has left the layer exposed as numerous escarpments. These are tailor-made for defensive purposes, and are used to great effect in the line of the Roman fortifications along Hadrian's Wall.

Dunstanburgh is the largest ruined castle in Northumberland. It is owned by the National Trust and is in the care of English Heritage.

The castle was started at the beginning of the fourteenth century by the Earl of Lancaster and was enlarged by John of Gaunt. A gaunt place it is too, with what little building remains standing like bare bones on a vast courtyard swept by the wind and rain. The nooks and crannies of the ruins and the cliffs now belong to the birds and the air is full of the screeching of gulls and kittiwakes. You may also see the odd pile of feathers where a peregrine has taken a fancy to the place, finding the pigeons in the keep an easy target.

From the castle mound you can see the village of Craster to the south. You can extend the walk there along grassy paths if you wish. Alternatively you should return north. Another way to extend the walk is to carry on along the coast to a nature reserve that is north beyond the golf course. However long you make the walk, I hope you'll be left with a memory of a spectacular site, and a sense of wonder about the castle.

The Coquet Valley

The classic view of Northumberland is one of wild open moorland stretching into a heathery distance. But a different picture is presented by the rivers, cutting their way through wooded valleys, twisting and turning along the route, and providing shelter for little villages that nestle in the crook of a bend. One of the prettiest of these river valleys is Coquetdale.

Even within the shelter of the valley, you are never very far from the elements. I came here first in patchy fog; walls of mist obscured the far view, while close at hand grey wisps hung like cobwebs in the trees, enclosing the road.

On a clear day, the wooded glades and winding course of the river are full of colour, from burgeoning green in the variegated trees in spring to the mellow silver and gold that stand out in an autumn sun.

The River Coquet begins high in the Cheviots and is fed by many tributaries rising in the hills near the Pennine Way. The dale was first settled in prehistoric times as evidenced by the hill forts dotted along its course. The Romans came here later, on their route ever-northward. They created a huge camp at Chew Green at the top of Coquetdale, near where one of the tributaries springs. Anglian farmers came here to the foothills of the Cheviots, looking for grazing land and shelter, too.

The middle ages saw the advent of monasteries, which owned much of the north and had rights to graze, sending their flocks up to the moorland in summer. Drovers' roads were created for the sheep traffic. Clennel Street and The Street still exist. They cross over Coquetdale and then go north over the border, meeting at Alwinton, which is the first of the ten towns of the dale. The hill-farming tradition has been carried on here and each year's season ends with the Annual Border Shepherds' Show.

Further down the valley is Rothbury, heralded as the capital of Coquetdale, but more fondly called by the locals 'The Village'. It is a pleasant place with a wide high street and shops well set back from the road. Just by the church is a triangle of green and a memorial cross, which is also a good place to park. There's a friendly feel here with visitors welcomed. As I was changing into my fell shoes an old chap asked me if I was off over the hills. When I said yes, 'Good on you lass,' came the reply.

The Simonside Hills

OS Map 1:50 000, Sheet 81
A circular walk of 7 miles (12 km). Allow 4 hours.

On either side of the valley, at Rothbury, there are attractive hills that are good for walking. To the south are the Simonside Hills. They form a most distinctive shape, climbing on a gentle slope punctuated by three slight lumps and then ending abruptly with a craggy full-stop. The silhouette can be seen from many parts of Northumberland, which is most satisfying if you've already walked up it. On the top you have reached a height of over one thousand feet (304 m), which means, strictly speaking, that it is a mountain, and a very accessible one, too.

Having said that, this expedition is quite strenuous as although the ascent is gradual, it is a climb after all.

The navigation is fairly easy, especially on a clear day when the peaks are obvious. There is also a very good path climbing the ridge, though the descent from the forest needs a little more care, but you can of course simply retrace your steps.

Do be well-equipped and prepared for sudden changes of weather. It is a good idea to have windproof clothing even in the best weather as there's almost certain to be a breeze which can be chilling. I think it is wise to have a compass, and something like a bar of chocolate just in case. The going underfoot will be wet in places, especially in the peaty parts of the moor and on the descent through the forest.

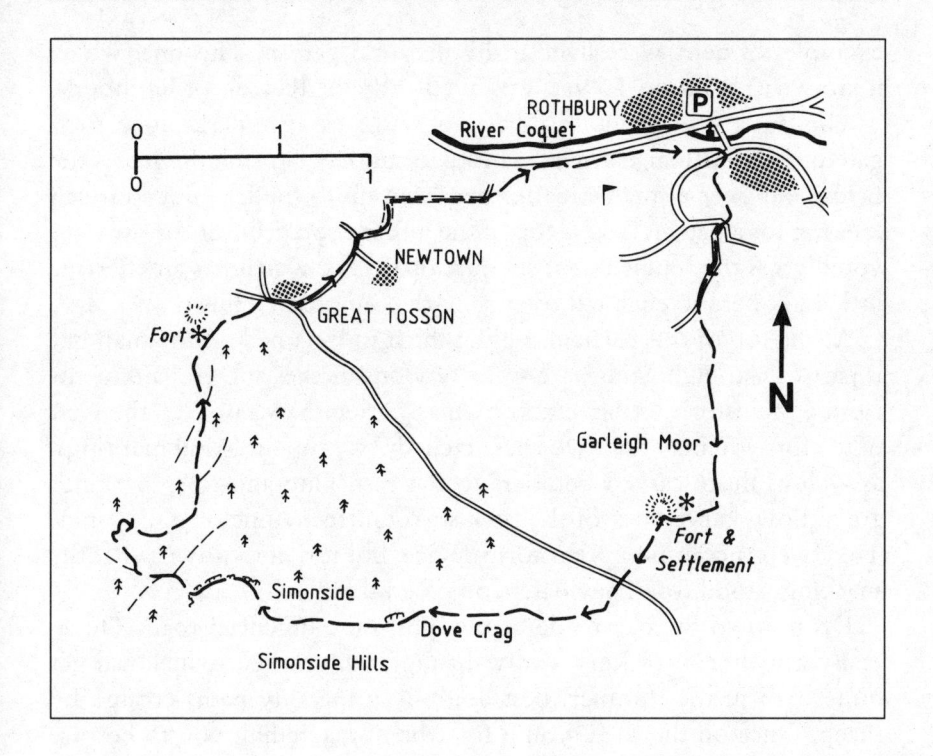

Car-parking and the start

Park in the centre of Rothbury by the church. In the church are buried the foundations of the original castle and hall built as border fortifications, which gave the name Haw (originally Haa) to the hill leading to the river.

You can cut down a small alleyway to the river. Then turn left towards the sturdy medieval bridge, originally built to carry the packhorses on the toll road to Hexham, but now somewhat altered for modern transport. Once over the bridge, veer slightly right and head up the steep hill on the narrow lane. Beyond here you come to a stretch of open land. Keep on climbing. Once over the crest there are a cluster of houses making up the small hamlet of Whitton, and a little gate where you come out onto the road. Turn right and then almost immediately left up a small lane towards an isolated circular tower. This was a pele, the name given to a fortified dwelling and a very necessary precaution so close to the border. It was certainly a style of architecture favoured by the church as some of the best remaining examples of peles were lived in by the local parson. This one, which is known as Whitton Tower, was lived in by the Rectors of Rothbury.

The lane curves around to the right past a caravan park. Look for a gate on the left marked with a footpath notice. Go straight across the fields, and over a small stream, then head up to the left, not so much looking for a path as for the top of the hill. As you get near the summit, you'll cross the boundary of the National Park which has an effective little kink here to enable it to enclose the Simonside Hills.

At the top of this particular hill, which isn't named on the map but is part of Garleigh Moor, are some obvious ditches and embankments from a prehistoric settlement known as Lordenshaw Fort. To the west of the fort you may find two rocks etched with cup-and-ring markings, as well as more carved boulders to the east. Cup-and-ring markings are hollows carved out of the rock surrounded by one or more rings. They were a common prehistoric device, but it is not known what the markings stood for. They date from 2000–1000 BC.

Drop down the other side of the hill to the unfenced road. This is really a matter of picking a way through the bracken, which can get quite high in the summer; best done by using tiny paths created by sheep. Once on the road, you'll find the notice telling you to beware of adders! So from here on I picked my way through subsequent bracken with a little more caution than before. With luck you won't be disturbed by the rattle of a snake. It is more likely to be grouse, which can fly out of nearby undergrowth at a tremendous rate, clucking and calling, and probably more startled than you.

The route crosses the road and starts up a clear track and then branches off to the right along the ridge. Climb along the ridge, over the first slight hill, the Beacon, and then on to a small outcrop of rocks known as Dove Crags. Here there is plenty of stone available to add one to the cairn on the top for tradition's sake.

Beyond is another craggy mass, Old Stell Crags, slightly to the left of the path, and finally a gentle slope brings you to Simonside. This stands at 1407 feet (429 m), so just creeps into the official mountain bracket. From the top of Simonside you get splendid views of the Cheviots and Rothbury and Thrupton in the valley below.

Don't go rushing over the top, as there is a very sheer drop down the other side, well-loved by climbers.

Apart from taking in the view, it is worth pausing to study the track layout below you. It makes it easier to choose the right path home for the circular route. The forest is mature and some felling may have taken place since your map was prepared. You should see where the path down from the crags meets a forest road, which then goes straight ahead over the next rise, joined by rides coming in from the left. The path you need goes off the forest road on a diagonal to the right.

The descent from the crags is quite steep. Once on the forest road, walk away from the crags and then look for the track to the right. This takes you through the forest for a short distance, and then ends at a T-junction with a rather overgrown wide but grassy track. Here, turn right, following the track as it winds around the top of a steep valley. After this, there's a crossroads of paths and you need to turn left. This footpath descends for some way, at first through rough wooded areas and then along a short section that is quite dark and deliciously pine-scented with good but soft going underfoot.

It comes out at a forest road a few yards from the bottom edge of the woods. Turn right to the stile that is just up the road on the left-hand side. Here, follow the footpath down towards the farm house, passing a clump of trees and the earthworks of yet another prehistoric fort.

Walk along the lane and then take the left-hand fork down the hill towards Newtown. At the junction, turn left and you'll see the bridle-way marked to Rothbury. This follows the line of the River Coquet, crossing on a footbridge where you can pause to admire the swans and the clear water, so clean you could see easily to the bottom. The rewards of Rothbury are at hand.

Cragside: The Palace of the Modern Magician

You may feel you have the energy to visit Cragside on the same day as climbing Simonside, but it really merits a visit on its own. There is plenty to take in, and a good two-mile walk (3 km) around just part of the estate.

Cragside is a National Trust property set in what is now described as a country park. It was the home of the nineteenth-century industrialist, William George Armstrong, who developed his company's Elswick works on the Tyne into a world-leading manufacturer of ordnance and industrial machinery. It advertised itself as the largest warship-building plant in the world in 1914. He was also an inventor and was fascinated by electricity, especially the hydro-electric sort. Through clever damming of streams on the Cragside estate, Lord Armstrong was able to have his home lit by hydro-electric power. This was only the second house in the country with electric lights; the first was that of his friend, Joseph Swan, the inventor of the light bulb. No wonder he was nick-named a modern magician.

The house is a massive Victorian pile designed by Norman Shaw. Pevsner's adjective for it is 'Wagnerian'. Every room is filled to the brim with memorabilia, furnishings, and all the 'stately home' trimmings. The result is, that although Wagnerian on the outside, it feels extremely cosy, friendly and attractive on the inside, more so than many houses one may visit. There is the most staggering marble fireplace in one wing, and an equally sumptuous Turkish bath in the basement.

Many rooms are hung with Pre-Raphaelite pictures of mermaids and other flowing-lock females frisking round or grappling with nature. The romantic feeling in the house continues into the garden where Lord Armstrong lavished much attention. He created a dramatic rock garden. He laid out a great system of roads for enjoyment of the estate. He planted literally millions of trees, many of which have grown to immense heights. In early summer the grounds are ablaze with colour from rhododendrons, which have taken so well to the soil that preventing them swamping the estate is a continual headache.

Through the grounds there is a walk called the Power Circuit, a well-marked route taking you around the elements of the hydro-electric system that powered the house. The machinery is not in use today and the cleanliness of it all is rather deceiving. There is, however, one pump that can be made to operate. I found it most satisfying to watch the slow-moving pistons, pushed by water, pivot a huge iron hammer until it fell with a resounding thump!

The Power Circuit also takes you through a romantic gorge, exactly what the Victorians thought was nature at her most spectacular, and across and alongside a series of bridges, some rustic in wood, some ivy-covered, and one impressive span, known as the Iron Bridge (but in fact made of steel), which was one of the first of its type in the world.

As well as the house and the walk, there are many other acres of estate to explore and a fascinating exhibition in the visitors centre about Lord Armstrong's life and his associations with leading industrialists and inventors of the day. There is a display on the various forms of electricity including how much electricity you can generate by holding hands, so take a friend.

Northumberland is known more for its castles than its stately homes, but there are some unusual houses that are interesting to seek out. I found two similar and yet contrasting houses, Belsay and Wallington, just south of the Simonside Hills and only separated by a few miles.

Visiting both houses, possible in one day if you wish, gives you a chance to compare different aspects of each estate as well as to see the influence of development due to living in the border regions.

I feel it is best to go to Belsay first, as it is here that you can see so vividly the transformation of a dwelling from times of border strife and conflict to days of peace. Belsay is also a shell, whereas Wallington has a packed interior, so there is more to look forward to by going there later.

Belsay

OS Map 1:50 000, Sheet 88
For a tour of the house and gardens allow 2 hours.

Belsay is on the main A696 Newcastle to Jedburgh road. The estate is in the care of English Heritage.

I was somewhat surprised on my first visit to drive up the sweeping estate road and find myself confronted with a classical-style hall where I had been expecting a castle. The castle is actually a short distance from the Hall, through the quarry that provided the stone for its building, and which is now an awe-inspiring garden. There is an excellent guide-book, so no fear of getting lost.

Belsay Castle, despite its obvious fortifications, is a very homely affair. It was built by the Middleton family in the late fourteenth century, when life on the borders was at its most precarious. The living quarters are more luxurious than castles built solely for defence. It is basically a single cube in shape. There was a kitchen on the ground floor, the great hall and principal chambers were above, and there was a little bit of privacy in small rooms within the corner towers. It was some three hundred years later, just after the accession of James VI of Scotland to the English throne, before anyone risked building an unfortified house. The Middletons were the first to do so, adding a central manor house right by the castle, and a large extra wing a hundred years later. This group of buildings, unoccupied and a little decayed, remains today.

In complete contrast is the classical Hall which is seen to good advantage on the sweeping carriage-drive through the grounds. This house was built by Sir Charles Monck, a Middleton by birth who changed his name to his mother's maiden name in order to inherit her parents' estates. It was on a two-year honeymoon that Sir Charles became interested in Classical architecture, being impressed by the Neo-Classical style of architecture in Germany, and also by the Acropolis in Athens where he stayed for a year. Whilst two years may seem long for a honeymoon, apparently it might have been even longer had the Napoleonic Wars not been raging over Europe at the time. His new Hall was started in 1807 and was ready to move into some ten years later.

The building is a perfect square of a hundred feet (30 m). I found the exterior rather severe, not helped by the sheeting rain, but the interior came as more of a shock. The place is completely barren of furnishings or fittings, a condition of English Heritage's guardianship of the property. It is like seeing a stately home in a very unstately condition with bare floors and walls, empty library shelves and echoing rooms. It made me realize how accustomed we are, now, to all the cosy trappings of country house interiors which can distract attention from the building. Probably Sir Charles would have been pleased to have visitors survey his design without distraction. I found the sense of desertion added a strange atmosphere.

The new Hall was built from honey-coloured stone quarried on the estate. Once the building was complete, Sir Charles and later his grandson, Sir Arthur Middleton, created a series of contrasting gardens from the strictly formal to the wildly romantic.

A tour of the gardens (which takes you round to the castle) is about one mile (1.5 km).

In front of the house is the beautiful formal terrace with a dazzling summer display of rhododendrons. Round the corner is the enclosed formal garden complete with croquet lawn and hoops. This is known as the Winter Garden as it is planted with a mixture of winter-flowering heathers and shrubs. Go on through a small door half-buried in ivy in true *Secret Garden* tradition, so much so that I almost expected to be greeted by a robin. Once across the lane, the atmosphere is quite different. There's a riot of plants with a backdrop of quarry cliffs, in some cases towering overhead. Ferns and mosses spring from the nooks and crannies, and trees cling precariously to the crags above. For students of flora, fauna or trees, this part of the garden is a must.

WALLINGTON

OS Map 1:50 000, Sheet 81
Wallington is off the B6342, a road off the A696 just south east of Kirkwhelpington.
Allow 1 hour for a tour of the house, 3–3½ hours for the Wannie Line Walk.

Wallington, some six miles (10 km) north-west has a different feeling. It too started as a pele, with a Tudor house added in more peaceful times, but signs of these buildings have vanished. Only the basement of the old castle exists today; it forms cellars under the present house. This was built at the end of the seventeenth century. Like Belsay, the design is square with an internal courtyard. The courtyard was roofed over in 1855 and filled with Romantic Pre-Raphaelite paintings by the Northumbrian artist William Bell Scott.

The interest comes in the interior. Whereas Belsay is stark, this place is packed from floor to ceiling with porcelain and paintings. Upstairs is a room christened 'A museum of Curiosities'. I would have transferred this title to the bathroom, which is filled with a range of extraordinary devices, including a bath that looks like a gargantuan metal boot! There is also a huge leather-covered stool, apparently for bouncing on to tone up muscles needed for riding. The guide told me shyly that one or two of them had given it a go.

The whole estate, which includes a good deal of land surrounding the house, was given to the National Trust in 1941 by Sir Charles Trevelyan Bt, who wished it to be kept as a complete unit and held in perpetuity for public enjoyment. It was one of the first houses to come to the Trust under the Country House Scheme, which permits the owner and his heirs to continue to live in the property after the Trust take responsibility for it.

The Wallington Estate is enormous and includes extensive gardens as well as the numerous farms. So pleasant walking can be had near the house, but at certain times of the year there is a rather special walk available.

The Wannie Line Walk (June to October only)

The Trust have devised an excellent walk they've called the Wannie Line to run for seven miles (11 km) through the Wallington Estate. It uses two disused railways joined by tracks and footpaths. I can recommend it as the way-marking is good, and it is all easy underfoot.

You'll need to get the leaflet, which includes a map, from the National Trust shop at Wallington. The walk starts and finishes at Scot's Gap, about three miles (5 km) away, behind a dark house that is the National Trust Regional Office. There are plenty of points of interest along the route. The two railway lines were the Wannie Line (1865) and the Rothbury Line (1870), which were both built originally to carry produce from the Wallington Estate. They were short lines of twenty-five miles (40 km) and thirteen miles (21 km) respectively, though this was quite common at the start of the railway boom particularly in Northumberland and County Durham where there were so many tracks that they were nicknamed Newcastle Roads. Apart from carrying lime, coal and livestock, they were also used by passengers. The line was single-track, sometimes with the signals for each direction being mounted on a single post.

On the walk you can see some distinctive ridge and furrow marks, signs left by the medieval farmer, and a most unusual lime kiln standing by a disused quarry. It is a four-arched structure, beautifully constructed. The fuel and limestone was put in at the top and the draught through the arches sent the fire burning at the base through the fuel and stone above, with the first lime ready to be drawn off two or three days later.

One of my favourite sections of the walk goes along a gurgling brook through the heart of a dense wood.

However, do remember that this walk is only open from June to the end of October in order that the lambing and calving seasons are not disturbed.

Driving from Wallington to the start of the walk you pass through the village of Cambo, a planned village and incidentally where Lancelot 'Capability' Brown was educated.

The North Tyne Valley

This walk explores the upper reaches of the North Tyne Valley. Like the Tees, the Tyne's character changes dramatically as it flows to the sea. In its early life it's a pretty mountain river, but by the time it reaches the conurbation at Newcastle it's a heavy-duty resource. The main river valley of the North Tyne and its tributaries of Tarset Burn and the River Bede run through remote countryside, but have always provided a natural communications route. Because of this the remoteness didn't stop it being a dangerous place to live when England and Scotland were separate kingdoms. These valleys were obvious corridors for Scottish raiders, so there were many fortified houses, some of which remain. Two of the finest, privately owned, can be seen on this walk, as well as one that although in a ruinous state is open to the public.

The first major town on the North Tyne is Bellingham, known as the capital of the valley. The last 'gham' by the way is pronounced 'jum' if you want to feel less of an outsider. It is an attractive, ancient market town, named after the De Bellingham family who were once foresters of the King of Scotland. They erected an earth and timber castle, though the only evidence of this, now, is a grassy mound by the old railway station. There are other signs, too, of a more turbulent age. The church has a roof of stone slabs, thought necessary after the previous timber roof was destroyed one night by one of the many Scottish raiding parties.

There are some gentle walks around Bellingham, the most well known being the two-mile stroll through a wooded dene (the local word for valley) up to Hareshaw Linn, a thirty foot (9 m) waterfall to the north of the town.

To the west of Bellingham, you'll find a series of open moors which give the essence of the lonely nature of the Tyne Valley. But there is plenty of interest here with an attractive picnic spot to discover, a look at the precautions taken against fourteenth-century invaders, and a chance to see a very different type of twentieth-century invasion of the landscape, Kielder Forest.

Black Middens and Bastle Houses

OS Map 1:50 000, Sheet 80
A circular walk of 5 miles (8 km). Allow $2\frac{1}{2}$–3 hours.

This walk is on very mixed terrain, starting with a forest ride that in parts is very boggy, continuing out onto open moor, and finishing on roads and grassland. There are fields to cross, bridges and a ford. There is some climbing but the gradients are gentle.

The overall navigation is not difficult and the area is bounded by roads should you get off course. But there are two sections where you need to look carefully for the path.

Car-parking and the start

The parking for this walk is in a secluded Forestry Commission picnic site just at the eastern edge of Kielder Forest (grid ref: 778 890) which is marked on the OS map.

To get there, drive through Bellingham towards the village of Greenhaugh. Carry on through the village, ignoring a turning to the right. After turning a sharp corner you'll find a bridge across Tarset Burn. Keep straight on this road heading towards Sidwood. The road is single-track and in places not in very good condition but it is quite suitable for ordinary cars. On entering the forest, keep going for about half a mile (1½km), then take the right-hand fork and almost immediately you'll find the car-parking place, which is well-signposted. It is a grassy rather than a hard-standing surface, but I went there on a windswept watery autumn day and had no trouble getting in or out.

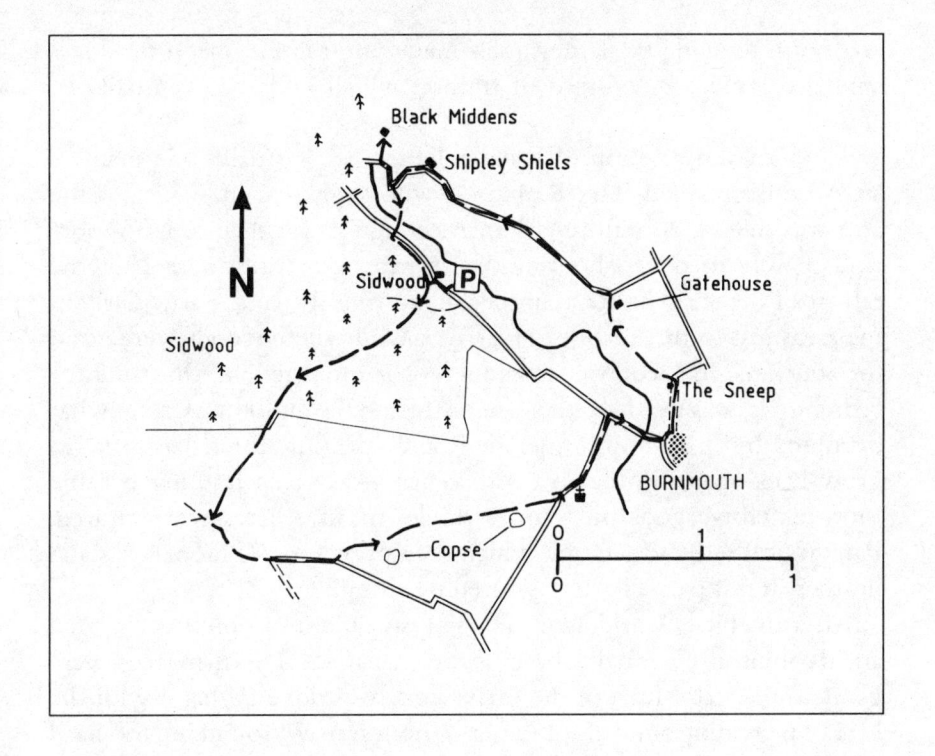

The walk begins with an uphill section. Start by going back to the forest road and turning right. You'll see a small house on your right, and opposite, a ride leading up to the left between the massive ranks of pine trees. If you have sharp eye-sight you may even spot the small blue tags fixed to the occasional tree, letting you know it is a public bridle-way.

Shortly after entering the forest there is a fork in the track, but keep to the right here, virtually following the course of the stream. Then it is about a mile (1½km) trek through the forest, climbing all the time. Keep to this ride, ignoring the many paths that cross it.

This mile or so of solid green is only the tip of the pine-covered iceberg. Kielder Forest is certainly the largest forest in this country and lays claim to being the largest man-made forest in Europe. It produces annually some 100,000 tons of timber, which will rise eventually to 300,000.

The idea and creation of Kielder Forest was virtually one man's — an Australian called Roy Robinson who suggested in 1910 that the area was suitable for afforestation. Although it was then rough moorland mainly used for shooting, there had been forest here after the retreat of the ice. The Romans began clearing the land, particularly in the areas just to the north of Hadrian's Wall where woods were good for attackers. In medieval times there was more felling, this time for farming. It wasn't altogether successful as the work was somewhat disrupted by the many border raids and often the forest had time to grow back again. In the sixteenth century, as sheep farming became more extensive and times more stable, massive areas were cleared. Paradoxically the vegetation which then grew, purple moor grass and heather, is not particularly favoured by sheep.

After the First World War, The Forestry Commission was founded and Robinson eventually became its chairman. The first trees were planted in 1920. Much of the early work was done by hand with the idea of providing rural employment, though many found life too hard and preferred to return to the cities. In the 1950s there was a women's brashing squad whose job it was to cut off the trees' side branches. These were usually left to lie on the forest floor. The women would work in a line, apparently like chattering birds, as the gossip spread from one to another. Now, Kielder is under pressure to become less of a monotonous timber factory and to provide more in the way of a country park, as well as providing a home for a wider selection of wildlife.

Eventually you come to the top of the hill, and it is just a short way till the trees are left behind. You should come out at a place where the forest boundary, which is basically east–west here, has a short north–south line for about a hundred yards (91 m). Go down the right-hand side of the wall here, heading roughly south, and more or less down the side of a burn, until you meet a very definite dirt track. The view over the North Tyne Valley as you descend certainly compensates for the climb up. The valley is pleasantly wooded and it comes as a great relief to see the variegated colour of the trees after the relentless green of the modern forest.

It all looks calm now, but the population of Tynedale and Redesdale were described as notorious thieves by the Bishop of Durham in the fifteenth century. Under threat of excommunication, the local families, the Dodds, Robsons, Milburns and Charltons all agreed to lay aside any weapon over nine inches (22 cm) long when they went to church!

Although there was never much of a road system here there was once the North Tyne Railway, opened in 1858 and closed after nearly a hundred years of operation. Most of the track has gone, though one of the most impressive parts to remain is further west at Kielder Water, where the viaduct is now a viewpoint.

Turn left along the dirt track and cross the burn at Slaty Ford, then continue round the hill. Up ahead to the left, is a large copse. Where the walls on the left-hand side of the track end, make for the top side of the copse following faint paths across the moor. Once above the copse, keep going in the same direction until you see on the crest of the hill a stone wall and two gates. Go through the topmost gate. On the slope below there is another large copse. Walk down to pass this one on the left, also, and beyond you join a road. You should continue along this to the left, soon passing a pleasant rural church.

This is the vale of Tarset Burn, another attractive valley, and the ridge immediately ahead is the route for the Pennine Way. To the far left is Padon Hill, topped with what could be a cairn at this distance but is actually a small monument. A mile downstream to the right, hidden in woods, are the ruins of Tarset Castle, another border fortification.

Continue for a few hundred yards until you come to a T-junction. (You can turn left here to get back to the car-park). To see the bastle houses (fortified farmhouses), turn right. Walk along the road and cross over the burn, then continue up the road to the house on the left. Just before the house is a gate and a faint path leading to a footbridge. Follow the path up the bank and then across to the farmhouse and cottages known as The Sneep. There's a little stretch of lane going by the side of these houses and a stile at the end. From here you need to make your way to the houses on the opposite side of the valley. The best route – to avoid climbing fences – is to drop down on the left, where you can cross the little stream, and then head up the hill, bearing right to a gate and a small stile in the fence. The path is not at all clear here but the route to take is over a marsh(!) between the buildings, which brings you out onto the road.

This is Gatehouse, where a pair of bastle houses stand guard with the small road between them. The bastle is a two-floored farmhouse strong enough to withstand a raid. The ground floor was used to shelter animals with just one entrance that could be closed from the inside, whilst sturdy stone steps led up to a main door on the upper floor to the living quarters. The staircase has a left-hand turn at the top, so that the occupier has the best position for right-armed swordplay.

It was common practice to build bastles in small groups, assuming you could at least trust your neighbour. Apart from these two, Black Middens is not far away, and there is another in the valley at Redhaugh. The bastle on the north side of the road here is the best-preserved in the area, dating from the sixteenth century. It is a very solid building with tiny windows and ventilation slits.

Carry on up this road to the crest of the next hill where you'll see before you the Kielder Forest, a farmhouse on the right and a small building beyond that is Black Middens Bastle. Unfortunately there is no direct route, so you'll have to follow the road round in a large loop to get to the entrance of the bastle.

This one, although in the care of English Heritage, is roofless, and only partially restored, enough to make it safe to explore. Again, there is the traditional design of thick walls and stone steps leading to the opening in the top floor where the farming family would live.

To get back to the car-park, retrace your steps to the large loop in the road. At the corner, aim diagonally across the field to the footbridge in the opposite corner. Here I was lucky enough to see the most enormous heron effortlessly flying along the path of the river and then disappearing over the tops of the trees beyond.

Follow the track straight ahead, until it turns a corner and takes you back to the small house and the car-park is just after that. You may decide it is time to take a well-deserved picnic lunch.

NOTTINGHAMSHIRE

If you think that the English are a quiet and reserved people then Nottinghamshire is the county with the style to match the country's people. Comparatively populous, most people will know little of it. The characters most have heard of are the fictional Robin Hood and the talented football manager Brian Clough (not a native of the county). The industries they may know of are the Nottinghamshire coalfield, Raleigh bicycles, and the Boots Company's products. The places they recall are likely to be Sherwood Forest and the Trent Bridge cricket ground. To those in the south it's a northern county, to the north it's south, to itself it's the East Midlands: quiet, reserved, and gets on with things – typically English.

The reality is that the above is not bad as part of a picture, but it doesn't really do the county full justice. Whilst you're never going to 'get away from it' in a county such as Notts, it is a very suitable place for a break. There is plenty of variety in unspoilt scenery, there are some great views, and some unexpected treasures and distractions for bad weather.

What I found most striking is the constant proximity of industry and the countryside. Sometimes there is a happy co-existence, often industry intrudes, but in some cases – a growing trend – industrial remains become valuable and enjoyable historical assets to the countryside.

The county is shaped like an upright beech leaf, an oval with its long axis north–south. The centre of gravity is Nottingham and its suburbs, which has the densest mass of population in the county. The city itself is a lovely place to visit if you have the time; the Lace Market, the Victoria Embankment and the Old Town are all great places to have a wander. Amongst many notable buildings you may like to view the castle and the nearby Trip to Jerusalem pub, which nestles in the sandstone at the foot of the castle rock. As you enjoy your drink you may like to contemplate what it would be like to live in a house where, if you wanted another room you just dug it out of the rock, for Nottingham was like that in medieval times. Coal has provided the strongest influence here through many centuries. It was the source of the Willoughby fortune that built Wollaton Hall, a grand Elizabethan mansion set in a large park, (a few minutes from the city centre) that is now the location of natural history and industrial museums. D. H. Lawrence grew up in Eastwood, just north-west of Nottingham, and the settings of his early work are the farmland and colliery landscape of this part of the county.

One of the great rivers of England, the Trent, enters the county in the south-west, flowing past Nottingham across to Newark in a north-easterly direction. It then heads almost north, becoming the county's eastern boundary for its last twenty miles in this county. It was long ago a principal highway, and is the reason why Nottingham was first established – on a sandstone cliff overlooking the river. Nowadays Nottingham seems to claim the Trent as its own; you can be pretty sure that anything with Trent in its name has a base in Nottingham.

Sherwood Forest, in the heart of the county, is only a shadow of its former self, but thanks to the activities of a group of dukes and earls in the eighteenth century, much of the land has remained undeveloped, as great parks. With the additional Forestry Commission-owned woodland, the county can boast an expanse of woodland and parkland that is truly delightful.

To the south-east is the Vale of Belvoir, a broad belt of land with, to the west, a softly undulating landscape that continues into Leicestershire, with the eastern end flattening out into Lincolnshire. The use of brick as a building material adds greatly to the attractiveness of many of the southern villages. Due to the amount of iron-oxide in the clay it is often a rich red colour and was used for the grander houses as well as the more humble cottages.

Two memorable discoveries here owe their existence to industry. The reclaimed gravel pits, so valuable along the Trent, now make up a huge nature reserve at Attenborough. In keeping with my theme of the proximity of industry and countryside it's interesting to note that gravel barges still move about the reserve as the works are just nearby. The other discovery is a piece of classic engineering of the Victorian age, the magnificent pumping station at Papplewick.

I like the way the countryside jostles with industry, and pockets of people intrude on every view. My lasting impression of Nottinghamshire is of a leafy scene, flat or undulating, with an elegant spire rising somewhere in the distance, proclaiming the presence of a small village or town. Or is it one of the power stations burning Nottinghamshire coal and cooling itself by the Trent?

Clumber Park

'The Dukeries' is an eighteenth-century term coined for the great private estates that lie in the central part of the county of Nottinghamshire. The estates Welbeck, Thoresby, Worksop and Clumber, belonged to the Dukes of Norfolk, Kingston, Portland and Newcastle and Earls Byron and Savile owned Newstead Abbey and Rufford Abbey, respectively. Sir George Savile's comment in 1769 was that 'four Dukes, two Lords and three rabbit warrens' took in half the county.

Thanks though to these estates enclosing vast tracts of land, much of what was the great royal forest created by William the Conqueror has been preserved, not all as forest, but as a mixture of woodland, parkland and country park.

The Clumber Park estate was part of Sherwood Forest until 1707 when a licence was granted to the Duke of Newcastle to enclose an area as a hunting park for Queen Anne. There wasn't much thought of landscaping the place and it was left as a scrubby heath. The predominant game seems to have been rabbit. It was described as 'a black heath full of rabbits, having a narrow river running through it, with a small boggy close or two.' In 1760 a house was started on the site of an old warren and work began to form a huge lake from the small River Poulter which trickled through the lands. It took fifteen years. The surrounding area was landscaped and the lake was crossed by a splendid classical bridge. There were attempts to convert some of the estate for agricultural use but the heathland soil was poor and so it was kept as grazing land, principally for sheep.

The dukes and earls, as well as creating grand estates and houses, added their own colour to the landscape. The four dukes were all descended from the energetic Bess of Hardwick. She had several husbands and estates in Derbyshire and built Hardwick Hall, described as more glass than wall.

The fifth Lord Byron was known as 'the Wicked Lord', retreating to Newstead Abbey after being found guilty of manslaughter. He was determined to make the estate valueless so that his son should have nothing to inherit, and began by killing the deer and cutting down all the trees, and continued by letting the house fall into decay. You can see the forts in the lake which were used in mock battles with a twenty-gun warship. The Duke of Kingston created a major scandal in the eighteenth century when he married a bigamist. As for the fifth Duke of Portland, unfortunately it isn't possible to visit the extensive rooms, tunnels and passages under Welbeck built by traction engine for this eccentric recluse. I was particularly sorry to miss the underground ballroom, apparently the largest room in Europe without supporting pillars. Employees on the estate were told to treat him as if he were a tree should they see him, unlikely as he drove about the estate with the blinds of the carriage drawn.

At Clumber Park, the fourth Duke, an opponent of parliamentary reform, evicted tenants and threatened to double rents if they didn't vote for his candidate. His empty mansion in Nottingham was burnt by a mob. The seventh Duke was fascinated by the gypsy life, so much so that he had a caravan built in which he could explore the countryside. There would have been plenty for him to see on his own estate alone, which comprises some four thousand acres (1618 ha) of parkland.

There is no longer a stately home or an eccentric aristocrat to provide a focus to the estate, but Clumber Chapel, its spire rising above the trees and descending deep into the reflection on the lake is a magnificent centrepiece.

There are several entrances to Clumber Park; one off the A57 at Manton Lodge, three from the A614, and two leading towards the B6005. Once in the estate there are three main areas in which to park, each having easy access to the lake.

Not to be missed is the avenue lined with a double row of lime trees. It is the longest avenue in England, stretching for three miles (5 km) from Apleyhead Lodge to Carburton Lodge. Not only is it interesting for its beauty and length but it also marks a change in the style of landscaping gardens and parks.

Capability Brown and his successor Humphrey Repton were responsible for creating 'natural' landscapes – softly rounded hills, strategically placed trees – to lead the eye, probably, to the strategically placed cattle who were thought to be appropriate rural ornaments. Formal terraces and layouts were obliterated to achieve this Sylvan ideal. Towards the end of the eighteenth century, Brown and Repton were attacked for producing unimaginative gardens and there was a plea for more formality and structure. Repton was influenced by this criticism and went a little way towards a new style when designing Clumber. He created the spectacular lime avenue, even though he allowed it to wind somewhat to make it less formal.

Another feature of many eighteenth-century parks is that the planting has reached maturity. Many trees need replacing, quite a headache for bodies such as the National Trust. Luckily the lime avenue still has many years ahead of it.

You can wander freely over the estate with its variety of woods and open land. Bicycles are available for hire near the restaurant. I find a walk around the lake gives you a chance to see many of the best features.

OS Map 1:50 000, Sheet 120
Round the lake, a circular walk of $3\frac{1}{2}$ miles (6 km). Allow $1\frac{1}{2}$–2 hours.

The going underfoot is all on good paths or park road. The route is virtually flat and the navigating easy as long as the lake is in sight.

Car-parking and the start

I like to park at the far end of the lake by Hardwick village, which can be easily reached by the A614 entrances. This car-park tends to be a little less crowded than the space by the tea-rooms. It also gives you a chance to work up an appetite.

Start by walking up the arm of the lake, away from the weir. The National Trust have been doing a lot of conservation work in this area recently to prevent the path across the far end of the lake becoming submerged. When orienteering here in the spring, I remember a very boggy area and muddy path, but on a recent autumnal visit, a new bank had been built across the end of the lake, and a spotless tarmac path was just being rolled into place.

You can either stay round the perimeter of the lake, or head through the woods to the left of the tarmac path. This way brings you through Ash Tree Hill Wood and then some open land with buildings beyond. This is the Kitchen Garden Exhibition Area including a walled garden, vineries and palm house. These have been renovated and replanted to preserve the range of nineteenth-century glasshouses. From here you can walk along the cedar avenue to the Victorian Pleasure Gardens, which are small grassy glades between groups of trees, all connected with a network of paths. At the eastern end is the Lincoln Terrace and to the west is Clumber Chapel.

The Chapel was built for the seventh Duke in the period of Gothic revival. It is built of red sandstone and contrasting white Streetly stone. The spire rises 180 feet (54 m) making it a dominating feature. Inside, you get a sense of height from the very narrow nave. Clumber Chapel has been nicknamed 'Cathedral in Miniature'.

From the Chapel, continue round the lake to the restaurant and shop. You may be able to cross the lake on the tiny ferry, but otherwise walk over the grassy lakeside areas to the bridge.

Large flocks of Canada geese seem very content to be nibbling at the grass and on the lookout for anything that visitors might throw at them. It is amazing how quickly news travels over just one crust of bread. Their big feet have been a headache for the National Trust though, as they tend to wear down the lakeside banks rather easily.

Once over the bridge, start back along the lake. It is from here you get the full view of the Chapel, standing in glorious solitude, surrounded by trees and reflected in the water. It is worth pausing, too, to imagine the grand house that was once on the lakeside beside it sharing the magnificent setting. It was demolished in 1938.

Clumber is near several other places you may like to visit. There are the soft pink ruins of the Cistercian abbey at Rufford, where the Country Park contains woodland, grassland walks, a lake, old yew hedges and plenty of views. Newstead Abbey, ancestral home of the sixth Lord Byron, poet, mad, bad and dangerous-to-know, and saviour of Greece is to the south-west. There is much to see there. Nearer is Thoresby, where the house is open to the public. I can recommend them all.

Southwell

Southwell is unusual amongst cathedral cities, being no more than the size of a small town. Its size makes the cathedral seem even more dominant, but far from overpowering the town, it adds a fairytale air. It is an easy place to explore, having an intimacy and great charm.

It is not clear from which well Southwell takes its name as there were four wells in the town; the Lord's Well, on the property of the Lord of the manor, Holy Well and Lady's Well in the precincts of the minster itself and St Catherine's Well. Further to the north of the town is the village of Norwell (Northwell) so perhaps 'Southwell' seemed an obvious choice. However, whilst one of the towns has remained a village, the other has developed.

The development began as Southwell became a place of pilgrimage. Here were kept the relics of St Eadburgh, daughter of the King of the East Angles. As time went on the minster replaced the Saxon church. It was started in the twelfth century and took over a hundred years to complete. For many centuries it was a Collegiate church, an outpost of the great Archdiocese of York. In 1884, when the Southwell diocese was formed, the minster became a cathedral.

Seeing the cathedral alone would make the town worth visiting, but the plethora of elegant brick buildings, numerous inns, and a chance to sip coffee on the site of Charles I's last hours of freedom, makes the place an absolute must. Southwell is enjoyable at any time of the year, but I feel the season that suits it best is autumn. The burnished hues of the numerous trees emphasize the warm glow of the brick buildings, especially if you get a clear blue sky as well.

Around the Town

OS Map 1:50 000, Sheet 120
1½ miles (3 km). Allow 1 hour.

This walk is virtually all on hard surface with only one very short section on a mud footpath. It helps to have a good look at the Town Plan at the Tourist Information Centre to get an idea of the overall direction, but the route is easy to find.

Car-parking and the start

There is a good-sized free car-park opposite the minster in Church Street. Start or finish your walk with a visit to the minster.

The walk starts by going away from the town centre along Church Street, a road that used to be known as Church Gate. Along here, and in West Gate – which you'll come to later in the walk – are many spacious houses. These were Prebendal Houses, the town houses of the Prebendaries, secular canons forming the chapter of the Collegiate church which was the minster's original function. Cranfield House, originally Oxton I Prebend, was built during Queen Anne's reign in 1709, by the Rev. George Mompesson. His father, William Mompesson, was brought to fame during the time of the plague as he was then vicar of Eyam. That village had the misfortune to contract the plague from clothing sent from London. Mompesson persuaded the villagers not to flee, spreading more infection, but to stay put. They isolated themselves and five out of six of the population died.

South Muskham Prebend, the last one on the left, originated in medieval times. The two before it are both mid-eighteenth century. Normanton Prebend has a three-storey classical facade. So too does Woodborough, but in its case that was added some seventy-nine years later. North Muskham Prebend was once a boys' school, known by the locals as 'The Gent's School'.

Beyond these, there's a pub on the left called The Bramley Apple with a gargantuan green apple used as a pub sign. The Bramley apple originated in Southwell though it might easily have been called a Brailesford. In the early 1800s, the two Miss Brailesfords planted two apple pips in their cottage garden in Easthorpe, which is now 73

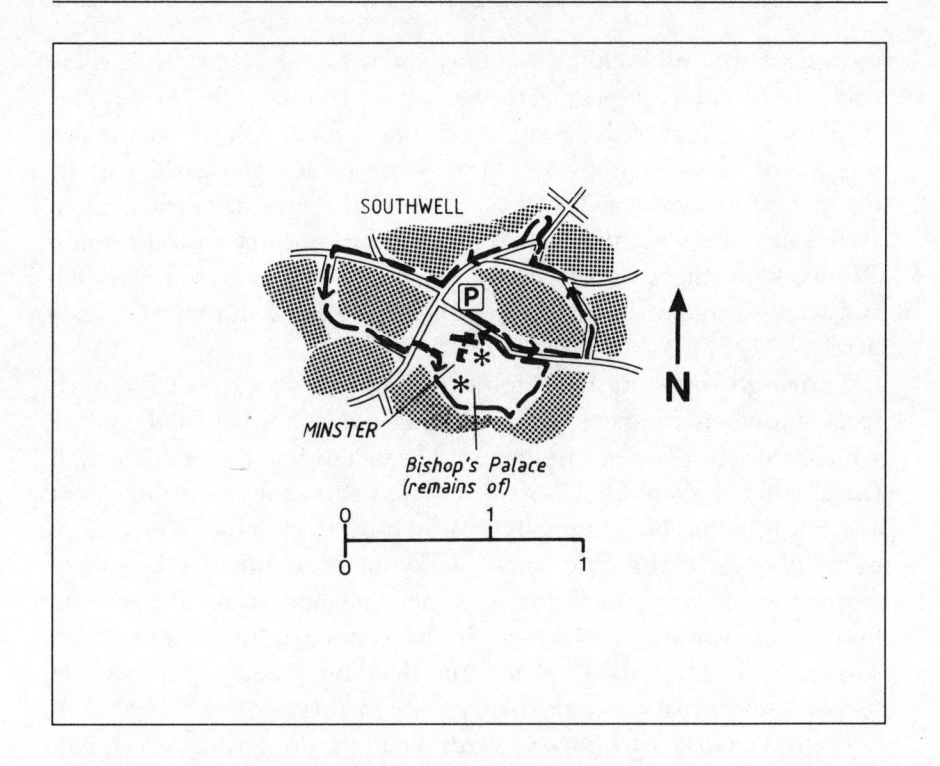

Church Street. One of these pips flourished into a tree bearing splendid fruit. Many years later, the fruit came to the attention of a local nursery man, Mr Merryweather. He was so impressed by the apples, that he wanted to grow them on a commercial basis. The then-owner of Easthorpe and therefore owner of the apple tree was Matthew Bramley. He agreed to cuttings being taken as long as the apple was named after him, and so it became known as Bramley's Seedling. The Merryweather family are still nurserymen, with a business just on the outskirts of Southwell.

Something that Southwell might once have been famous for was the number of inns, taverns and beerhouses, apparently totalling nineteen in 1832. You'll not be surprised to find that only yards behind The Bramley Apple is The Hearty Goodfellow. Just beyond this is a footpath on the left, known as Shady Lane, probably because for much of the way it is overhung with small shrubs and trees.

There is a slight climb up to the area known as Burgage. At the junction with the road, turn left and ahead on the left is Hill House.

Now a school, this building was once owned by the Rev. Becher. He was one of the first people to encourage Byron with his writing. Byron's mother rented a house on Burgage for several years and her son stayed in Southwell for a few years during the early part of the nineteenth century. The Reverend Becher may have encouraged Byron in more ways than one by urging him to mix with mankind. Womankind might have been more appropriate, as Byron was well and truly distracted by several Southwell ladies during his few years here.

Turn right opposite Hill House and you come into a wide open space known as Burgage Green. Burgage Manor is here – the house which was let to Byron's mother. You can also find the police station (1884) and the old police house. It is quite an area for law enforcement as the forbidding building halfway down is the House of Correction, or to give it its full title, the County of Nottingham's House of Correction. It was built for 36 prisoners and then extended to hold nearly 150 including 18 women. It also contained a treadmill which was used for hard labour. When the building was closed in 1880 it played a somewhat different role as a lace factory.

From the Green turn back towards the town along King Street, past the modern market place and another good selection of pubs. There were so many places to drink in the town that many publicans had to find other work, to supplement their earnings. One advertised as a chandler, and one as a sanitary inspector.

At Queen Street, turn right and walk up here to Chatsworth Avenue, then turn left. This is new housing but settling in well under a plentiful supply of trees. At the top of the slight hill, take the footpath ahead and keep going along the ridge. You come out on a curiously named road, Lowes Wong. 'Wong' is the old name for a meadow or lea, and this land once belonged to the Lowes family.

At the bottom on the main road, turn left and then right down Bishop's Drive. You can see the minster to the left and the gates of the bishop's manor which is the residence of the Bishop of Southwell. Behind this are the ruins of the Bishop's Palace, but those are best seen from the grounds of the minster.

Turn left by the curved arches of the war memorial and then keep to the lane and a footpath off on the left. This brings you round the boundary of the school fields, and then after a sharp left turn, back onto Church Street where you can then return to the car-park.

The Minster itself is fascinating, both externally and internally. The twin Norman towers capped with pyramidal roofs, nicknamed pepperpots, create a unique facade. Unusual in today's England, they would have been more typical in the twelfth century, unlike the needle-sharp spires now seen throughout the rest of the county.

Inside, the main body of the church is Norman with massive stone piers, simple decoration and low, rounded arches. The smooth creamy stone, which came from Mansfield, has a pleasing look and the whole effect is solid but not heavy. The surprise comes as you venture further down the nave into the Early English section with its delicate feel and more uplifting appearance due to the use of a more pointed arch and slender columns. Best of all is the Chapter House built at the end of the thirteenth century. It is unusual in having no central column. Spanning such a space in stone was a remarkable feat; it leaves a breathtaking feeling as does the wonderful stonework. There is a wealth of carvings with masses of detailed foliage. Some of it is so fragile it looks as though it could be just snapped off. The leaves around the arches and doorways stand out boldly because of the depth of stone removed from behind. As is often the case with the best stone masonry, there are many individual touches to look for such as the darting lizards, mythical beasts and caricature faces hidden in the foliage.

Don't forget to look at some of the sculpture on the outside. There are some remarkable faces, my favourite being the lady with the very square headdress and expression to match.

Just by the minster, opposite the end of Church Street, is a striking black and white building, The Saracen's Head, which claims to be the oldest inn in Southwell and once an important staging-post. It was here that I sipped coffee and Charles I spent his last day of freedom before giving himself up to the Scots just outside Newark. This came rather full circle for Charles as it was at Nottingham that he originally raised his banner calling for troops, and so began the Civil War. The inn used to be called The King's Arms (luckily not The King's Head), changing its name in the eighteenth century.

Apart from enjoying a walk around the town, there are many good footpaths locally and pretty villages too. It is easy to get from here to the Trent.

A Great English Industrial Monument

No visit to Nottingham should miss Southwell but there is another gem only a few miles away – the Papplewick Pumping Station. It was built in the late nineteenth century to supply water to the mushrooming City of Nottingham, a marvellous monument to the Victorian age. It seems fitting that a fine building such as this has been preserved in a county where the industrial side is so intertwined with the countryside.

Papplewick Pumping Station is just outside the village of Papplewick on Long Lane, an unclassified road that runs between Oxton and Ravenshead (grid reference 584522).

The setting of the building is magnificent as it stands almost like a stately home in front of an elegantly curving lake, which functions as a cooling pond, and neat landscaped gardens. Adjacent are two sizeable houses built for the superintendent and his assistant, and there are smaller stokers' cottages opposite.

The entrance is through a massive oak door, supported on rollers, leading to an absolutely stunning interior. There are cream painted columns covered in a riot of intricate cast-iron work, fashioned with great delicacy to represent reeds and fish. The capitals are adorned with golden cranes, following through the theme of water. There is stained glass in the windows, again inspired by water, with fish, water lilies and bulrushes. Add to this, ornate lamps, coloured tiles and a picture of Queen Victoria, and you have the makings of a grand foyer. What is even more remarkable (and says a good deal about the times) is that the inside of the building was only seen officially by three people. This was the domain of the superintendent. If the stokers or gardeners wanted to see him, they had to knock at the great door, and remove their shoes if they were to be allowed in.

At the end of the seventeenth century, the original Nottingham Waterworks Company built pumps driven by water wheels to take water from the River Lean to a small reservoir, from which it could be piped to most parts of the town. However, with the establishment of framework knitting and the lace industry, the population of Nottingham increased in the next hundred years or so from 10,000 to 50,000. All this extra population was housed within the boundaries of the old medieval town. The water supply was not only inadequate, but filthy. There were constant outbreaks of cholera and typhoid, although the causes of this were not then linked to the condition of the water. Several new pumping systems were developed, making use of the sandstone beds on which Nottingham is built. Sandstone, a porous rock, is able to act as a sponge and also as an effective filter for storing pure water.

By 1880, it was apparent that there was an urgent need for increased capacity and water storage, and the result was the Papplewick Pumping Station. It was designed by Marriott Ogle Tarbotton and built in 1884. This splendidly named individual was Nottingham's Borough Surveyor, and was the first municipal engineer to use subways under streets to carry services.

The Pumping Station was operated by steam and worked until 1967, when the system was electrified. The cost of that equalled the cost of the original building, the machinery and the construction of Mapperley Reservoir. The Pumping Station, though listed, was eventually abandoned. Luckily the machinery was too big to get out of the main door otherwise it would all have gone for scrap.

In 1974 a Trust was set up to restore the place, renovating and repairing the pumps and it was able to open for 'steaming' days when the machinery is activated. You'll see the massive beam-pumping engines, thought to be the last made by the famous firm of James Watt and Co. The feats of engineering equal those at Southwell. Here, the massive fly wheels either side are skilfully cut into the supporting piers, leaving a space of about half an inch. You can climb up the cast-iron stairs and see the tops of the giant engine cylinders, each needing so much oil for lubrication that they have a battered copper kettle apiece for the purpose. These are also original to the building.

On the top floor, the beam floor, there are the great engine beams, hauled up originally by means of pulleys and a good deal of sweat, I should imagine.

Behind the engine room are six Lancashire boilers, the stone steps leading between these are well-worn, despite having been turned over once already.

It is marvellous to go when the place is in full steam, but fascinating just to view the massive machinery, hear some good stories and of course enjoy the building itself. It is only open on certain weekends, though if you contact the custodian it is possible to make a private appointment (donations are greatly appreciated). I went in a party of two, but larger groups are welcome.

There are some facilities in the grounds and they are planning to have refreshments; meantime, just down the road, within easy walking distance is the Burntstump Country Park where there is a good picnic site.

Attenborough

As you turn off the main road from Long Eaton into Nottingham (A6005, the old A453), down what quite quickly becomes a quiet leafy lane, you feel as though you are entering a different world. The lane ends in a large car-park which gives you access to the Attenborough nature reserve along the banks of the River Trent (the reserve is named after the nearby village rather than the famous naturalist).

Every city should have a hidden corner of greenery and water such as this. Within minutes of walking here you can forget the noise and the traffic and enjoy a range of different sounds, mainly from the many water-fowl that gather here. The only traffic jams in the car-park at Attenborough are caused by little bands of ducks, marching in unhurried single file across the stone.

Although I say you get away from the bustle of the city, you don't get entirely away from the industrial side of the county. I feel, however, that a chugging gravel barge complements rather than intrudes on the scene, and even the Ratcliffe-on-Soar Power Station has a peculiar way of blending into the view. It is as much a feature of modern Nottinghamshire as the church spire of Attenborough.

The lakes here are the result of gravel extraction from beds alongside the river. They are extensive. The area is predominantly water, with tree-lined paths following the sinews of remaining land. The area changes with the seasons, frozen and bare in winter, soft and bright in spring, baked hard and languid in summer. In times of heavy rain the region is still liable to flooding, but the river rises quite gently so you needn't fear being caught. If you do want to be impressed by the power of the river, there are marks on Trent Bridge at Nottingham showing how much the river has risen in the past; some of those marks are extremely high.

In normal times the efficient drainage means no water should be in the wrong place and the more permanent environment has attracted a great variety of wildlife. There's coming and going all year round. As the waders and winter ducks move off, the first spring birds of passage and summer visitors arrive.

There are several easy walks from there that all go on good paths, You can take in every lake to either side of the car-park, or go on down river to Beeston Lock and back.

The Attenborough Nature Reserve

OS Map 1:50 000, Sheet 129, GR 521343
Circular routes of 2½ miles (4 km), 4½ (7 km) and 7 miles (11 km). Allow up to 3–3½ hours.

The going underfoot is all good and flat but there may be some seasonal flooding. Navigation is not really difficult as the route is around lakes and alongside the Trent on well-defined paths.

Car-parking and the start

Turn south off the A6005, just west of some traffic lights down Attenborough Lane. Continue on across the level crossing and although the lane makes a couple of turns you should have no trouble finding the car-park entrance on the corner just as the cricket field comes into view.

From the car-park, head across the little stream on the high curving footbridge. After a short distance you come to the broad expanse of the River Trent. The partially wooded hill on the opposite side is very clear, rising to over 200 feet (60 m) very quickly. Gotham Hill rises slightly to the right, but before your eye gets as far as the cooling towers.

The Trent has been a major water highway and trading route since 1000 BC, known from the two Bronze Age dug-out canoes which were found in the riverbed just near Nottingham. The river was used by the Romans, and later by the Vikings as an invasion route. During the Industrial Revolution river traffic increased considerably and at one time, Shardlow, at the eastern end of the Trent–Mersey canal and just over the border into Derbyshire from here, was the country's largest inland port. Now, most of the trade on the river is nearer the sea, between Gainsborough and the Humber.

At the Trent turn left, walking downstream, and follow the line of the river for about one mile (1½km). Shortly after crossing a low bridge, where the water from one of the lagoons spills into the Trent, there is a path off to the left. This takes you on a short loop back to the top of the car-park.

If you want to continue a longer walk, then carry on along the Trent to the Beeston Canal Lock and Keeper's Cottage. For the next five hundred metres you can walk on either side of the canal, but be sure to be on the far side, after the little bridge, at the time the road called Canal Side curves away to the left. Walk on the track rather than the towpath as the latter narrows to a barrier further down.

Over the canal to the left are the Boot's Pharmaceutical Works. Jesse Boot, founder of the company, was the first Lord Trent. He was known for his philanthropic works which included developing the site of the university on the rising ground just to the north of here. He bought the park at Lenton, then a village close to the centre of Nottingham, and built the first parts of the university. It is a remarkable campus. I was given a guided tour by a former student (my husband) and it is well worth making a detour here when you are exploring Nottingham. The campus, reflecting in some ways the county as a whole, has tree-lined drives and many open grassy spaces around the halls of residence in what was once the park.

Just before the university playing fields at Grove Farm, you'll see a right-hand sign pointing down a field hedge towards the Trent.

On reaching the Trent, turn right back along the bankside path. Here the river is very shallow and virtually un-navigable. This was the reason for the construction of the Beeston Canal, which passes very close to the centre of Nottingham, linking into the now-abandoned Nottingham Canal.

Walk back along the river to the turning off the towpath that I mentioned earlier. This leads up through the lagoons to a high footbridge. The place is teaming with wildlife, yet just beyond is all the noise of the local Trent gravel works, the reason for the pits in the first place. The gravel is no longer dug here but is brought in by barge from Derbyshire. At the works it is washed and graded by means of mechanical sieves. The birds seem unflustered by the presence of the industry and nature is busy reclaiming the once barren pits. There are many shrubs such as ash, elder and willow to look for as well as the ubiquitous, but nevertheless attractive, Rose Bay Willow Herb.

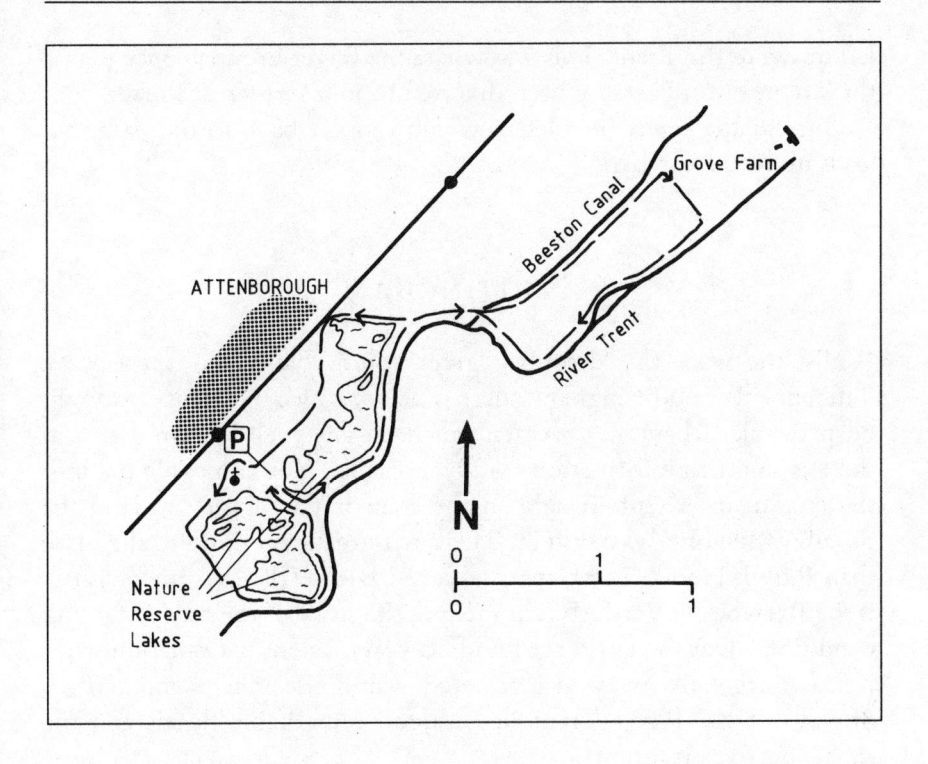

Bird-lovers may well be able to spot Coots, Moorhen, and Great Crested Grebe, the latter especially if it is courting in early spring when the wedge of feathers on the head stands up like a fan. Young birds can sometimes be seen riding their parents' backs.

Follow the path round to another humpback footbridge and then follow the obvious path along to the little lane called The Strand at the top of the car-park. Many of the houses here are most attractive and have a pleasant view over the local cricket pitch.

You can finish the walk here, but to complete the other part of the figure of eight, turn the corner and walk towards the church up Church Lane.

Beyond the church is a footpath leading to a track where you turn left down to the Trent. This was where the River Erewash once joined the Trent, but it has now been diverted to join further upstream.

Once at the river, turn left and you can get back to the path that leads up to the car-park.

Nottingham

Whilst the walk I've described gives you a chance to experience a different side of Nottingham, there is plenty to see in the city, though, on principle, I have not written much on any well-known places as there is so much information readily available. You can easily get into the city from Attenborough on the train if you want to avoid the pitfalls of the one-way system. There is a great deal more to the place than Robin Hood. The recently opened Lace Hall is worth a visit as is the Brewhouse Yard Museum telling the story of the city's working conditions over the last three hundred years. There is a canal museum just a short walk away in a restored warehouse where you can see displays of the River Trent, its bridges, remarkable floods and the canal and river transport.

The Vale of Belvoir

This area to the south-east of Nottinghamshire is shared with Lincolnshire, Leicestershire and what was once Rutland. The best-known feature of the Vale is probably the castle located in the Leicestershire part. It stands on a wooded ridge with a good view of the surrounding countryside. The original castle was built by the Norman conquerors but was destroyed and rebuilt in both civil wars, and again after a fire in 1816, so the present castle dates from then.

Within the Nottinghamshire part of the Vale there are many quiet lanes and attractive villages. Parts of the countryside are very flat, having a Lincolnshire/East Anglian feel about them, but there are some gently undulating hills and many small woods.

Throughout the area weaves the Grantham Canal. The fourth and fifth Dukes of Rutland did much to bring about its construction and the waterway was opened in its entirety in 1797. It prospered for about fifty years before better road and railways forced it into decline. There are now plans to reintroduce boats and there are miles of footpath to explore.

Churches and Cheese

OS Map 1:50 000, Sheet no. 129
A circular walk of 4–5 miles (7–8 km). Allow 2–2½ hours.

This walk, based around the broadest part of the Vale, gives you the essence of this part of the countryside. It starts in the pretty village of Colston Bassett with the inevitable church and spire. The walk takes you over a gentle hill, then across a mixture of arable and grazing fields to the village of Langar, returning along a flat-gated lane. There is plenty to see in both villages.

The going underfoot can be very muddy as there are several ploughed fields to cross so make sure you have suitable footwear. The second part of the walk is easier going along a good quiet lane.

The route on the way to Langar is marked with a mixture of faded and newish yellow markers which give you confidence in places where the path seems to be lost to the plough. The churches provide good landmarks if you feel you are wandering off-course.

Car-parking and the start

There is a no through road behind the church at Colston Bassett and here there is room for several cars to park without blocking the entrances to the houses opposite or the farm. Park on the verges as some farm traffic will be coming through.

Walk back along the lane towards the church, and turn right along the road. Almost at the corner, by the side of a house on the left, there's a small footpath leading out to the parkland that once belonged to the Great Hall. The Hall in the distance stands out from the countryside as it is painted white and comes as a surprise after the predominance of brick in so many places in Nottinghamshire. Walk across the parkland by the cricket pitch and towards the church on the hill. This was abandoned in 1892, when a grand church was built by the squire in what was then the estate village. He was ordered by the Church Commissioners to unroof the old church and create the ruin that is there today. Even though a ruin, it is still a lovely place, set on the small hill with views over the valley. Much of the building left is being overrun with ivy and undergrowth, but vivid stone faces high up on the tower look down with almost a challenging and mocking air. It is possible to go round but inadvisable to try to climb inside.

Double back to the cricket pitch and go out at the gate on the left that brings you onto the road. Here, turn right, crossing the infant River Smite. At the next corner is a footpath post pointing you to the left. My heart sank as the path disappeared straight into a ploughed field. However, it was possible to keep to the grassy field alongside.

At the far end of this field, the path takes a diagonal to the right, again over two ploughed fields, though a slight path was starting to be trodden down, and then into more grazing land. Aim for the top corner of this field and a makeshift bridge over a tiny ditch. The planks are in need of repair as they are broken in the centre, but with one gigantic stride, it is possible to get safely across.

You can see a ruined building in the next field, and the path goes to the north of this. The planking over the next, wider stream is in good repair, and shortly afterwards the path curves left to bring you over a litle bridge onto the road.

Here, cross the road and turn right. It is just a short walk beyond to Langar Hall with its attractive entrance drive lined with lime trees. There is a small gate immediately after the drive and a footpath leading across a field to the church.

Here is something of an oddity – a Nottinghamshire church without a spire. The present church was heavily restored by the Rev. Thomas Butler, father of Samuel, who rebuilt the tower and renewed much of the external stonework, choosing a yellow Ancaster Stone from Lincolnshire, which gives the building a mellow air. It is a large church for a comparatively small village and has been christened 'the Cathedral of the Vale of Belvoir'. You are more or less at the centre of the Vale now.

Inside, there are a number of striking monuments including one to the Scroope-Howe family in black and white marble. The clothing on the recumbent Thomas, Lord Scroope and his wife is extraordinarily detailed. He is dressed in armour with the collar, cap, mantle and garter of the Order of the Garter. There is also an engraving of the Rt Honourable Richard, Lord Howe, Vice-Admiral of Great Britain, who was the British hero of the sea battle between the French and British in 1794, known as the 'glorious first of June'.

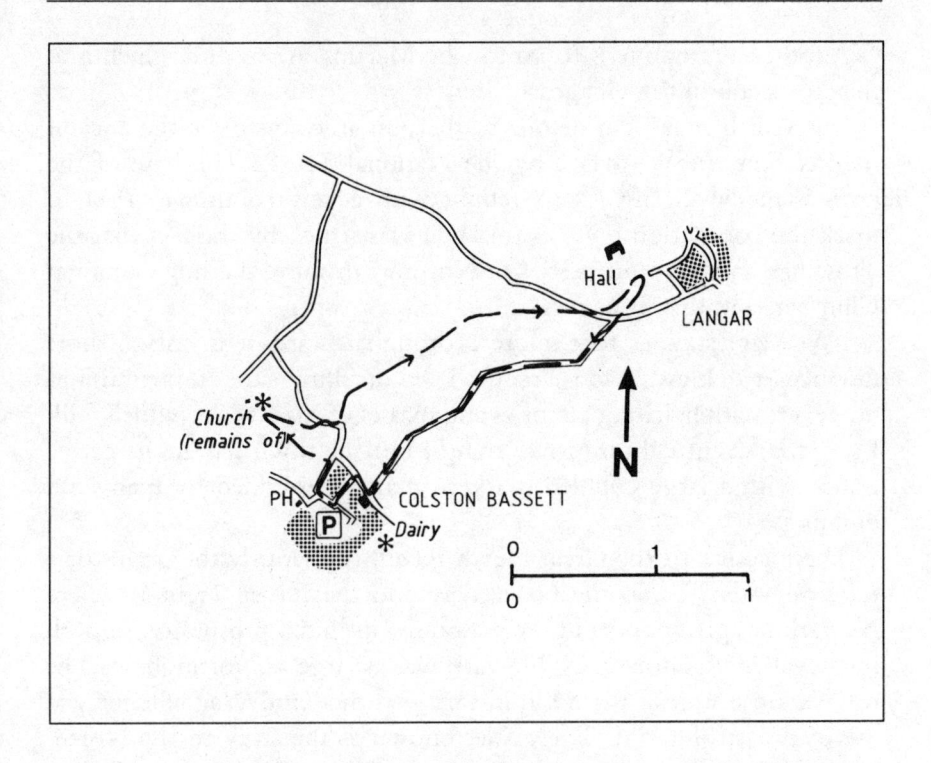

From the church, you can see the elegant rectory where Samuel Butler was born. In his novel *The Way of All Flesh* he refers to Langar under the name of Battersby-on-the-Hill.

Either walk through the village or go back through the meadow to the road. Opposite the gate is a small lane, not signposted, which leads back to Colston Bassett. It is gated and so scarcely used by traffic which means it is very pleasant to walk along.

At the far end of the lane, you come out directly opposite the Colston Bassett Dairy which specializes in making Stilton cheese, very handy if you've timed your walk to finish at lunchtime and you've got the makings of a sandwich on hand.

Another alternative is to go to The Martins' Arms pub which is at the crossroads in the village.

It is worth making a detour to the pub anyway to see the ancient market cross (now owned by the National Trust). The base of the cross is medieval and it was rebuilt with a new column in 1831 to mark the coronation of William IV. I was struck by the fact that the Trust has only two properties in Nottinghamshire, the huge estate at Clumber, and this tiny cross.

If you are staying to explore Nottinghamshire, it is only a short distance to Newark-on-Trent. The outskirts are unpromising, however, with belching factories and masses of roadworks, which will, I suppose, eventually improve things, but the town has an attractive centre with a large cobbled market square surrounded by many old buildings.

The meeting of the Great North Road, (previously the prehistoric track Sewstern Lane) the Fosse Way and the River Trent is where Newark has grown up and the reason for its initial prosperity. In both medieval and Tudor times, Newark was as large as Nottingham. The town's most famous period in history was the Civil War when it was a Royalist stronghold. The castle, known as the 'Key to the North' was beseiged three times. It is hardly surprising that Cromwell then ordered its destruction. However, the Norman gatehouse survived and the whole castle is being restored.

West Leake and Gotham

The countryside here is pleasant rather than breathtakingly pretty, but it does bring you face to face with the typical Nottinghamshire blend of industry and countryside. There are views of the Vale of Belvoir and the East Leake Gypsum Works, a foreground of gentle wooded inclines and curving crop-laden fields, with the cooling towers of Ratcliffe in the distance. The walk starts in the charming village of West Leake, and then views the urban sprawl of Gotham. It is rather like escaping to the country with your feet firmly on the ground.

I've already mentioned the eccentricities of the aristocracy in the Dukeries, but madness wasn't confined to the upper echelons. On this walk I encountered Cuckoobush Wood and the madmen of Gotham, of which more, soon.

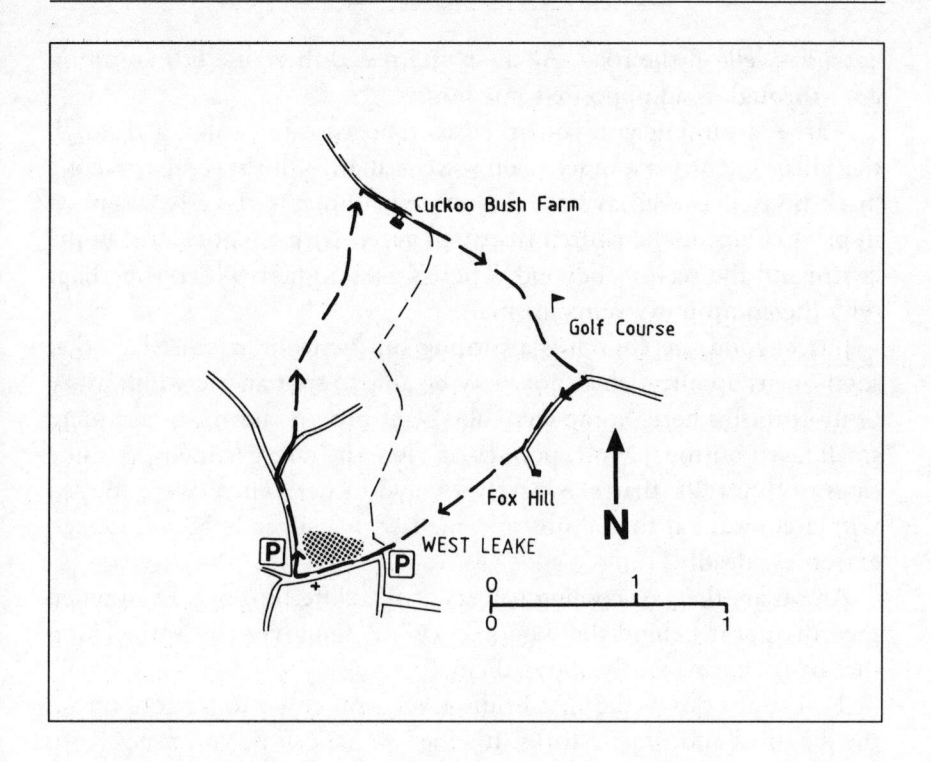

OS Map 1:50 000, Sheet 129
A circular walk of around 4 miles (6.5 km). Allow 2 hours.

The going underfoot is on lane, dirt track and grassy paths. One section at the entrance to a field was mucky and it can also be muddy along the field edges. There is one short, fairly gentle climb.

The walk begins in West Leake, a small attractive village between Nottingham and Loughborough.

Car-parking and the start

There is some parking in West Leake. The best place is at the eastern end of the village where, just off a sharp bend, there is a reasonable flat area well off the road. At the western end there is a little room in a no-through road opposite some houses.

Start – assuming you've parked to the east – by walking through the village. It is very much a one-street affair, with several attractive brick houses, as well as several new developments cleverly disguised in brick. Outside the church is a small green with a mature tree in the centre and the rectory beyond. There's no pub here which is perhaps why the community remains small.

Just beyond the church is a turning on the right, a quiet lane that soon opens up into fields. You may be able to spot an incredible array of mushrooms here. Some were like giant brown saucers, others mere small fawn buttons. Most spectacular were the tall specimens, in some cases with a stalk that was nearly twelve inches. These were topped with a conical hat that almost gleamed with a silver light and looked extremely deadly.

Ahead are the vast cooling towers of Ratcliffe-on-Soar. Even when they disappear behind the wooded skyline, the giveaway is the cloud that hangs permanently above them.

Turn right down the first bridle-track you come to. It goes off on the diagonal and shortly forks. It's the left-hand fork you need. Keep going in the general direction of the wooded ridge.

Just before the woods, where the field is edged by a hedged ditch, I disturbed a large number of pheasants hiding in the undergrowth. They fluttered in all directions across the fields and into the woods.

The main track swings round to the left in the direction of the farmhouse, and branching off is a wide grassy path that goes up between the two areas of wood.

Follow this path over the crest of the hill and then down the rather rough lane that continues in the same direction. Just past a modern farmhouse on the left there is a T-junction and you can look down the hill to Gotham.

The view is quite a contrast from West Leake village, with the old village now indistinguishable from the mass of new houses. There are many different stories concerning the madmen of Gotham and not much explanation as to why they got up to all their foolish things. It is said that they tried to drown an eel in a bucket, and thinking the moon is made of cheese, they tried using nets to catch it in a pond. But they may have been shrewd after all. The story goes that they wanted to prevent King John coming to their village as it was commonly thought that wherever the king had been would become a public road.

At this T-junction, turn right towards the isolated farmhouse, known as Cuckoobush Farm (the capturing of cuckoo was also among the madmen's exploits). Where the track ends keep going in the same direction across the fields, with a little copse, known as Cuckoo Bush, to your left. Where the copse ends, the path goes straight on, but you will need to walk on the lower side of the hedge boundary. The upper field ends in a dead-end of hedges, as I found out.

From the top of the lower meadow, you can again see Gotham filling the valley, the larger sprawl in the distance is Nottingham, and the surrounding countryside is the Vale of Belvoir.

Walk along the top edge of the meadow and through the spinney to the golf course. Ahead is the East Leake Gypsum Works. The area here has been quarried for many years for gypsum, which is found at Gotham and nearby Kingston-on-Soar. Nottingham produces 45% of the national output of gypsum. In Victorian times it was used to make a very durable flooring found in many old Notts houses. Now it is mainly converted into a range of plasters for the building industry. I wonder if, in years to come, you'll be looking down at a nature reserve here. Already, near Newark, an exhausted gypsum quarry has been turned into a lake with the surrounding area planted, rather like the gravel pits at Attenborough (p. 187).

Continue along the top of the golf course which is quite a lumpy affair as it goes over what remains of Gotham's medieval strip-farming system. The path forks off to the right to run along the side of the fields parallel with the golf course.

At the far edge of the field is a hardcore track; turn right, walking in the direction of West Leake. The main track leads to the farm, but just before it is a grassy path which takes you down into West Leake, coming out at the sharp road bend.

WARWICKSHIRE

In this small and rewarding area of the country, I discovered a huge variety of things from cabbages and kings and kingmakers to contrasting castles and canals. And there's a good deal more. I so enjoy the vivid and romantic history to be found in Warwickshire. It is surprisingly easy to experience despite the county being squashed between a proliferation of roadways, vast blocks of urban sprawl, electrified fences, Shakespeare, and notices warning you to Beware of the Bull!

The tourist tag for Warwickshire is the 'Heart of England'. My heart warms to this county, not so much in the geographical sense but for the time when it was centre stage in the great struggles for power, starting with the rivalries of those tempestuous houses, York and Lancaster. The realm was divided by war and intrigue. Following the long-drawn-out Wars of the Roses and the emergence of the Tudor dynasty, Warwickshire had a close involvement with the Civil War with its curtain-raiser, the Battle of Edge Hill.

The towns and castles of Warwick and Kenilworth and the surrounding areas have many connections with this period of history and are marvellous focal points for reliving some of these events. Associated with Warwick is the best-known kingmaker, the man who supposedly 'made' King Edward IV, Richard Neville, Earl of Warwick. He completed a unique feat in history by having two kings of England imprisoned at the same time. Henry VI was in the Tower of London, whilst Edward IV was a prisoner at Warwick Castle. Neville added some glorious complications to an already very involved period of history, and seemed to put somewhat of a jinx on the title of Earl of Warwick. The next few Earls met various unfortunate ends usually without their heads. Neville himself died at The Battle of Barnet in 1471.

Kenilworth, too, played its part in the affairs of kings, or perhaps strictly speaking, queens, as it was at one time owned by Robert Dudley, favourite of Elizabeth I. He played host to her on several occasions, and the grand ruins of this castle have an air of romance. (Cynics say that these remains are probably more attractive than the original castle.)

Warwickshire isn't all about the doings of royals, there's plenty to enjoy on an ordinary scale, which I suppose brings me back to the cabbages! It is easy to be put off by the thought of so much tarmacadam and forget that Warwickshire has a strong agricultural tradition from medieval times. There are still some tell-tale signs of the old-style farming techniques. Lumps and bumps in the fields reveal the ridge and furrow system, which tended to be quite regular, adding a wonderful rhythm to the land. The more chaotic humps and depressions can be sites of deserted villages and it's fascinating to trace out long-deserted streets and lines of moats. The county is still important to farming with the National Agriculture Centre just near Warwick, and in the more recent National Centre of Organic Gardening, but more about that later.

I didn't always find the agricultural nature of Warwickshire conducive to my progress as a walker. You will often have to contend with ploughed fields and barbed wire where sometimes there are supposed to be footpaths. Fortunately, there are some active local walking groups with the main objective of keeping paths open and well-marked.

Finding ways round sticky ploughed fields where the clay clings in wet weather, and in dry conditions where there are gaping cracks ready for the unsuspecting ankle, led me down to the towpaths and a part of Warwickshire I hadn't really been aware of. Three great canals cross the county, the Grand Union, the Stratford-upon-Avon, and the Oxford Canal, and there are miles of peaceful stretches to explore plus many places where it's worth climbing the banks to find friendly pubs and pretty villages.

You may also come across less-predictable obstacles of the four-footed variety. I particularly liked a short note in one local book that stated frankly that all bulls were a potential danger (and probably more so when they're calmly grazing in the field you want to cross). But if you don't feel you can tell a Charolais from a Friesian or an Aberdeen Angus from an Ayrshire, then it isn't worth the risk. As my knowledge of bulls goes no further than the horns, I took these words of wisdom to heart and ended up scouting round the outside of two fields with one eye firmly fixed on the beast in the centre, and the other eye gauging what damage I might do to myself leaping over the fence into the hawthorn hedge beyond. Don't worry, though, I have now found some alternative routes to suggest here.

My choice of activities in Warwickshire is centred around Warwick and Kenilworth. I wanted to reflect the mixture in this county from the doings of the great and the powerful to the everyday. Everything takes place in a fairly small region so there is little driving involved; go by bike if you prefer. One big advantage of all the major roads is the way they draw off the heavy traffic and leave many of the country lanes pleasantly quiet.

Warwick and Kenilworth are popular but I hope with my suggestions you'll be able to find a different side to see. In the surrounding areas I found a host of entertaining things from a moated manor, and medieval tea-rooms, deer park and deserted village to windmills and waterways. You'll also discover the local countryside. To the east is a delightful area around the Oxford Canal, and to the west, where I began, the remnants of the ancient forest of Arden, about the nearest I let myself get to Shakespeare.

Baddesley Clinton

OS Map 1:50 000, Sheet 139
A circular walk of 6 miles (10 km). Allow 3 hours and extra time to visit the house.

I first found myself at the moated manor house of Baddesley Clinton really by accident. I was in search of a good picnic spot on a long drive north. Nearing Birmingham, I spotted the trusty 'blue table' sign on the map and turned off the road to Hay Wood. Things looked promising as within minutes of leaving the roar of the A41 the route to the picnic site went down a tiny lane marked unsuitable for heavy traffic. A mile or so down was a pleasant forest parking place, unspoiled, where someone had gone to the trouble of providing a few wooden tables and benches – the 'blue table' on the map.

Exploration of the area in the immediate vicinity is somewhat limited by the private sporting rights. There is a footpath which takes you nowhere much except back to the A41, though lack of success in this direction was a blessing in disguise, as turning the other way, I came across the National Trust notice 'Public Footpath to Church and Baddesley Clinton only'. Needless to say I decided to explore.

The name sounded rather like something, or someone, out of a spaghetti western, so it was lovely to find a delightful manor house, made all the more romantic by its wide moat and single entrance over the bridge through the gate-house. It has remained virtually unchanged since the early 1600s. What I liked about it was the feeling I could live in it. Whilst there is much to admire in many grand houses, the rooms are too vast and too daunting to imagine I could ever fling my shoes off and curl up on the *chaise-longue*. Here, there is a refreshingly different feeling, a sense that the house has been well and truly loved and lived in. If only walls could talk these would have many a tale to tell. There are a fair share of intriguing stories concerning the various owners, some of whom have names to match that of the house itself.

Baddesley Clinton was built in about the thirteenth century and many improvements were made by Nicholas Brome, renowned for his 'building and violence'. A curious combination. There is some gruesome evidence of the latter in the upstairs parlour, but I won't give too much away. In the Elizabethan period, the house was owned by the Vaux sisters, Catholic sympathizers. They sheltered many a priest in the numerous ingenious hiding-places that you can still see around the house. By the nineteenth century, the buildings had fallen into disrepair; it was lived in and restored by the last of the Ferrers of Baddesley, Marmion, with his bride Rebecca Dulcibella. They shared the house with Rebecca's aunt and her second husband, Heneage. This quartet became a partnership as both the aunt and (after a decent interval) Rebecca's husband, died, and eventually Rebecca married Heneage. On his death she lived on in the house until 1923.

The panelled rooms are beautiful; there are splendid fireplaces and most interesting old armorial glass. The place is staffed by well-informed guides who have a wealth of stories to tell.

Entry to the house is by timed ticket so it doesn't get too crowded, and in case of a fire everyone can get over the moat via the causeway without getting their feet wet.

Despite its proximity to the busy A41 trunk road, this small area is a surprising backwater, surrounded by peaceful country lanes and close to both the Grand Union and the Stratford-upon-Avon canals. There are many possibilities for long and short rambles around the grounds of Baddesley Clinton via the villages of Rowington and Turners Green.

I've described one of the longer options, a circuit of approximately six miles (10 km). It is best to time your walk so you can look around Baddesley Clinton house, and enjoy the delights of the tea-room in the stables there. This walk is full of contrasts, from open fields and parkland leading across to the massive Wroxall Abbey, through quiet lanes, to a very attractive mile or so along the Grand Union Canal. The going underfoot is mostly good on short grass, lane or towpath. I went after a week of rain and it was still wet underfoot, but soggy rather than boggy. There are a couple of ploughed fields which can be muddy and some of the gateways get a little waterlogged, so wear sturdy shoes or wellies. Dogs are fine on the walk, though will need to be on leads across the grazing area and they are not allowed in the house and its immediate grounds.

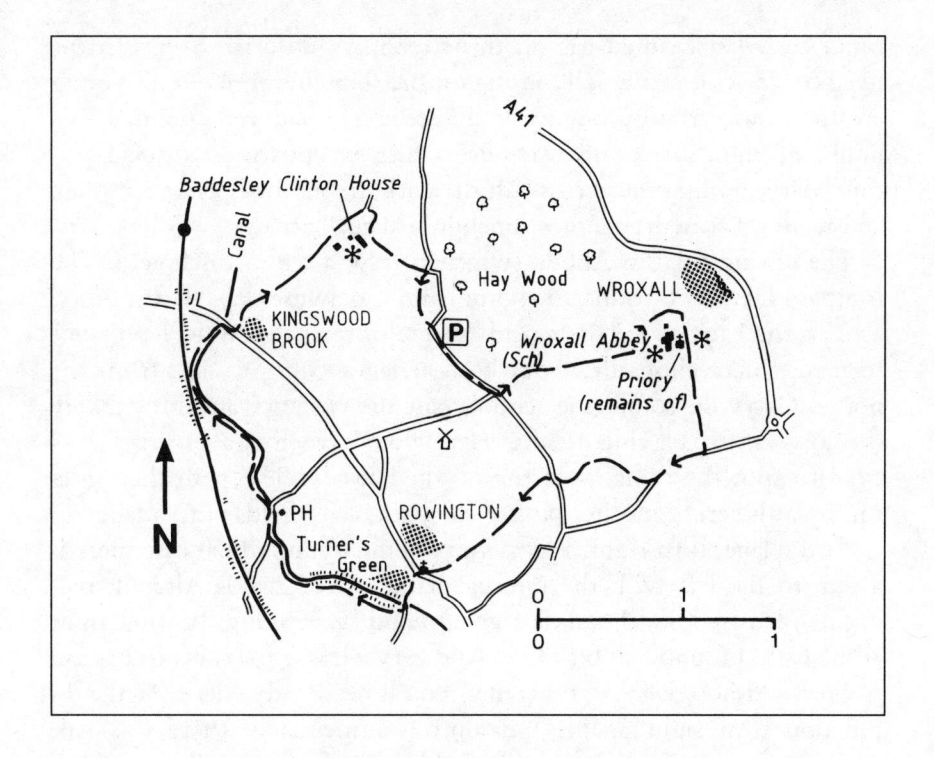

Car-parking and the start

You can either park at Baddesley Clinton itself, or in the designated car-park at Hay Wood. I parked there as I like the idea of coming across the house as a special treat at the end of the hike, so I'll give directions from there, but you'll see from the map the possibilities of starting from the house.

From the car-park, turn left out of the wood and along the lane to the T-junction. Just beyond this is a footpath sign to the left marking two routes, one straight on and one diagonally to the right. Go for the one straight ahead which leads down the side of the field and then into the parkland that belongs to Wroxall Abbey. This stretch is super, typical 'sheep may safely graze' English parkland with occasional solitary trees. These grounds stretch up to the impressive Victorian house. The footpath marches boldly through the centre of the open space which I think is much more fun than timidly creeping around the edge. There are helpful yellow markers on the trees to keep you on line. It was shortly after lambing and I nearly came away with more than I bargained for on this stretch. A little lamb decided he liked the look of my woolly jumper more than his mum's. This young creature was certainly out to be different. He had very pointed ears unlike all the others, and was pure white except for jet black knee-caps. After trailing me across half the park, he suddenly changed track and went off to worry a most uncuddly wheelbarrow.

The setting for the Abbey (which is now a school) is lovely. The footpath takes you round the school anti-clockwise. It is worth going around the back to see the grand avenue of trees that must have once formed a marvellous driveway for carriages going to and from the house. Carry on round the school, past the entrance and most likely the lower-fifth playing tennis. Here you have to be rather sharp-eyed to spot the remains of the original abbey. The path then goes southwards across another part of the park, over fields onto a lane.

At the lane, turn right (unless you are thirsty, in which case there is a pub to the left with the unusual name, The Case is Altered, recommended by a local walking group) and walk along, bearing right at the fork. I found this bit of the lane very narrow for cars rather than walkers. Although I saw no traffic, you'll need to be alert. At the T-junction turn right again, and almost immediately there is a stile opposite marking a way across the fields to Rowington Village. I don't know who this path was designed for as the green way-marker is at ankle level. Nevertheless it is a good route along pleasant fields, going over a little stream and eventually leading up to Rowington Church. This is a delightful setting, with the church on the top of a slight hill and the apron of the churchyard stretching out towards you as you approach. I was lucky to pick a time when the sun shone from behind me, lighting up the church windows and the many graveside flowers.

The church is on a busy corner so take care as you cross. But on that corner is a lane, marked as a footpath, that leads you shortly down to the canal. This is a lovely meandering section of canal, almost hidden in a deep cutting which in spring is covered with harebells. It wiggles along wooded meadows to Turner's Green where a small road crosses over the top. It's worth climbing up here, perhaps for the pub, but also for the pretty setting and charming cottages.

Carry on along the canal to the next road junction at Kingswood Brook. This section goes extremely close to the Stratford-upon-Avon

Canal and the two waterways are joined by a small spur with a reservoir at the junction. It's a popular area for boating.

To find the route to Baddesley Clinton, leave the canal and cross the road to the Navigation Inn. Just by this pub, there were ominous signs saying 'Works Entrance' and my heart sank as I thought the new M40 was destined to ruin this lovely spot, but I breathed a sigh of relief when I found the work was merely a section of the canal being repaired. The right way for the walk is to head diagonally across a rather scruffy, unpromising-looking field, through a hedge and onto a track. Then, a series of decent, newish stiles takes you towards the house. You can't see it easily because of the surrounding wood. These trees are some of the few remaining of Shakespeare's Forest of Arden.

At last you come to the house. It's very relaxing to walk around and the stable tea-rooms are good. From the house, it is a short walk up to Saint Michael's Church *en route* back to base. If you look just inside the church, there's a stone by the front door inscribed 'Nicholas Brome', 1517 (he of the violent temper). It was a condition of his will that as penance for his violent crime he should be buried thus and so trodden on by all who enter the church.

From the church, continue on the track to the road and turn right to the car-park at Hay Wood.

If you want a shorter outing, you could treat this circuit as two loops, either doing the tour of Wroxall Abbey and coming back along the lanes, or alternatively, walk along the lanes via Rowington Green to Turner's Green and onto the canal there. If you take this route, do look out for the old windmill (now sail-less) which has been converted most cleverly into a private home.

Kenilworth

Having slogged my way up the long, narrow high street of Kenilworth Town behind a stream of large lorries and vans all trying to turn the road into a dual carriage-way, and competing with push chairs and pedestrians for right of way, I was quite unprepared for the spaciousness and relative tranquillity of Kenilworth Castle with greens to one side and vast meadows to the other.

The surrounding land was at one time all part of the royal manor of Stoneleigh which was given to Geoffrey de Clinton in the twelfth century. He divided it into two sections; downstream was the priory and upstream a large space was reserved for building his castle. Fortunately, little of this has been encroached on by modern builders. From the northern end of the high street there is a good view over the old Abbey fields and a route down by the river leads to the main entrance of the castle.

The ruins of Kenilworth are most striking, not least because they are massive, but also because they are a rich red sandstone which really glows in sunshine. I've got strong memories of this deep colour as I've been lucky to have good weather every time I've been here.

Both Kenilworth and Warwick, the other major fortress of this part of England, are well known and well-publicized, but crowds tend to come at weekends and Bank Holidays leaving mid-week days relatively uncrowded. There is also plenty of good walking in the vicinity.

Around the Castle and Through the Lake

OS Map 1:50 000, Sheet 139 and 140
A circular walk of about 5 miles (8 km). Allow 2–3 hours.

This walk gives you some marvellous views of the castle as the setting is quite equal to the ruins. Early on, you can look down on Kenilworth from a small hill, and at the end of the walk approach from almost below the foundations across what was once a grand lake, known now as The Mere. The going underfoot is very good for two-thirds of the walk as it is mostly track and lane with the odd muddy patch, but the route home over the meadows can be wet, even after long spells of dry weather. The paths are easy to follow, well-signposted with yellow arrows. The first time I went round this route, I only had half an OS map with me and even then didn't get too lost. The castle acts as quite a beacon for getting you back onto the route.

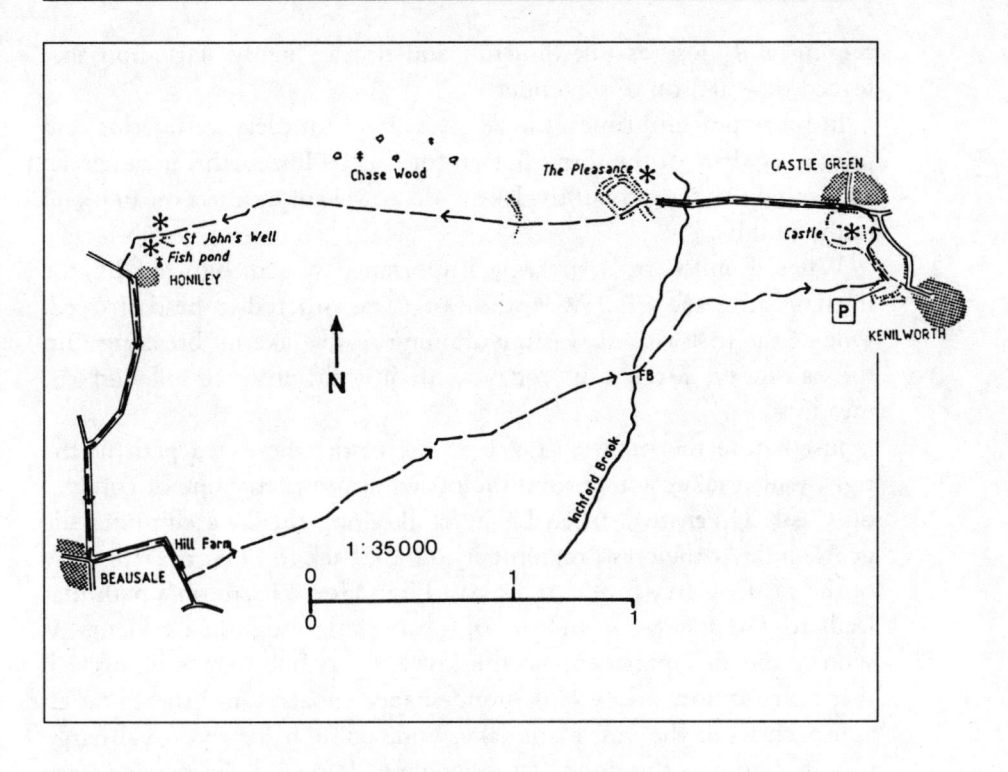

Car-parking and the start

There is ample parking at The Brays, an old name for the ponds of water that collected between the locks and dams surrounding the castle in medieval times. Now it is quite dry.

From the Brays you can follow in Elizabeth I's footsteps as she made her progress along this causeway when visiting the castle. It must have been some occasion. Poets and musicians were along the way to greet her, and gifts were laid in her track. Robert Dudley, Lord Leicester, had built for her some grand staterooms, now known as Leicester's Building. She stayed for some nineteen days of entertainment.

Whilst on the causeway, look over to the meadows to the left. It is hard to imagine that this was all once a great lake known as The Mere, over half a mile wide, created by damming Inchford Brook and other streams. It formed the main defence of the castle to the southern and western sides first. It proved valuable in a thirteenth-century siege of the supporters of Simon de Montfort. The width of the lake made mining and close assault difficult, and it was finally starvation that forced the garrison to surrender.

In more peaceful times, the lake was used for pleasure-boating and pageantry. Part of the show put on for Queen Elizabeth I included an appearance by the lady of the lake and a couple of nymphs on an island in the middle.

When Kenilworth's strategic importance was recognized by the Puritans after the Civil War, the castle was ordered to be destroyed. One of the first actions was the draining of the lake by breaking into the causeway, leaving us today with just the little brook and the meadows.

Just before the main entrance to the castle, there is a path to the right which takes you around the castle, near a pretty line of cottages on Castle Green to Purlieu Lane. Walk along this lane climbing the gentle hill. At the crest, remember to look back for a wonderful view of the castle. Carry on the track past High House Farm on a path that leads to The Pleasance, the site of a summerhouse built by Henry V who found the apartments in the castle too public for his liking. All that remains now are two diamond-shaped moats. Once there was an approach from the vast castle lake, wide enough for the royal barge to sail almost to the door of the pavilion. It must have made a very special retreat. The area is quite boggy, but note, to compensate, it's a rich source of marsh-loving flowers such as bittercress.

The path carries straight on west across the fields with Chase Wood up to the right. This wood, at least according to my OS map, used to come right down to the path, but has now sadly been cut back. Along the fields to the left you'll soon see the pretty spire of St John's Church at Honily. There's a little bridge over a stream, and then a slight walk up the hill towards the church. Just below the church is an overgrown area, the site of St John's Well and some old fishponds. You can just about see some indentations under the brambles. Follow the path around until you come out on a lane. Here, turn left. It's a quick detour to nip into the church, an attractive building of pale sandstone. The ruins of Kenilworth can just be seen from the churchyard from its Baroque tower. Then there's a mile or so along a pleasant country lane to the village of Beausale. At these crossroads, turn left and follow the road round a corner past Hill Farm. Just beyond there's a way-marked track leading you back along the meadows towards the castle.

This part of the walk takes you across Inchford Brook through the area that was once all lake. It is easy to imagine when you are standing in some of the boggier bits. But even if you get wet feet it is not too long to the end and dry socks in the car. The last meadow is known as Echo Meadow and is a wonderful approach to the castle as you come virtually underneath the foundations, which makes the outer walls seem massive.

Just by the car-park, I found a noticeboard advertising the local walking society. There is information about this group in the local library. For anyone staying longer in the area, they produce a small booklet of local walks.

Lord Leyster's Loaf

I like the compactness of Warwick centre, its twisting streets, antique market, and availability of parking space. It took me several visits to the town before I braved the castle, mostly because I felt it would be overcrowded and commercialized. I was pleasantly surprised by how much I enjoyed my visit.

It is popular, certainly, and you'd be well-advised to avoid weekends, but inside there is plenty to see and ample space to accommodate a large crowd.

As for the commercial side, much of the older part has been left alone, giving an excellent impression of the sparse living quarters of medieval times and this balances the luxurious state rooms. I didn't think I would enjoy these – static table settings, endless portraits, and the long red ropes keeping you away from all the interesting objects – but the rooms are brought to life with the famous Tussaud (the group owns the castle) waxworks, recreating a royal house party. I found it worked really well especially when Field-Marshal Lord Roberts fixed me with a steely glare whilst adjusting his bow tie!

A good walk has been created from Guy's Tower, a climb of 128 feet (39 m) but worth it for the terrific views over Warwick and the surrounding countryside. From here, you go down another staircase, along the battlements into some of the older quarters. Each suite has a tiny bedroom, sitting room and loo. The original tower block!

Caesar's Tower, at the other end of the wall, is equally massive with foundations going down practically to the level of the river. This tower houses the dungeon and torture chamber, and is not for the faint-hearted as I found out. There is a grisly display of torture instruments and gruesome descriptions of their effects. The dank space of the dungeon below is quite horrible, and even more so, a wretched tiny hole virtually underground, where some unfortunate could be left and forgotten. I felt the atmosphere was quite disturbing and it was a relief to get into the fresh air and walk in the lovely grounds surrounding the castle. There is 'natural' (Capability Brown) parkland leading down to the river, and some formal gardens dotted with many peacocks. I had forgotten how noisy they are.

Although the castle is probably Warwick's most well-known attraction, there is a very good (10 p) town trail to follow around some of the less well-known sites which takes about half an hour. It was this that brought me to Lord Leycester's Hospital just next to the West Gate, and also to the tea-room, a gem neatly hidden inside.

The hospital buildings are some of the oldest in Warwick and they enjoy using the old spelling of Leicester. In spite of being timber-built, they miraculously survived the fire that destroyed much of the town in the seventeenth century. They have all the crooked charm of old houses, with top floors that lean precariously over the street. Originally they were used as meeting places for the guilds and the burgesses of Warwick until abandoned during Henry VIII's time of persecution. Robert Dudley, Lord Leycester and favourite of Elizabeth, took them over in 1571 and founded a hospital for a master and twelve brethren. These 'brethren' were old soldiers who had fought for Queen Elizabeth I. The tradition continues today as accommodation is still provided for ex-servicemen.

The Brethren's Kitchen is a wonderful tea-room tucked inside these buildings. It overlooks the half-timbered inner courtyard surrounded by Elizabethan gables. The inside is furnished in dark oak and the walls hung with all manner of curiosities, including some hand embroidery belonging to Anne Neville.

You can visit the tea-room here without necessarily going through the hospital. I have a passion for tea-rooms, strange for a non-tea-drinker, but I find good tea often brings with it good coffee, sandwiches and baking. The Brethren's Kitchen is no exception. There is a good, simple menu of sandwiches, toasted and plain, various filled potatoes, salads, amazing hot chocolate, and do leave room for it, Lord Leycester's Loaf. Served in a thick slice with butter, it is quite enough to restore the most intrepid traveller. I was told very modestly that it was just Bara Brith. Maybe it is cooked in an Elizabethan oven for extra flavour.

A quiet sitdown here is exactly what is needed after a tour of a busy town. Since discovering it, my subsequent trips to Warwick have begun with a beeline here. There is an exclusive little car-park at the back, solely for visitors to the hospital, though I think one or two canny souls sneak in there unofficially as it seemed very full considering the number who were actually in the café. Maybe it would be appropriate to mount a guard like Taylor's in Suffolk.

The Oxford Canal

I spent two days discovering this lovely area to the east of Warwick. It has quite a different feel to the western parts; gentle undulating hills and valleys, occasionally punctured by a more dramatic feature such as Napton Hill or Burton Dasset. The area is crossed North/South by the Oxford Canal.

If you are heading in this direction it is not much of a detour to visit Ryton Gardens, The National Centre for Organic Gardening. My only other experience of organic gardening on a large scale is The Centre for Alternative Technology in Wales. That is housed in a rambling quarry, a location that fits very well with the promotion of a self-sufficient and organic lifestyle. Ryton Gardens is a complete contrast, its surroundings are busy roads, industrial sites and urban development. Its neighbour is another type of plant, the well-known Talbot car manufacturing one.

The centre's success is, for me, all the more inspiring because of its position. I found a visit absolutely fascinating and I went away with visions of DIY compost bins and a very non-vegetarian desire to go slug hunting. More practically, I loaded up with organic wine, vegetables, and wholefoods, and environmentally friendly house-plant food (well it's a start), all from the well-stocked shop. You can either wander around the gardens on your own, or go on a guided tour.

These are led by organic enthusiasts and take place twice daily, lasting between one and two hours. Apart from the gardens and shop, there is a handy small café overlooking the grounds.

The café's menu is simple but excellent. Much of the produce used is supplied by the garden. It's quite a challenge working out all the different ingredients of the leafy salads, despite some helpful illustrations on the wall. There's a good range of hot savouries, delicious cakes and some particularly good fruit (organic) puddings. There is a charge for looking round the garden, but it's free if you only want to eat. Simply explain at the entrance and go straight into the café. There is ample parking in the grounds.

The roads around Ryton are so hazardous it's worth going on towards the Oxford Canal to find some decent walking. In search of this, I came across Napton-on-the-Hill. You can't really miss it as the village is literally built on the hill, a fact well-emphasized in the name as 'nap' means hill and 'ton' means town. You also can't fail to see the wonderful windmill that faces towards Warwick. The Oxford Canal bends round the hill and just to the north is Napton Junction where the Oxford Canal joins the Grand Union. Napton turned out to be a lovely place to explore.

In Napton, there is a limited amount of roadside parking but choose carefully as some of the streets are narrow. I made a bee-line for the windmill on a path that led through the churchyard. Needless to say, I nipped in for a quick look at the church, and here discovered the village trail devised by the local Women's Institute in the 1970s. A plan of the village is mounted on a large board hung just inside the nave. The route for the trail is marked in red. Surrounding the map are snippets of history about the village and drawings of many of the flowers and shrubs that you are likely to see *en route*. the trail is about two-and-a-half miles (4 km) long and certainly worth doing, though it may take longer than expected, as it did me, due to the many distractions that Napton has on offer. There are plenty of curiosities here, and I don't just mean buildings.

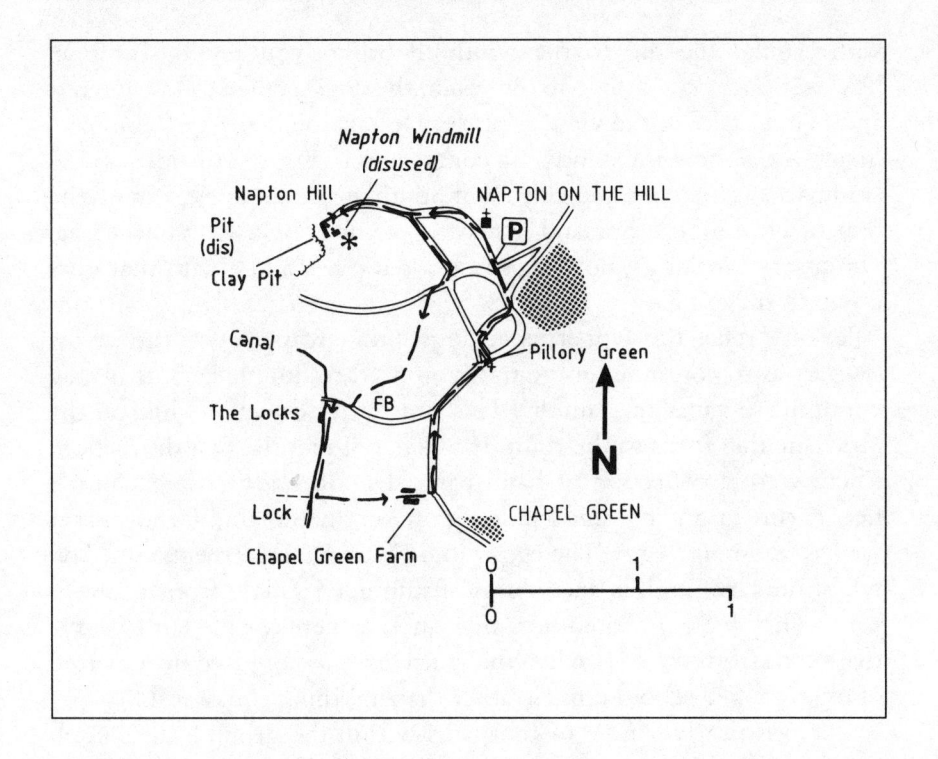

In and around Napton-on-the-Hill

OS Map 1:50 000, Sheet 151
A circular tour of $2\frac{1}{2}$ miles (4 km). Allow up to $1\frac{1}{2}$–2 hours.

This is just the sort of walk that you could do spontaneously. You don't really need a map and it is fine in ordinary footwear. The one place you do cross a field can be avoided, if conditions are wet, by using the quiet lanes instead. Dogs and children are welcome.

To start the walk, go behind the church and up the lane to the windmill, where there is a wonderful view west towards Southam and Warwick. The windmill is no longer in use and has been converted to a private residence. You become very well aware of this when two huge Dobermann pinscher dogs come leaping out, jaws wide open, barking a ferocious greeting. Yes, there is a fence, but I felt I could have done with another couple of feet on the netting for safety. The path around the hill to the windmill brings you perilously close, however once down this narrow patch, the dogs seemed to lose interest and I could take in the view at peace. Do take binoculars, if you have them, as the view is extensive, a compass, too, is good for identifying landmarks. The town and church of Southam are quite clear, with the blur of Leamington Spa and Warwick beyond. Below, you'll see the old quarry workings, now mostly grassed over, and a path that goes down to the canal.

To my relief the Dobermann dogs didn't reappear on the return journey as to continue on the trail you need to double back from the windmill towards the church. This time walk down the hill on the little lane that forks to the right. It was here I met the first distraction. There were a collection of hand-painted notices advertising Church Leas Farm, an organic small-holding offering nature and farm trails as well as free-range eggs. The eggs can be had any day except Saturday, whilst the farm itself is open on most summer Sundays from 11 am to 5 pm. They have practised organic principles here for the last twenty-five years, from the days when the word 'greens' conjured up a picture of over-cooked school dinner rather than anything ecological.

There is nearly a mile of footpaths within the grounds at Church Leas. One trail I saw was curiously called The Old Tramway. An old farmer told me it was made from some of the sleepers which were part of the line that used to go to the quarry workings near the windmill. There are some interesting trees and shrubs to see and inevitably free-range chickens enjoying the trails as much as any visitor. There is a dairy herd here too, as well as other livestock, and I was struck by the fact that the place, unlike many farms, didn't smell.

From the farm, the trail goes on down the lane and onto a road known as The Butts, an old term for the strip-farming used from Saxon times until the land enclosures. From here, go diagonally across the fields (or via the lane if it is very wet) down to the Folly Bridge, which you can see below. This is an attractive area of the canal, and a popular place for the barges to stop. They are probably trying to summon the energy for the eight locks just beyond Napton going south towards Banbury.

Don't cross the Folly Bridge, but walk south to the next bridge, one of some 250 that span the canal. Then leave the canal (again without crossing it) and walk along the track to Chapel Green, so-called because it was the site of the Chapel of St Lawrence at the end of the fourteenth century. The route then goes back to the village via Pillory Green where, as the name implies, the village stocks were sited.

Here's another oddity, the Napton Christadelphian Reading Room. I don't know if it's still in use, but I needed a swift look in the dictionary at home to check who the Christadelphians are. (They are nothing to do with peculiar hybrid flowers, but a sect who reject the doctrine of Trinity and expect the second coming of Christ). The road twists round to the village green with a magnificent chestnut tree planted to mark the coronation of George V, which is now truly one of the 'underneath the spreading' type.

Don't miss the Napton Nickleodeon Museum, yet another local distraction. In fact, if you are interested in mechanical music machines, this could be a very major diversion, as the presentation featuring the Hurdy Gurdy Man, a mechanical violin and Bruno the Smoking Monkey, lasts $1\frac{1}{2}$ hours. The museum is really designed for visiting groups but individuals can be shown around as long as they (you) telephone in advance. Otherwise, go to open afternoons, usually on Bank Holidays, or open evenings on the last Saturday of every month except July and August, starting at 7.30 pm.

This wasn't the last of the Napton entertainments on offer. I came across the local theatre which is open-air. Are you surprised? It was started by the locals a couple of years ago and they put on one show during the summer which has proved very popular. As the director told me, they have a very mixed community in Napton.

What I thought was going to be a ten-minute walk up to the windmill took two hours as there was so much to enjoy here.

Close by Napton, within walking distance if you like, is the Shuckburgh Estate with ancient parkland and a herd of fallow deer which I was anxious to see. I couldn't tell from the map whether the Estate was entirely private so I started out by driving to what I considered the back door, but which is really the main route to the grand house. I was a bit disheartened by the notice there saying 'Private Deer Park' and wasn't entirely convinced that the footpath on the map was valid. Luckily, at the gates of the park, I met an estate worker who told me of the splendid footpath that came up to the other side of the park from Lower Shuckburgh and then 'way over yonder by the woods'. He didn't need to say much more besides mentioning some pretty lakes and attractive woodland and I was off, back to Lower Shuckburgh to find the route up to The Cannon Bank.

The Cannon Bank and the Fallow Deer

OS Map 1:50 000, Sheet 151
A circular walk of about 3 miles (5 km). Allow 1–2 hours.

You could probably manage this without the map if you just walk straight up from Lower Shuckburgh to the park and back, but as I always find circuits more interesting, I've described a route that takes you on to Beacon Hill and down another way. So the map may help.

This is a lovely stroll, mostly on springy sheep-nibbled turf, which is very pleasant underfoot. There are all sorts of things to see, deer and rabbits as well as attractive woodland and good views from the top.

Car-parking and the start

There is limited parking (just for one or two) by Lower Shuckburgh Church. Do look at this curious building with its unusual hexagonal steeple. It doesn't fit very readily into the typical country church scene and was apparently altered to this eastern style following the fancy of one of the Shuckburgh family when he returned from the Crimea.

From the church, cross the (main and rather fast) road and almost opposite is the footpath leading diagonally up the hill behind some cottages. There are a couple of white metal gates to aim for and then it is really a matter of a steepish climb across the fields to the top. Although there isn't a very distinctive track, there must once have been more traffic from the 'big house' to the workers' cottages. Near the top of the hill is a substantial iron swing-gate, the type you normally see in a churchyard entrance, which now looks rather isolated. Continue to go up beyond this, and to the right there is what appears to be dense dark woodland. Getting closer I found it was an illusion, just a reflection of the trees in the very still waters of an almost hidden lake. There wasn't a ripple in sight despite a slight breeze in the open. There is an old wooden gate leading into this wood, but the padlock and noise of shooting decided me against exploring. Just beyond in the open is a large gate into the park. It's a bit of a struggle to deal with the chain and stiff catch but it does eventually open. From here there is a bank to the left where at first I thought I saw a telescope, then realized this must be the 'cannon' of Cannon Bank. It's splendidly sited and on a good day from here you can see the Black Mountains.

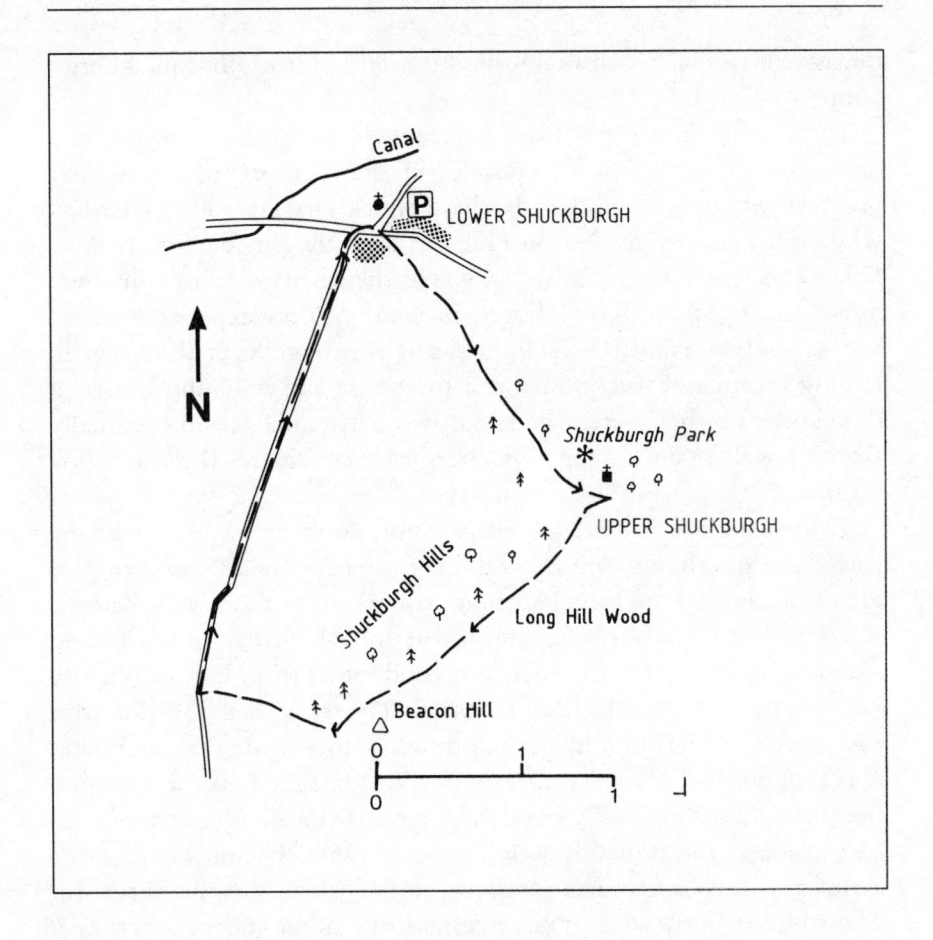

Once in the park you'll see a path running straight ahead which is the route home, but to see the estate church and the deer, keep going left. The church comes in sight just around the corner, and so do the notices saying the public are to go no further. But there is a good view of this lovely park, dotted with ancient oaks. You should be able to see the deer which wisely have chosen to live on the far side of these notices. If you are particularly keen on churches, I was told that you can ask for special permission to visit the church from the Shuckburgh family.

The family have owned the estate since the twelfth century, and one of the most colourful episodes in their history concerns their involvement in the Civil War. Richard Shuckburgh met King Charles I while out hunting on Beacon Hill and later fought for him at Edge Hill some ten miles (16 km) away. He then had to fortify his own house and fight the Roundheads on his own doorstep. Sir Richard was severely wounded and imprisoned for a while in Kenilworth, leaving Cromwell to commandeer the house and stable his horses in this church on the Estate. The house was left standing, and eventually all went well again for the Shuckburghs once Charles II came to the throne.

To find the route home from this point, double back, then take the path that goes slightly left. You'll leave the park by another gate and then continue up the ridge, keeping to the side of the wood. Known as Long Hill Wood, it leads you to the top of Beacon Hill (of King Charles I's hunting fame). There are good views from here of Napton Hill and the valley of the Oxford Canal. The track then goes due west past a group of farm buildings and down onto a road. Turn right and it is downhill all the way to Lower Shuckburgh. I like a downhill finish and this is especially good. The road is almost all unfenced, and gated too, so you probably won't see any traffic. The only car I came across was full of a courting couple, not too happy to be disturbed. The route is lined with grand trees and the adjoining pastures are a mass of lumps and bumps showing very clearly the medieval ridge and furrow system highlighted for me by the shadows of a gentle evening sun.

Back at Shuckburgh, if you have a little extra time, it is just a few minutes down the lane beside the church to the canal, not the Oxford as you might expect, but the Grand Union.

You could combine a visit to Ryton Gardens with either a tour of Napton or a walk to the Shuckburgh Deer Park as both these would while away the afternoon.

If you are in a mood for a whole day of walking and a picnic it is easy to combine these two walks. In that case it is best to park at Napton where there is more space. After wandering around the village, leave on the road to the west signposted Priors Marston. It is a fairly quiet road leading up towards Beacon Hill. At the T-junction, turn left and a little way down the road, you'll see the footpath on the right up to Long Hill Wood. This takes you into the deer park and from there you can walk back to Lower Shuckburgh. Then come back to Napton-on-the-Hill along the canal passing Napton Junction where the Oxford Canal heads south. It is about seven miles (12 km) all round and an extra two-and-a-half miles (4 km) to include the Napton village trail as well.

The Wormleighton Loop

I spent a second day to the east of Warwick itself. I found a good walk along a winding section of canal, some good views, and some interesting history. I went south down the line of the Oxford Canal Valley by car, which made a lovely, traffic-free drive. The lanes wind around the canal, crossing to and fro over a number of alarmingly steep, humpbacked bridges. My heart is in my mouth every time I flop over these. It's not just a case of leaving your stomach behind, but a case of will the car manage the hump? There is a descriptive warning sign with a lorry precariously balanced mid-hump, as it were, wheels in the air. I'd like to know how they get you afloat again if this happens.

The Oxford Canal is very meandering in its course, as it was designed by Brindley to follow the natural lie of the land rather than going straight, which would have necessitated major engineering feats such as deep cuttings or aqueducts. But going around the bend is not good for business. The contour-style canal was soon considered outdated. When the new Grand Union opened in 1800 and was a quicker way to get to London, trade on the Oxford Canal dropped off. Luckily for its owners, the Grand Union had to share a section north of Napton and very high rates were charged, making sure the Oxford Canal still made a good profit.

Later, once the canal was in use, the more dynamic, and possibly ruthless, Brunel shortened the northern part of the Oxford Canal by some thirteen miles (20 km). You can see the redundant loops on the map. Going south, Brindley's meandering design remains unchanged and I was particularly attracted to the Wormleighton Loop. It is a section of canal that makes a three-mile (5 km) journey around a spur of land (New House Farm) to make almost a complete circle.

Modern Wormleighton is an attractive village with some interesting sandstone buildings. I say 'modern' really to distinguish it from Old Wormleighton, the site of a deserted medieval village, in this case due to conversion of arable fields to pasture in the sixteenth century, effectively putting sixty villagers out of employment. I'm not sure it would have made the tabloid headlines even if there had been such a thing, as the business of enclosure was fairly common. Deserted villages are plentiful throughout Britain, but particularly in the Midlands where there are some thirteen hundred known sites.

To find the site of the deserted Wormleighton, walk through present-day Wormleighton towards the canal. This is along a lane which forks to the left, leading out onto fields which are the site of the abandoned village. All that's left now are grassed over hollows, ridges and other alterations in the land. You can find the path of a narrow village street, bordered by flat platforms showing the bases of small houses. The upper part of the street was at some point converted into fishponds, long since emptied, now just shadows in the ground. Near the canal are the remains of a rectangular moat, which may well have surrounded the original manor house, as that too was left to ruin. Outside the 'village' are the regular ridges, traces of the old farming system. Since discovering so much about deserted villages, I've never quite been able to look at a lump without wondering if it represented man or nature, and wondering what story it had to tell.

Simply walking along the canal around the loop makes a pleasant stroll. It is not an especially popular part, with no pubs or locks, just a natural towpath. In this instance that's a euphemism for narrowness sometimes to the point of disappearing for a stride or so, and a little muddy in places. But whilst walking on the section near Wormleighton, you get a good view of the Burton Dasset Hills about four miles (6 km) west. They rise, quite dramatically for Warwickshire, out of the plain, like the giant knuckles of a crunched up fist. Then, as the loop winds back east, the sails of the Napton Windmill may be seen, and further to the right are the woods of Beacon Hill. At Bridge 129, there's a good dirt road to bring you to the village.

I finished off my tour of this section of the county by attempting to look at Edge Hill, but I found the battlefield is now army land, guarded by very believable pictures of fierce Alsatian dogs, high wiring and areas of dense undergrowth which we call 'fight' in orienteering. The 'hill' of Edge Hill is well-wooded and I didn't find anywhere to get a good view. What I did discover, though, was the excellent viewing platform on the top of the Burton Dasset Hills in the Country Park. And it's also a good spot for a picnic lunch.

Burton Dasset Country Park covers about a hundred acres (40 ha) including this spur of five hills. If your interest in lumps has increased after Wormleighton, you'll have a field-day here as in between Magpie and Pleasant hills is a marvellously pock-marked area of land, the site of former quarries worked in the latter part of the nineteenth century, and briefly during the First World War. Once rich in iron ore, and now botanically rich, a nature trail leaflet is available for this area.

It is worth having a ramble around the entire area including Burton Dasset. Of Saxon origin, it was once occupied by Mr Bur and family. A burial place containing thirty-five skeletons was discovered at the beginning of this century on the not-very-aptly-named Pleasant Hill. On top of another hill is a stone beacon, probably lit at the time of Edge Hill to show that fighting had started. The signal would be seen from beacons up to forty miles (64 km) away on the Malvern Hills. The viewing point, to help you identify distant sites, is on Magpie Hill. There is a terrific view of Edge Hill and the site of the battlefield in the plain below. Other landmarks include Warwick, some eleven miles (17 km) away and Coventry (17 miles/27 km) and Cleeve Hills near Cheltenham, an optimistic fifty-two miles (83 km). In the next year or so, you'll also get a panoramic view of the new northern section of the M40 which bisects the valley below.

Further south down this valley is the National Trust property of Farnborough Hall. This is good to visit if you are interested in the Civil War as the Edge Hill Museum is housed there.

The gardens are interesting, landscaped two hundred years ago. Going from Avon Dasset, you soon see the slender obelisk which marks the end of a three-quarter-mile terrace walk. From here, too, there are good views of Edge Hill and the Warwickshire Plain.

For a county that isn't really known for its hills, I saw rather a lot on this trip – Napton, Burton Dasset and Farnborough. I'm probably being cynical in thinking that they are the few places that are bound to escape motorways.

I found one more hill on the way back to Warwick that is well worth making a detour to visit (this time by car), Windmill Hill, just west of Harbury. It is the windmill rather than the hill that you should go for. Designed by Inigo Jones (though he seems to be credited for most things around the mid seventeenth century and there is some doubt), it is quite the most unusual windmill I have ever seen, standing elegantly on slender columns. Doubt too has been cast on whether it was really built as a windmill as there is no permanent access to the upper floor. Nevertheless, it makes a very pleasing sight for the end of the day.

SUFFOLK

Discovering Suffolk is such a pleasure, and so relaxing that I scarcely know where all the time goes. I have a feeling that the whole county moves along at a very respectable pace, mostly in low gear. In fact you need to slip into this gear fairly frequently when driving down all the twisting, turning country lanes. Rumour has it that the roads wind so much because when the first travellers were pounding out the original trails, they were constantly turning to keep the wind at their backs.

I love exploring all these corkscrewing cross-country routes. You get a constantly changing view of the countryside, never quite knowing whether you'll come across a shallow valley, a cluster of pretty pastel farm cottages or a vast stretch of open fields, a concession to modern farming techniques.

Many of these little backwaters are quite deserted, especially noticeable if, like me, you've just come from a crowded city. Amongst all this solitude it's hard to imagine that East Anglia was once one of England's more dynamic industrial regions and considered quite densely populated. Admittedly this was in the seventh century, when the contemporary idea of overcrowding was different from now. What happened to all the people? Why did they leave? This started me on the 'disappearing' theme in Suffolk, and to my amazement I discovered a disappearing town. I say 'disappearing' rather than 'disappeared' as it has not all gone, so hurry to catch the last glimpse.

The place I'm referring to is Dunwich on the mid-Suffolk coast, I first noticed it mentioned as 'the ancient capital of East Anglia'. To me 'ancient capital' conjures up thoughts of places such as Winchester with its great cathedral, or the sturdy city of York with its massive walls. I found that Dunwich was no more than a pin-prick on the map. What had happened to this once flourishing town? The answer is extraordinary, and a visit there is so rewarding. It's a magical spot, a place to ramble and meander, to absorb the atmosphere and let the imagination run riot.

Surrounding Dunwich are some very beautiful coastal areas. Corn-coloured marshland is a haven for wildlife, accessible yet seemingly remote under vast tracks of sky. I was completely distracted, too, by the charming old-world quality of the neighbouring seaside towns, not ruined by rows of amusement arcades and cheap souvenirs.

In addition to disappearing Dunwich, I had great fun delving into a great many other reminders of bygone days and glimpses of a vanishing world in mid-Suffolk. It's a joy to be able to find so much with an old-fashioned charm that is far from twee. Places are left untouched to speak for themselves – an isolated minster, once part of a powerful bishopric and now an ivy-covered ruin providing a home for rooks rather than bishops; sturdy castles, strongholds of powerful families, whose names now are virtually forgotten; unspoiled market towns and grocery shops with a style that might be more familiar to our grandparents. There are reminders too of old working Suffolk – signs of once-busy ports when the coast was linked by trade with the Flemish nations, and lovingly restored mills to be driven by wind and water.

All these sights evoke such different feelings, sometimes nostalgic or eerie, melancholic or magical, but above all very compelling, and the region provides the necessary tranquillity to let all this sink in. No wonder Suffolk has a reputation for a timeless atmosphere, a world untroubled in the main by modern influences such as huge motorways and urban expansion. It was quite a shock after two or three days' exploring to come across the bustling traffic on the A12.

Whether you have gone to East Anglia to visit the well-publicized Norfolk Broads, the famous 'Wool Churches' of Lavenham and Long Melford, or the Aldeburgh Festival, do try to find an extra few days to explore Suffolk, or, as I did, make a special trip. There is not just a great deal to see but so much to experience.

The focus for my journey was Dunwich, and I decided to spend time discovering the surrounding mid-Suffolk coast and the Blyth Estuary. You can certainly lose two days here and still feel you've not had enough time. I then wandered inland, first to the extraordinary River Alde, which refuses to go into the sea, and north to Framlingham. From here it's a short distance to the pretty valley of the River Deben and down to Woodbridge. My longer meanderings were by car, interrupted with the inevitable rambles. If you have plenty of time, the quiet lanes are excellent for biking along, especially as you only ever meet the gentlest of hills.

If you are walking, the coastal areas and marshy river estuaries are superb. Inland, true cross-country walking is more difficult because, as often happens in farming areas, many footpaths have been ploughed up. Those that are left can be terribly claggy due to the heavy soil. I always feel as though I'm walking in moonboots once I've gone but a few yards. I found country lanes were a good deal easier.

I decided to wend my way down a few of these *en route* to the coast, leaving the main road between Diss and Bungay and heading for South Elmham Saint James. I have friends there and had always thought it was a curiously long address. I discovered on the map that there are at least six other South Elmhams, all named after individual saints except for the all-embracing South Elmham All Saints. These scattered villages have between them a collection of ruined and isolated churches, like St Cross, the site of a romantic ruined minster. In my search for the 'disappearing world', I discovered a lovely series of country walks.

South Elmham and St Cross Minster

OS Map 1:50 000, Sheet 156
A variety of circular farm walks, 2 miles (3 km) to 7 miles (11 km). Allow from 2–3 hours.

South Elmham Hall and the St Cross Farm have been farmed by the same family for nearly a hundred years, though the present owners have only lived at the Hall for the last two. In that time, they have installed some wonderful walks around the farm with help from the Upper Waveney Valley Trust, a body responsible for promoting the area.

Car-parking and the start

There is a large car-park near the Hall, (you are asked for a pound donation per car). A noticeboard here gives information about what to see on the routes and a leaflet including a sketch map of all the possible walks. There are a good variety of lengths from a two-mile circuit (3 km) up to a seven-mile (11 km) trek around the boundary. The walks are distinguished with different letters and clearly marked with yellow arrows on gates and trees.

I really enjoyed sauntering around here. It makes a change to be on a farm that welcomes walkers, preserves its footpaths, and provides decent stiles, direction-finders and even little bridges to cross some of the deeper ditches. I found I had time to gaze at the scenery instead of watching every step over uneven ground, taking in the wildlife, the working farm itself and clues to the history of the land.

All the walks start along an old sunken lane across a meadow, and then meet Debb's Lane at right-angles. This is a green lane, a term used where an old track or bridle-way has just become greened over as it has dropped out of use. Nineteenth-century maps apparently show that this lane was just as prominent as many of the other lanes that went through the village. I wondered if the reason for the loss of popularity was the sad story of Debb. Local folklore has it that this unfortunate girl hanged herself here. The field opposite is known as Debb's Grave, her supposed burial site. Just to reassure the faint-hearted, the farmer told me he has never yet found any evidence of the wayside grave.

Debb's Lane is bordered by an ancient hedgerow thought to be between 800 and 1000 years old. I thought it was a good chance to try out Hooper's Rule, an unproven yet often-used yardstick to work out the age of a hedgerow. All you have to do is count the number of different shrub species growing in a thirty-yard (27 m) stretch. Allow a hundred years for each species you find. It's really an exercise for the sharp-eyed and the patient, but it's very interesting to compare findings with newer hedges around the water meadows near the minster.

At Debb's Lane, turn left for the short route, or take the longer way to the right which leads more or less around the farm's boundary in a large loop. Both walks meet up again along the low water meadows at the side of the beck, near the Minster.

This area of the farm was once part of an old deer park, in use when South Elmham Hall was used as a hunting lodge by the bishops of Norwich who kept a sizeable herd of deer. Large hornbeams grow along this section. They are similar to beech to look at but with broader leaves having crinkly edges. These trees have been pollarded – a system where branches above the reach of grazing animals are lopped off to make the most of the tree without impairing its growth – another clue to the former use of the land. Huge amounts of timber were needed in medieval times, for building and for fuel. At South Elmham, there was an on-site brick works which gobbled up a large amount of wood.

Gone now are the deer, and the meadows are grazed by British White, a rare breed of cattle, bred for the last 150 years mainly in East Anglia. Shortly after the war, numbers of British Whites dropped dramatically and the breed has been rescued with help from the Rare Breeds Survival Trust and specialist farmers such as the ones at South Elmham. The cattle vary from white to speckled but all have endearing black ears, noses and feet. Other livestock are the Oxford Down Sheep, again a less-familiar breed. I would be hard-pushed to tell one sheep from another. Oxfords, though, are fluffier than the more common Suffolk breed, and have rather attractive woolly faces.

Halfway down the meadows, just set back from the stream, are the ruins of the Minster, surrounded by a shallow ditch and virtually hidden by a thick wood. This ruin had its days of glory nearly a thousand years ago. It is hard to imagine, now, as it stands so lonely and desolate in its leafy shroud with the one unobtrusive notice, 'The Minster'. Nature is gradually reclaiming the place, and ivy smothers some of the tumbled-down walls. But you can trace out the nave and some internal divisions, peer through the glassless windows and walk under the side arch with just half a curve hanging in the air. Approach quietly as you may be lucky enough to catch sight of the owls that now inhabit the upper storeys.

Beyond the Minster, the trails go around the remainder of the farm along pretty hedgerows where I saw masses of sunny yellow cowslips. You can stroll back to the Hall, an attractive sixteenth-century building, surrounded by an impressive moat.

If you still have the energy, a walk around any of the local lanes will bring you to one of the many South Elmham saints. It would be the best part of a day, though, to visit the lot. One of the prettier routes, and very close to the St Cross Farm, goes to the church of St Margaret's.

From the entrance to St Cross, carry on straight ahead along the lane, ignoring the junction to the right. The lane turns a corner and just beyond is a drive leading through a delightful orchard, and then across meadows to the church. This was inhabited by some very curious rams (well, horned sheep at least). Instead of doing the normal sheep-like thing of running away, they herded together and came towards me *en masse* in a most disconcerting fashion. I was glad to get to the safety of the churchyard. If you are not so concerned with the rams, do look back at the Old Rectory, a lovely house by the meadows surrounded by a most attractive garden.

From South Elmham, I headed towards Dunwich and the coast through Halesworth, stocking up there with provisions from the local health shop (just by the main square), which had a marvellous range of breads, organic fruit and vegetables, and a terrific apricot slice, highly recommended, whether you've walked to earn it or not.

The Sandlings

The Sandlings (or Sandlands) is an old word for this part of Suffolk and exactly conjures up the mixture of marsh, heath and sea found here. It is a lovely area for walking, both through the open countryside, the main town, Southwold, and neighbouring villages. Many of the footpaths in the area are very well marked. The coastal areas, especially, are a haven for bird-watchers, though they tend to flock(!) more to the very well-known Minsmere, further south.

I started at Southwold, arriving there on a dull murky day in late spring, after driving from Halesworth along winding Suffolk lanes. The world just suddenly opened up before me. Directly ahead was the wide estuary with its broad marshes and the splendid Blythburgh Church dominating the view on the right.

Southwold is four miles further on, following the line of the river. I loved the description of this town in the *East Anglian Good Beach Guide*: 'Uncommercialised, but pots of teas are available on the beach.' It rather sums up the old-fashioned quality of the place.

I found the town was a delight with its mixture of fisherman's cottages and houses, some typically East Anglian in pretty pastels. Others have a Dutch or Flemish influence thanks to the trading that took place with Northern Europe when Southwold was a busy port. Dotted in amongst the houses are 'The Greens', tiny open spaces created by a fire in 1659 which destroyed many buildings which were then never replaced.

There is a good street plan worth getting from the Tourist Information Centre. It marks all the greens and footpaths and I wandered happily around for an hour or so. The church at Southwold is a beauty. I still find the sight of these window-full churches a marvel. I came to it in the evening gloom, the walls blended in with the mist and the windows just seemed to hang in the air.

I was rather surprised to come on a lighthouse in the heart of the town. Its towering hundred feet or so made the houses below seem of doll-like proportions. There can't be many lighthouses that are so accessible. I expect the keepers manage to do their job and get a social life as well! Nor are there many places where sailors are entertained by the likes of The Sailors' Reading Room (on East Street). It is crammed full of sea-faring portraits, models and maritime books.

I should also mention that Southwold is home of the famous Adnams Brewery, in case the sea air gives you a thirst.

Apart from exploring the town itself, there are all sorts of possibilities for walks around this area. Two very pleasant short circuits begin in Southwold. For neither of these do you really need an OS map, the town plan is quite enough.

'The Isle of Southwold'

A circular walk of about 4 miles (6 km) around the outskirts from the centre of Southwold. Allow 2 hours.

This walk is literally a circle of the town which is bounded to the North by Buss Creek and to the south by the River Blyth. It's fun to do because you discover that, with a slightly wider ditch and a fuller river, the town might have been named 'The Isle of Southwold'. Its hold on the land is very tenuous. The creek and the river have served as a limiting factor to the development of the town and have probably helped to preserve its charm. This walk also gives you good views of the Blythburgh Estuary, and takes you over a variety of marshes where there is abundant birdlife.

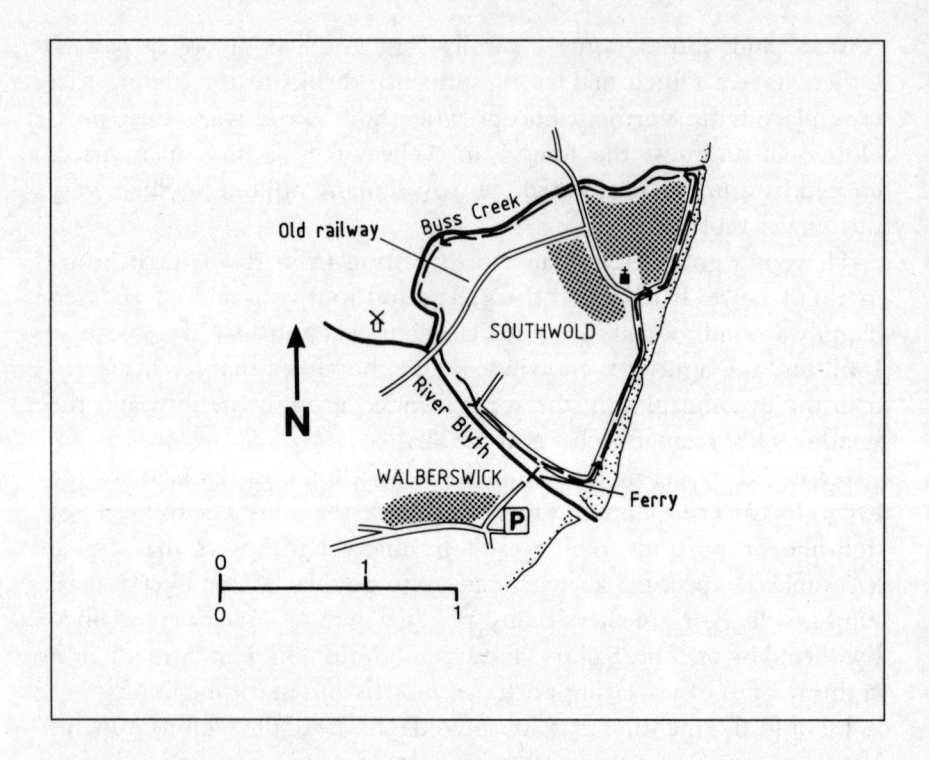

The going underfoot is fine in the town itself but tends to be rather slippery and muddy along the edges of the creek and river. Occasionally, work is going on to preserve the banks, too, which can make it worse.

Catch the ferry to Walberswick

A circular walk of around $3\frac{1}{2}$ miles (5 km). Allow 2 hours.

I hadn't realized, at first, that you can walk along the old railway line from Southwold to Walberswick. There's a splendid old iron bridge, which used to carry the narrow gauge railway into Southwold from Halesworth. Another way of getting to Walberswick, though less predictable, is via the ferry at the very mouth of the river. Ferry may be too grand a word as it is actually a rowing boat holding six or eight people. I discovered that the 'ferryman' is in his seventies. He's still going strong, probably due to the fact that he's been rowing for the last forty years, ever since the old chain ferry was sunk after the war. I didn't like to be a pessimist but tentatively enquired how long he might continue. All's well. His father who rowed before him got to his mid-eighties! For the future, there is a nephew to carry on the tradition. Prices are fixed before each season and in the past it has been 10p. To catch the ferryman you'll have to pick a decent day between Whitsun and mid-September, and not when 'there's a nor'westerly wind with the tide going out'!

You can do a circular walk when the ferry is operational or a there-and-back using the footbridge. To get to the ferry, go down Ferry Road, or ferry footpath opposite Queen's Road, at the southern end of Southwold. The footbridge is about a quarter mile (0.4 km) further up the river. It is also well-signposted from Walberswick if you want to start walking from there.

Walberswick is worth a wander. Don't miss both the excellent tea-rooms. Mary's is set back in the village, near the church. I like to think she was in love with a sailor as the walls of the café are thick with maritime memorabilia and fishing nets. The coffee is good and there's a great Apple Spice Cake. The Parish Lantern serves food too, as well as having a wonderful display of individual pottery and pictures. There are some unusual postcards with artists' impressions (quite a colony at Walberswick) of the village and surrounding countryside.

Much of the area in between the village and the river is a nature reserve with a mixture of mud flats, rough heath and marshes, attracting a great variety of wildlife.

Instead of either of these walks you could take some time to visit Blythburgh Estuary.

Walberswick to Dunwich

OS Sheet 156 or Pathfinder 966
A there-and-back walk of 7½ miles (12 km). Allow 4–4½ hours.

It is worth planning to spend the best part of the day on this marvellous walk. Much of the charm is simply the tranquillity of the surroundings. The first part takes you into the heart of the lonely marshes with the added benefit of so much birdlife to see as you go. You end up at Dunwich and can see for yourself the village's battle against the sea.

It's a longish walk and you'll also need to allow some time at Dunwich. I took a just-in-case packed lunch, but there is a pub in Dunwich serving food.

The going underfoot is excellent for running or walking. The path across the marshes has a few slippery patches but is generally fine. There is a good track through Dunwich Forest, and a short amount of road leading to Dunwich itself.

Car-parking and the start

There are plenty of road-side parking places in the village of Walberswick and several footpaths leading south out of the village. Choose one for going and one for returning. They all lead down to the main footpath along Dunwich River (really hardly more than a broad ditch) towards a deserted windmill in the midst of the marshes. I walked this route early one April morning. The silence is impressive. It is broken by the sudden fluttering of startled mallards and the 'tseep-tseep' call of the reed bunting. The large embankment along the coastline shuts off the sea and the ominous booming of the waves on the shingly shore is lost as you venture further into the marshes. On parts of the track it's like walking in a golden tunnel as the reeds grow well over head height.

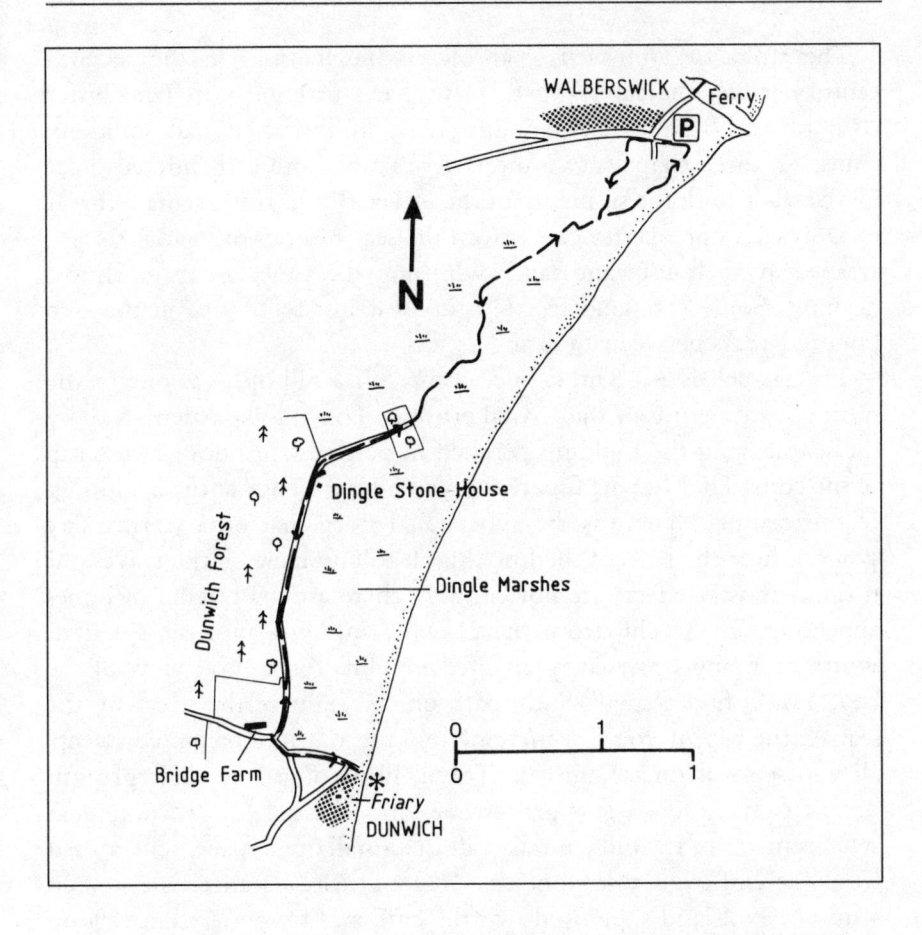

Near the ruined windmill, there is a path leading west to Westwood Marshes and the main area of Walberswick Nature Reserve. Don't take this path however but keep south, aiming towards two lumps in the marshes. Despite one of these being called Dingle Great Hill, according to the contours on the map it is only thirty-nine feet (12 m) high. After rounding these hills, the track goes along the edge of the forest, climbing slightly, until you can see the distant sea beyond the shingle wall. Here, I came across a flock of wild geese enjoying a brief rest in a sunny field. Simply keep on this track along the forest edge until it rounds the corner by some farm buildings and meets the lane. Turn left to Dunwich and the sea.

The story of Dunwich is absolutely fascinating. In the seventh century it was the capital of East Anglia, a thriving port (and bitter rival of Southwold), and an important bishopric. It had some six churches, three chapels, two monasteries and a mint. It suffered great loss of trade with the silting up of the River Blyth. But the main threat to Dunwich's prosperity came from the sea. A series of vicious storms washed away houses and land, whittling the town away to almost nothing. Some thousand feet (304 m) was lost to the sea in the two hundred years between 1550 and 1750.

The chapel of All Saints, once secure on a hilltop, was one of the most recent victims of the coastal erosion. The hill was eaten away by the sea, leaving the building perched in perilous splendour at the top of the cliffs. The last part finally toppled over the edge at the beginning of this century. There is the apocryphal story that on a stormy day you can hear the bells of the lost church tolling beneath the waves. As if these ghostly effects are not enough, there are grisly tales of bones appearing on the cliff from the graves crumbling into the sea. It is worth climbing up what is left of these cliffs for a good view of the bay. You'll find a small sandy path on the right of the street by the sea. At the top, if you can imagine looking out in a half-mile sweep, all you see was once Dunwich Town. In amongst the undergrowth here, I came across a few gravestones and realized I was walking in what remains of the old churchyard. In a small open space, only a yard from the cliff edge, one stone stands alone. Already there is a sunken semi-circle of land slipping down the cliff, and I wondered how long this lone tombstone would remain.

Further inland from the clifftop graveyard are the ruins of the Franciscan monastery.

Dunwich is a very special place to visit, not so much for what there is to see, but with all there is to imagine. Try to pick a weekday (and not such good weather) as it is best to have the place to yourself. According to local gossip, it's always busy on bank holidays and through the height of the summer. In my visit in April, I saw no one at all except for the fishermen on Dunwich Beach.

There is a small museum in the main street. This has exhibits which tell the story of the ancient town. There are a number of models to show its battle with the tides. Try to time your walk to coincide with its afternoon opening times. In August it is open daily, 2.30–4 pm;

June, July and Sept, Tuesday, Thursday and weekends, 2.30–4 pm; March to May, and October only weekends, 2.30–4 pm; otherwise closed except for special parties.

I should mention that it is easy to drive to Dunwich, if the walk from Walberswick is rather too long for your taste or time. There is a large car-park on the beach, and some car-parking in a forest picnic area about a mile (1½ km) from the sea. You can walk further on down the coast (the route is part of the Suffolk Heritage Coast Trail which goes all the way down to Bawdsley, near Felixstowe) and also along the beach at Dunwich, though it's not advisable to go under the cliffs. I'm sure you can imagine why.

Blythburgh and Angel Marshes

Which ever way you go to Southwold or Walberswick (unless you have walked the coastal trail) you can't fail to notice Blythburgh Church. Dominating the estuary, it is appropriately nicknamed 'Cathedral of the Marshes'. Its size, quite out of scale with the needs of the present village, acts as a testament to the changing fortunes of this part of the coast. Once Blythburgh was a bustling port, with houses and market stalls bordering the quays on a river that was navigable to Halesworth. The town boasted its own mint and gaol, and of course wanted a splendid church to accommodate the needs of the parishioners. The one at Blythburgh was built in the fifteenth century. Sad to say that more or less as this grand building was being finished, the town fell into decline. The demise was caused by the river, which had once brought prosperity, silting the estuary and making shallow channels. These could not cope with the new larger ships that were being built and so trade went elsewhere. In 1478, the paltry sum of sixteen pence was recorded as the total harbour revenues, hardly enough to justify a church mouse, let alone a church. Now all that bustles in Blythburgh is the busy A12 which cuts between the church and the wide salt marshes.

The unimportance of the town doesn't diminish the magnificence of the church. It has a typical East Anglian fragility due to the predominance of window lights. If the sun is shining the whole exterior dances with light glinting on the windows and the flint facets. At night the church is floodlit, providing an amazing beacon for miles around. The interior is just as interesting as the exterior, with all manner of stories and things to discover. There is the usual worthy guide leaflet, but also one for children with an I-spy theme, which is far more fun.

Can you remember the seven deadly sins? I'm rather alarmed to find I always remember Greed and Sloth first. Here, there are carved bench ends to remind you of the full complement, including the splendid Slander, with a protruding slit tongue.

The carved roof and wonderful wooden flying angles are quite remarkable. They, too, have a tale to tell. The attack on Blythburgh came from the reformers of Oliver Cromwell's day and was particularly severe. Hundreds of bullets were shot through the door and into the magnificent angels in the roof. The close-ups on the postcards show the bullet-holes. Horses were ridden into the nave and signs are still there of tethering rings and trampled brickwork.

Another unusual wooden article is the Jack-o-the-Clock which originally struck the hours of the clock. This is one of a few remaining in England (there is another in Southwold).

Today, Blythburgh Church seems set to remain a magnificent landmark, though it had a very lucky escape, nearly becoming part of Suffolk's disappearing world. By the mid-1800s, the building was in a very sorry state of repair. Luckily, a restoration fund was set up towards the end of that century. It was just in time to save the church, and repairwork has gone on ever since. The twentieth-century struggle has been against some less picturesque invaders than Oliver Cromwell's men, the deathwatch beetle.

A Walk Along Angel Marshes

This is virtually a stroll just to get away from the busy A12. Allow approximately 30 minutes. It gives you a chance to see a little of the estuary if you haven't the time to spend at Southwold and Walberswick. As this is the widest part of the estuary, there are lovely views over the marshes. Around the edges of the bay are areas of attractive hilly woodland. It is amazing how quickly you can get taken over by the tranquillity of the marshland. I walked here when the widening of

Blythburgh Bridge was in progress. As I set out, some enormous foundation pillars were being hammered into the ground with a continuous wearisome pounding. It didn't take many minutes of walking for the sound to melt away.

To get to the marshes, just walk from the church down a lane, full of an interesting mixture of old houses, to the main road. By the pub opposite is the footpath along the side of the estuary. Watch out for very fast traffic.

There is a choice of walks either along the side of the marsh, or for the more adventurous, a path into the centre. I had intended to go for the latter until I saw that, owing to the high tide, some of the route consisted of no more than reed-covered lumps interspersed with several feet of water. A man in the post office told me that even at low tide, you need very high wellingtons and a certain amount of luck if you don't want to be waterlogged.

The path along the marsh edge, although not marked on the OS map as a footpath, is well signposted as part of the nature reserve. There's plenty of birdlife to see and hear. I got close to several pairs of shelducks. They are quite large birds, mostly white, but with bold streaks of black and chestnut that is very distinctive. Do take binoculars as you can get some marvellous close-ups of the birdlife. One distinctive sound to listen for is a loud 'tu tu' yelping from the redshanks. For keen bird-watchers there is a small hide about halfway along. The path follows the curve of the marshes for a mile or so and the going under foot is mostly dry. Eventually you come to a pretty woodland area on a slight hill. This track goes on as far as Walberswick, but I walked just a short way into these woods, curving round to make a circuit joining the grassy track known as Lodge Lane. This brought me back, slightly away from the marshes on the southern edge of Blythburgh, where it is just a short walk back to the car-park.

After visiting Blythburgh, it is a short drive to Southwold, Dunwich and the coast, or inland to the interesting towns of Framlingham and Woodbridge.

From Dunwich and the coast, I went slightly inland to another main Suffolk river, the Alde. This area of Suffolk has achieved fame through the Aldeburgh Festival, much of which takes place at The Maltings, an old brewery near the village of Snape.

An Isolated Church on the Salt Marshes

OS Map 1:50 000, Sheet 156
A circular walk of 5 miles (8 km) with the possible addition of a visit to the church $\frac{1}{2}$ mile (1 km). Allow 2–3 hours.

This is a beautiful walk with all of what must be best about Suffolk – wide marshland with interesting wildfowl, isolated buildings which suggest some colourful or mysterious past, open fields and leafy lanes. The constant change of scenery adds much interest with peace by the river, and farming life to be seen inland, especially if the free-range pigs are in evidence. The first part of the walk linking The Maltings with the Iken Picnic Site is popular, so if you want to have the place to yourself, it is best to go early and avoid the main weeks of the festival, held in June.

The going underfoot is mostly fine, though it's bound to be a little slippery on the path around the marshes. Forest tracks are good and so is the section across the fields, which despite having had two days of rain when I went, was unusually dry, with almost sand-like soil. The walk is virtually flat.

Car-parking and the start.

There is plenty of parking at The Maltings, and you will probably feel obliged to visit the craft centre or coffee shop, which won't be too much of a hardship. Otherwise, there is a small triangular patch of green with room for five or six cars just beyond The Maltings where the B1069 and a minor road to Orford divide.

The Maltings is now recognized as a premier concert hall having some of the finest acoustics in Europe. A far cry from the days of the nineteenth century when most of the sound heard would have been the unloading of barges of American barley for the brewing industry. The buildings were used for malting until 1965.

The path starts on a track just by the side of The Maltings complex and goes along the marshy edges of the River Alde. It is clearly marked, crossing the wetter parts of the marsh on a sturdy boardwalk. I thought I was looking across another estuary, like the Blyth. In fact this is not the case, since the Alde behaves in an extraordinary fashion.

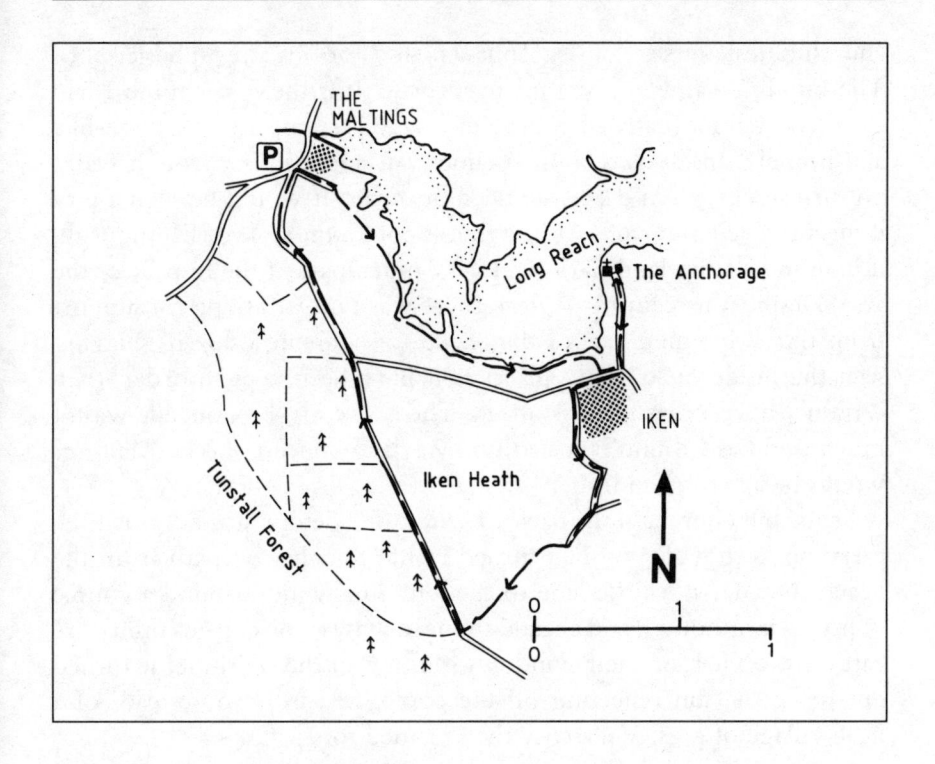

The river broadens out as you would expect at its mouth, but then, within yards of the sea, it turns an abrupt right angle and runs parallel to the coastline until it gushes into the sea much further south. An odd thing about the coast here is that, far from eroding, it is increasing in size by the year, quite noticeably.

Looking down the marshes you can see the isolated church you are aiming for, though not as far as it looks. The predominant feature is marshland, and there's plenty of birdlife — sheld ducks and red grebe.

After about a mile, you come to the Iken Picnic Site, a large grassy area with a noticeboard about the nature reserve. From here the path goes on along the side of the bay. I found the tide was at very low ebb, so parts of the walk were on sandy stretches. It's evident from a seaweed line that the water comes quite high so you may find the need to scramble along the bank; either that or have wet or webbed feet. At the very end of the bay do look back at The Maltings in its golden marshland setting.

The path curves slightly inland onto the road. Turn left towards the church (a mile or so 'dog leg', but worth it for this atmospheric spot). The building came as a complete surprise. It is the first church I had ever seen with a thatched roof. This made it seem rather cottage-like and homely. Inside was another shock, an uneven floor, rough walls, no furnishings, all in desperate need of repair. It would be such a pity if this place fell into ruin. Although it is not on the scale of Blythburgh, it is an interesting landmark, and very much part of the history of the area. Despite the seeming neglect, there was a notice asking for support from the active members of the parish (only about a dozen). Having seen the inside of so many places that have been kept in order, they certainly have a massive task ahead. The collecting-box outside wasn't much good as I found it sealed up. Maybe a concert at The Maltings would be a better fundraiser.

From the church, walk back to where the detour started, this time carry on as though you had turned right after the footpath from the beach. Not far is a little lane to the left. This winds around a couple of pretty farmhouses, and ahead I thought I saw some curious miniature caravans, or at least their windows glinting in the sunshine. It turned out to be the sun reflecting off the corrugated-iron homesteads of a little village of pigs. Very cosy they seemed too.

In case the pigs have gone and you miss the well-worn signpost, the track you need leads away from the road almost at a hair-pin bend. It goes up the side of a field towards a small wood, skirts around that and over another field. Ahead you can see the line of Tunstall Forest. Here, I came across more pigs and quantities of pheasants fluttering in and out of the hedges. This section of the walk, though inland, is part of the Suffolk Coastal Trail.

Once on the road, there is supposed to be an easy footpath joining a northerly ride through the forest to Blaxhall Heath. Sadly the forest is in a terrible mess from windblow and workings. The rides and paths are virtually obscure. The most direct route back to base is to turn right up the lane. It is a pleasant walk for approximately $1\frac{3}{4}$ miles (3 km), which comes out at the junction by The Maltings. If you decide to go through the forest, it is probably best to have a compass to make sure you are on a northerly route. I was rather blasé, thinking by looking at the map that the ride would be easy to follow, and I got myself completely lost. For a start the forest wasn't at all what I expected. Apart from the inevitable windblow and random felling, there were vast areas bare of trees. The scorched look of the old bracken made the land look as though it had suffered a major drought. In one particularly overgrown section, I followed what I thought were some helpful orange markers wiggling in and out of the fallen trees. I had a tiny suspicion that if I was going north the morning sun shouldn't be behind my left shoulder, but confident in my natural instinct for direction, I strode on. I was rather dismayed to find myself at the village of Tunstall, some two miles out of my way, having made a ninety-degree error. Out came the compass, a not-too-happy retracing of steps, and after that I stuck firmly to a bearing, refusing to be enticed by any more helpful markers, and got back to The Maltings a little more exhausted than I expected. The nicest part of the woods was the area around Blaxhall Heath.

From Snape, you are in easy reach of Orford. This is a village which used to be on the sea, but is now well and truly inland due to a great gravel bank thrown up by the sea at the rate of fifteen yards (14 m) a year. Rather the reverse of Dunwich. Here it's worth going to the top of Orford Keep, the castle built by Henry II, where you can look over to Aldeburgh and Havergate Island, breeding ground of the wading bird, the avocet, and now owned by the Royal Society for the Protection of Birds (RSPB).

In search of more castles I went north to Framlingham. Top of the list of the 'most oft-quoted facts of Framlingham' is that Mary Tudor was staying here when she learnt that she had become queen.

The castle is now owned by English Heritage and is a rather curious sight. Its massive curtain walls and sturdy square towers are topped with incongruous Tudor brick chimneys. I thought if they were all alight it would look like a great stone birthday cake, but apparently many of the chimneys were only ever ornamental. Framlingham was built on the site of an older castle. The ring shape was an innovation, brought back by the crusaders who learnt that a circle was defensively more effective than a square. It had its fair share of owners, including Bloody Mary, who probably needed as much protection as possible. The Bigods, Mortimers and Howards were all pretty treacherous and all wheeler-dealers when it came to the crown. Framlingham's eventual fate was to become a poorhouse once the Great Hall inside the castle had been destroyed.

Although there is little to see once you go through the entrance, there is a splendid wall walk that is well worth the climb. I'm a bit dizzy when it comes to exposed heights like this, but the walkway going all the way round has been very well constructed. (It is not recommended for children.) You can look out over the castle grounds to the defensive lake on one side, and way beyond. There are grim reminders of life for some in the castle when you get to the Prison Tower. It has no entrance at ground level, just a first-floor trapdoor opening onto the space below.

It is worth walking around the castle grounds. On the opposite side to the entrance is a footpath leading over the fields quite close to the large lake. This path joins a road where, if you start walking back towards the town, you'll find a wonderful (and most-photographed) view of the castle across the lake. This route takes you into the town via the spacious market square with its lovely old shopfronts. Up Castle Street, you'll find the church of St Michael's. Inside is a most interesting painted alter-piece. I was first struck by its luminosity (in my innocence I hadn't noticed the spotlight). It is a beautiful radiating wheel of colour, with the ancient Greek monogram for Jesus in the centre. Just opposite the church is a good place to get coffee (*cappuccino*) in a little café tucked in behind a gift shop.

I liked the unspoiled atmosphere in Framlingham very much and was pleased to find it so un-touristy. The nearest you get to Bloody Mary probably is a stiff drink in the bar of the local hotel. Enjoying the castle is a rather do-it-yourself affair, a case of spending time, gazing and imagining. It was an ideal way to spend a restful afternoon after walking at The Maltings in the morning.

Easton and the River Deben

OS Map 1:50 000, Sheet 156
A circular stroll of $2\frac{1}{2}$ miles (4 km). Allow $1\frac{1}{2}$ hours.

After Framlingham, it is a short trip across country to the River Deben. It starts, hardly surprisingly, at Debenham, and meanders through some very attractive areas of Suffolk such as Cretingham and Kettleburgh. The place I found to stop was the little village of Easton. Here was the oddest wall construction I've ever seen. Officially it is a ribbon wall. Unofficially and much more descriptively, it's called a 'crinkle-crankle' wall. (Crinkle-crankle isn't in my dictionary, but I found crinkum-crankum, meaning a thing full of twists and turns, which sums it up.) This curving wall built of warm red bricks snakes some way along the road and on around the estate, making it the longest of its kind in England.

The main house of the estate has long since gone, but behind some very impressive gates you can see several delightful cottages and a brick summerhouse. The estate was built during the nineteenth century by the local landlords, the Earls of Rochford and the Dukes of Hamilton, in a style deliberately romantic and ornate. It sounds like an early bid to attract tourists, but these *villages ornées* were much ridiculed at the time. The Duke of Hamilton also built the model farm on the outskirts of the village, which is now known as Easton Farm Country Park and it is open to the public. In addition to the rare breeds on show, there is the original Victorian dairy with its ornate tiles and central fountain. In contrast to this is a modern milking parlour. There are nature trails in the farm park but you may prefer to wander around the surrounding lanes which are nearly all unfenced.

Car-parking and the start

There is parking opposite the church in Easton, and then it is a short walk along the 'crinkle-crankle' wall and across the main road to the farm park. Going anti-clockwise you come first to the little village of Letheringham at a quiet leafy T-junction at the bottom of the hill. Go on round to a delightfully situated moated Hall. Someone here takes pride in the garden as I could see a mass of flowers on the banks of the moat. Just round the corner is the Letheringham Watermill, now fully restored. There is a short footpath across the fields, over the Deben back to Easton Church, and time for morning coffee, which I found in Wickham Market.

Wickham Market might have been a grander place except for the fact that the market of the title was lost to nearby Woodbridge in the sixteenth century. Now the main square is a car-park and bus stop. There are plenty of comings and goings so after a couple of turns round the square I was able to park in the central spaces. I asked a lady laden with shopping where she would recommend for coffee and was told there was no choice, Taylor's or nothing. This turned out to be the grocers-cum-wine-merchant-cum-restaurant-cum-meeting-place for locals on the corner of the square. It was great! The restaurant is up a few stairs, above the interlinking shops, in a quaint old part of the building. Half the area has conventional tables and chairs, but the small back room is furnished with a couple of comfy sofas and armchairs. A huge drum (ex-Wickham Market Boys' Brigade) acts as a coffee table. I don't know if you have to have Wickham Market Ancestry to qualify for this part as it was obviously a very regular meeting-place for locals and a good place to gather gossip. There was a very friendly atmosphere and I enjoyed a cup of coffee and a chance to eavesdrop. The latest scandal was all about the owner of the shop. He had been reported by the 'big boys' for selling his wine too cheap. This had made the headlines and also encouraged me to take home a bottle he recommended (Cahors 1982; a present from Suffolk).

My other reason for stopping at Wickham Market was to seek out the Museum of Grocery Shop Bygones (admission free). It turned out to be in a minute shop just round the corner from Taylor's, and not a great surprise to find it run by one of the Taylor dynasty. This Mr Taylor started his collection with one or two items from the days when he ran the shop. He added to his collection with some marvellous fittings from the splendidly named Gobbitt and Kirby, old grocers at Woodbridge. There are some large scales and an old coffee grinder, which brought back memories of the one I had in my shop at Scarborough. In pride of place are some large drawer units originally used for storing rice and sago. Look closely at these to see the holes made by what must have been very cheeky and probably very chubby mice.

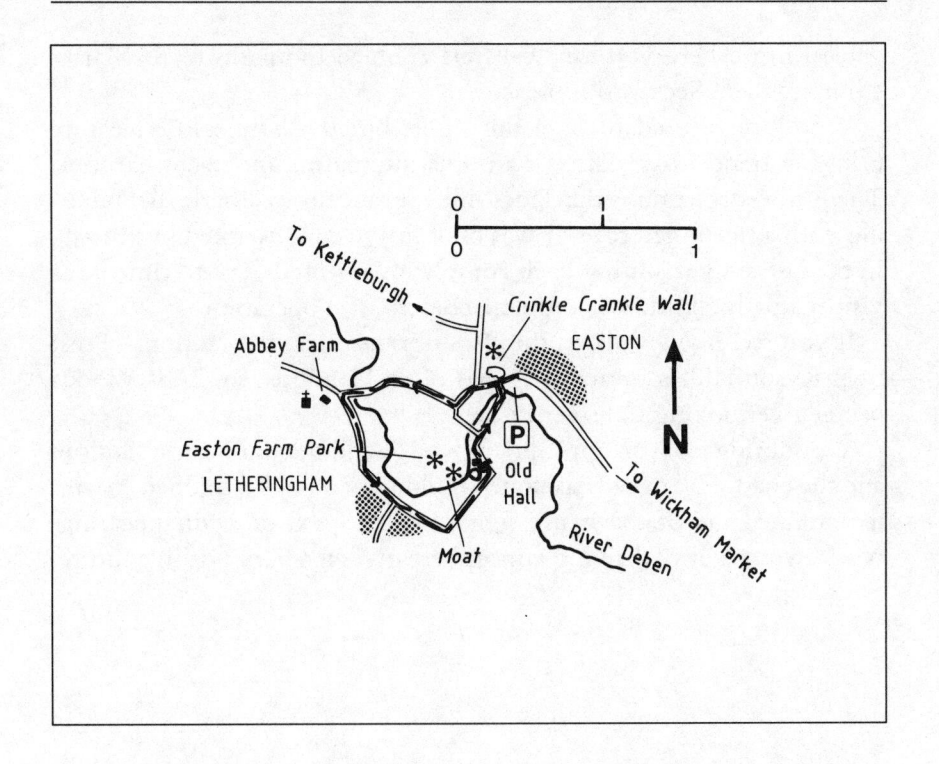

On a top shelf are a series of large tin tea caddies which, when in the right order, tell a story. One of the smallest items in the museum is a tiny tin. It looks as though it should hold Parma Violets but actually contains a ladies razor discreetly known as 'The Ladies Boudoir'.

The place is an Aladdin's cave of coloured treasures and instant nostalgia. Mr Taylor has a wealth of stories about the origins of his collection. It has grown so much over the years there is scarcely room to display everything. Space is limited to two or three visitors.

I found out later that Taylor's have their own car-park, closely guarded so it is used only by genuine customers.

Further down the Deben is Woodbridge, the main town of the area and a splendid place to while away an afternoon.

A book like this owes quite a debt to one of Woodbridge's benefactors, Thomas Seckford, who commissioned the first systematically surveyed maps of England. He was also responsible for building the striking Shire Hall which dominates the main square (called Market Hill). It is built of red brick and ornamented with high Dutch-style gables. From here you can walk via cobbled footpaths to St Mary's Church where Seckford is buried.

Woodbridge used to be a busy port but the business of pleasure brings in trade, now. There is a miniature marina and yacht harbour. The prime attraction is the Tide Mill, a beautiful weatherboard building with a steep tiled roof. It was built in 1793 and worked until 1957. In the last ten years it has been completely restored. Try to time your visit with a high tide when the machinery is in operation.

If you feel like a walk in the Woodbridge area, the National Trust own Kyson Hill, four acres (1.5 ha) of parkland just south of Woodbridge overlooking the river Deben.

Woodbridge was an appropriate way to end the tour of mid Suffolk and the coast. Full of old-fashioned buildings and old-fashioned charm, it reminded me of the many sights I'd glimpsed of a 'disappearing' world, yet, its busy thriving atmosphere gives it a very positive future.

The Chilterns

I first became more aware of the Chilterns when I started taking part in an annual orienteering competition known as 'The Chiltern Challenge'. It was always an event to look forward to, as running through the mature beech woods for which the Chilterns are renowned, is a wonderful experience. The steep slopes and the brambles were, however, something of a challenge to rapid progress.

Paradoxically, although the Chilterns themselves are well known as a region, you might be hard pushed to think immediately of any famous places or major tourist attractions in the Buckinghamshire area. There's a good reason for this as there are no famous castles, palaces or cathedrals in the vicinity. Yet despite the lack of obvious attractions, I discovered the Chilterns has much to fascinate and there's plenty here to see and do.

Although in modern terms the Chilterns are considered close to London, until less than a hundred years ago the area was thought to be quite wild and dangerous. Not many people chose to live in the isolated hills and lack of water on the porous ground limited settlement. Travel was very difficult with the main routes going either side of the ridge, using the Thames Valley to the south, and the gap at Luton to the north. The daunting northern scarp was not favoured as a coach route and the thick woods were ideal hiding-places for ruffians and robbers. The unsafe nature of the area led to the setting up of the office of the Steward of the Chiltern Hundreds, the origin of the parliamentary expression. The steward's job was to catch as many thieves and highwaymen as possible, and probably swing them from the nearest tree.

Yet, in spite of such disadvantages this part of England has been the home of many people who have had a strong influence, though an often little-publicized one, in Britain's history. This is perhaps particularly true in relation to political matters and religious affairs. You can encounter the beginnings of the revolt against King Charles I that led to the Civil War. You can look over the vast estates of one of Europe's most wealthy and influential families, the de Rothschilds, who made the Chilterns their English country home. Near High Wycombe is the former home and burial place of one of the leading statesmen of the Victorian Age, Disraeli. On the edge of the region is Cliveden, once home of the Astors, a fascinating place to visit, tinged from its conception with scandal.

I've come to think of the area as full of 'places of quiet influence'. This chapter includes visits to all those places with a walk around, to or near them.

The walking in this region is excellent and there is more to the Chilterns than the beech woods. The land itself is varied with its jumble of hills interspersed with dry steep-sided valleys, known locally as 'bottoms'. It is easy to imagine the whole range as a clenched fist with the hills gradually flattening out to meet with the River Thames, whilst to the north there is the dramatic drop onto the Oxford plain. On the ridges there are some good places to get expansive views.

It's not all countryside of course. There has been much modern development here to cope with the inevitable commuting that goes on from a region so close to London. Major towns such as High Wycombe and Aylesbury, the county town of Buckinghamshire, have grown considerably, and are not so attractive. There are, however, some delightful smaller towns and many of the villages tucked into the hills have changed little.

One advantage of this area being part of the commuter belt is that it's possible to get access to a reasonable amount by train from London (for the fifth of the British population who live in the London area). Wendover, Marlow and High Wycombe all have stations. Some of the walks in this chapter can be started from these.

You are still in the crowded southern half of the country in the Chilterns, but it is easy to find peace and quiet as well as a wealth of interesting history and personalities; it's certainly worth finding time to come here.

Disraeli Day

OS Map 1:50 000, Sheet 175 and 165
A circular walk of 5–6 miles (8–10 km). Allow 3–4 hours inclusive of visiting either of the houses.

This walk gives you the chance to take in two very different politicians, separated by a few miles, a hundred years, and a completely different outlook on life, Benjamin Disraeli and Sir Francis Dashwood. The former spent some of his boyhood in the quiet village of Bradenham. From 1847 until his death he lived at Hughenden Manor, just a few miles further south. Also a few miles south of Bradenham is West Wycombe, the Dashwood family estate, made most famous, or infamous, by its eighteenth-century eccentric owner, Sir Francis.

This circuit goes around those three places via some typical Chiltern landscape of wooded hills and valleys.

Car-parking and the start

There is a small car-park just off the A40 near West Wycombe House at the foot of West Wycombe Hill. The church on the top of the hill with its extraordinary golden ball is clearly visible. It makes a good landmark at the end of the walk. If the car-park is full, there is parking at the top of the hill by the church. This area was once all part of the Dashwood Estate and is now owned by the National Trust.

West Wycombe – village, church, caves and house – was the creation of Sir Francis Dashwood, a most colourful character of the mid-eighteenth century. He played a brief role as a politician, first as a disastrous Chancellor of the Exchequer, and second as a capable Postmaster General. He is mainly remembered today for the goings on of the Hell-Fire Club, of which he was the founder member.

The club, also known as the Monks of Medmenham, or the Knights of St Francis of Wycombe, consisted of a group of rakes who got together for drinking sessions, card parties and orgies with the 'nuns' of Medmenham. Some of these meetings were supposedly held in the West Wycombe Caves in the hill under the church, but there was also 'The Globe Tavern'. This was what one wit termed the golden ball on top of the St Laurence church. Sir Francis had the tower of the church heightened to accommodate the globe which was fitted out inside with enough seats for a card party. The motto of the club was *Fay ce que voudras* – Do as you please.

It is hard to believe that Sir Francis had time for anything else. But his other passion was architecture. He founded the Dilettanti Society, a group devoted to the study of classical architecture. He used ideas researched in that group to build and remodel the house in West Wycombe Park. Its serene setting and elegant exterior come as something of a surprise after the tales of wining and whoring. The contrast in the man makes the place more intriguing, and I wonder what Sir Francis would like best to be remembered for?

Inside the house are wonderful painted ceilings, elaborate fire-places and fine furniture.

I particularly liked the gardens. As you enter, the proud column of Britannia stares down to the lake where there are cascades with more statues in the distance. The winding stream is crossed by all manner of pretty stone bridges and various temples are dotted around the park. At the back of the house there is a huge sweeping lawn with an impressive statue at the far end. The opening times of the house are quite limited, though the grounds are open a little more frequently.

From West Wycombe House, walk down the small parade of shops along the busy A40 to the roundabout. Here is a sign of former days, a curious stone mile-post giving distances to the capital, the county town, and the university (Oxford). It was put here by Sir Francis in 1752 to mark the opening of this road. At the roundabout, just to the left of the garage, is Cockshall Lane. Walk up here, keeping to the right-hand forks, to the village of Downley. The path brings you round by a school and out on a road junction near the post office. Here turn left, walk a short distance and then turn right down the next lane. Not far down is a church and turning area. A good bridle-path goes straight down into the woods and you start to get that typical Chiltern feeling of being surrounded by beech trees, and unless you are very lucky, a little mud underfoot. Keep going downhill, ignoring the many paths that criss-cross this section. The woods suddenly give way to a large field area and you get the first glimpse of Hughenden Manor high up beyond the trees.

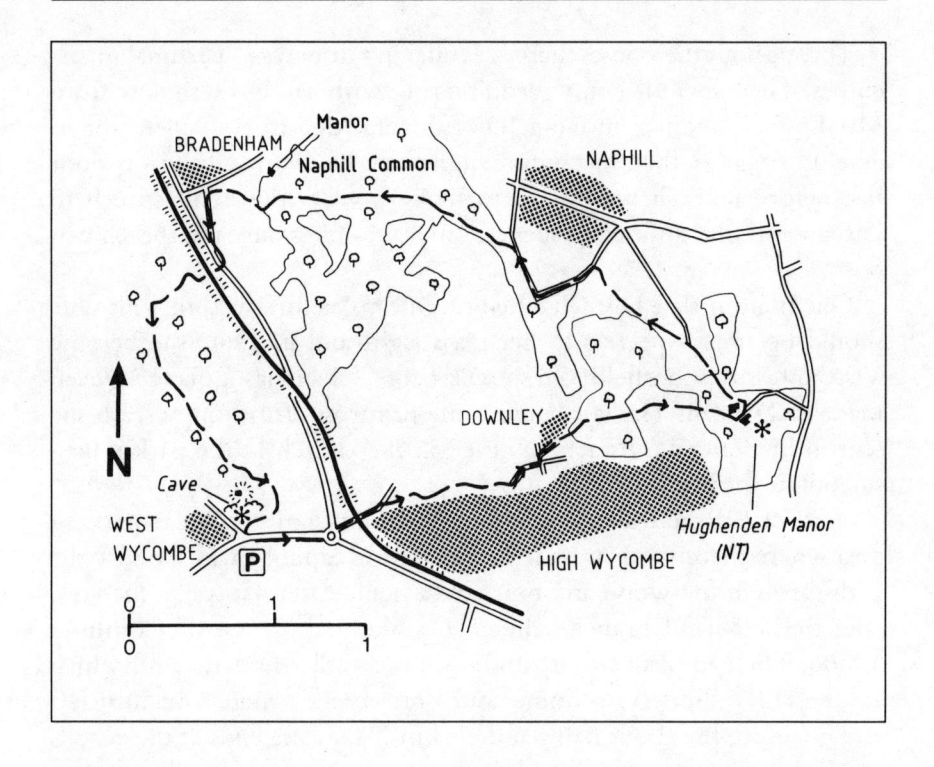

Follow the path over the field and into the next patch of woodland. There's a short but gradual climb which brings you out at the side of the house. Turn sharp left and up a short flight of steps which takes you into a car-park area just by the National Trust Shop. To see the house, turn right, to continue the walk, turn left.

The House is a sober but friendly place. In 1848 it cost Disraeli £35,000, most of which he had to borrow from a friend. But it was a shrewd move giving him the 'Englishness' and respectability necessary for a politician, especially one who was to end up as party leader.

I particularly liked the library, lined with hefty, bound volumes, overlooking the garden. Disraeli wrote to a friend of his passion for books and trees. He would come to the house and first stroll around the garden to look at all the trees before coming inside to study his many books.

Throughout the house, there are touching displays of personal mementoes. These include a tiny wedding ring with handwritten note from Mrs Disraeli about removing 'Dizzy's ring' due to a swollen finger. The story goes that his wife caught her hand in a carriage door just before Disraeli was about to make a very important speech to Parliament. She suffered in silence, only swooning once the speech was over.

One honour that Disraeli asked of Queen Victoria was that his wife should become a peeress in her own right and in 1868, she became Viscountess Beaconsfield. On show are the first and last gifts the Queen made to Disraeli. The last being some primroses from the wreath she sent to his funeral. Disraeli is buried in the church in the park which surrounds the house.

To continue the walk, follow the 'Way Out' signs to the car-parking area where there is a National Trust sign to Naphill Farm. Follow the path through the wood and out onto a field. After 250 yards (200 m), take the left-hand branch which goes along the edge of Common Wood. The end of this footpath becomes a rather narrow path which can be fairly slippery. It comes out onto a lane where you turn left and go along for about half a mile (1 km). The lane ends at the woods of Naphill Common, and from here you need to head north and then west to Bradenham. I'm giving compass directions because there are a multitude of paths through the woods, and at least you can trust the compass.

I suggest that you start by turning right where the lane ends, past a couple of cottages and a large gate (still painted green when I last went). Take the track to the left of the gate which then swings round in a large curve through a narrow strip of wood and comes out at a wide open area of fields. Just before these is a bridle-path, marked, to the right. Follow this until it seems to bend away from the fields. There are then white arrows marking a path that keeps you fairly close to the edge of the open space. Eventually, you come through the woods to the corner of the field. Here, continue through the woods, taking the central of the three possible paths. It drops slightly into a shallow valley and then joins an earthbank, going roughly west. Keep going in this direction until you come into a large glade with a clear bridle-track. Going left, this takes you near the fields of Bradenham Hill Farm, and then out onto Bradenham Village Green.

It won't really matter, except for time, if you do get a little lost as these woods are a pleasure to walk in. They are very peaceful and seem so remote despite being minutes from the busy A4010 on one side and the sprawling village of Naphill on the other. I caught sight of both a fox and a deer last time I was there.

When you get to Bradenham, it's a good place to picnic if that fits in with your itinerary. I had a long sit down in the sunshine, admiring the peaceful triangular green and the pretty grouping of the warm brick-built house, flint church and village houses, with a back drop of beech woods. My munching of sandwiches was accompanied by the munching of two tethered horses on the grass.

From Bradenham, go down to the main road, which is fast and busy. Turn left towards High Wycombe, and after a short distance, cross the road and take the farm lane under the railway to Averingdown Farm. At the farm entrance the footpath goes slightly right up into the woods behind the farm. There are two turnings left along either side of the ridge towards West Wycombe Hill. The first one gives you views of the valley but the traffic along that busy road is audible. The second turning joins part of a nature trail organized by the Chiltern Society with the help of the present Sir Francis Dashwood. Notes on this part of the trail include some interesting comments on the damage done to the woods by grey squirrels. You should look out for the way the bark has been stripped off some of the younger trees.

These paths lead out to open grassland on West Wycombe Hill, and the church topped with the golden ball. On this hill the village of Haveringdon used to stand, but it disappeared some two hundred years ago, probably due to lack of water, a problem for many Chiltern areas because the surface land is porous. Apart from the church, there are the remains of a hill fort, and a huge mausoleum built by the infamous Sir Francis in 1763. Pevsner describes it as 'a spectacular and passing strange structure', a fitting folly to this extraordinary character.

Beneath the hill are the caves, also attributed to Sir Francis, and apparently the scene of meetings of the Hell-Fire Club.

This walk, although it would be a bit longer, could be done from High Wycombe. The train service from London is frequent, and a day return reasonably cheap. The only drawback is the final section through the town which seems long and tiresome after the restful countryside.

If you go into High Wycombe it's fun to spend half an hour or so at the High Wycombe Chair Museum. It is an odd little place, not least because it closes for lunch. There are only three rooms downstairs, crammed with an amazing selection of chairs, so much so that you can never quite see, or rather sit on them again in the same way. There are all manner of designs with bow backs, fan backs, triple splats, roman and gothic spindles. Rooms upstairs contain some 'personality' chairs, including the one Disraeli used at the Junior Carlton Club. The word 'bodger' comes from the chair-making industry. Then, it referred to a craft requiring considerable skill, unlike its present-day slang meaning.

The chair industry of the Chilterns was centered on High Wycombe, and made good use of the surrounding woodlands. What began as a cottage industry developed into production of over a million chairs a year. At the back of the museum is a Bodger's Hut and typical workshop. Summing up the work is a 1920s old Music Hall song:

> I'm Jurkins of Wycombe, High Wycombe in Bucks.
> Where I lives with mi' wife and mi' fowls and mi' ducks,
> And I turns up the spindles and makes all your chairs,
> Aye! I guess I'm the man at the seat of affairs.
> And whether you're high-born or proud as can be,
> You'd look very 'low' if it wasn't for me!

Wendover is a compact town with an attractive high street dominated by the clock tower. It is a busy place for walkers as the main road forms part of the Ridgeway long-distance path. That path goes through the town, turning off the main street just before the clock tower and winds its way through a pretty part along a brook and around by the church. If you are only able to visit Wendover briefly, do go along this back route, and visit the church where there is the marvellous brass commemorating William Bradschawe and his wife, plus nine smaller kneeling figures of their children and the names of twenty-three grandchildren below that.

Power and Politics

OS Map 1:50: 000, Sheet 165
A circular walk from Wendover of 5–6 miles (8 km). Allow 2½–3 hours.

This area of the Chilterns involves you in various aspects of political life, past and present. There's a chance to see the country residence of the Prime Minister, a walk through a place closely associated with one of the first politicians to make a stand against the power of the throne, and a view over the estates of one of the most influential families of the nineteenth and twentieth centuries.

Going underfoot is varied as the woods can be muddy and the chalky areas a little slippery. There is a fair amount of climbing up to Coombe Hill which is the highest point on the Chilterns. Most of the route is very clear, especially the first part which follows the same route as the Ridgeway. This is also likely to be the most populated part, but not all that many people walk on beyond the Coombe Hill monument.

Car-parking and the start

There is good parking in Wendover by the library which is midway down the high street.

This is also a good area to come to by train since you can start and finish at Wendover Station.

Start the walk going down the high street away from the clock tower. It is the B4010 to Ellesborough, but was once known as the Upper Icknield Way, an ancient road through England. Shortly the path goes off to the left up a steep-sided chalky track. It is a hefty climb taking you out onto the open and the ridge of Bacombe Hill. Follow this ridge along to Coombe Hill and the monument. This was erected to commemorate the dead in the South African (Boer) War. It's a good spot to get a sense of the Chiltern geography. To the north is the very obvious scarp face, dropping abruptly to the plain and the Vale of Aylesbury, whereas looking south, the ground slopes away much more gently.

From the monument, the path continues south along the ridge. I prefer to drop down slightly and stay in the open, though there is a track through the woods on the top. There's a steep hill over to the right covered with a glorious wood which, at this distance, looks like numerous balls of wool in every shade of green, packed into a huge basket. This is Beacon Hill topped with Cymbeline's Castle, an Iron Age fort.

Almost hidden in the valley to the left is Chequers, the large country house given to the nation in 1917 by Lord Lee of Fareham. He requested that it should be used exclusively for prime ministers in the hope that the fresh air and pleasant surroundings would help them make sound judgements. Apparently prime ministers are not allowed to leave anything personal in the house. Legend has it that Stanley Baldwin was always having his pipes forwarded on. Apart from the associations with prime ministers, Chequers was also a prison for two years for the unfortunate Lady Jane Grey.

This walk brings you closer to Chequers. Follow the footpath through the woods (this is still the Ridgeway) crossing a minor road. Then go on through more woods where there are a confusing number of paths; you should look for the Ridgeway signs. The path contours around the side of a hill and then drops down into the valley on a wide track, bringing you out onto the road at the southern end of Chequers Park. The Ridgeway path, as I discovered when I completed the section from Ivinghoe Beacon to Princes Risborough, goes across the bottom of the park and across one of the muddiest fields I've ever encountered.

To continue the circuit, you can either double back and take the bridle-path to the left where the path divides, or for easier navigating, walk up the lane past Buckmoorend Farm. Where the lane ends there is a bridle-path, going straight on. Shortly, there's a small footpath off to the left which should take you around the edge of the fields, and some nice-looking houses plus tennis courts. The path goes around these and then drops steeply down into Hampdenleaf Wood.

Hampden is a well-known name in these parts. In the seventeenth century, the Hampdens owned much of the land, including Wendover, and the villages of Hampden and Little Hampden still bear the name. The best-known member of the family was John Hampden, who made a stand against King Charles by refusing to pay the £1 tax known as Ship Money. It was a levy imposed by the King without the agreement of Parliament. The protest happened at the church at Great Kimble,

THE CHILTERNS

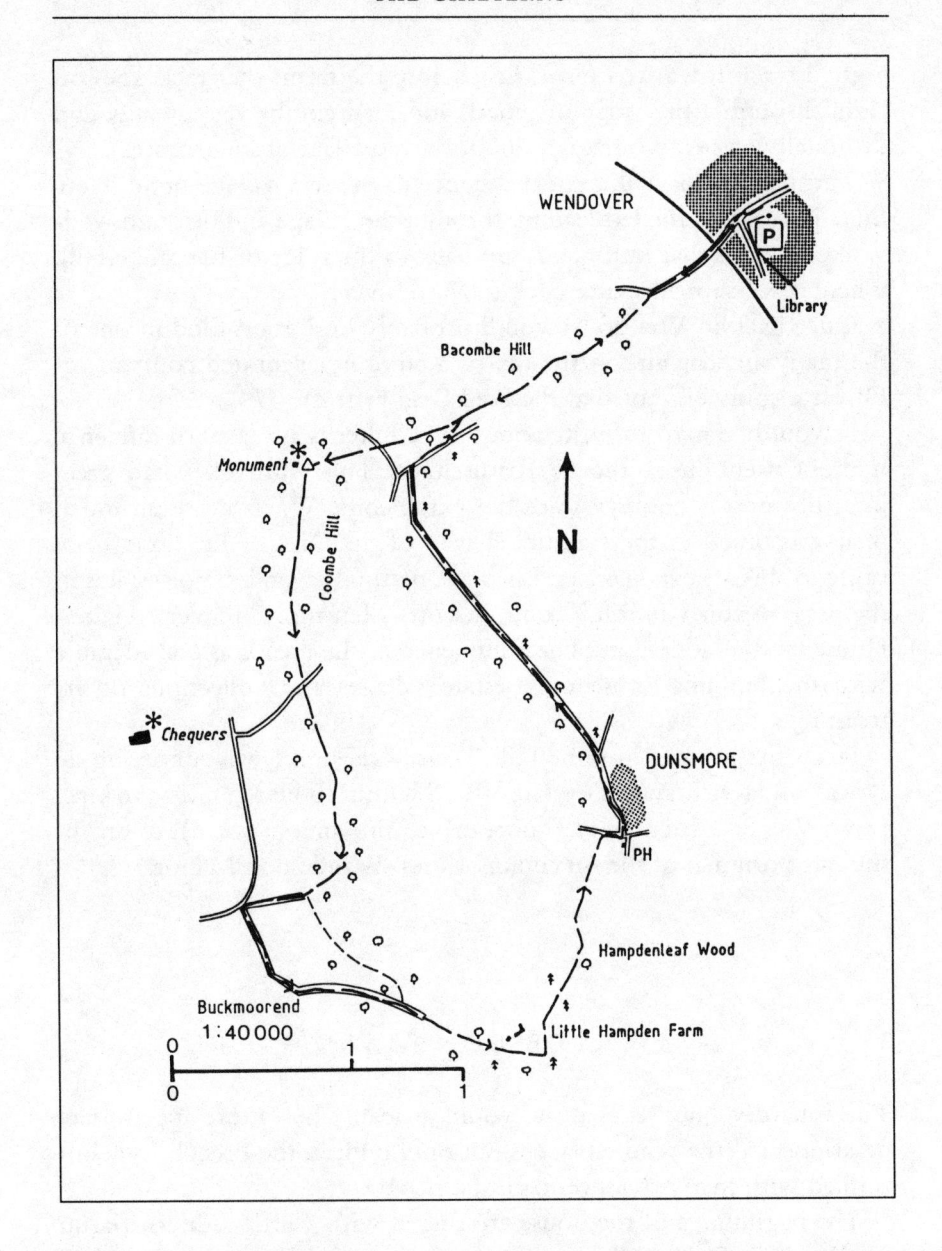

just over the hill from Chequers, and is said to be one of the causes of the Civil War. Hampden later fought against the king, was mortally wounded at the Battle of Chalgrove, and subsequently died at Thame.

At the bottom of the valley, follow the path to the left (north) on a good track towards a farm. Just before the farm, the track goes off right through a tiny strip of wood, and then climbs very steeply and diagonally across two fields and out onto the lane at Dunsmore.

Turn right and walk a short distance to the tiny village pond. Here there is a road to the left leading through the village and through well-walked woods that lead gently up back to the ridge of Bacombe Hill, where it is a short distance back to Wendover.

Once back in Wendover you'll probably find good food in one of the many ancient inns in the town. You're in celebrated company as Oliver Cromwell stayed at the Red Lion in 1642.

It would be hard to write about the Chilterns as places of influence without mentioning the de Rothschilds. This family has had great influence on the country since the Napoleonic Wars, although much of it was quiet, in the traditional way of the City of London. They came to this area *en masse* and had at one time several major estates in the area, Aston Clinton, Tring, Ascott, Mentmore Towers, Halton House, and Waddesdon. Their influence in the area was considerable with the building of schools, estate villages and collections of art treasures.

From the top of Coombe Hill, I felt as though I was surveying de Rothschild territory as the estates are all within about ten miles (16 km). From Wendover it is only a short drive, nine miles (15 km), to one of the most original of the surviving houses, Waddesdon Manor.

Waddesdon Manor

This is hardly a house; château would probably be a more appropriate description as the whole place is not only built in the French style but is filled with many treasures from France too.

The beginnings of the house are tinged with a little sadness. Baron Ferdinand de Rothschild came to settle here after his young wife died in childbirth. He spent the rest of his life building the house and adding to its marvellous collection of furniture and paintings. His sister, Alice, who succeeded him, continued the collection, and so too her great nephew, James de Rothschild, who succeeded her. He too died childless, but left the property, plus an enormous legacy for its upkeep, to the National Trust.

Every room is a treasure store whether you are interested in paintings, porcelain, furniture or fabrics. The de Rothschilds were collectors of treasures, not just for their appearance, but also out of interest in their history and associations. Some of the items that are particularly evocative are the ones brought from France after the Revolution. There are miniatures of Madame de Pompidour's dogs and a petite desk made for Marie-Antoinette. I liked the story of the carpets. There are thirteen Savonnerie or royal carpets in the house. All made in the most vivid colours from vegetable dyes which have certainly stood the test of time. They too were bought in the days when aristocrats were busy getting rid of anything that might link them with the king. Perhaps the most interesting is one carpet, in the Morning Room, where the *fleur de lys* emblem has been carefully unpicked and replaced with something less innocuous. I wonder if that action saved the owner from the guillotine.

My favourite piece of all was the travelling dinner service. At first glance it looks like a rather superior picnic set made in Meissen porcelain and silver gilt. When unpacked, there is a place setting for one, with a platter and vegetable dish, and condiment containers, plus tea-pot and two cups. The spare one was for the coachman who was allowed a drink of tea whilst his master had the full dinner!

A fascinating footnote is that the house was used during the war as a centre for East End evacuees. I should think the children thought they had arrived in fairyland when they drew up to the château, and the guides told me that many of them have since been back.

Hidden in the bend of the Thames

OS Map 1:50 000, Sheet 175
7–8 mile (11–12 km) circular walk. Allow 3–4 hours.

This walk is a lovely tour in a backwater of the Thames with continually contrasting surroundings: open fields, typical Chiltern beeches, riverside footpaths, orchards and attractive village roads.

It is a ramble especially suitable for terrible weather as much of the going underfoot is on firm ground, either flat grassy embankment or chalky track. There are one or two short routes through the woods which can be muddy but quite negotiable. If the weather is bad, there are plenty of places (pubs!) to shelter in on the way, and plenty to look at close-to-hand if thick cloud spoils the view. It sounds more as though I'm preparing you for the wilds of Northumbria rather than for a stroll along a very picturesque meander of the Thames.

Most of the route is very clearly marked with good footpath or bridle-way marker posts, thanks to the diligence of the East Bucks Ramblers who have erected many of them. You will need to take a little care on the route through the woods above Bisham (Quarry Wood) where new tracks and forest working mean there are more tracks on the ground than on the map.

An interesting feature of this walk is the way it goes through so many tiny patches of National Trust land. I had previously associated the Trust with large-scale tracts or parks and the grounds of stately homes. Quite the opposite can be seen here, with some areas not much bigger than a pocket handkerchief.

As this jaunt is long with no obvious short-cut, I have suggested an alternative start if you prefer a shorter loop. That variation is all on good surface and would be good if you simply wanted to walk off lunch.

Car-parking and the start

You begin this walk, if you are doing the full distance, in Marlow. There are plenty of car-parks in the town. I was able to park in a little spot just by the bridge in Higginson Park, where there is room for four cars.

THE CHILTERNS

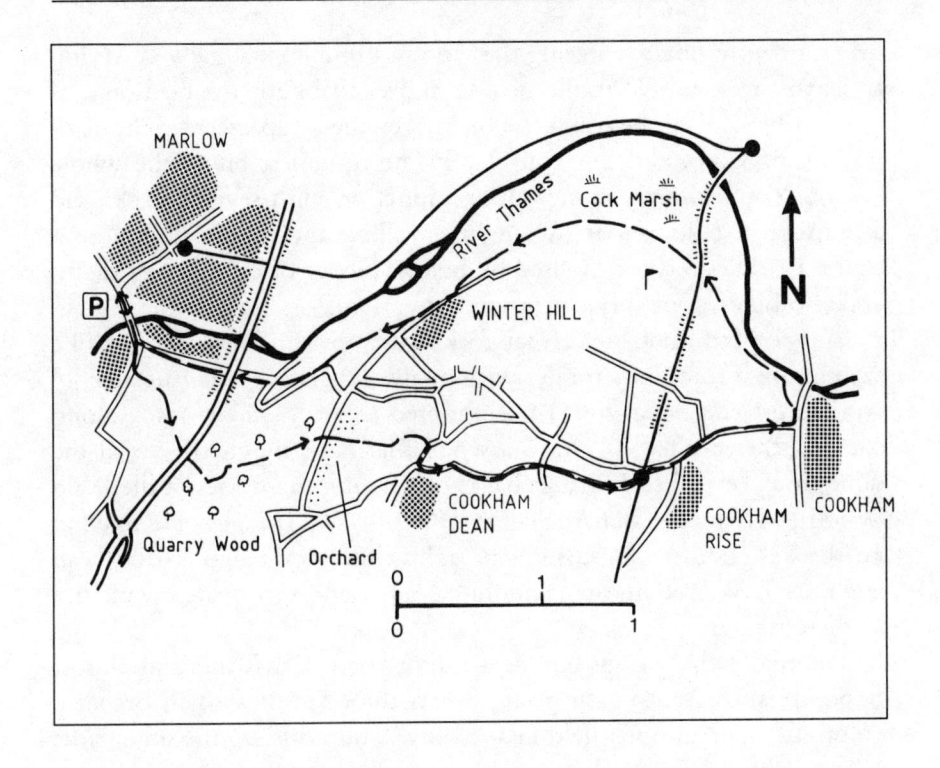

Start off down the high street towards the suspension bridge. (I didn't know previously that the present capital of Hungary used to be a Buda and a separate Pest, but the man who spanned the river between the two, William Tierney Clark, also designed this bridge.) It is full of interesting detail with pretty, almost flower-like, tops to the side posts making them look a little like drooping daisies. It was completed in 1836 and nearly scrapped in 1966 but these plans were fortunately defeated. At the far side, I got rather a surprise to see boat ends poking out from underneath, but there seems to have been some very inventive use of space here by the local rowing club. There is a good view from here of the Thames, All Saints Parish Church and a very dramatic weir. It was there that an old timber bridge used to span the Thames providing the main crossing-point into Marlow.

Once over the bridge, walk along the road until you see a footpath sign to the left taking you across some fields to the ridge and the woods ahead. Look for the stile in the far right-hand corner. Here you need to cross the very busy A404, and then a little stream (there is a small bridge) before finally entering the woods. I find it extremely satisfying to leave the sound of traffic behind and exchange it for birdsong, as you do here. It almost makes you forget the steep ascent. The path goes straight up, and this is probably the muddiest bit of the whole circuit. You'll shortly come out at a junction with several tracks and a number of coloured arrows, white, yellow and blue. The blue is a sign for bridle-ways to be used by horses, plenty of evidence of them, and also bikes, probably the mountain variety.

Aim for the main track that forks away to the left. It is just like walking in a tree-lined tunnel with banks either side rising up steeply and almost enclosing you. I felt tempted to stray off the track along some of the tiny paths. This is a wood that has a magnetic, yet at the same time, eerie feel. It brings back very strong memories of the Wild Wood in Kenneth Grahame's *The Wind In The Willows*. He lived at nearby Pangbourne but spent some of his childhood in Cookham Dean and must have used his own childhood experiences to create the picture of these woods.

Eventually the woods end at a minor road. Cross this and almost opposite is a narrow path going down the edge of a small orchard. Continue over an open field in a shallow valley and up the other side. When I think back to this part of the walk, I remember enjoying its neatness; the well-laid-out orchards, the hedged fields, the glimpses of old timbered houses through the trees and a gentle valley stretching out ahead. It's strange to think that less than two hundred years ago, the whole of the Chiltern area had a reputation as a hideout for highwaymen in the wild stretches of woodland.

This section brings you out at the Hare and Hounds and via a small stretch of open land owned by the National Trust onto the road at Cookham Dean. Here, turn left up the road to the church. This part of the village is very pleasant with all sorts of houses and cottages creating an attractive whole.

Go along the road to the right up to the church. The route goes behind the church, seemingly straight down a private drive marked Huntsman's Cottage, but it is a right of way. As you round the corner, the view is down onto Cookham, though the scene is dominated by the gas works.

At the bottom of the track, take the minor road straight ahead which brings you through the back streets of Cookham Rise. Being naturally nosey, I enjoy a section like this, looking at all the different houses, gardens, names and so on, and there are some delightful domestic cottages and buildings here.

Join the main road at the station, and turn right, passing a few more shops and houses, then go on through Cookham Moor where the old road and bridge now form the footpath. As you go by the station, don't miss the beautifully illustrated information board and some of the instructions such as 'you can feed ducks here'. There is a small short-cut if you head left off Cookham Moor towards the Thames, but I think it is worth walking on through Cookham village to the road junction, the church and Cookham Bridge. Cookham is the location for the annual counting of Thames swans and the Keeper of the Royal Swans has offices in one of the houses just below the bridge. The painter, Stanley Spencer, who lived for nearly fifty years at Cookham, captured the scene in his painting 'Swan-Upping' which now hangs in the Tate Gallery. The place seems to have changed little in the eighty years since the work was executed. Spencer often used Cookham and the surrounding area for his paintings. 'The Last Supper' hangs in the church.

Go through the churchyard. It is a delight. I was there in the spring at the beginning of the blossom season, and the air seemed full of the delicate petals.

Once through the church grounds you are on the side of the River Thames, which has swept around in a massive bend from Marlow. The river setting is lovely, needless to say it has a Ratty and Mole feel to it.

The walk now follows the line of the Thames, though after about five hundred yards ($\frac{1}{3}$ km) you need to cut away from the river slightly to get under the railway line. The Thames comes in view again on the other side at Cock Marsh, another piece of land owned by the National Trust. I liked the going underfoot here, a short grassy embankment, and the gradient – flat. Away to the right, across the very large expanse of marsh, is the Thames. There's quite a long section on the flat before you begin to climb a more chalky part towards Winter Hill. You gradually get an aerial view of the Thames, the massive reservoirs and the wooded hills beyond. Once on Winter Hill you can see Marlow spread out before you and look over the Hambleden Valley and Chiltern Ridge. Someone has thoughtfully positioned a very handy seat, so I felt no guilt in taking a long time enjoying the view.

Don't miss the little footpath at the end of the Winter Hill stretch that takes you off the road behind the houses and back through the woods. This is a most lovely section of beeches. It appeals to me because the trees are tall and mature and there is little undergrowth (good orienteering terrain which is why I'm biased). Simply follow the track down to the very bottom of the hill and onto the road. Then head for Marlow and home.

If you want to shorten this walk, start the circuit at Cookham Dean. Park either at Winter Hill, though this is a popular viewing-from-the-comfort-of-the-car spot on sunny week-ends, or in Cookham Dean, and wend your way to the Hare and Hounds. This makes the circuit about four or five miles (6–8 km) long.

You can partake of tea or luncheon at the very well known and beautifully sited Compleat Angler, though I'm not sure what they would think of muddy boots. It is just by the suspension bridge. I found a friendly continental-style café just up the high street (open on Sundays too).

There are some interesting buildings to see in Marlow. Shelley, who lived here briefly in 1817, had a house on West Street which is a left turn further up the high street. During that time his wife Mary wrote *Frankenstein*.

My favourite part of Marlow goes down by All Saints Parish Church (again just by the suspension bridge). There's a little passage leading to St Peter Street, which has many interesting cottages including The Old Parsonage at the northern end, probably the oldest building in Marlow. From the bottom of the street you can get another view of the weir and look back at the famous bridge. Nearby is another little alley taking you to Mill Road and down to the lock.

CLIVEDEN HOUSE AND ESTATE

The wonderful estate of Cliveden, although not on the main Chiltern ridge, is located in the Chiltern Hundreds. It is worth coming here if you are in the vicinity of Marlow, and you might prefer a stroll around this estate to the walk around Cookham. It is substantial, a fact that is obvious from both the map and the view of Cliveden Reach from the wooded spur above Cookham. Yet nothing can quite prepare you for the scale of the property. The magnificence of the grounds is breathtaking, and remains so however many times you visit.

The house with its numerous owners has certainly played its part in influencing events, from its origination to one of the major political scandals of this century. Knowing a little of this makes a wander around the grounds even more fascinating.

The original home was built in 1666 by William Winde, who later went on to build Buckingham Palace. It was commissioned by George Villiers, the powerful second Duke of Buckingham. He eloped here with his mistress having killed her husband in London in a duel.

The next owner was Lord Hamilton, who distinguished himself in the Napoleonic Wars, and was the first Englishman to hold the title of Field Marshal.

The house was then let to Frederick, Prince of Wales, father of George III. In his time here, the Masque of Alfred was performed in the open-air theatre in the grounds. That might not ring any bells, but it included the aria Rule Britannia, which is today practically a national anthem. It was while playing with his children in the grounds of Cliveden that Prince Frederick was hit in the chest with a cricket ball, an injury which was later to prove fatal.

Just before the nineteenth century, Cliveden was burnt to the ground leaving little but the original terrace. A new house was put in its place only to be burnt down again, so the present house was built by the Duke of Sutherland.

In 1893, Cliveden was bought by the millionaire William Waldorf Astor. The Astors were the first owners to be succeeded by two generations of the same family. The first Lord Astor planted many of the trees that have now reached maturity in the estate. He also commissioned the Fountain of Love, a vast evocative, or rather provocative, marble statue.

William Astor and Nancy, the first woman to enter parliament, were given the house as a wedding present. She and her husband made the place a major political and literary centre between the two world wars. The term for those in this clique was The Cliveden Set.

After the war the house parties continued and the man who achieved notoriety through his role in the Profumo scandal, Stephen Ward, was a frequent guest. He was a particular friend of William Astor. Ward was allowed to renovate a dilapidated cottage in the grounds, for which he paid a peppercorn rent. Both Christine Keeler and Mandy Rice-Davies came to this cottage, along with other notables. The Profumo Affair was the outcome, a huge political scandal of the early 1960s. It involved government resignations, suspicion of espionage, and the suicide of the unfortunate Ward.

Now the National Trust own the property and the grounds. The grounds are open to the public, whilst the house has been converted into a luxurious hotel. Two rooms in the house are shown but access is limited.

It is the garden, the exterior of the house, and their position some two hundred feet (60 m) above the Thames that is so stunning.

It is worth getting the estate walks leaflet which describes four walks around the gardens lasting from thirty minutes to three hours. If you are interested in maps, this one has a most interesting cartography, done in monochrome shades of green. It is almost more of an aerial photograph than a map. The main features, such as the house and various statues are finely drawn in (not to scale). It makes it easier to find them and feel you are in the right place, although there is very little opportunity to get lost, despite the size.

I went around in the late evening and felt something of a pauper skulking around in my running kit whilst watching the 'black tie' guests enjoying their pre-prandial drinks on the terrace. All this added to the atmosphere, and you shouldn't miss the view from the Parterre.

There are plenty of places to escape other people. I had the fenced rose garden all to myself, or so I thought. I noticed a tiny brown animal just like a small dog, but it turned out to be a tiny deer. It let me get quite close before darting off. I was told in the information kiosk that there are quite a few deer in the grounds, and they wage a constant war with them over the rose garden in particular; roses are their favourite food, hence all the fencing to try to keep them out. Not entirely successful, I would say.

Try to set aside at least two hours for a fleeting visit to Cliveden, as it is memorable in so many ways.

The Hambleden Valley

I have chosen a walk taking in two lovely villages at the head of the Hambleden Valley, but the whole area is worth exploring. Many other villages are pretty, pubs are good and churches interesting. You could make a whole day's expedition by starting at Mill End, the little settlement where the Hamble River runs into the Thames. Mill End has a picturesque weatherboarded mill and an exciting weir across the river which is popular with white water canoe enthusiasts.

Heading up the valley, you'll come first to the village of Hambleden with its very pretty central green. It seems a typical English scene with a cluster of cottages, pub (very good) and church. I popped in to see the D'Oyley memorial. It is an extravagant tableau which I find fascinating and repellant all at the same time. Mother and father D'Oyley, who 'multiplied themselves with 5 sons and 4 daughters' are shown as near life-sized carved figures. The children, also life-size, are differently dressed, Roundhead or Puritan, depending on which side they supported during the later Civil War. Slightly more conventional is the sad sight of those who did not survive, represented by their father holding tiny skulls.

If you haven't time to go further up the valley, a good short walk can be had around the back of Hambleden up to Rotten Row and Pheasant's Hill.

Turville and Fingest

OS Map 1:50 000, Sheet 175
A circular walk of 6–7 miles (10–12 km) with ample opportunities for short cuts. Allow up to four hours.

This walk epitomizes the essence of the Chilterns and takes you through some of the best of the countryside. The scenery changes constantly with open fields, quiet beech woods, chalky hillside and shaded lanes.

It is not just the excellent countryside that makes the walking so good, but the reliable footpaths and good marker posts. The network of paths is extensive and very well-maintained. I was most surprised and pleased to find a well-trodden way through a field of fully grown rape, a plant which is notorious for getting everywhere.

You can time this walk to take in a visit at both excellent village pubs, The Bull and Butcher at Turville and The Chequers at Fingest. Otherwise, go on a Sunday, share the place with a few other folk, and enjoy Sunday tea served on Fingest Church Green.

Because of the nature of the Chilterns, there is a fair amount of climbing up and down on this walk, something you may like to brood upon at the bottom of a steep ascent. The going underfoot is good most of the way. The tracks are well-worn, though there are a few places across fields that may be muddy after wet weather. The routes should all be obvious both on the map and on the ground but there is some navigating to do as the route twists and turns quite a lot on the circuit.

Car-parking and the start

One, perhaps the only, drawback of this walk is the lack of suitable parking spots. All the more reason for walking, I suppose, but if you do drive up to this valley, many of the roads here are very narrow. Depending on what you plan to do later, park at either Turville, Fingest or Skirmett. I started at Turville with the steep climb to the windmill.

This is such a pretty village, with warm brick and flint buildings, and a charming church with an unusually squat tower. The path goes straight up the side of the valley, right under the windmill. The windmill is now a private residence and does have a splendid setting overlooking the little village sitting in the valley below. It is a peaceful rural scene, though it has not always been so. I discovered that there's an unsolved mystery here. Under the mill a thirteenth-century coffin was discovered with a murdered woman inside.

Walk up by the side of the mill to the top of the ridge and cross a minor road. There's a path leading you down through some more woods to the bottom of another valley. I soon began to appreciate why 'bottom' is a favourite Chiltern term.

From here you can turn right and go directly down the road to Fingest. If you prefer, take the footpath up the next hill (the start of that is just a little way down the road) into Hanger Wood, and then follow the path down into Fingest Village.

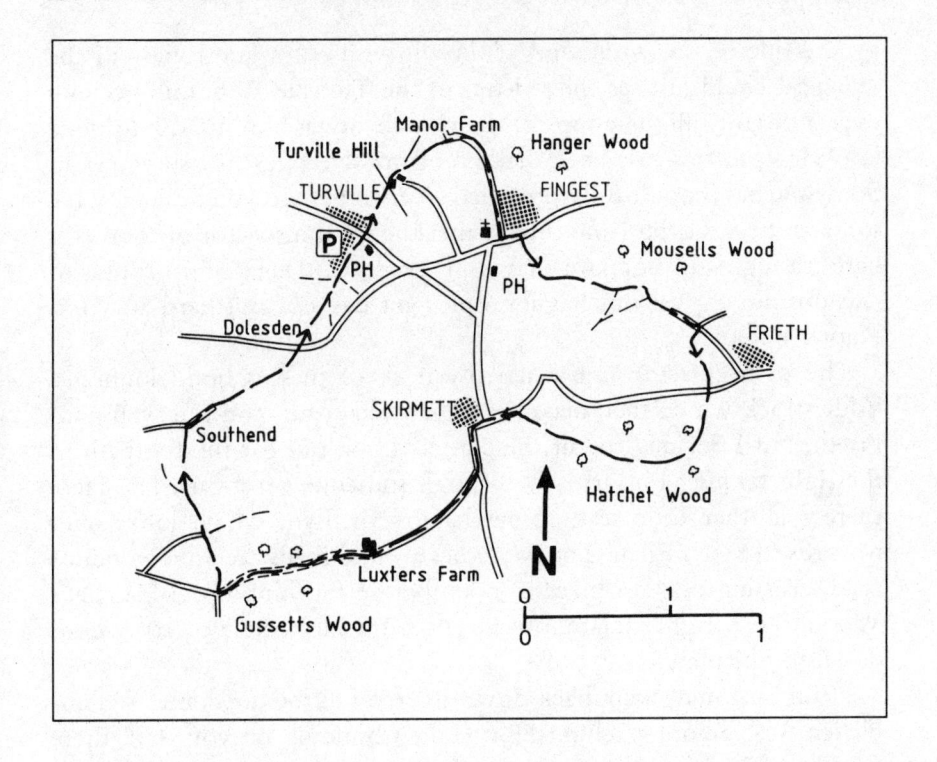

Fingest is another ancient and charming place. It's name has gone through several variations including Vengest, Tingehurst and – my favourite – Thinghurst. These are all of Saxon origin from the word 't'hing' or 'hing' in turn from 'hangen' meaning 'at the hanging wood'.

The church here is most striking. The outstanding feature is its enormous square tower, dating from Norman times, which is topped by a very unusual twin saddleback roof. It rather dwarfs the rest of the building. There's a short history of the church and the village written by 'Cassandra' of the *Daily Mirror*, the pen-name of a journalist who lived locally. It is just by the entrance gate. I particularly liked the way local events were related to some of the major happenings (Battle of Bosworth and so on).

This is where you'll get afternoon tea on a fine Sunday, but year-round refreshments can be taken in the Chequers Pub, which is at the road junction. From the junction of roads by the church, facing the pub, turn left, and after a short distance there is a footpath to the right leading up yet another slope towards Mousell's Wood. The path runs by the side of the wood and at the top you get a good view of the village. I could just see the sail-tips of the Turville Windmill peeping over a distant hill. The tops of the church tower also just about poke into view, in this case over the line of massive trees that surround it. Someone has thoughtfully provided a bench here so you can enjoy the scene and rest at the same time. I met the local inspector of footpaths here, though I'm not sure that is his correct title. He did his best to reassure me he was not having a pleasant day out but hard at work. Rather like me.

The path cuts through a narrow neck of these woods, joining a bridle-track which then becomes a metalled road. You can walk into Frieth, but I decided to cut the corner. Look out for the footpath to the right taking you virtually through someone's front garden. Here there's another little seat, somewhat overgrown, which looks over towards Luxter's Farm. The path goes around fields then over a minor road, crossing one last piece of open before finishing up in Hatchet's Wood. Turn right and follow the path through these pretty woods down to Skirmett.

From Skirmett, walk back down the road in the direction of Hambleden. Just before reaching Flint Hall, a building on your left, there is a footpath to the right. It starts off running between two fences, then goes around the fields and into a strip of woodland. There are several tracks in this part but the direction you need is up, aiming towards Luxter's Farm. You should meet the path which climbs the hill, coming out in an open area just below the farm, then going below a vineyard and onto the road. I wonder whether it will soon be possible to do a spot of wine tasting here as the vineyard looks quite well-established.

Once on the road, turn right up the hill, go past the farm and up into the woods. It does suddenly go very dark under the trees, the wood coming right up to the roadside. Although these woods look open and are very tempting they are in fact private. Carry on up the road until the wood on the right comes to an end. In the adjacent field there is a footpath sign on the right pointing you across the field and back into the woods. There is a small path here that takes you down the steep-sided valley.

At the bottom, cross over and climb up the other side, heading towards Southend, a cluster of houses. This is the top of a small plateau, and there is a trig point close by. There are fine views with Henley-on-Thames to the south, the main Chiltern Ridge to the north-west, and north-east is the Turville Windmill, which consolingly looked further away than it really was.

The path continues along a small lane which ends at a building, but you should continue in the same direction along the spur. Then, drop through some woods and down to a minor road and Dolesden Farm. Keep going straight on across more fields, gently climbing until you meet a bridle-track and from here it is just a short distance to Turville.

At this point, you are within very easy reach of either Henley or Marlow if you need an injection of town after the countryside. But as you are so near to the Chiltern Ridge, it is worth driving on up to Christmas Common.

You could come here as an alternative to the Hambleden Valley as there are some good short walks, or simply add it on to the Hambleden day.

Christmas Common and Ewelme

I picked out Ewelme as a place to visit after finding out it had a connection with William de la Pole. I had a fascination with this character after witnessing his fate in the awesome Royal Shakespeare Company's production of *The Plantagenets*. He was beheaded, according to Shakespeare at least, for his antics with, and loyalty to, Margaret of Anjou, wife of King Henry VI.

William was married to Alice Chaucer, granddaughter of the poet, in 1430. Together they probably rebuilt the church and founded the almshouse here less than ten years later. De la Pole was created Earl of Suffolk in 1448, but killed two years later. Alice retreated here after his death and is buried in the church.

I also met one of the friendliest church cats, who accompanied me on the whole visit after a rather daring leap onto my shoulders!

To get to Ewelme, go on from Turville along the narrow tree-lined road to Northend and Christmas Common. This makes a very good spot for a picnic assuming you haven't indulged in all the village pubs. There is the most wonderful view of the Oxford Plain, as you are now on the northern face of the Chilterns. Drop down into Watlington and then it is only a short drive to Ewelme. Parking is just possible outside the church.

The Tomb of Alice Chaucer is quite a sight. Carved in alabaster, she reclines peacefully on the top, whilst underneath is a macabre emaciated half-shrouded figure representing the poor woman in death. It sits in a beautiful side chapel, decorated with an engraving of the initials IHS, *Iesus Hominum Salvator* (Jesus Men's Saviour). Apart from the tomb, one of the other furnishings worth seeing is the font. It has a huge wooden cover, some ten feet (3 m) high, with a huge carved Tudor rose as counterpoint.

The almshouse next door is charming. It was instigated by William and Alice for the benefit of thirteen poor men and two chaplains. There were very specific directions to the chaplains concerning their duties, and detailed regulations for the conduct of the almsmen. They had to be present at two daily services and wear a uniform cloak with a red cross on the breast. The uniform has been discontinued, but the present almsmen still attend church once a day and say daily prayers for the founders.

The tiny houses are brick-built, and arranged as a block around a square courtyard. There wasn't much brick used here at the time. It is thought that William brought in labourers from his East Anglian estates to do the work as the style is similar to work of a similar period in Suffolk. It is hard now to imagine how styles of work and material could be so isolated, but brick was not a material readily available in the Chilterns. Over the years the building has taken on a warm, mellow appearance. Considering it has stood for well over five hundred years, the walls looked in remarkable condition.

Browsing around this peaceful spot makes a good end to explorations in this area.

Sussex

'Sussex by the sea'. This well-known phrase conjours up this county's cosy feeling of gentle hills basking by a sunny English Channel and soothing, grey stone villages nestling in the graceful contours of the hills. There are still plenty of small villages down quiet winding roads that appear to have avoided the inevitable modernization and development. Probably the more preserved the village, the worse a commuting rail journey to the capital really is.

The history of Sussex, even up to fifty years ago, belies this quiet picture; it is perhaps more appropriate to think of Sussex as Britain's frontline. The sea that it nudges up to is also the sea which has brought scores of invaders from the earliest times. Romans, Vikings, Saxons, Danes and Normans have all landed here, and more recently there have been invasion threats from the principal continental powers of the time, the Spanish, the French and the Germans. The popular TV programme 'Dad's Army', based on a unit of the Home Guard established for home defence in the Second World War, was set in Sussex.

One of the most interesting maps I've come across recently was one showing the distribution of pillboxes in Britain. These underground forts sprang up in 1940, during the early part of the war, because of the invasion threat from Germany. As well as being sited to assist the defence of specific places, they were used to strengthen military defence lines across the country. Sussex was cut off from the rest of Britain by one such line.

All the invaders, Saxons, Danes, Romans, Vikings and Normans have laid claim to bits of county one way and another and have left some evidence of their stay. The sea, too, was once a stronger invader, filling up the rivers so they were navigable some ten miles (16 km) further inland than they are now, leaving wide valleys as evidence of its retreat.

Invasion didn't always have an aggressive side. Not all were military ones, some were just immigration. But whether they forced their way in or not, all who came and settled in the county brought skills with them, such as the Huguenots (French Protestants) and their glass-making.

Long periods of peace were enjoyed after some of the invaders had settled. The Romans were able to establish a way of life over centuries of residence, and one of the biggest Roman palaces known in Europe is at Fishbourne.

The threat of invaders also altered the use of the land, and gave rise to fortifications such as the famous Iron Age camp at Chanctonbury Ring, one of the most prominent features of the West Sussex Downs. There are fine castles built to control the five areas of Sussex into which William the Conqueror divided it, called 'rapes'. Incidentally, we know him as William the Conqueror but in his time he was known as William the Bastard, for strictly factual reasons, of course. Each of the rapes controlled a portion of Sussex where a river broke through a gap in the downs. These castles were thus part of the national defensive framework of that time, as well as being the way that Norman rule was enforced on the native population. The five castles were at Arundel, Bramber, Lewes, Pevensey and Hastings, and some-thing has survived to the present from them all.

In Sussex, I feel very much on home ground, as I was born in its heart and brought up from the age of three on its coast. Now, when I return after fifteen years living elsewhere, it is extremely pleasant to visit old haunts, discovering that some places seem smaller and nearer than how they felt as a child. Of course, I also delight in discovering and finding new things to see.

In this chapter I've gone to some of the many places where invasion has left its mark either by people or by nature. The important Roman sites at Fishbourne and Chichester are included. The walks take in visits around the central Norman rapes of Arundel and Bramber, where the sea swept up the gap in the downs, and also around Highdown, an interesting area where several individuals have left their mark.

I've avoided walking much on the downs themselves as the footpath – The South Downs Way – is already very well known, and is well signposted for anyone who wants to do it (and well worth it if you do). Instead, I've gone for some back door approaches, with good views of the north face of the downs, explorations of the delightful, spacious river valleys, and stopping-places in neglected outposts on the downs and at quiet harbours of the coast.

The Most elegant Tea-Rooms in Sussex

OS Map 1: 50 000, Sheet 198
A figure-of-eight walk of 11–12 miles (18–20 km). Each loop is about six miles. Allow $2\frac{1}{2}$–3 hours for each section, or a day for the whole expedition.

This may seem rather a strange title for a walk. Let me explain. Desperate for a drink after walking on one of those really hot summer's days forced me to scour Bramber. I found, hidden in St Mary's, a striking half-timbered house, in a spacious eighteenth-century music room, the most amazing place for tea. On some days you may be lucky enough to have a little accompaniment as you sip your drink.

After diving in for the tea, I went around the house rather as an afterthought. Thank goodness. It is not to be missed. The whole place is completely enchanting, and there is so much to every room. You get a personal tour by the owners whose infectious enthusiasm brings everything to life.

You can of course cheat and just go to the tea-rooms with no walk at all, but this stroll along the banks of the River Adur and the old railway line is most pleasant.

The walk makes a really splendid day out exploring the quiet Adur Valley and the villages of Beeding, Bramber, Steyning and Ashurst. You can time it to have lunch in the cosy country inn, The Fountain, at Ashurst, and then get back for tea and a tour of St Mary's House, Bramber. There are marvellous views of the north scarp face of the downs and it is possible to pick out some of the well-known landmarks.

The alternative is to start at the Ashurst pub and do a shorter circuit, and then explore Steyning and Bramber afterwards.

The going underfoot is all good with a few wetter patches by the river and some slower going if the grass along the embankment hasn't been cut recently. You can walk on either side of the river. I found it was a case of the grass being greener on the other side, as, whichever bank I opted for, after some minutes the other side looked better going.

Most of the route is easy to find, especially with the river running down the centre. The railway track is also very clear, and most of the footpaths are signed with finger posts. There are two occasions where you seem to be on the verge of trespassing into a back garden. Just when you start to lose confidence, there's a stile and it turns out to be the right way. It is suitable for dogs, though there is livestock grazing in most of the fields along the river.

Car-parking and the start

If you are doing the whole figure-of-eight, or just the bottom loop, then park near Upper Beeding Priory. There is some space just outside the Priory grounds.

If you want to do the top loop, park at The Fountain Inn at Ashurst, though do check with the landlord.

The footpath starts just by the Priory, down some steps leading to the river flatlands.

For the first part of the walk, follow the river northwards as it meanders gently towards Henfield. Don't be fooled by the Adur's sluggish appearance, low water-level and slimy banks into thinking that it is no more than a trickle through the countryside. The Adur, like the Arun, is a strong tidal river, so much so that when the tide turns the river turns too and gives the impression that it is running backwards.

The Adur has carved out for itself a very wide valley and it is surrounded on either side by fertile stretches of flat land. This is a reminder of the time when the sea came much further up the valley with navigable waters as far as Steyning.

I walked here on a humid July day with a feeling of a lazy English summer. The riverside grasses were bejewelled with butterflies. Several families of swans were grouped along the river, closely guarding some quite grown-up sygnets. A huge cob hissed loudly and fluttered his wings as I got close. One look at the strength in those wings ensured that I gave him a wide berth.

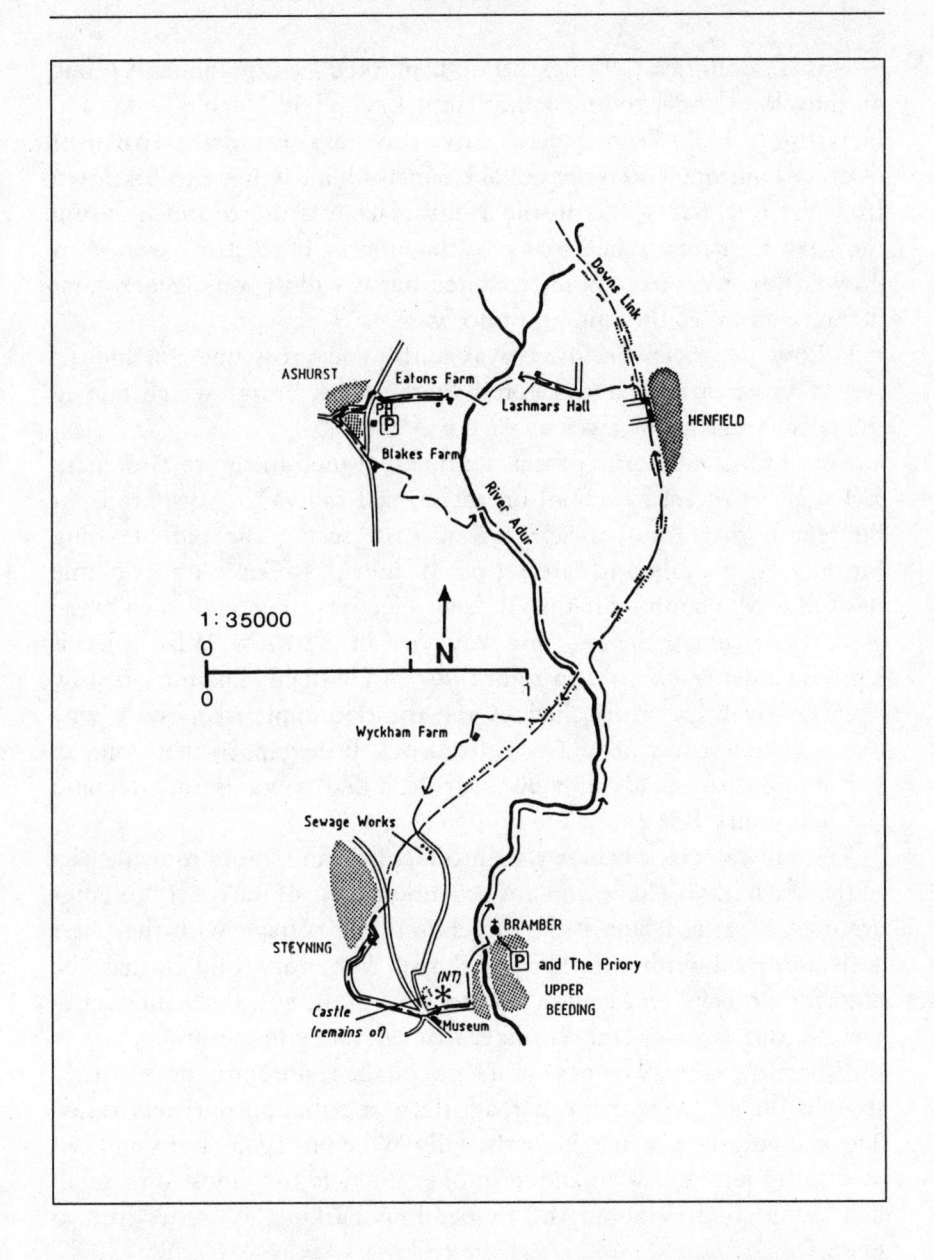

From here you get a good view of the steep northern face of the downs. Looking east, Truleigh Hill is marked by a pylon, and is one of the closest hills to the Adur Gap; beyond is Devil's Dyke and Newtimber Hill. To the west, above Steyning, is a dense crown of trees on a hilltop. This is the site of Chanctonbury Ring, a well-known Iron Age fort. Sadly, the profile of this place was altered much during the 1987 hurricane when many of the ancient beech trees were torn down. New trees have been replanted but it will be some generations before we can see the ring as it once was.

Follow the river for some way until you cross under a line of marching pylons and ahead you'll see the black bridge which carried the railway across the river.

I have fond memories of this old line that used to run to Shoreham as I used to travel to school on the coastal railway to Brighton. At Shoreham there was always a chance of seeing the old Steyning Steamer, as we called it, rattling out of the Adur Gap with its plume of smoke. Much more fun than the staid electric trains. Sadly it chugged along the river for the last time way back in the 1960s. What is left is a good cinder track, so turn right towards Henfield. The track is now enclosed by high shrubs, hedges and the odd apple tree. Some way along, there's a seat provided in front of a little gap, so that you can rest and look at the lovely view over the valley towards Steyning and Chanctonbury Ring.

The railway track brings you into Henfield in a more modern part of the town. If you have time for a wander, some of the older buildings are on the eastern side. Near the church is a cottage with the outer walls adorned with cats holding birds. The story told is that the cottager's canary was caught by the vicar's cat, and these silhouettes were meant as a constant reminder (for the cat or the vicar?).

Where the railway comes into Henfield, the route continues virtually straight on, via a short bit of road, up to a pub, appropriately called The Cat and the Canary. Here the railway begins again, but you need to turn off left very soon and head over the field to a house on a small lane. Don't worry about the tremendous barking, it comes from a kennels.

Follow this lane to Lashmar's Hall, a most charming house with a beautiful garden. Follow the path down the side wall towards another small cottage. Keeping close to the cottage, and getting that 'back garden' feeling, you will find a stile in the hedge which leads out to the open and the river. Just down the river is a footbridge by a wind charger.

Follow the footpath straight across the next field by a large farm, then turn left around the buildings onto a lane and head towards the main road. There, almost immediately on the left, is The Fountain Inn. It is a gorgeous old pub with a typical dark, wooden interior and two delightful gardens. They have a splendid range of real ales to quench the thirst, including some local brews such as Pompey Royal; there's some good food too,

You can walk straight on down the road to Blake's Farm. It isn't very busy, but there is no footpath. I prefer the route through Ashurst Village, which is a pretty mixture of buildings. Take the footpath at the recreation field which brings you, cross-country, back to the road, almost at Blake's Farm. Here, there is a newish coloured sign indicating the footpath. It's well-timed too, just as you begin to feel it is not the right way. Just inside the yard to the left is a broken stile and a faint path leading along the meadows beside a ditch. Follow this along a tall hedge. When the hedge turns the corner to the right, you should follow too. Follow it to the next field and then go around the side of that and up over the small hill. Bear right over another couple of fields and eventually you come out via a large gate onto a bridle-track. Turn left to get back to the river.

From here, cross back over the river and head down towards Bramber.

When you come to the railway line you can turn right in the direction of Steyning. After a short distance, the route leaves the old railway line, going off to the right, then left through Wyckham Farm and on down the farm road. Where this road crosses over the old railway track, there is a footpath on the right to Steyning. Watch out for the busy A283.

Coming this way you face the downs and look down through the Adur Gap. Quite low on the right-hand side is a huge chapel, part of the school, Lancing College. Although Gothic in appearance, it was started in 1868 and only finished recently.

Steyning is packed with ancient buildings, timbered gables, tile-hung frontages and fine windows. The story of its origins is most endearing. St Cuthman (Cuthbert), from Devon, fell on hard times and was forced to wander the countryside pushing his mother along in a wheelbarrow. It broke on the site of what is now Steyning, and here he stayed, building a church and starting a settlement that was later to become an important place for pilgrims. Steyning was important for William the Conqueror, too. It had been given to the Abbé of Fecamp, in Normandy, by Edward the Confessor, and was subsequently confiscated by King Harold. One of William's excuses for invading England was that he wanted to restore Steyning to Normandy. Steyning's importance as a town diminished as the sea receded and it changed from a port to a peaceful market town.

From here walk into Bramber and to the castle on the outskirts of the village. William saw this gap in the downs as strategically important, and Bramber was the key place in one of the five Sussex rapes. The castle was built by his henchman, William De Braose, and ruined in the Civil War. Now one rather lonely wall, a fragment of the keep, points some seventy feet (21 m) to the sky and the sheep nibble the surrounding sward.

Further along the main street a discreet notice tells you if St Mary's is open, and don't miss it. Although what remains is large, it is only half the original house. It was built as a monastic inn lived in by four monks who were wardens of the original bridge over the Adur. This stretched virtually from the present front garden of St Mary's when the river was much larger. Pilgrims travelling to Canterbury along the South Downs or the old Pilgrim's Way, would bed down in the upstairs dormitories. Changes were made to the house in the sixteenth century with the addition of partitions, splendid fireplaces and wooden panelling.

Famous visitors have included Queen Elizabeth I, for whom The Painted Room was especially decorated. It is most remarkable with extraordinary pannelling which creates an optical illusion and leads the eye to beautifully detailed miniature landscapes.

Charles II also called in as he fled the country after the defeat at Worcester in 1651. In his memory is a picture of a certain Miss Eleanor Gwynn. The adjective fruity comes to mind.

There's something fascinating in every room, not just the stories of the great and powerful. There are many facts that relate to commoners, and personal mementoes of the present owners' family that all tell a little bit of history. There are many interesting details – medieval shutters, beaten-leather panelling, doors from a sunken galleon, and I particularly liked the patchwork foot-stool, made from scraps of uniform from pre-1900 soldiers.

A visit here is the most wonderful way to end a day in this part of Sussex.

The route for the top loop only goes from The Fountain Inn through Ashurst to Blake's Farm, then on to the river, and down to the railway line; only turn LEFT for Henfield and back to Ashurst.

Highdown is a part of the downs although it's somewhat isolated from the rest. Its skyline is one of my strongest childhood memories as I was brought up at Goring-by-Sea, the village lying near the foot. It was a point to aim for on walks and bike rides, and despite the distance to the top, apparently diminishing as I've grown up, the steady slope is still a challenge. After the October '87 hurricane, it was a terrific shock to see the total change in outline to the clump of trees at the top. It had always seemed such a sturdy crown, thick and evergreen. After the swirling winds it was sadly reduced to bare bones. The summit does still have a wonderful appeal, though, with the remains of an Iron Age fort as well as a wonderful view along the coast. With good (very good) conditions, I have seen the Isle of Wight.

A Touch of the Eccentrics

OS Map 1:50 000, Sheets 198 and 197
A circular walk of $4\frac{1}{2}$–5 miles (7–8 km). Allow 2–3 hours.

This walk takes you to Highdown hilltop, and over to the villages of Clapham and Patching. As well as some lovely downland scenery and pretty woodland, you'll come across several sites created by, or in memory of, strong individuals, perhaps seen as slightly eccentric, but in my opinion all the more interesting for that.

The going underfoot is good though there may be slippery patches in the woods and one stretch across open field is ploughed up in the early spring, although it's soon flattened into a decent path by the ever-watchful local ramblers.

The route is fairly clear on track, road and way-marked path. The villages of Clapham and Patching, as well as the summit of Highdown Hill, will help you get your bearing if you get off course.

Once at Clapham it is possible to walk right up onto the main body of the downs. It takes the best part of the day, but is worth it if you only have one chance to get into the heart of downland scenery.

Car-parking and the start

There is ample parking about halfway up Highdown, signposted Highdown Gardens, off the A2032 Worthing to Chichester road.

You can begin or end your walk with a stroll around the garden here (admission free), meeting the first of our individuals, the creator of the Chalk Gardens, Sir Frederick Stern.

He lived at Highdown Towers and began the garden at the turn of the century. All there was to start with was a bare chalk pit, and probably a lot of scepticism from friends and acquaintances who thought that nothing would grow in these chalky, windswept conditions. Sir Frederick was able to travel widely and, in those days, bring back many species that were already growing in similar conditions in such exotic spots as China, India and South America. The most glorious garden can be seen today, full of unusual plants and shrubs.

Lady Stern presented the gardens to Worthing Corporation, in memory of her husband and for the pleasure of the public. There is no entry fee, just a small donation box at the entrance. The gardens are quite large but they are divided up into a number of different areas creating an intimate atmosphere. I particularly like the less-formal part that is almost overshadowed by the surrounding chalky cliffs. Here is a little stream, cascading, albeit in miniature, down to a series of pools.

Climbing up to the highest point of the gardens you get a good view of the coastline. In the distance is Castle Goring, built for Shelley's grandfather, with the odd distinction of being Gothic-style on one side and Italian on the other. I wonder if he had similar sides to his personality?

Further east you'll see the sprawl of Worthing, and beyond is the one remaining chimney of the Brighton 'B' Power Station, the south-coast version of Battersea. In the far distance you can make out the cliffs of the Seven Sisters.

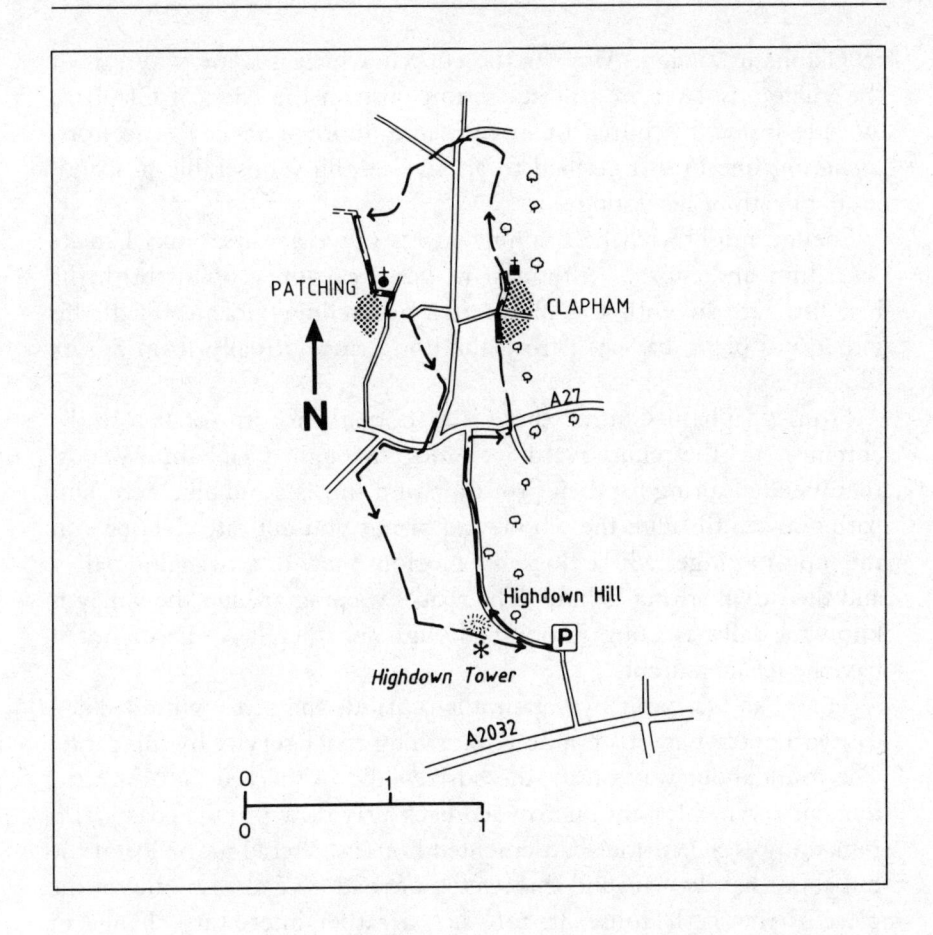

In the other direction look for the spire of Chichester Cathedral and a misty off-shore shape which is the Isle of Wight.

Leaving the gardens, take the footpath to the top of Highdown. The top itself will be visited on the return, so rather than continue all the way, find some huge chalk pits just before the top. Here, look for a small path leading out of the open area into some woods to the north – this soon joins a track that takes you down the northern side of the hill. Follow the track all the way down until you meet the busy A27. Here, turn right. Don't cross immediately but walk just around the corner where the road becomes a dual carriageway. It is easier to cross there.

A footpath points you north and brings you more or less directly to Clapham Village. Aim for the church which is some way out of the village, isolated in a pretty setting just on the edge of Clapham Woods. Inside the church are memorials to more of Shelley's ancestors, including one brass inscribed to an 'everlastingly miserable husband' on the death of his young wife.

Shelley might well be spinning in his grave at these links I make with him and Sussex. Although it was the county of his birth, he had little to do with the place after quarrelling violently with his father and being banished from the house and virtually from Sussex too.

From Clapham Church there is a footpath north, just before the entrance to the churchyard. It goes through Clapham Woods, renowned in spring for their profusion of primroses and bluebells. This path goes on through the woods and brings you out into the open on the top of a ridge, where there is a glorious view of a sweeping valley and the downs rising behind. The road sweeping around the valley is known locally as Long Furlong, though whether it is one or not, I have never measured.

This road was built by yet another curious character, who decided to try to make a go of a London–Worthing coach service by this route. The roundabout way meant the business didn't succeed, but the road remains a very pleasant uncrowded back way down to the coast. Also remaining is the curious battlemented house sheltered in the lee of the hill about halfway around this stretch of road. I've always known the place as the Toll House. It, too, had a rather interesting change of fortune.

For many years the building was very shabby with a rundown and forlorn appearance, as if about to be taken over by ivy and undergrowth from the garden. One day, to my family's surprise, we turned the corner at the top of the valley and looking across were amazed to find the Toll House immaculate, painted in brilliant white. The reason for this unexpected face-lift came a few days later when the house was prominently featuring in paint advertisements. The setting was perfect. With clever photography, the road had disappeared from view and the house stood alone in the midst of green hills and hedgerows. To the credit of the firm, the brilliant white did last for many years.

From the top of the ridge, turn left and drop down to the road (another rather awkward place to cross) and then take the bridle-track on the other side along to Patching Village. The woods just behind Patching achieved fame as a good source of truffles. These were discovered by a Frenchman, naturally enough, when he was staying locally.

When you get into Patching Village walk on past the church, and, at the T-junction, turn left. The footpath is just down this road between two blocks of houses. It crosses the fields diagonally (these are the ones that may be ploughed up) and brings you out on the road (Long Furlong again) just above Patching Pond. In winters past, when the season seemed more definitely cold, rather than just a succession of dreary days, I have skated here.

Turn right down the main road to the large junction with the A27. Cross here and turn right, then left down the first main road, just opposite the pub. A short distance along this road is a footpath, just by a water tank, taking you up Highdown Hill again, approaching the summit from the west. You'll find a trig point and possibly a digger or two. One good result of the hurricane was that with the uprooting of the trees, it was possible for archaeologists to explore the site more thoroughly. Finds have been made from several prehistoric ages as Highdown Hill has had a fair share of settlers. There was a Bronze Age camp, an Iron Age fort and a pagan Saxon cemetery.

Before walking back to the car-park, take a short detour to visit the last eccentric, John Olliver. He is buried in a simple tomb just below the hedge line that borders the hill on the eastern side. He was the local miller, hence the nickname The Miller's Tomb. John Olliver had an obsession with death, building his tomb some thirty years before it was needed, and then sleeping with his coffin under the bed!

From here it is a short walk back to Highdown Gardens car-park.

If there is drama to be found in the landcape of Sussex, it is here in the Arun Valley with the towering chalk cliffs formed by years of quarry workings. In complete contrast is the wide flat valley of the river which has cut its way through the downland ridge in search of the sea. The retreating sea left fertile river wetlands that are now rich in wildlife. Like the Adur, the Arun is a tidal river that once was navigable to a point upstream. In the case of the Arun, that point was the village of Amberley. It is round this region that I planned a walk.

Chalk Pits and Churches

OS Map 1: 50 000, Sheet 197
A circular walk of 6–7 miles (10–12 km). Allow 3–4 hours.

This walk will take you through a spectrum of lovely Sussex scenery: a river trail, a climb on the downs, and dizzy cliffs that are a leftover from when the land was quarried for lime, as well as a visit to two secluded hamlets.

Isn't it a real pleasure to walk and know it's quicker on foot that it would be by car? This is just the feeling you get when going between North and South Stoke. They are two remote villages, each with no more than a handful of buildings. Walking between the two is a mere half mile (1 km) and by road it would be at least seven miles (12 km). This thought drew me back to the days when the pace was slower and often the only way to get anywhere was setting off across the fields.

The going underfoot is all good though, as usual, liable to be wet near the river. Remember too that chalk as a surface also gets quite slippery after rain. During the summer months, some of the narrower paths may get quite overgrown, again especially by the river.

This walk is suitable for dogs though there is livestock grazing by the river and on parts of the downs.

You can also treat this walk as three short loops if you prefer. First, the section around Amberley and the river, secondly, the visit to North and South Stoke, and thirdly, the section on the downs.

Car-parking and the start

There is a good car-park at Amberley Station and the Chalk Pits Museum. The museum is popular at weekends and with school coach parties in term times, but there is ample space and you may well wish to visit the museum later.

Start by walking across Houghton Bridge, a good solid medieval structure with squat arches, and handy stone inlets for dodging the traffic, though that probably wasn't their original purpose.

Don't take the first footpath sign, as you need to get to the western side of the Arun and follow its course in a large sweep all the way round to South Stoke. There is a second footpath sign to the left just after leaving the bridge. From here you get a good view of the Amberley chalk pits. Now, they are part of the landscape, but were created by a family firm, Pepper and Sons, who began quarrying for lime here over a century ago. The chalk pits were first worked for lime in the 1840s and then Pepper and Sons became the main lime producers until the closure of the pits in the 1960s. Their speciality was called 'Amberline'. In later years, the business changed into a general builders' merchants, reflecting the changing needs of Sussex when the coming of road, rail and charabanc brought light industry to the county.

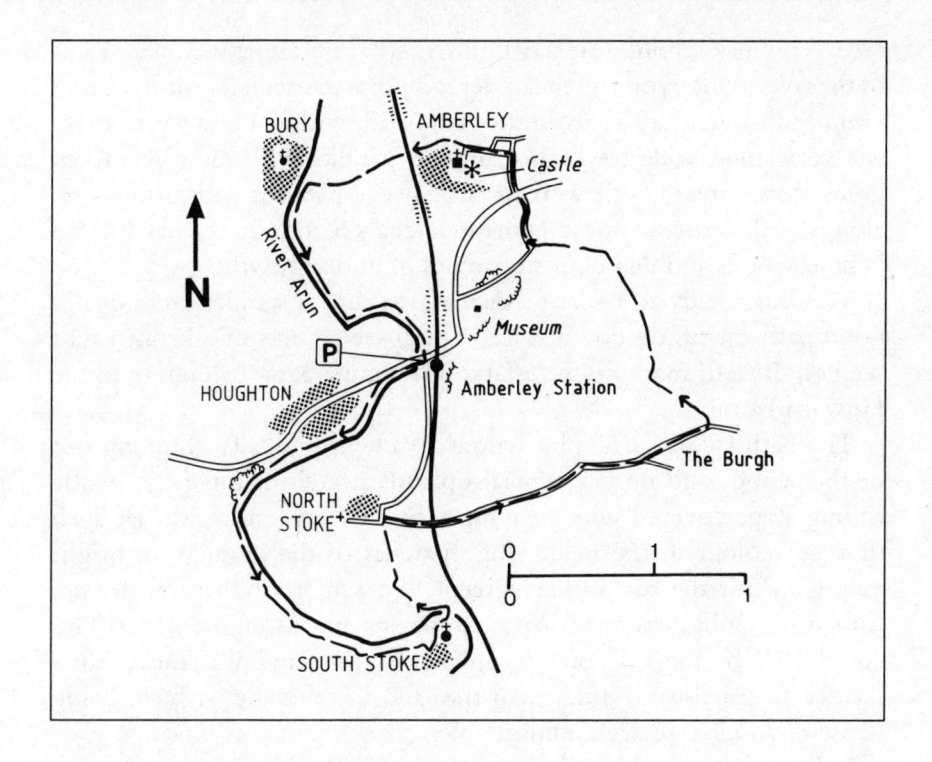

When you turn off down the footpath on the far side of the Arun, follow the embankment of the river until it curves away near a modern house. Then, stay close to the river's edge. At the far end of the field is a rickety wooden bridge over a ditch. After this, the footpath gets quite narrow and overgrown. I armed myself with a stick for a bit of nettle bashing and, even though wearing shorts, escaped from being stung. This little path seems to twist and turn through a jungle of reeds, cow parsley and rose bay willowherb, but it does stay quite close to the river. Once you feel the undergrowth is particularly intimidating you need to strike away from the Arun and, within a few yards, there is a very good wide track also running parallel with the river. Keep going downstream, as it were, and this very pleasant path brings you along to the base of some enormous chalk cliffs, somewhat hidden behind woods and dense green patches of undergrowth.

The track ends at a sort of picnic area, but a smaller and equally good path carries on down river. You'll see chunks of a broken flint wall on the left, marking the estates of Arundel park, belonging to the Howard Family.

The path swings around a wooded valley, gradually climbing out of the woods and onto a typical uplands stretch of Sussex, a gentle rolling slope covered with swaying wheat. It was curious to see such different colour in the field. Huge patches of the grain were bright yellow whilst the rest seemed green. Different growth in plants can sometimes indicate a disturbance to the soil up to centuries ago. This could well be the case on the uplands as this land was more often farmed in prehistoric times than the land in the valley which, being densely wooded, proved inhospitable.

Follow the path along the edge of this field, round a sharp corner, and the top of the church of South Stoke will come into sight. It is just a slender short tower topped with a pretty pointed cap.

This remote village is just a handful of flint and brick buildings built in a little hook of the river. Wend your way amongst the houses down to the river. Just over the footbridge there's a finger post signing left to the twin village of North Stoke, which is the next target. The path goes left at the sign and then turns right along a good path through woods, following the line of a ditch. It was here that it was so easy to imagine the days when roads and tracks were created by plodding village folk. Halfway along you come to a well-built and well-maintained wooden bridge. With modern road travel, a bridge like this linking two quiet places would never get built since the needs of walkers are mostly ignored.

North Stoke, like its southern counterpart, is hardly more than a tiny hamlet, but it has another delightful little church. You'll see the outline of an unusual tower as you approach the village. It is so low that it almost disappears from view behind the houses. Part of its lack of height is that it is not on the gable of the roof but instead built across one of the transepts. It is worth diverting to the church to look at the interior too with its cool white colour, and remnants of wall paintings between the nave and chancel. One delightful touch, put in by a medieval craftsman, is the tiny primitive hand carved as a corbel to hold up the arch.

For a shorter option on this walk, you can take the footpath back to Amberley Station from North Stoke.

To continue the main walk, turn up the road to Camp Hill and The Burgh. It is a pleasant road to walk on, soon becoming unfenced. As it is a dead end, there is little traffic. I was passed by a solitary tractor. This climbs on a high ridge where you get a good view down the Arun Gap. Just over a spur in the far distance you can catch sight of the towers and spires of Arundel's castle and church.

The Arun Gap was seen by the Norman invaders as vital to their defences and so the Rape of Arundel, with compulsory castle, came into being. The original castle took a severe battering in the Civil Wars of the seventeenth century, from guns conveniently mounted on the neighbouring church, and it was left in a ruinous state. The present castle belies its medieval appearance, being mostly built in the nineteenth century. It is the seat of the Premier Duke and Earl Marshal of England and for the last four hundred years has been in the possession of the Howard family.

Presentday Arundel is less important than its Norman ancestor as though the receding tides sapped its strength. What is left behind is a striking landmark at the southern end of the gap and it is certainly worth a detour (driving) to view the town closer at hand.

Carry on up the track passing some farm buildings, and then take a left-hand fork. The road now flattens out onto a plateau and, after a short distance, a footpath crosses over this track. Here, you need to turn left, heading north towards Amberley. If you prefer a little more downland walking you can carry on along this track as it eventually brings you on to the well-marked South Downs Way at Springhead Hill.

My route goes down into a deep, sheltered valley. The sides of the valley are covered with those little ridges that are evidence that medieval farmers used this land. From the valley floor, the path climbs up around the spur on the opposite side, again marked with a post.

This part of the walk brings you along a stretch of land that is cultivated on one side and with wild meadow on the other. It impressed me here how much man imposed on the landscape, creating crop patterns and patchwork field systems. But, looking behind, nature is always ready to reclaim. The wilder land on the other side of the path, though once changed greatly by nibbling sheep, has reverted to meadow with a profusion of delicate flowers. Look out for the tight, but slightly spongy-looking, greenish-yellow plants known as bed straw, so-called because they were used as a soft lining to sleep on, and sometimes put in shoes. It's the country folk's equivalent of cushion lining. I've yet to put it to the test in my trainers!

At the end of this stretch there are a great many paths cross-crossing, but you need to go along to the sign for the South Downs Way, which runs along the northern edge of the escarpment. It is here you find company as this is one of the most popular long-distance footpaths. It follows the length of the downs with one end in Hampshire, and the other at Beachy Head.

Turn left and follow the track down to a little lane and then turn right towards Amberley Village. This is the second opportunity to curtail the walk by carrying on along this path back to Amberley Station.

Amberley Village is a good mixture of houses and cottages of all shapes and sizes. This diversity and the wide range of building material used – timber and flint, tile and thatch – stops the place being twee. The attractive gardens unify the picture, and dominating the end of the village is the church and the massive curtain walls of the castle.

Unlike Arundel and Bramber, this castle was never meant to put up much of a fight, and it never had to either. The manor of Amberley used to belong to the bishops of Chichester who decided to create a summer palace here – and subsequently built the bridge at Houghton to make it easy to reach.

It started off as a fairly humble house, but fear of the French, reinforced by the sacking of Rye and Winchelsea, probably encouraged the bishops to fortify the place. The footpath down to the river leads you right under the curtain walls, giving a false sense, perhaps, of the strength of the building.

Follow the footpath down to the river and pause to look at the outline of Amberley with castle, church and cottages. Then go on towards Bury, the little village just across the river, where once there used to be a ferry.

This river area is rich in wildlife, both flora and fauna. It is known as Amberley Wild Brooks. 'Wild' in this case is derived from the word 'weald'. The main nature reserve is to the north of Amberley. (It isn't open to the public, though there is a footpath that does go straight through the middle, and there is quite a lot that you can see from that.)

Unless you want to detour to the heart of the Wild Brooks, turn downstream along the river's embankment and in a mile or so (1.5 km) you come back to Amberley Station.

There is a huge choice of things to see close to this walk. If you are interested in industrial history, the Chalk Pit Museum has extensive displays. It is best to make sure (from the sign at the entrance) how much is actually working. I found instant nostalgia when I rode on the open-top double-decker bus, only wishing that we stopped for petrol at the hand-operated pump at the quaint mock-up of a country garage. It was harder to relate to some of the static exhibits. Arundel is worth a visit and so too is Parham House, in the opposite direction, an impressive stately home set in acres of ancient parkland.

ROMAN PALACES AND SAXON PIERS

OS Map 1:50 000, Sheet 197
Taking the footpath ferry, this is a linear walk of $2\frac{1}{2}$ miles (4 km). Allow 1–$1\frac{1}{2}$ hours.

There is a wealth of things to see around Chichester and this part of Sussex with the palace at Fishbourne and the picturesque village of Bosham (pronounced Bozzum). It is probably a good idea to walk to Bosham, or go on the ferry as there is a danger that if you park at Bosham Harbour you will find your car underwater when the tide comes in. It has been known.

There are really two ways to enjoy seeing this area. The first, via the ferry, is very exciting, but it is a service restricted to the summer months at weekends and during the day in the peak season, so I have included an inland alternative as well.

Car-parking and the start

To catch the ferry, go to West Itchenor which is some ten miles (16 km) from Chichester along the A286. A turning to the right off here takes you along a narrow winding lane which ends very abruptly at the harbour's edge. There is parking just off this street. The ferry goes from the end of the pier, as do the Water Bus Tours, altogether grander affairs that last one-and-a-half hours.

It is probably best to try to arrive somewhere around the even hour (10 am, 12 noon etc.) as that is the time the ferry picks up anyone on the Bosham side of the harbour, some two hundred yards away. The other alternative is to ring the Chichester harbour office to book a trip.

The official service from Itchenor to the opposite bank is known as the footpath ferry. I wondered if the name, and indeed service, was unique. In the old days, there used to be a large brass bell for travellers to ring when they arrived at the Bosham side of the estuary. This would summon the ferrywoman, and she would leave her cottage and row over to bring the folk to Itchenor. Nowadays the 'ferry' consists of a Dory with an outboard motor, not so romantic maybe, but still a pretty exciting experience.

The Dory is a traditional flat-bottomed skiff, made locally to a design that has been around here for the last two hundred years. Now made of modern materials rather than wood, it still looks rather precarious, being not much more than a flat rectangle with turned up edges. I was cheered up by the ferryman's comment that he'd seen her full of water to the brim plus eight, presumably wet, adults, and she still hadn't sunk! Oh well, time to put that to the test.

In order to go to Bosham Village, (rather than Bosham Ferry Hard which is the jetty on the opposite bank), you need to negotiate with the ferryhand to take you to Bosham Quay. The trip takes about twenty minutes, and will be possible at the ferryhand's discretion, as so much depends on the weather. Although it may look calm in the harbour, once you round the deep-water mark, the winds can make the sea a little choppy, not the ideal for a boat where there is just four inches of rim between you and the water!

It is marvellous fun being in the little boat, threading your way through all the bobbing yachts in the harbour. The route goes round in a huge 'C' shape up the Chichester Channel, turning at the deep-water mark into Bosham Channel and up towards the main village.

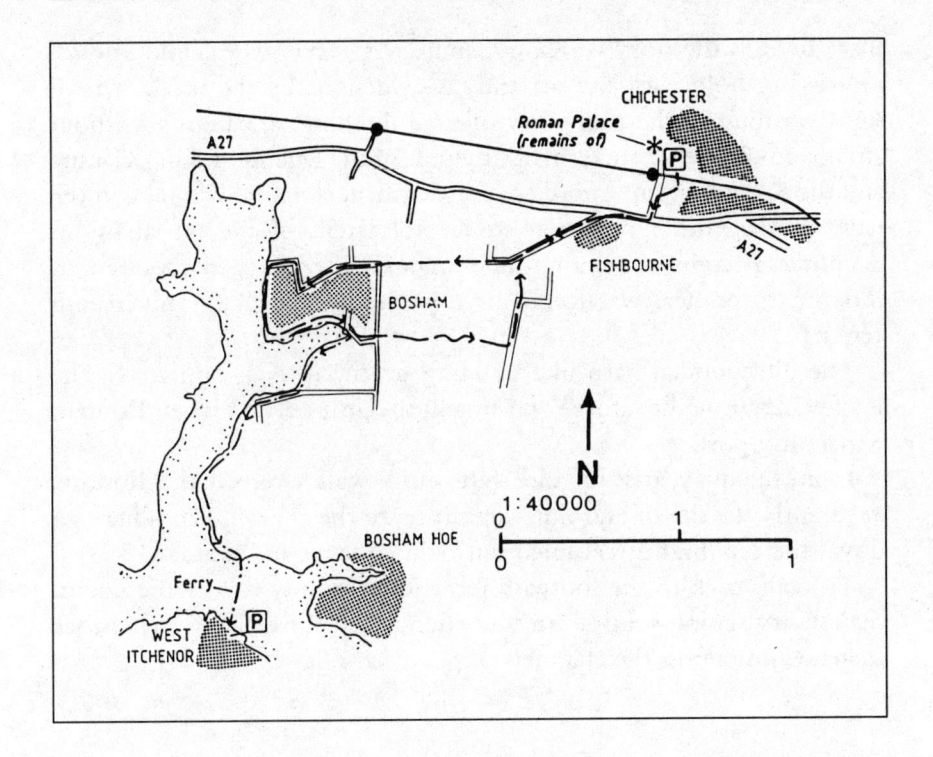

The approach from the water is very pretty. The low cottages cluster around the shore with the classic lines of the church rising behind, the white tower and the shingled grey spire making a focus on the skyline.

More yachts are anchored up this channel above Bosham with the downs fading into the blue distance beyond. No wonder it's a classic venue for artists. Take your sketchbook if you have one.

Plan your trip so that you have time to wander around Bosham. There are plenty of distracting tea-rooms and galleries, and you can have a gentle stroll around the harbour mouth before being picked up again at Bosham Hard.

Bosham is an old settlement, lived in at one time by the Emperor Vespasian in the first century AD and it was from here that Harold set sail for Normandy, a voyage which was to have serious repercussions later. His visit to Bosham Church is recorded in a section of the Bayeux Tapestry.

Perhaps the most famous incident that is supposed to have taken place here, is the story of King Canute. As every schoolchild knows, he tried to hold back the sea and, as evidenced by the modern road signs warning of the possibility of tidal flooding, apparently without any great effect. Whatever truth there is in the legend of King Canute and the sea, you'll find more concrete evidence that he was here in the nave of the church where a stone tablet tells of the burial of his daughter. A coffin containing the remains of a child aged about eight, thought to be her, was found here in the middle of the nineteenth century.

The old wooden barn-like building on the quay is known as The Raptackle. It used to store rope and all the gear needed when Bosham was a busy port.

From the quay, past the old water-mill, walk over Quay Meadow, apparently the site of Harold's departure, to the church. From here go down the tiny high street lined with old cottages and houses.

To walk back to the footpath ferry jetty, simply follow the line of the estuary going south until you round the spur of land and can see Itchenor just across the channel.

A Winter Alternative: from Fishbourne to Bosham

OS Map 1:50 000, Sheet 197
A circular walk of 5 miles (8 km). Allow up to three hours.

This very pleasant walk takes you from the remains of one of the finest Roman palaces discovered in Britain along quiet country lanes and fields to Bosham Village.

The going underfoot is fine, mostly along lane, road and track. You might only get your feet wet if the tide is in.

Car-parking and the start

There is a good car-park and facilities at Fishbourne, which means you are in an ideal place to see the museum devoted to the history of the site, either before or after the walk. Parking here does mean a short stretch of busy road-walking as there isn't a suitable footpath.

Walk back along the road on which you drove into the museum to the main road. Here, turn right and after a short distance there is a lane on the left called Old Park Lane. Walk down here and at the junction you'll see a footpath. It goes straight down a private road lined with a row of coppiced poplar trees, which create a good shade or wind break. Keep going along this road. When you meet the junction of another track, take the footpath directly ahead which brings you over the fields to the lane leading to Bosham.

Carry on along this lane lined with modern houses for some way until you get to the Millstream Hotel, then turn right up the tiny lane by the side of the hotel. Ahead you'll see a footpath to the left which brings you through an old boat-yard to the estuary above Bosham. The sudden opening out on to the water is delightful, and if you are there at low tide you'll be able to walk along the shingle around to the main part of the village. If the tide is in, there is a footpath just above, but it is somewhat uneven.

You'll come round to the water-mill and Quay Meadow with the church just behind. From here you can easily explore the rest of the village.

To get back to Fishbourne, follow the line of the estuary along the indentation that runs to the south of the village, (This is the same route as you would take to get back to the footpath ferry.) There's a low white house at the head of this and a narrow footpath close by taking you eastwards. This seems to come out in someone's backyard, but immediately across the lane is another footpath across the fields with a slight diversion around a curious little house in the middle with, as far as I could see, no main access.

The path runs on beyond this along the edge of some interesting apple nurseries. Fruit-growing and nurseries are very much part of the landscape here, making good use of the flat and extensive fields with their rich and fertile soil. This particular nursery had a huge variety of different types of apple, each arranged by row. It reminded me of the days when there was more to life than the Golden Delicious, with James Greave, Ida Red, Discovery and one of my favourite 'old-fashioned' apples, Egremont Russet. Perhaps there is an apple renaissance due, but I suspect the trees are for domestic rather than commercial growers.

Where the path ends at the lane, turn left and at the next corner take the footpath which goes along the private road and leads you back to the track with the coppiced hedge. Here, turn right and retrace your steps to Fishbourne.

It seems appropriate enough, with the theme of invasion, to visit one of the most striking remains of the Romans, significant invaders of Britain. For once, the story of Fishbourne is not one of bloody skirmish and battle. The kingdom at the time of Fishbourne's construction belonged to Atrebates, who had had a long allegiance with Rome. He provided a friendly welcome. The other big advantage was the site itself. The harbour was largely unoccupied, and the water deep enough in the upper reaches for barges to come close to the shore. The area to the north of the harbour was protected by massive earthworks.

Roman remains around Fishbourne were found in the nineteenth century, but finds were not recorded in any detail, sadly, as much of the palace has now gone under the main road. In 1960, a workman digging a water-main trench across the fields found ancient rubble. This initial find sparked off some eight years of major excavations revealing most of the northern wing of a palace and uncovering some beautiful mosaic floors.

The site is now covered over by a low and most unpalatial building, but it does mean the remains can be viewed in comfort, and your imagination can take you back to the civilized life of Rome.

Index

Abbey Dore (Hereford), 62, 64–5
Abbotsbury (Dorset), 13–17
Abdon Burf (Salop), 92
Abdon Village (Salop), 91, 93–4
Abercrombie, Catherine, 57, 58, 60
Abercrombie, Lascelles, 57, 58, 60, 61
Adderley (Salop), 81
Addleborough (Yorks), 134, 135
Adur Valley (Sussex), 275–81
Agglestone (Dorset), 5, 6
Agricola, Julius, 135
Ainsdale Nature Reserve (Lancs), 118
Alde, River, 225, 237, 238–9
Aldeburgh (Suffolk), 237
Alton Barnes (Wilts), 40
Alwinton (North'd), 157
Amberley (Sussex), 285, 286, 287, 289, 290–1
Angel Marshes (Suffolk), 236–7
Armstrong, William, Lord, 162, 163
Arnside (Lancs), 103
Arnside Knot (Lancs), 97, 102, 103–4
Arts and Crafts Movement, 52, 54
Arun Valley (Sussex), 285–91
Arundel (Sussex), 274, 288, 289
Ashurst (Sussex), 275, 276, 279, 281
Astor family, 265–6
Attenborough (Notts), 186, 197
Attenborough Nature Reserve (Notts), 175, 186–90
Attingham Park (Salop), 81, 84
Avebury (Wilts), 30, 31, 32, 39
Avoncliff (Wilts), 44

Baddesley Clinton (Warw), 201–3, 205
Bainbridge (Yorks), 131, 135

Baldwin, Stanley, 79, 256
Ballard Down (Dorset), 7
Bamburgh (North'd), 153, 154
Barnard Castle (Durham), 141–4
Bastard brothers, 25
Beacon Hill (Bucks), 256
Beacon Hill (Warw), 216, 218, 219, 220
Beacon Hill (Wilts), 36, 38
Beausale (Warw), 208
Beeston Canal (Notts), 188
Beildi Hill (Yorks), 140
Bellingham (North'd), 167–8
Belsay Castle (North'd), 163–4
Belsay Hall (North'd), 164–5
Belvoir Castle (Notts), 190
Belvoir, Vale of, 174, 190–4
Bewley Common (Wilts), 48
Black Middens Bastle (North'd), 172
Blacker's Hole (Dorset), 10
Blackmoor Vale (Dorset), 24
Blandford Forum (Dorset), 25
Blaxhall Heath (Suffolk), 240, 241
Bloody Ditch (Wilts), 37, 38
Blythburgh (Suffolk), 228, 235–6
Blythburgh Estuary (Suffolk), 230, 232
Bog, The (Salop), 75, 76, 78, 79
Bosham (Sussex), 291, 292–4, 295
Bovington Camp (Dorset), 20
Bowden House (Wilts), 45, 48
Bradenham (Bucks), 249, 252–3
Bradford-on-Avon (Wilts), 27, 42–4
Bradschawe family, 254
Brailesford, Misses, 180
Bramber (Sussex), 274, 275, 276, 280
Bramley, Matthew, 181
Brewster. Rev. William, 79

INDEX

Briantspuddle, (Dorset), 18, 21
Brindley, James, 219
Brockhampton (Hereford), 51, 52, 54
Brome, Nicholas, 201, 205
Brooke, Rupert, 50, 57
Broome (Salop), 86, 88
Brown, 'Capability', 34, 167, 177, 210
Brown Clee (Salop), 74, 90–4
Brown Moss (Salop), 80
Brownsea Island Nature Reserve (Dorset), 6
Brunel, Sir Marc Isambard, 219
Buckingham, George Villiers, 2nd Duke of, 265
Bulbarrow Hill (Dorset), 22
Burntstump Country Park (Notts), 186
Burt, George, 6
Burtersett (Yorks), 131, 133
Burton Dasset Country Park (Warw), 221
Burton Dasset Hills (Warw), 220, 221
Burtons Well (Lancs), 101
Bury (Sussex), 291
Butler, Samuel, 192, 193
Butler, Rev. Thomas, 192
Byron, 'Mad Jack', 5th Lord, 176
Byron, George Gordon, 6th Lord, 178, 182

Caen Hill locks (Wilts), 39
Caer Caradoc (Salop), 78, 85, 88
Cambo (North'd), 167
Cannon Bank (Warw), 217
Canute, King, 294
Capler Camp (Hereford), 52, 54, 55
Caractacus, 88
Carlow Stone (Yorks), 135
'Cassandra' (Sir William Connor), 269
Cautly Spout (Yorks), 139
Chanctonbury Ring (Sussex), 274, 278
Chapel Green (Warw), 214
Chapman's Pool (Dorset), 11–12
Charles I, 183, 218, 256
Charles II, 280
Chequers (Bucks), 256
Chesil Beach (Dorset), 1, 2, 13, 14
Cheviot Hills, 149, 153, 157, 160
Chew Green (North'd), 157
Chichester (Sussex), 274, 291
Chillingham (North'd), 149, 150–2, 153
Chiltern Society, 253
Christmas Common (Oxon), 271
Church Preen (Salop), 86, 88, 89
Churchtown (Lancs), 122

Clapdale Drive (Yorks), 130
Clapham (Sussex), 281, 282, 284
Clapham (Yorks), 126, 129, 130
Clark, William Tierney, 261
Clavell Tower (Dorset), 11
Clee Hills (Salop), 75, 90–4
Clee St Margaret (Salop), 94
Clive (Salop), 81, 82
Cliveden (Bucks), 248, 264–6
Clouds Hill (Dorset), 17, 20–1
Clumber Park (Notts), 175–9, 194
Cock Marsh (Bucks), 263
Colston Bassett (Notts), 191–2, 193–4
Connor, Sir William ('Cassandra'), 269
Cookham (Berks), 262–3
Cookham Dean (Berks), 262, 264
Coombe Hills (Bucks), 255, 258
Coquetdale (North'd), 157–61
Corbet, Sir John, 81
Corbet Wood (Salop), 80, 81, 82
Corfe Castle (Dorset), 1, 2, 3, 5
Corndon Hill (Powys), 79
Cotherstone (Durham), 141, 142, 145
Countersett (Yorks), 131, 133, 135
Country House Scheme, 166
Crag Foot (Lancs), 98, 99
Cragside (North'd), 161–3
Cranberry Rock (Salop), 78, 79
Cranbourne Chase (Dorset), 24
Craster (North'd), 155, 156
Cromwell, Oliver, 24, 81, 194, 218, 236, 258
Crummack (Yorks), 127, 128
Crummackdale (Yorks), 124, 126
Cuckoobush Wood (Notts), 195, 197
Culpepper's Dish (Dorset), 18
Cuthbert, St, 280

D'Oyley family, 267
'Daffodil Trail' (Glos), 58, 59
Dancing Lodge (Dorset), 10
Dashwood, Sir Francis, 249–50, 253
De Braose, William, 280
De la Pole, Alice, 271, 272
De la Pole, William, 271, 272
Dean, Forest of, 50–1, 65–73
Deben, River, 225, 243–6
Devil's Chair (Salop), 75, 76, 78
Devil's Den (Wilts), 31
Devizes (Wilts), 27, 35, 36, 38–9
Disraeli, Benjamin, 249, 251–2, 254

INDEX

Ditton Priors (Salop), 91, 92
Dorchester (Dorset), 17
Dorset Coast Path, 14
Dorset Heathland Forum, 4
Dove Crags (North'd), 160
Downley (Bucks), 250
Drinkwater, John, 57
Dudley, Robert (Earl of Leicester), 199, 207, 210
'Dukeries, The' (Notts), 175, 194
Dunsmore (Bucks), 258
Dunstanburgh Castle (North'd), 153, 154–7
Dunwich (Suffolk), 223–4, 232–5
Dunwich Forest (Suffolk), 232, 233
Dymock (Glos), 57–8, 59, 61

East Bucks Ramblers, 260
East Leake Gysum Works (Notts), 194, 197
Eastnor Park (Hereford), 61
Easton (Suffolk), 243
Eastwood (Notts), 174
Edge Hill (Warw), 218, 220
Egglestone Abbey (Durham), 142, 146
Elizabeth I, 199, 207, 208, 210, 280
Ellesmere (Salop), 80
Embleton (North'd), 155
English Heritage, 113, 156, 163
Ewelme (Oxon), 271–2
Ewyas Harold (Hereford), 51, 62, 63, 65

Farnborough Hall (Warw), 221
Farrer, Reginald, 130
Fell Beck (Yorks), 129
Ferrers, Marmion, 202
Ferrers (later Heneage), Rebecca, 202
Fingest (Bucks), 268–9
Fishbourne (Sussex), 274, 291, 294–6
Fishpool Hill (Hereford), 56
Five Springs (Salop), 91, 92
Fleet (Dorset), 14
Forest Sculpture Trail, 68–70
Forestry Commission, 67, 69, 168, 170, 174
Formby Hills (Lancs), 117
Formby Point (Lancs), 118
Fownhope (Hereford), 51, 52, 53, 56
Framlingham (Suffolk), 241–2
Frederick, Prince of Wales, 265
Frieth (Bucks), 270
Frost, Robert, 57, 58
Fyfield Down (Wilts), 29–30, 31

Gait Barrows (Lancs), 97
Gallops, The (Wilts), 29, 32
Gaping Gill (Yorks), 129, 130
Garleigh Moor (North'd), 160
Gatehouse (North'd), 172
Gibraltar (Lancs), 100
Gibson, Wilfrid, 57
Gillow family, 102, 105, 108
Glasson Docks (Lancs), 105, 106–7, 110
Glasson–Lancaster Line, 107–8
Glendower, Owen, 65
Golden Valley (Hereford), 61–5
Gotham (Notts), 187, 194, 196–7
Grahame, Kenneth, 262
Grand Union Canal, 199, 202, 212, 218, 219
Grantham Canal (Notts), 190
Great Kimble (Bucks), 256
Greenhaugh (North'd), 168
Greta Bridge (Durham), 146
Grey of Fallodon, Viscount, 152
Grinshill (Salop), 80, 81–2, 88
Grinton (Yorks), 137
Grosmont (Gwent), 65
Gunnerside (Yorks), 141

Halesworth (Suffolk), 228, 235
Hallgarth Hill (Yorks), 145
Hambleden Valley (Bucks), 267–71
Hambledon Hill (Dorset), 1, 23
Hamilton, Field Marshal Lord George, 265
Hampden, John, 256
Hampdenleaf Wood (Bucks), 256
Handfast Point (Dorset), 4, 7
Hardy, Admiral Sir Thomas, 14
Hardy, Thomas, 1, 7
Hardy's Monument (Dorset), 14, 17
Hareshaw Linn (North'd), 168
Harold, King, 293
Haugh Wood (Hereford), 56
Haughmond Hill (Salop), 84, 88
Havergate Island (Suffolk), 241
Haveringdon (Bucks), 253
Hawes (Yorks), 135
Henfield (Sussex), 276, 278
Henry V, 208
Hepburn Crag (North'd), 152
Hepburn Wood (North'd), 152
Herefordshire School of Norman Architecture, 52, 54
Hesketh, Sir Thomas, 122
High Wycombe (Bucks), 248, 253–4

INDEX

Highdown (Sussex), 275, 281, 282–3, 285
Hilton, Abraham, 145
Hoarwithy (Hereford), 52, 56–7
Hod Hill (Dorset), 1, 23
Hodgson, John, 105
Holy Island (North'd), 154
Honeystreet (Wilts), 40
Honily (Warw), 208
Hope Bowdler Hill (Salop), 88
Horton-in-Ribblesdale (Yorks), 129
Housman, A. E., 74
How Caple (Hereford), 56
Howard family, 288, 289
Howe, Richard, Lord, 193
Hughenden Manor (Bucks), 249, 251–2

Iken Picnic Site (Suffolk), 237, 239
Inchford Brook (Warw), 207, 209
Ingleborough (Yorks), 124, 129
Ingleborough Cave (Yorks), 129, 130
Ingleborough Hall (Yorks), 126
Iron Pear Tree Farm (Wilts), 36, 38
Iwerne Courtney (Dorset), 24

Jack Scout (Lancs), 100
Jenny Brown's Point (Lancs), 99, 100

Keeler, Christine, 266
Keld (Yorks), 136, 137, 140
Kenilworth (Warw), 198, 199, 200, 205–9
Kennet and Avon Canal (Wilts), 39, 46
Ketford (Glos), 61
Kielder Forest (North'd), 148, 168–70, 172
Kilpeck (Hereford), 52
Kimmeridge Cliffs (Dorset), 1, 11
King's Caple (Hereford), 56
King's Play Hill (Wilts), 36
Kisdon Force Waterfall (Yorks), 138
Kisdon Plateau (Yorks), 136, 137
Kyson Hill (Suffolk), 246

Lacock (Wilts), 44, 45, 48–9
Lambsquay Mines (Glos), 68
Lancaster, 104–5, 106, 108, 110–11
Lancaster Canal, 110–11
Lancing College (Suffolk), 279
Langar (Notts), 191, 192–3
Lawley, The (Salop), 85, 88
Lawrence, D. H., 174
Lawrence, T. E., 2, 12, 17, 20–1
Lee of Fareham, Lord, 256

Leighton, William, 89
Leighton Hall (Lancs), 102
Leighton Moss (Lancs), 97, 99, 101–2
Lethaby, W. R., 54
Letheringham (Suffolk), 243
Litton Cheney (Dorset), 14
London-to-Bath Coach Road, 48
Long Bredy (Dorset), 14
Long Furlong (Sussex), 284
Long Mynd (Salop), 74, 78
Lordenshaw Fort (North'd), 160
Lower Shuckburgh (Warw), 215, 216, 219
Ludlow (Salop), 75, 94–5
Lune, River, 105, 107, 111

Magpie Hill (Warw), 221
Maiden Castle (Dorset), 1
Maltings, The (Suffolk), 237, 238, 239, 240, 241
Manton (Wilts), 28
Marden (Wilts), 40
Marlborough (Wilts), 26, 27, 28, 30, 33
Marlow (Bucks), 248, 260–1, 263, 264
Marsett (Yorks), 133, 134
Mary I, 241
Mayall family, 83
Merryweather family, 181
Middleton (Salop), 79
Middleton, Sir Arthur, 165
Mildenhall (Wilts), 34
Mill End (Bucks), 267
Milton Abbas (Dorset), 25
Mitchell's Fold (Salop), 79
Mompesson, Rev. George, 180
Mompesson, Rev. William, 180
Monck, Sir Charles, 164
Morecambe Bay (Lancs), 103, 108
Moreton (Dorset), 18, 19–20
Moreton Corbet (Salop), 81
Morgan Hill (Wilts), 36
Morris, William, 54
Mother Anthony's Well (Wilts), 38
Moughton Scar (Yorks), 126, 128
Mousell's Wood (Bucks), 269–70
Much Wenlock (Salop), 75, 85, 89–90
Muker (Yorks), 136, 137, 140

Naish Hill (Wilts), 45, 47
Naphill (Bucks), 252, 253
Napton-on-the-Hill (Warw), 212, 213–16, 218, 219, 220

INDEX

National Agriculture Centre (Warw), 199
National Centre of Organic Gardening (Warw), 199, 211–12
National Sedum Collection, 64
National Trust, 44, 45, 49, 56, 72, 73, 84, 97, 102, 103, 117, 118, 122, 152, 156, 161, 166, 177, 178, 194, 221, 246, 249, 251, 259, 262, 266
Nature Conservancy Council, 29, 31
Newark-on-Trent (Notts), 194
Newcastle, Dukes of, 175–6
Newstead Abbey (Notts), 175, 178
Nordy Bank (Salop), 90, 92
North Stoke (Sussex), 286, 288–9
North Tyne Railway, 171
North Tyne Valley, 167–72
Norwell (Notts), 179
Nottingham, 173–4, 183, 184, 186, 190
Nottingham University, 188

Okeford Hill (Dorset), 22
Old Gang Smelt Hill (Yorks), 141
Old Harry Rocks (Dorset), 1, 3, 7
Old Stell Crags (North'd), 160
Oldbury Castle (Wilts), 29
Oliver's Castle (Wilts), 36, 37, 38
Olliver, John, 285
Orford (Suffolk), 241
Overton Down (Wilts), 30
Oxford Canal, 199, 200, 211–12, 218, 219–20

Padon Hill (North'd), 171
Papplewick Pumping Station (Notts), 175, 184–6
Parham House (Sussex), 291
Patching (Sussex), 281, 282, 285
Pen-y-Ghent (Yorks), 124, 128, 129
Pendle Hill (Lancs), 114
Pennine Way, 134, 137, 138, 140, 149, 157, 171
Pepper and Sons, 287
Percy Beck (Yorks), 146
Percy Myre Rock (Yorks), 145
Perkins Beach (Salop), 78
Pillory Green (Warw), 215
Pimhill Farm (Salop), 83–4
Plaish (Salop), 86, 88–9
Pleasant Hill (Warw), 221
Polissoir, The (Wilts), 31
Poole, Rev. William, 57

Poole Harbour (Dorset), 6
Portesham (Dorset), 14
Portland, Dukes of, 175, 176, 178
Preen Manor (Salop), 85–6, 87
Priest Weston (Salop), 79
Purbeck Hills (Dorset), 22, 24
Purbeck, Isle of (Dorset), 2–12
Puzzle Wood (Glos), 67–8

Raby Estates (Durham), 146
Ramsbury (Wilts), 34
Ratcliffe-on-Soar (Notts), 186, 194, 196
Redhaugh Bastle (North'd), 172
Redmarley D'Abitot (Glos), 61
Reeth (Yorks), 141
Rennie, John, 44, 111
Repton, Humphrey, 84, 177
Reybridge (Wilts), 46
Ribble Valley, 111, 114–16
Ribble Way, 115
Ribchester (Lancs), 111–16, 134
Rice-Davies, Mandy, 266
Ridgeway, The (Bucks), 255, 256
Ridgeway, The (Wilts), 30, 31
Rimsmoor Pond (Dorset), 18
Robinson, Roy, 170
Rock Walk (Yorks), 146
Ros Castle (North'd), 152–4
Rothbury (North'd), 158, 159, 161
Rothschild family, 248, 258
Roundway Hill, Battle of (1643), 35–8
Rowington (Warw), 202, 204
Rufford Abbey (Notts), 175, 178
Rufford Old Hall (Lancs), 122
Rutland, Dukes of, 190
Rybury Camp (Wilts), 41
Ryton Firs (Glos), 58, 61
Ryton Gardens (Warw), 211–12

St Aldhelm's Head (Dorset), 10
St Briavels (Glos), 66
St Catherine's Chapel (Dorset), 13, 14, 16
St Cross Minster (Suffolk), 225, 227
Sanctuary, The (Wilts), 30, 32
Sandlings, The (Suffolk), 228–30
Savernake Forest (Wilts), 33, 34
Savile, Sir George, 175
Scott, William Bell, 165
Scroope, Thomas, Lord, 193
Seckford, Thomas, 245
Sedgwick, Adam, 135

INDEX

Sedgwick Geological Trail (Yorks), 135
Semer Water (Yorks), 124, 131–5
Severn Bore, 71
Severn Way, 72
Shardlow (Derbys), 188
Shaw, Norman, 85, 89, 162
Shelley, Sir Bysshe, 282
Shelley, Mary, 264
Shelley, Percy Bysshe, 264, 284
Shelley, Timothy, 284
Sherwood Forest (Notts), 174, 175
Shobdon (Hereford), 52
Shoreham (Sussex), 278
Shrewsbury (Salop), 75
Shropshire Union Canal, 80
Shropshire Way, 92
Shuckburgh, Sir Richard, 218
Shuckburgh Estate (Warw), 215–19
Silbury Hill (Wilts), 32
Silverdale (Lancs), 97–105
Simonside Hills (North'd), 153, 158–61
Skeb Skeugh (Yorks), 138
Skenfrith Castle (Gwent), 65
Skirmett (Bucks), 270
Slaty Ford (North'd), 171
Snape (Suffolk), 237, 241
Sneep, The (North'd), 171
South Downs Way, 275, 289, 290
South Elmham Saint James (Suffolk), 225–8
   South Stoke (Sussex), 286, 288
Southend (Bucks), 270
Southport (Lancs), 96, 116–22
Southwell (Notts), 179–83
Southwold (Suffolk), 228–30, 231
Spencer, Stanley, 263
Spring, Tom, 53
Staindrop (Durham), 146
Stalling Busk (Yorks), 132
Stern, Sir Frederick, 282
Steuart, George, 84
Steyning (Sussex), 275, 276, 278, 279–80
Stiperstones (Salop), 75–9
Stonehenge (Wilts), 31, 32
Stourhead (Wilts), 25
Stratford-on-Avon Canal, 199, 202, 204
Studland (Dorset), 4, 6, 7
Sulber Nick (Yorks), 129
Swaledale (Yorks), 123, 124, 136–41
Swan, Joseph, 162
Swanage (Dorset), 7, 9
Swinner Gill (Yorks), 140

Talbot, Matilda, 45
Talbot, William Henry, 44, 48
Tan Hill (Wilts), 29, 41–2
Tarbotton, Marriott Ogle, 185
Tarset Burn (North'd), 167, 168, 171
Tarset Castle (North'd), 171
Taylor family (Wickham Market), 244–5
Tees Aqueduct Bridge (Durham), 143, 146
Tees Valley Viaduct (Durham), 144
Teesdale (Durham), 124, 141–7
Thieves Moss (Yorks), 128, 129
Thomas, Edward, 57
Thoresby (Notts), 179
Three Peaks Walk, 124, 129
Thwaite Lane (Yorks), 126, 127, 129
Titterstone Clee (Salop), 90, 91
Tottenham House (Wilts), 34
Towler Hill (Yorks), 144
Trent, Jesse Boot, Lord, 188
Trent, River, 174–5, 187–9
Trevelyan, Sir Charles, 166
Trow Gill (Yorks), 129
Tunstall Forest (Suffolk), 240–1
Turner, J. M. W., 142, 144
Turners Green (Warw), 202, 204
Turnworth Down (Dorset), 24
Turville (Bucks), 268, 270, 271

Upper Waveney Valley Trust, 225
Urchfont (Wilts), 40

Valley of the Rocks (Wilts), 31
Vaux sisters, 202
Vespasian, Emperor, 293

Waddesdon Manor (Bucks), 258–9
Wainwright, A., 140
Walberswick (Suffolk), 231–2, 237
Walkers Hill (Wilts), 40
Wallington (North'd), 163, 165–7
Wannie Line Walk (North'd), 166–7
Wansdyke (Wilts), 39–42
Ward, Stephen, 266
Wareham (Dorset), 3, 12
Warkworth (North'd), 154
Warton Crag (Lancs), 97, 98
Warwick, 198, 200, 209–11
Warwick, Richard Neville, Earl of, 198
Webb, Mary, 75, 79
Wendover (Bucks), 248, 254, 255, 256, 258
Wenlock Edge (Salop), 85, 86–9

302

INDEX

Wensleydale (Yorks), 123, 124, 125–35
West Itchenor (Sussex), 292
West Kennet Avenue (Wilts), 32
West Kennet Long Barrow (Wilts), 32
West Leake (Notts), 195–6, 197
West Wycombe (Bucks), 248, 249–50, 253
Westbury-on-Severn (Glos), 51, 70–3
Whernside (Yorks), 124, 129
Whistler, Laurence, 20
White Castle (Gwent), 65
White Horse (Wilts), 40–1
Whitton (North'd), 159, 160
Wickham Market (Suffolk), 244–5
Wigan (Lancs), 96
William the Conqueror, 274, 275
Wiltshire and Berks Canal, 46
Windcross Public Paths group, 59

Winde, William, 265
Windmill Hill (Warw), 222
Winspit (Dorset), 9–10
Winter Hill (Bucks), 263–4
Wolf House Gallery (Lancs), 98, 100
Wood Well (Lancs), 101
Woodbridge (Suffolk), 244, 245–6
Woolhope Dome (Hereford), 56
Wormleighton (Warw), 220
Worth Matravers (Dorset), 9, 12
Wrekin, The (Salop), 74, 78, 85, 86
Wren, Sir Christopher, 1
Wroxall Abbey (Warw), 202, 203–4
Wroxeter (Salop), 81
Wye Valley, 51, 52, 53–7, 70
Wytch Farm Field (Dorset), 6

Yorkshire National Park, 123, 124